Opportunities in Emerging Markets

Opportunities in Emerging Markets

Investing in the Economies of Tomorrow

GORDIAN GAETA

John Wiley & Sons Singapore Pte. Ltd.

Other Wiley Editorial Offices
John Wiley & Sons, 111 River Street, Hoboken, NJ 07030, USA
John Wiley & Sons, The Atrium, Southern Gate, Chichester, West Sussex, P019 8SQ, United Kingdom
John Wiley & Sons (Canada) Ltd., 5353 Dundas Street West, Suite 400, Toronto, Ontario, M9B 6HB, Canada
John Wiley & Sons Australia Ltd., 42 McDougall Street, Milton, Queensland 4064, Australia
Wiley-VCH, Boschstrasse 12, D-69469 Weinheim, Germany

ISBN 978–1–118–24717–4 (Cloth)
ISBN 978–1–118–24720–4 (ePDF)
ISBN 978–1–118–24719–8 (Mobi)
ISBN 978–1–118–24718–1 (ePub)

Typeset in 10/12 pt. SabonLTStd by MPS Limited, Chennai, India.
Printed in Singapore by Ho Printing, Pte. Ltd.
10 9 8 7 6 5 4 3 2 1

To my wife, Michelle, thank you.
To our daughter Manon and son Dorian,
happy investing.

Contents

Preface

It is foolish to assign any permanence to current economic balances, growth patterns, or trajectories. Very fundamental event risks are systemic. Yet it would be equally foolish to miss early opportunities afforded by the inevitable rebalancing of the global economy.

Investing in developing markets, including emerging and frontier economies as well as some unclassified investment destinations, is a broad subject that cannot be treated adequately in one book. It covers public and private securities (direct investments), debt and equity, large and small investments. They all are very different and all deserve much consideration on their own. We have therefore taken an inductive approach to elaborate on some of the more unusual aspects of developing markets investing to provide the ingredients for a holistic view on the subject.

The objective of this book is that in 5 or 10 years, you may still want to read certain contributions and refer to some market selections. This book is not meant as a short-term perspective or investment guide, but as a long-term view of what will become a necessity for every investor.

If you believe statements of the leading investment bank[1] that any economy less than 1 percent of global GDP is frontier and below 0.5 percent of global GDP is not going to influence the world, this book is not for you. This view restricts the universe of meaningful economies to some 20 countries (and including frontiers, to some 30 economies) globally by 2050,[2] if at all. This will cause an overinvestment problem and largely miss the current rebalancing of the global economy.

We rather believe the sum of around 50 to 60 economies, each below 0.5 percent of global GDP, with huge endowments in natural and human resources and often adequate financial reserves, will individually and collectively have a very significant impact on global trade, consumer developments, and business activity and therefore are investable markets to consider. Moreover, regionalization will give those economies new impetus to grow and prosper and their political voice will increase. Far from sidelined, they will gradually increase their share of attention and in many cases deservedly so.

This book is for those who agree that it may take another few years, possibly longer, before the true impact of smaller, less-developed economies is fully appreciated. As investors, you do not want to wait until the future is history; now is the time to reflect and act.

On such a broad subject there cannot be only one view. Thus a number of contributors who have experience and insights into the trajectory of developing markets and are not hypnotized by China, India, or some of the other mega-economies are included. Undoubtedly, China will dominate the global economy in size and impact, but they will face as many issues down the road as the United States and Europe are confronting today.

Elephant hunting is not the only solution for the rational investor. Being nimble and alert is often the better play. To adopt a stratagem of *The Art of War* (Sun Tzu), when all investors target the relatively big markets and they become more expensive, the rational investor will be nimble and fast and target the less popular opportunities. This we argue throughout this book to the extreme of talking about Lao PDR, the Kingdom of Cambodia, or even Haiti as a possible investment destination in a timeframe of a few years to a generation's lifetime.

Parts of this book are written from the perspective of a private equity investor (direct investments) because private equity investors are less concerned about the initial stock market framework or comparative analytics from a Bloomberg/Reuters screen and more about the specific investment and its value creation. They are more adventurous and find more interesting investment opportunities; they tend to outperform more passive public equity investors. Much can be learned and in developing economies even listed companies often present themselves and behave in way that is better suited to the assessment and approach of private equity investors.

In today's world, the asset management industry that manages most of anyone's financial assets faces great challenges. As with listed companies, the focus is on the shorter term when investing should be a horizon beyond five years. It is about capital concentration and the rewards asset managers get for investing other people's money in line with traditional wisdom even as the world changes fundamentally. It is about sharing accountability with others when markets decline or blaming global economic factors for value destruction. We argue that with respect to the potential of developing economies, the train has left the station. Hard work, flexibility, and significant due diligence will be required but there can be no escape from investing in smaller developing markets.

Most of the growth will come from economies that are still weak in key areas such as the rule of law, governance, and economic freedoms; these economies are dominated by informal structures. We see these bandit economies as no different than where European kingdoms or territories were a few hundred years ago, or the United States maybe 200 years ago. However, at the current rate and catch-up, this time frame has been compressed. Developing economies generate three times marginal GDP compared to developed nations and create three times the population. They all want to become economically independent and prosperous. A hundred years becomes 20 years, and in the case of South China it was only 5 to 7 years. In 5 to 10 years, the discussion about developing economies will be very different than it is today and our arguments will be old hat. Such is the pace ahead of us.

Moreover, in a few years' time, we may no longer be focused on GDP but on more advanced concepts such as the *inclusive wealth*[3] of an economy, which go beyond the income view of GDP to measure the assets and sustainability of an economy along its produced capital, human capital, and natural capital. Then, the relative importance of some of the smaller developing economies will become clear: They are the main source of growth and resource supply to the rest of the world, which is increasingly depleting its resources and has little opportunity for substitution or augmentation. Since investment success ultimately depends on economic growth, these sustainable economies will continue to outperform more advanced economies and investors will increasingly bet on sustainable growth.

We see developing markets as the upcoming middle class of the world, the necessary driver of all economies. They save, consume, start companies, and create value. Sharing in the growth of this group of economies is imperative. As with the middle-class customer, the individuals may not be attractive as customers, but as a group they are increasingly dominant.

In the end, investing is all about making money and this book offers general and specific, theoretical and practical approaches to this subject. With several contributing authors, this book offers different perspectives, styles, and ideas that reflect the multidimensional nature of investing in emerging markets, both in private and public securities and across the globe. Every reader should find something useful, interesting, or beneficial but should accept that this is only one book. There are already many publications and there will be many more to come and in only a few years we will rewrite history in these markets that can double in size and attractiveness over such a short period.

As always, all errors, omissions, unsupported facts, or political incorrectness remain my responsibility. I ask all those who are critical of some points or phrasings to look for the substance and intent and not the form. Many of the markets described are considered countries in one part of the world and not so in others. Many economic judgments invoke philosophical and emotional reactions. National sentiments are high, arbitrary country borders injurious, and inequalities great. Anger is prevalent and may be fueled. That is not intended.

This book is about investing money for profit and thereby ultimately providing a future for every individual, family, company, economy, and regional market that is willing and able to perform. This as the only stable way I know to increasingly align legitimate global interests and individual aspirations across the arguably widest range of possible markets and cultures. If we can achieve this through rational investing, politics and conflicts will have a much smaller role, as they deserve to have.

■ ■ ■

The book is divided into three parts.

The first part discusses more conceptually the nature of developing markets and the current state of selection of investable markets by major service providers and asset managers. We take a critical view on the prevailing classifications that guide and benchmark capital flows. We also suggest that the emphasis on stock market attributes is not the necessary condition for investors—for traders yes, but not for investors. We argue that stock market attributes are the sufficient condition but that the endowment of an economy in terms of legal and governance frameworks, economic freedoms, and resulting competitiveness is the necessary condition. Essentially, we take the view that although both are required, quality outweighs size. This aspect is largely missing in current perspectives.

We take some guidance from private equity that traditionally is at the forefront of investing. Based on their considerations, flows, and outlook, we develop a framework that harnesses both quality (enabling conditions) and quantity (size) of an economy and its capital markets. This makes for interesting results.

The second part is an advocacy for developing markets investing, largely in emerging economies, from a variety of perspectives. The allure of investing in emerging markets has a solid foundation. Several contributors generalize this theme and offer insights and arguments for taking an investment position. They highlight some of the risks but remain fervent supporters of emerging market investments. Mostly they are regional specialist investors, analysts, or general economists.

Both the outlook of developed economies and the resource endowment of developing economies are analyzed and commented on. The merits of investing in developing economies stands to reason from two angles: (1) the weakness of developed economies and their imminent plight (moderate growth with large debt burden and unemployment as well as depletion of their resources) and (2) the refreshing nonconformity and potential of many developing economies on their own merits based on their resources and human capital.

A review of regions such as sub-Saharan Africa, Southeast Asia, or the wider Middle East–North Africa, demonstrates where future market value and growth could be found. They are no longer or not much longer blips on the radar screen.

The third part takes the advocacy for developing markets investing one level deeper. More pragmatic aspects on developing economies and even some hereto unclassified economies dominate the contributions. A true and different insight into the global elephant China aptly demonstrates that size does not overcome structural boundaries. Economies grow faster than they can build foundations. Accepting some inherent weaknesses in any accelerated economic development is critical to investors fascinated by macroeconomic statistics and population size.

Credit markets, frontier economies in the wider sense, economies with newly established stock markets, and property markets across some of Southeast Asia are other more real-time subjects treated. These outlying countries and assets are on the way to making a name for themselves and are on the way to joining the group of investable economies. Although they have the narrowest of bases, they can deliver valuable returns and are determined to increase their offerings for investors. They could be but a few steps away from becoming worthwhile frontier economies. To complete the picture we take a current "non-market" and review their prospects for joining the ranks of an economy to think about much further out.

We consider a few subjects traditionally not considered by many investors. They address some critical business and operating issues such as the growing coverage of UK and US anticorruption laws, a subject very relevant to any developing economy investment, the substance of marketing, and the complexities of information aggregation and collection. It is but a glimpse into what direct investors have to deal with every day but also a reminder to public market investors that not all that seems to be, actually is. We complete the book on the lighter side with some experience and advice by pioneer investors and advisors.

These contributions highlight the inherent contrast and contradictions in developing economies that mirror the very challenges emerging markets investors face. While frameworks are often in place, they may not be applicable or institutions lack any practical experience as to how they should be applied. Not all that is legislated, written, or said about frameworks, rankings, or even ratings in emerging markets—and is true on paper—also happens in reality. This lesson is the most realistic and insightful balance to the allure of investing in emerging markets.

■ ■ ■

My profound and primary thanks go to all the contributors who have mostly stayed within the (moving) timetable and provided material and support as and when required. They are the spice and backbone of a multiperspective publication. Without them and the multitude of their backgrounds, this book would be a one-sided affair and could not even aspire to be valuable to some readers.

Thank you, Nick Wallwork, of John Wiley & Sons, for inviting me to this largely insane commitment of writing and editing a book. As it is customary but not less sincerely, I thank the Wiley team for their forthcoming support and hope that this will be plain sailing despite the quirkiness of the authors and commensurate quirkiness of publishers today about what you can/should say, the use of the English language, and how to discuss or display matters.

I thank Robert-Jan Temmink, a contributor who also kindly edited some of the writing using his fine command of (British) English, which was then largely Americanized. In the end, it does not matter which linguistic rules are used although for any classically educated reader some of the language and wordings may seem at odds with past usage.

NOTES

1. Jim O'Neil, Goldman Sachs, "Investing in Frontier Markets," Clear Path Analysis (London, 2010).
2. Karen Ward, "The World in 2050," HSBC Global Research (2011).
3. UNU-IHDP and UNEP, *Inclusive Wealth Report 2012, Measuring Progress toward Sustainability* (Cambridge: Cambridge University Press, 2012).

Selected List of Acronyms

ADB	Asian Development Bank
ADR	American Depository Receipt
AFTA	American Free Trade Association
ASEAN	Association of South East Asian Nations
BEM	Big Emerging Markets: Brazil, China, Egypt, India, Indonesia, Mexico, Philippines, Poland, Russia, South Africa, South Korea, Turkey
BRIC	Brazil, Russia, India, China
BRICK	Brazil, Russia, India, China, South Korea
BRICM	Brazil, Russia, India, China, Mexico
BRICS	Brazil, Russia, India, China, South Africa
BRIIC	Brazil, Russia, India, Indonesia, China
CEE	Central Eastern Europe
CIS	Commonwealth of Independent States
CIVETS	Colombia, Indonesia, Vietnam, Egypt, Turkey, South Africa
CME	Chicago Mercantile Exchange
COMECON	Council for Mutual Economic Assistance
DM	Developed Market
ECB	European Central Bank
EIB	European Investment Bank
EIU	Economist Intelligence Unit
EM	Emerging Market
EMDB	Emerging Markets Data Base
EMI	Emerging Markets Index
EMPEA	Emerging Markets Private Equity Association
ETF	Exchange-Traded Fund
EU	European Union
FDE	Frontier Developing Emerging Markets
FDI	Foreign Direct Investment

FIBV   *Fédération Internationale des Bourses Valeurs*/International
           Federation of Stock Exchanges
FM   Frontier Market
FMCG   Fast Moving Consumer Goods
FTA   Free Trade Agreement

GCC   Gulf Cooperation Council
GDP   Gross Domestic Product
GES   Growth Environment Score
GDR   Global Depository Receipt
GNI   Gross National Income

IFC   International Finance Corporation
IFCI   International Finance Corporation Index
IFRS   International Financial Reporting Standards
IMF   International Monetary Fund
IPO   Initial Public Offering
IRR   Internal Rate of Return

LATAM   Latin America
LP   Limited Partner

M&A   Mergers & Acquisitions
MBO   Management Buy-Out
MENA   Middle East North Africa
MTN   Medium Term Note
MSCI   Morgan Stanley Capital International
MSIM   Morgan Stanley Investment Management

N-11   The Next Eleven: Bangladesh, Egypt, Indonesia, Iran,
           Mexico, Nigeria, Pakistan, Philippines, South Korea,
           Turkey, and Vietnam
NYSE   New York Stock Exchange

OECD   Organisation for Economic Co-operation and Development
OTC   Over the Counter

PE   Private Equity
PEI   Private Equity International
PPP   Purchasing Power Parity

QFII   Qualified Foreign Institutional Investors

R&D	Research and development
RMB	Renminbi
S&P	Standard & Poor's
SEE	South East Europe
SME	Small Medium Enterprises
SSA	Sub-Saharan Africa
UAE	United Arab Emirates
UN	United Nations
WIPO	World Intellectual Property Organization
WTO	World Trade Organization

One

On the Selection and Classification of Developing Markets

Part One frames the various general concepts and perceptions of developing markets as they are commercialized by index, service, and asset management providers. From a terminology to group economies into similar stages of development for analytical purposes, the various names, categories, and grouping of developing nations have taken on a life of their own in the investment community. This has created boundaries that are not necessarily useful.

At the outset we demonstrate that from being a minor player on the global stage only a few decades ago, emerging markets as a group and distinct from developed markets (traditionally the United States, European Union, and Japan), have come to the forefront of growth and economic success. They now dominate world economic growth with their commercial activity, economic output, and population. At the margin, for any one additional unit of world gross domestic product (GDP), developing markets account for double the value of growth of developed markets.

This reversal from only two decades earlier is fostering immense and exciting opportunities for businesses and investors. Thus, investors no longer can afford to ignore developments and opportunities in developing and emerging markets as a group or in select individual emerging markets.

The informal nature of developing markets is often considered the key impediment—there is hardly any reliability in bandit economies, markets dominated by connected entrepreneurs and opportunistic bureaucrats. Investors most value good information. A survey of institutional investors on key issues likely to deter investment in developing markets shows that lack of information or lack of reliability of information is one of the major reasons not to invest in certain markets. The information gap is often more important than liquidity concerns and more important than political risk concerns.[1]

Yet these bandit economies may be about to bloom. Macroeconomic analyses may not help. An experienced private equity investor outlines a very pragmatic assessment of economies as to their potential and future opportunity. Without resorting to economic data or third-party analyses, indicators of booming economies and growth are identified. They are hands-on and only depend on the powers of observation.

In addition to the touch and feel approach, institutional investors need some benchmarks to allocate investments in developing economies. The question on all minds is how to develop the tools or use existing tools to select which market to focus on or, even more broadly, how to select the likely high-performance markets of the future.

We look into prevailing classification approaches to developing markets. Principally, these markets or country economies are segregated based on some varying criteria, largely dominated by stock market requirements, into two main categories: emerging markets, considered investible by the investment community at large, and the less investible frontier markets heretofore reserved for contrarians, private investors, and long-term, often public financiers.

We review approaches to classifying developing markets and conclude that combining vastly different economies with fundamentally different structures into one basket or category simply because the stock market fulfills to some degree size, regulatory, and transaction criteria is not well-suited to guide investors. For all investment, the single most important aspect is the individual company or security to be invested in and the overall conditions for industries, sectors, or companies to prosper. Macroeconomic aggregates of the country as a whole and stock market standards are not the sole compass for investors as most service providers postulate.

The prevailing classification of economies into emerging markets excludes a number of well-performing economies with attractive public or private securities or opportunities for investment; however, the prevailing classification benefits a number of economies that have little else to offer than a stock market that meets the criteria with very limited worthwhile securities. This leads to an artificial market and price for these few securities. Moreover, the much hyped BRIC (Brazil, Russia, India, and China) economies are dominating by their sheer size, but some of them less so on their merits. In fact, they are hardly comparable and constitute an artificial group, ranging from the global manufacturing leader to a major economy with some of the weakest public governance structures.

Therefore, in the context of investing in developing markets, frontier economies and heretofore excluded economies must be considered more deeply and in a similar category as a matter of principle. We review some of the approaches and indexes dedicated to frontier markets. Frontier markets represent the next wave of emerging markets and should not be excluded solely because their stock market is too small, illiquid, or restricted. Small stock markets may have some very good stocks and companies about to be listed or seeking private equity. There are multiple ways to participate in these markets and the investment community offers a large number of vehicles that allow participation in frontier markets. Going further into unclassified economies, several such markets have stock exchanges and several markets have investible instruments even if the market or economy as a whole does not meet other standards.

By strictly segregating developing markets into a first class (emerging), a second class (frontier), and a third class (unclassified), investors assume some sort of quality rating attributable to these markets when in reality only access to and tradability of public equities is truly assessed. Sovereign ratings of these markets are often relatively strong—even when accounting for the inherent limitations of the ratings process—and even more so when considering the possible ratings or assessments of individual securities.

Since current approaches are not entirely satisfactory, we suggest looking at developing markets from different angles, namely less from stock market attributes and more toward enabling economic framework conditions and economic structures. It is not the stock market on which companies trade that matters ultimately but rather the fundamental modus operandi of an economy, in particular the relative importance of the informal economy.

In considering the nature of developing economies, we argue first and foremost that the texture in which the economy operates, that is their level of organization and relative structure, matters most. We call this *governance* or *the formal economy*. Organized economies have a small informal sector. Economies that lack institutional or administrative frameworks tend to have more important informal structures.

Markets with predominantly informal economic structures (lack of rule of law, institutions, transparency), also referred to as *bandit economies*, should not be considered universally investible even if the stock market has attained certain benchmarks and qualifications. Caution is equally appropriate when considering listed companies operating in informal markets. As part of the system, companies operating in informal markets tend to adopt a more informal approach to business. The market listing and associated trading conditions are not the drivers of the opportunity or risk.

Smaller companies operating in smaller markets with a dominance of a formal economic structure (prevalence of rule of law, institutions, transparency), tend to outperform in the long term comparable companies in informal or bandit economies. This holds true even if the latter economies have a better developed stock market.

Many current approaches of analytical service providers may value some bandit economies higher than those economies developing more slowly or from a smaller base albeit along an orderly path. We conclude that current service providers do not adequately cover the universe of investible economies or markets.

Leading academics provide a solid analysis of indexing and passive investment requirements from an Asian investor perspective. They underline the widespread usage of equity indexes and concerns about the concentration of investment that defeats the very essence of diversification into developing markets. Given the importance that investors attach to indexes with a market development focus, a point argued in the issues section, the emphasis on huge BRIC (Brazil, Russia, India and China) and fairly advanced markets (Next 11 or CIVETS) at the expense of interesting but less developed markets supports the concern that capital flows are guided by indexes rather than fundamental investment considerations since most in the investment industry rely on or use extensively external analytics. A more dynamic approach of analytical service and index providers would stand to reason.

This leads us to discuss alternative definitions of investible developing markets based on the critical factors for investors: rule of law, proper treatment of shareholders, and absence of government interference/shadow economy. The world's Heritage Freedom Index covers many of these hallmarks and based on their latest ranking, we define a subset of attractive developing economies.

We also review global competitiveness of economies, their economic global governance ranking, and ease of doing business. Many popular economies and investment destinations, indeed the BRICs, do not fare that well.

We also consider the strength of economies outside macroeconomic and structural aggregates. As a substitute for support service industry and overall capital market attractiveness, we look at a financial center index for the relative strength in financial services and at a manufacturing competitiveness index for the equivalent in the real economy.

A summary indicator seems to be private equity flow. Growing and significant private equity flows provide a lead indicator for future market potential. Private equity is less constrained by capital market development, in fact they substitute the lack of growth funding. At the same time, private equity investors enhance governance and company prospects through active management participation. Thereby, they enhance the stock of companies and provide the first stage of liquidity for company shares when they exit or trade. Comparing relative private equity flows and relative market capitalization suggests that high private equity flows in economies with relatively low stock market capitalization is a lead indicator for upcoming stock market growth.

Those developing markets with the highest private equity when eliminating certain anomalies such as extraction industries or energy-related investments already demonstrate many of the core elements of an attractive market.

The World Bank and its affiliates have been investing in private equity in developing economies for several decades, initially in infrastructure but increasingly in core industries to support the development of a country. Their International Finance Corporation (IFC) makes a case for private equity investment that is not only compelling but based on what is probably the longest systematic experience of any developing market investor of significance.

Some of the advantages and myths of private investing are dispelled on the base of the IFC private equity data base. Private equity investments in developing markets are not inherently riskier and provide very attractive returns. It is simply a matter of time and effort until formalized stock markets catch up.

Enabling economic framework conditions outside the stock market and the propensity to further improve these conditions foster attractive companies and make all the difference for the developing market investor. Economic endowment and activity have a mutually reinforcing effect on stock markets. Stock markets require improving governance structures, and with improving governance structures, stock markets tend to grow, all else being equal.

In applying this principle, we find that a number of hereto highly valued developing markets should not be at the forefront of principal attraction except for the sheer relative size of the stock market. On the contrary, the most attractive markets based on the criteria of solid governance structures—always given similar growth rate and development potential—are a different selection. They seem most relevant in fostering solid long-term investment performance.

We provide a metric of the emerging markets along a scale of governance that is outside traditional aspects as well as their stock market size in recognition that small but highly attractive economies may not have the absorption capacity required for larger investments. Thus investors with long-term capital appreciation aspirations but not guided primarily by the overall stock market size can consider some of the likely winners of the future. At the same time, investors mainly guided by the potential for capital absorption, crudely measured by stock market capitalization, can select other markets.

The resulting groups of economies looks somewhat different than traditional classification providers suggest. The key difference lies in addressing the opportunity of developing markets along two axes: size (stock market) and quality (underlying structures). In this way, both small and big investors can participate in the opportunity, select their targets, and assess the systemic risks before selecting the security itself. Looking at any one aspect alone either increases principal risk (quality) or liquidity risk (market attributes). Only together do they form the necessary base for investment for any investment type, size, or objective.

Some attractive markets are only accessible through private equity, but many are accessible through public equity. All of them are or can be made investible through listed securities, be they ETFs, country funds, dedicated investment companies, tradable indexes, or other instruments. It would be up to the investment community to provide appropriate vehicles that give investors better choices. It is not the access vehicle that matters when unlocking opportunities in developing markets but the choice of the specific investment-country combination.

Further down the road, even these metrics of GDP growth in combination with a more formalized economy may take second stage to the economic sustainability of an economy. The recent work of the United Nations University International Human Dimensions Programme on Global Environmental Change (UNU-IHDP) and the United Nations Environment Programme (UNEP) has started to look at the wealth creation of an economy covering all its factors: human; productive; and natural. The resulting measure indicates the sustainability of an economy in terms of growth and resource replenishment.

Ultimately, the long-term investor may choose economies with strong sustainability (purely from a commercial perspective and ignoring any ethical aspects) over economies that are depleting resources. This would quite fundamentally change today's perspective from being fixated on GDP growth (for example, one that only irreversibly pillages natural resources), as a necessary condition and a decent formal economy as a sufficient condition (as we argue) to a world where sustainability of all resources is the necessary condition. After all, GDP is nothing but the income calculation of an economy and its outlook is driven by sustainability. Growth and economic success is the consequence of decent economic framework conditions but only in sustainable economies. This would provide a great base measure of investment attractiveness but we are still a good step away from assessing these sustainability metrics.

NOTE

1. EMPEA Special Report, Asian LP Sentiment Toward Private Equity (2012).

CHAPTER 1

On Developing Markets in General

The concept of developing markets and its subcategories of emerging and frontier markets evolved over several decades. This chapter looks at the nature and rise of developing markets outside the traditional perspectives of most analytical service providers.

THE NOTION OF DEVELOPING MARKETS

Postwar finance of economies with severe infrastructural deficiencies, an old-fashioned way of describing developing economies or those economies with postwar rebuilding requirements, was pioneered by the World Bank and its associated lending organizations. In 1971, the World Bank created its Development Research Centre[1] and started with an impressive array of research reports primarily on economies in the process of rapid development. The resulting findings supported a categorization of such developing economies to adequately group various economies by similar stage of development and potential growth outlook.

To this effect and during the 1970s and 1980s several group terms were used: Third World economies, least developed countries, less economically developed countries, newly industrializing countries, rapidly developing economies, or high performing (Asian) economies. Eventually, in 1981, Antoine van Agtmael[2] of the World Bank's IFC coined the overall notion of emerging economies or markets because most other terms were considered too negative or too exclusive. If, for example, the traditional Asian Tigers (Hong Kong, Singapore, Taiwan, and South Korea), were named high performing then by inference all other Asian economies were not high performing. This caused some discomfort. However, which economy wants to be termed Third World or less economically developed? Thus the origin of the notion of an emerging or developing economy (the terms were used more or less synonymously) rests more on political correctness and marketability than on analytical insight. In themselves, they are of little relevance to the investor.

Essentially, emerging or developing economies are those that are neither the poorest economies nor a developed economy (traditionally the United States, Western Europe, and Japan). They are in a transitional phase toward becoming a fully developed (or high income) economy.

Emerging or developing markets were made a household name by a number of studies by the World Bank, the IFC, the Asian Development Bank, and other multilaterals or government agencies. Subsequently, market participants started using the term and the industry of emerging market observation, analyses, and investment began its life in earnest.

The World Bank, in its seminal report "The Asian Miracle"[3] in 1994, classifies for its own purposes economies by GDP per capita into low income, middle income, and high income economies. However, they go on to say:

> *Low and middle income economies are sometimes referred to as developing economies. The use of the term is convenient; it is not intended to imply that all economies in the group are experiencing similar development or that other economies have reached a preferred or final stage of development. Classification by income does not necessarily reflect development status.*

For the investment community, the notion of development status and growth potential is paramount. Since the transition toward a developed economy is by no means assured for any of the emerging economies, further refinement is necessary. The investment community and their service providers needed to create a categorization of countries to segregate those worth investing and those still under construction.

This refinement was done generally on the basis of size/growth of the economy and capital markets, in particular stock markets. The notion of emerging markets was born. Based on fundamental criteria for an orderly stock market such as accessibility, regulations, liquidity, size, and transparency, a host of popular groupings of investible emerging markets were created: BRIC (Brazil, Russia, India, China).[4] BRICS (+South Africa), BRICM (+Mexico), BRICK (+South Korea), Next Eleven (Bangladesh, Egypt, Indonesia, Iran, Mexico, Nigeria, Pakistan, Philippines, South Korea, Turkey, and Vietnam),[5] CIVETS (Colombia, Indonesia, Vietnam, Egypt, Turkey, and South Africa),[6] and BEM—big emerging markets (Brazil, China, Egypt, India, Indonesia, Mexico, Philippines, Poland, Russia, South Africa, South Korea, and Turkey)—to name a few. There are few limitations to what asset managers and service providers can come up with in terms of groupings and targets. By today, they cover most all the countries projected to generate high incremental GDP in the next decade and generally have sizeable populations. They are all defined by stock market factors.

The drawback is that most of these groupings exclude a number of highly interesting countries and markets. They are sometimes considered frontier markets or are not considered at all. Excluded countries either do not have a stock market or the securities market is less developed or they do not meet some other criteria. In the broadest sense we therefore need to deal with two distinct groups of economies: (investible) emerging markets and (less investible) frontier markets.

THE NATURE AND STRUCTURE OF EMERGING MARKETS

Developing markets are economies in which to a varying degree business and capital markets legislation exists, but the registration and prosecution of business interests, commercial dispute resolution, or the execution of security does not in reality follow a book of rules. It is therefore fraught with process uncertainty and overriding collusion of local interests.

In other words, almost all developing economies are increasingly regulated on paper in favor of business but the implementation of these regulations suffers from unpredictability and a lack of an organized institutional framework dedicated to implementing business laws and rules. At the same time, prevailing behavior patterns and some cultural norms are not aligned with legislation that is seen more as a guide, recommendation, or objective than a book of rules.

The level of economic development, growth patterns, and outlook for continued success, typically the main aspects to consider for developing economies as investment destinations, do not reflect the true nature of developing economies. Therefore, pitfalls and barriers are not readily discernible. Institutional development in support of business undertakings, freedom of contract, and freedom of capital flows matter more than any one macroeconomic measure or a somewhat organized stock market. Therefore, a stage of development that differentiates between investible and high risk markets should be measured by the ability of investors to execute, protect and exit investments with some degree of confidence. This should not be confined to stock markets or developed market attributes of stock markets.

The underlying fallacy is not that a well-regulated stock market does not provide in principle for an orderly buy and sell process—this is generally the case—and subsequent repatriation of funds is possible but that the investment itself suffers greatly from deficient framework conditions. As a consequence the underlying investment does not perform as well as it could or a majority of value generated is diverted away from the investor. This is a lesson private equity investors learn the hard way and public equity investors tend to ignore. For the latter, a properly governed stock market looks like the key criterion. For the private equity investor, even in a market with a well-governed exchange, the real rules applicable to the underlying investment are the key criteria.

Frontier markets most generally provide some formal legal base to conduct business but do not always provide for reliable realization or implementation of business interests. A set of informal but real rules define business success. Emerging economies are further down the development path. They provide both a better quality of business legislation and a more rules-based execution and resolution of legitimate interests.

There is a huge difference between the two. To illustrate, take the ongoing set of business contracts and agreements necessary to ensure licenses, supply, operations, and distribution or sale of products and services. Every one of these processes and agreements holds the potential for bureaucratic costs, transfer payments, dispute, disagreement, or renegotiation. In the case of frontier markets, there is, more often than not, no purpose to even seek access to the local administrative or justice system for redress. Expensive and frustrating expeditions are the consequence. Commercial interests need to be exercised based on connections, influence, and relative (commercial) power. The informal economy dominates for business problem resolution. This fundamentally shapes contracts, choice of business partner, investment target, and business focus. Business in frontier markets is more of an art and interpersonal skill than a science. It is more suited to liberal entrepreneurs and less to technocrats. The professional advice of accountants and lawyers has more value in providing influence on public decision-makers than their advice has substance. Offshore financing and security arrangements dominate.

In developing economies, the balance of power shifts from the informal system based on influence and relative power to the formal, generally state managed administrative and legal systems. Still, uncertainties and local interests prevail but there is a fair chance to find redress in the formal system without the need to regularly resort to the informal system. More often than not time is a major barrier and the institutional systems work slowly, but eventually all parties get to a reasonable outcome.

At this juncture, institutional investors from abroad find markets interesting enough to take additional risk for an adequate reward. The gradual development path toward an institutionalized economy can be summarized by the transition in Figure 1.1.

This seems a very formalistic approach that many entrepreneurs, investors, or asset managers may consider insufficiently relevant to qualify

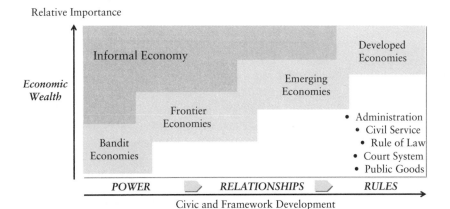

FIGURE 1.1 Structure of Economies

or disqualify a market for business. Many believe that as long as on the face of the regulations and practices they can invest and get their profits and investment back out, there is a business and investment case to be pursued. This is of course largely true and also applies to a bandit economy. More often than not, however, successes are achieved by sheer good fortune, selecting the right partners with power and influence, and lucky timing before the advent of rivalry and infighting. The sustainability of such investment approach is in question and the occasional winner or superstar do not distract from fundamental flaws in such markets.

The only real basis for making continued, long-term investments and getting an adequate reward with some confidence based on analytical insights is either a formal or an informal institutional framework that safeguards the implementation of business decisions, including but not solely the trading of investments.

It does not really matter whether institutions or organizations are in the self-organized market or whether an informal economy systematically protects such transactions through informal channels, as would often be the case for frontier markets. For example, money markets are often informal in developing economies but they protect through self-regulation the integrity of transactions in the same way if not better than if they were under license by a central bank in a country of comparable economic development. In fact, more often than not the supervisors or related administrative branches have to deal with issues in their own ranks that leave investors exposed. Many early emerging markets investors can attest to that.

In distribution or production of goods, channels not designed for private commercial use can provide a very effective access to disparate locations or source of product. A national navy may have an interest in providing waters not generally accessible for local seafood sourcing and supporting the local fisheries industry. In the natural resource and agricultural industries, provincial authorities may support and protect local companies that provide technology transfer, employment, and tax revenue to their specific location and may use their influence to provide more conducive rules in interpretation of some federal rules. The early development of South China is a good example of an effective yet rather informal style of a well-organized but not always federal-law–based economy.

Self-interest can be as good as if it were replacing a (missing) country-wide law. There is a difference between supplementing missing or vague countrywide legislative frameworks and violating or circumventing existing laws. The line between the two is a fine one. The latter falls into the category of illicit or corrupt practices but the former can provide legitimate comfort, albeit in a narrow application. In many cases, self-organized structures simply provide for solutions and rules on gaps; sometimes they bring about specialized regulations applicable to certain regions or industries.

What matters is the confidence in some form of platform to deliver the desired result—sourcing of investment (information), investment prosecution (access), supervision of investment (transparency)—with some degree of predictability. That should be the necessary but not sufficient assessment factor to establish whether an economy is investible. The quality of the stock trading environment is the sufficient condition, not the other way around as seemingly adopted today.

THE SPECTACULAR RISE OF DEVELOPING MARKETS

There are many reasons that developing markets should be considered by all types of investors. Key macroeconomic indicators in Table 1.1 are elements of evidence.

Over the past three decades, the global economic landscape has changed dramatically. A number of new countries emerged and the economic performance and future of many countries (economies) changed fundamentally. A glance at the composition of the gross domestic product (GDP) of the world and its major economies underlines this point.

While between 1980 and 1990, the United States, the European Union, and Japan, traditionally considered highly developed economies, accounted for around 62 percent of incremental (additional) world GDP at purchasing power parity (PPP) and for around 73 percent of incremental GDP at prevailing exchange rates, the tide turned rapidly in favor of developing economies over the subsequent two decades. During the period of 2000 to 2010,

TABLE 1.1 Global Population and GDP Growth Rate, 2011F to 2013F (F=forecast)

World Economy—Growth in % (Population in Millions)	2011 (F)	2012 (F)	2013 (F)
G-10 (911)	1.5	1.4	1.2
US (313)	1.9	2.0	1.8
Euro Area (408)	1.7	.02	0.4
Japan (128)	−0.6	1.2	0.5
UK (62)	1.2	1.0	1.2
Top Emerging Markets (3,130)	**6.4**	**6.0**	**6.2**
China (1,347)	9.3	8.1	8.6
India (1,210)	7.3	6.6	6.8
Russia (143)	4.7	4.5	4.0
Brazil (192)	3.7	3.5	4.0
Indonesia (238)	6.6	5.6	6.2

Source: IMF, OECD, Themes Investment Management analyses, Eurostats, national statistics.

the share of incremental GDP growth of the United States, the European Union, and Japan fell to around 32 percent at purchasing power parity and to around 43 percent at prevailing exchange rates.[7]

IMF projections for the period 2010 to 2016 extrapolate this trend: The United States, the European Union, and Japan are predicted to account during this period for around 26 percent of incremental global GDP at purchasing power parity and for around 34 percent of incremental GDP at prevailing exchange rates.

This complete reversal from roughly two thirds of the world's growth happening in developed economies in the period 1980 to 1990 to about one third in the period 2000 to 2010 and further declining to about one quarter by 2016, demonstrates the rise and importance of developing economies.

In absolute terms, the sea change is equally stark. From 1980 to 1990, developed economies (always the United States, the European Union, and Japan) generated around US$7.5 trillion additional GDP (PPP) or US $8.4 trillion nominal GDP growth. The rest of the world generated only US$4.6 trillion additional GDP (PPP) or US$3.1 trillion of nominal GDP growth.

During the period 2000 to 2010, developed economies generated some US$10.3 trillion additional GDP (PPP) or US$13.1 trillion of nominal GDP growth while the rest of the world achieved US$21.8 trillion additional GDP (PPP) or US$17.6 trillion nominal GDP growth.

Figure 1.2 shows what happened to economic output over the last few decades in percent of world incremental GDP at purchasing power parities.

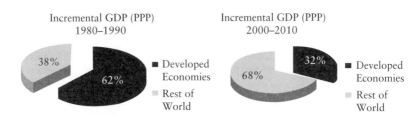

FIGURE 1.2   Incremental GDP (PPP) 1980–1990 and 2000–2010
Source: International Monetary Fund.

FIGURE 1.3   Origin of 100 Wealthiest Individuals, 2000 and 2010
Source: Rising Star AG Research.

If anything, these numbers are benign in regard to developed countries because the European Union includes economies that on their own would not qualify as developed economies.

In a nutshell, so-called developed economies more than halved their growth contribution to the rest of the world and economies heretofore considered developing account for the majority of the world's economic growth.

Not surprisingly, this has had a significant impact on the net worth of individuals. While only some 10 years ago the wealthiest individuals were from developed or industrial nations, today, one third of the richest 100 individuals are from emerging markets (see Figure 1.3).

Looking at the near-term future, global growth in the aggregate will also be driven by non-OECD economies. In 2012, some 80 percent of total world growth will come from outside the OECD, and about half that will be generated by China. A further 25 percent of the remainder will come from economies deeply related to China, such as Hong Kong, Singapore, Taiwan, Korea, Thailand, and even beyond.

For example, a large component of Japan's growth in 2012 will come from exports to China; the same is true for Australia and others.

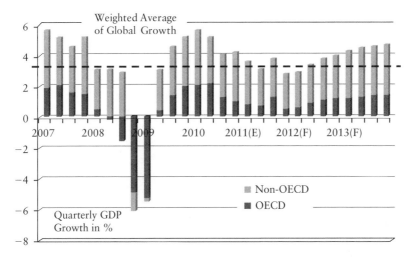

FIGURE 1.4 Annualized Quarterly GDP Growth—OECD and non-OECD, 2007 to 2013
Source: OECD, Themes Investment Management analyses.

Figure 1.4 shows the contribution to annualized quarterly world real GDP growth in aggregate for OECD and non-OECD economies until 2013.[8] The dotted line represents the weighted average of global growth.

The center of economic activity has shifted irreversibly away from developed economies. This does not mean that the role of developed economies necessarily will diminish to the same degree. For example, in financial markets, for innovation and technological progress, in service industries and consumer activity, and possibly in military, political, and global leadership functions, developed markets will retain much of their coveted role for some time to come.

For investors, however, the shift in economic activity is a critical measure. In the past, investing in developed economies gave them access to about two thirds of the world's economic output—if not more, if we factor in sourcing and buying from developing economies—and arguably with much less risk. There was no case for Main Street or traditional fund managers to consider developing economies as an investment target.

Today, even Main Street investors need to consider countries where every day two thirds of the world's new economic activity is located. While China, India, Russia, and Brazil (BRIC) arguably account for the lion's share of people, output, and activity, many other countries are growing at very high rates and are producing excellent returns. Some of them have large populations and are poised to challenge smaller, highly developed economies.

Between 2010 and 2016, according to IMF sources, it is projected that out of the 20 economies with the highest incremental GDP (PPP), only eight will be what we term today a developed economy, namely the United States, Japan, Germany, the United Kingdom, France, Canada, Australia, and Spain. The majority will be what we consider today emerging economies—China, India, Russia, Brazil, Indonesia, South Korea, Mexico, Taiwan, Turkey, Iran, Argentina, and Saudi Arabia. Among the second 20 it is even clearer: Only Italy, the Netherlands, and Sweden make the ranking while Thailand, Poland, Nigeria, Egypt, Malaysia, Pakistan, Colombia, South Africa, Vietnam, the Philippines, Bangladesh, Peru, Hong Kong SAR, the Ukraine, Singapore, Chile, Kazakhstan, and Iraq will replace some of the most advanced economies such as Switzerland, Austria, Finland, Norway, or Belgium.

Emerging economies are at the forefront of economic success. Investors have to deal with this phenomenon.

PRACTICAL PERSPECTIVE ON FRONTIER ECONOMIES

Chris Tell
CapitalistExploits.com

What exactly is a frontier market? By my definition a frontier market is one that is less developed than an emerging market. This reads similar to writing "red is not blue." but bear with the argument.

Frontier markets are distinctly different from failed markets, which are popularly referred to as failed states by the media. Examples of failed markets/states' would include Afghanistan, Somalia, and Honduras.

We could add to this list of failing states. In this category, we would include the United States, Europe, and Great Britain. These states have just not yet quite figured out that they are failing.

A couple of core or guiding concepts have led me to invest so enthusiastically in frontier markets:

- It is my contention that people all over the world are pretty much the same when it comes to the desire to increase their own living standards.
- Each incremental dollar earned has a converse effect on the desire to earn an additional dollar once certain thresholds are met.

Take for example a country such as Rwanda, with a per capita income of somewhere around US$600. Earning an additional $1 per day translates into a 61 percent increase in income. I do not know of many people who would not wish to increase their income by 61 percent. Incentive is therefore high. At the same time in a country such as Qatar, with a per capita income of roughly US$109,900, earning an additional $1 per day translates into a 0.3 percent net income increase. Hardly an incentive and certainly nothing that will have any noticeable impact on the spending habits of a Qatari.

Finally, but just as importantly, we want to invest in markets with as little correlation to the failing states just mentioned as possible.

It is a paradox that the countries that have been closed off to the global marketplace are less affected by trouble in the world's developed markets. At the same time, some of these countries are moving toward opening their markets. The base level at which they are starting is likely to rise even in an environment where the world's developed markets are de-leveraging. The risk/reward setup is greatly in favor of certain frontier markets in comparison to developed western markets.

Closely related to this point is the fact that frontier markets, since they are coming off of such a low base, allow for any small increase in per capita income to create a disproportionately large return for investors.

With that said, there are frontier markets that can languish for many years and simply drain capital. What is required is a trend change. Things need not necessarily get good, but merely get less bad for an investor to make multiples on his or her money.

Some Factors to Consider in Frontier Markets

There are significant nuances to investing in frontier markets that are 180 degrees different to investing in developed, liquid capital markets.

Contracts are often worthless. Even if you are armed with lawyers, have reams of documentation and can cite the laws of the land ad nauseam, all that is more often than not a waste of your money and time. If there does not exist a reliably functioning judiciary, you as a foreign investor will *always* find yourself drawing the short straw. Instead, we believe it is better to focus on people, and on acquiring a reliable network of locals to assist in transactions.

Often in frontier market countries the social stigma of a poor reputation, and what it means to the person who is stigmatized, is your greatest weapon. Reputation has meaning to people within a small community. As a disconnected foreigner you are just an outsider, and often it is seen as being acceptable to rip you off. Not so for a local.

So, finding local partners whom you can trust decreases your risks substantially. Try to find people with a lot to lose if their reputation is tarnished. They will typically be people who are successful because of having added value to people's lives.

In frontier markets price discovery is difficult and erratic, and liquidity is poor. Both of these "disadvantages" are arguably the strongest reasons to invest in frontier markets!

Price Discovery

The argument has been made that an outsider cannot better understand price than a local. This is a false assumption. As an outsider we often have a broader arsenal of experience available than a local does.

Bringing with you that broad view of the world, and having the ability to supplant knowledge, capital, and expertise into a frontier market, allows an investor and/or entrepreneur the ability to see how adding (technology, capital, marketing, product distribution, etc.) value can increase cash flows. Rising cash flows are a precursor to rising asset values, which will ultimately provide multiples on the capital investment.

It is far easier to find deeply undervalued and mispriced assets in frontier markets than in well-developed, normally functioning markets. All else being equal, the lower the foreign direct investment (FDI) into a country, the greater the opportunity to find and negotiate favorable terms as an investor.

Liquidity and Front-Running Liquidity

Emerging markets have liquidity; frontier markets have little to none. As such, the absence of the stress associated with the daily, weekly, or monthly price fluctuations inherent in liquid, deep markets allow a frontier market investor to focus on the fundamentals of a particular investment. The lack of liquidity itself goes hand-in-hand with the price discovery previously discussed.

Liquidity can be produced by a number of things but they all add up to greater demand.

My favorite strategy for investing, and this is true not only for frontier markets but also applies to any investment market, is to look out for situations where liquidity is likely to increase.

A few examples will better illustrate my point. Infrastructure creates liquidity in many instances. A block of land in the middle of nowhere that is easily accessible will become worth many multiples once a road is run through it. The provision of infrastructure such as power, water, and sewerage increases liquidity. Rezoning of land from rural to residential or rural to industrial and so forth all create greater levels of liquidity. Investing ahead of these events has proved worthwhile.

Many other events create liquidity. A lifting of sanctions imposed on a nation, the repealing of, or relaxing of, red tape, and/or punitive bureaucratic costs can have wonderful effects on profits and valuations for businesses. Large trade deals can create a similar situation for investors to participate.

As of this writing, Mongolia is on a parabolic upward curve. The liquidity is coming in for myriad reasons. The requirements to build roads and pipelines in addition to upgrading power, among other things, are all necessary in order to exploit the many resources that have been found in the country. This translates into per capita income rising sharply, as mentioned. As such, there are multiple opportunities in the country for investors.

Noncorrelation

Traditionally, frontier markets have shown a very low correlation to highly developed markets. This is often due to isolation. Frontier markets have often been cut off from the rest of the world. As a result they are somewhat insulated from things like global recession, or even depression. These countries will not feel those effects, but rather manage to grow less rapidly than they might when the outside world is booming.

Coming full circle, any incremental increase in living standards in frontier market countries has the very real potential to create significant returns on an investor's capital.

This is the present day situation in countries such as Myanmar, Rwanda, Cambodia, and Zimbabwe. Others are at differing stages of advancement, like one of our favorites, Mongolia.

Consider that as little as 10 years ago investing in China, India, and Brazil was considered risky. Those were exotic investment markets not long ago, yet today they occupy large percentages in many a fund manager's portfolio, and have provided the early investors and speculators with life-changing returns.

Conducting Research in Frontier Markets

Statistics are dangerous and never more so than in frontier markets. What does get reported is wildly different from reality and what does get reported is twisted by governments to achieve what they want to achieve with these numbers. Forget about statistics.

You will likely learn more from talking to your taxi driver than any official.

As soon as you cross the border you will be able to find out a couple of interesting things. If there is a black market for the currency you immediately know that the free flow of funds is hampered. The greater the discrepancy between the market rate and the official rate the greater the problems.

The ease of entering and exiting a country provides you with insights into the level of control the bureaucrats have, and bureaucrats always hamper the free market. It is simply in their nature to do so, much like giving an alcoholic free access to the liquor cabinet and expecting responsible behavior. Do they wave you through after a simple procedure or do they extract your firstborn before letting you enter or exit?

When traveling to a new country, instead of letting your mind wander aimlessly, ask yourself some questions as you watch your surroundings. What do their actions signify with regard to their social status, attitudes, fears, and desires? Economics is all about people when you care to break it down. Most people's sense of the world is captured in their actions and words.

Consider two scenarios:

1. A mother carrying bulging shopping bags, wearing the latest fashions, walking aimlessly down a sidewalk with a child in tow. She window shops casually, passing an ice cream vendor where her child performs the natural action of requesting a much-needed treat. The mother nonchalantly hands the vendor payment while chatting on her cell phone. A little further on she stops at a sidewalk café and orders a latte and a muffin. She pays with her credit card and still drops a tip into a jar.

2. Now consider the same sidewalk, but in this instance a mother hurries her child past a toy shop. Her clothes have seen better days and she carries a half-empty shopping bag. She too purchases her child an ice cream, but conceals her purse and guardedly pays the vendor, forgoing a tip. She glances furtively at the sidewalk café before pushing on.

You will find both of these scenarios unfolding in the cities and towns of the world—New York, London, Ulan Bator, Luanda, and Almaty. What you are watching for is a prevalence of one set of actions over the other in any given country; or, an increase in sightings of one sort of behavior over another on successive visits to a country. This can help tell you what is happening in a country's economy and even its political environment. Are people free to discuss politics or is it taboo?

Watch to see what sorts of goods people are buying in the shops. In fact, watch to see what shops are cropping up. Are they high-quality shops selling higher-priced goods, or is it basic and lower-quality goods?

Watch to see whether people are paying with credit cards or with cash stuffed into clothes. The use of credit cards is ubiquitous with the middle class, while the use of cash is more prevalent in a populace that is living hand-to-mouth.

When you see small children playing in the park, are they being watched by a big brother, sister, or are parents nearby? Who is watching them? If big brother is watching them this is more typical of a family setup where the parents are working and do not have the ability to watch these children. Disposable income is likely very low. Contrast that with a mother who sits at a nearby coffee shop with friends while a nanny keeps a close eye on the children.

Every country has different norms and cultures. Find out if tipping is part of the culture, and if it is, ask waiters, bellboys, and taxi drivers what the tips are like.

When staying in hotels, see whether they offer complimentary breakfast and if so, what's the quality? Watch how the hotelier talks to others. Is there a high level of service being offered? What sort of toilet paper is being used, and is the air conditioning or heating only on when you rent a room or is it run continuously? When business is good the turnover will be high and vacancy rates low enough to mean that running the air conditioning or heating continuously is warranted.

Are the shops in hot countries routinely air conditioned and in cold countries heated or are they turning down the air conditioning and heating to save money? Does the inventory look dusty and old when sitting on the shelves?

When you hire a taxi, notice whether your driver overcharges you for the trip. Does he run his taxi on just over empty and fill up when you hire him? This is a clear sign that margins are thin and business is tough. There is little to no working capital. If there is no working capital there is little chance of sufficiently large amounts of savings and capital that can be used to grow a business. It goes without saying that a large pool of capital is a prerequisite for an economy to grow.

Another matter that needs to be considered is social norms. For example, in the West it has become increasingly normal for wealthy businessman to wear more casual clothing. Suits are no longer necessarily consistent with wealth. One need only look at Silicon Valley as an example. Understanding these cultural nuances before coming to any conclusion in a foreign country is important.

Actions speak louder than words. Therefore, we pay careful attention to actions.

It is not unusual to find a taxi driver in Lusaka grinning from ear to ear as he tells you that life is great. In reality he is living hand-to-mouth in a country that stifles investment and suffers from a crumbling infrastructure, government interference, and violence.

Life might be great because his wife just had a child, or more frighteningly he may have just finished a joint and be feeling the love. He might be telling you this while swigging liberally from a bottle of beer as he takes on a blind curve at high speed (yes, I have been there).

Taken individually these actions may not mean a great deal; however, collectively they paint a picture that government statistics will not tell you. Government statistics may even actively misguide you regarding the reality on the ground.

The bottom line: Trust yourself and trust your instincts. Like someone once said, "If it walks like a duck and quacks like a duck, it's likely a duck." A little observation and awareness can go a long way.

CONCLUSION

Developing markets in general are not only at a different stage in their economic development with, for example, lower GDP per capita, they are different in their structure and texture. Macroeconomic data and overall socioeconomic indicators underpin the rising importance of developing markets to the world in numbers, but they only paint one aspect of the picture. In fact, close to all developing markets grew rapidly between 2003 and 2007[9] and the most populous ones received the most attention. This alone should not suffice to redirect investment flows.

For the investor, sustainability of economic growth and development is critical. Sustained development depends mainly on two factors: the economic potential of the country and the framework conditions under which this development takes place. Solid foundations for increased consumer spending or manufacturing output, to take two examples, are relevant to investors (as opposed to speculators) only if they take place under conditions that suggest longer-term viability.

Understanding the starting position of developing economies in a generalized form is required reading. Analyzing the shift in texture from a largely informal economy to a more institutions based one, assessing economic freedoms and the rule of law, observing the change in population behavior, or feeling the pulse of an economy on the spot should prove to be more important initial investor criteria than short term blips on the growth curve or the size of the market. They are some of the necessary indicators of a stable growth pattern, but not always components of the analytical fare provided to investors.

NOTES

1. The World Bank, Chronology, www.worldbank.org.
2. Antoine van Agtmael, *The Emerging Markets Century* (New York: Free Press, 2007).

3. World Bank Policy Research Report, *The Asian Miracle* (New York: Oxford University Press, 1993).
4. Goldman Sachs, Global Economic Paper, "Building Better Global Economic BRICs" (November 2001).
5. Goldman Sachs, Global Economic Paper, "N-11: More than an Acronym" (March 2007).
6. Attributed to Robert Ward, Global Forecasting Director, The Economist Intelligence Unit (2009).
7. All data is from IMF Statistics.
8. Data and graph courtesy of Kenneth S. Courtis and Themes Investment Management.
9. Ruchir Sharma, *Breakout Nations: In Pursuit of the Next Economic Miracle* (London: Allen Lane, The Penguin Group, 2012).

CHAPTER 2

Developing Market Classifications and Categorizations

Aside from the BRIC (Brazil, Russia, India, China) economies, possibly Mexico for US investors, Taiwan or South Korea for Asian investors, South Africa for African investors, and maybe one or two other economies, there is little consensus on what constitutes an investable emerging market. Given the rapid growth of a large number of economies but equally the size of event risk for many economies, it seems quite challenging to clearly define any group of emerging markets. This may not hinder contrarians or specialist investors to invest in unclassified markets, but it poses issues for traditional and passive fund managers.

We review several prevailing classifications and their assessment criteria for investable emerging markets and less investable frontier markets.

INVESTABLE EMERGING MARKET CLASSIFICATIONS

A range of classifications of emerging countries by major index and classification providers and selected players with different approaches are reviewed, in no particular order, to illustrate prevailing perceptions.

Standard & Poor's (S&P)

The S&P Global Equities Index Series[1] has three main indexes and thus country selections: developed markets, emerging markets (emerging plus to include South Korea), and frontier markets. The first emerging markets were included in the composite index in 1995 and cover today 46 advanced and emerging economies.

The country classification system is based on macroeconomic conditions, political stability, legal property rights and procedures, and trading and settlement processes and conditions. In addition, the majority view of institutional investors is taken into account and adds a judgmental and dynamic factor to these country assessments.

As a result of these assessments, S&P qualifies 26 economies as advanced and 20 as emerging.

Based on research and discussions with clients and investors, the following factors are considered (edited from the original index methodology document):[2]

1. Economic and political
   - Macroeconomic measures, such as GDP per capita, rate and variability of real GDP growth.
   - Risks of war, civil disruption, and disturbance.
   - Restrictions imposed by other governments.
2. Relative market size
   - Large enough to make a difference to the overall portfolio.
3. Market size and structure
   - More than five listed companies.
   - Float adjusted market capitalization above US$100 million.
   - Number of non–trade days for stock market.
   - Annual trading volume of at least US$50 million.
4. Related investment considerations
   - Settlement procedures.
   - Foreign exchange access and procedures.
   - Capital controls and restrictions on foreign investment.
   - Rules on short sales, availability of futures contracts, and so on.

All primary market share classes are admissible and adjusted to reflect foreign share ownership limits or restrictions. As with most country classifications systems that are meant as a base for indexes, advance warning is provided to investors and a suitable process is defined to allow investors to adjust to changes in the index.

Table 2.1 enumerates the countries that are currently designated as emerging economies by S&P.

FTSE International Country Classification

In 2003, FTSE International Limited, the index company, launched a public consultation with a large number of global investment organizations to establish a classification system for markets in general and specifically including frontier markets. This effort resulted in a classification framework to categorize economies for inclusion in the FTSE Global Equity Index Series.

TABLE 2.1 S&P Emerging Economies

Americas	Europe, Middle East, and Africa	Asia
Brazil	Czech Republic	China
Chile	Egypt	India
Colombia	Hungary	Indonesia
Mexico	Morocco	South Korea (EM Plus)
Peru	Poland	Malaysia
	Russia	Philippines
	South Africa	Taiwan
	Turkey	Thailand

Source: Standard & Poor's, author's analyses.

Markets[3] were classified based on a number of criteria and principles (see Table 2.2) into:[4]

- Developed—high-income countries with developed market infrastructure.
- Advanced emerging—upper-middle–income countries with developed market infrastructure or high-income countries with lesser-developed market infrastructure.
- Secondary emerging—lower middle income and low income countries with reasonable market infrastructure and upper middle income countries with lesser developed market infrastructure.
- Frontier—lower-income countries with a stock market that meets a minimum set of criteria.

The specific criteria for the FTSE classifications are listed in Table 2.2. Most of them are quantitative and can be measured, but some require judgment.

These criteria from the outset represent a decent foundation for assessing a market for public (listed) equity investment purposes provided we assume that the economic structure and performance is worth investing in and thus capital markets are the relevant differentiating factor.

As of September 2011, 73 countries have been classified. Of them, 25 are developed, 10 are advanced emerging, 12 are secondary emerging, and 26 are frontier markets. They are shown in Table 2.3.

This classification of markets within FTSE's Global Equity Index Series is assessed and considered on an ongoing basis, with changes in designation between developed, advanced emerging, secondary emerging, and frontier status agreed to annually in September. Although assessment of all markets within the FTSE indexes is a continuous process, FTSE, in conjunction with

TABLE 2.2 FTSE Classification Criteria

Market and Regulatory Environment	Developed	Advanced Emerging	Secondary Emerging	Frontier
Formal stock market regulatory authority monitors market	X	X	X	X
Fair and nonprejudicial treatment of minority shareholders	X	X		
No or selective incidence of foreign ownership restrictions	X	X		
No objections or significant restrictions to capital repatriation	X	X	X	X
Free and well-developed equity market	X	X		
Free and well-developed foreign exchange market	X	X		
No or simple registration process for foreign investors	X	X		
Custody and Settlement				
Settlement—rare incidence of failed trades	X	X	X	X
Sufficient competition to ensure high-quality custodian services	X	X	X	
Clearing and settlement—T + 3 or shorter, T + 7 or shorter for frontier	X	X	X	X
Stock lending is permitted	X			
Settlement—free delivery available	X			
Custody—omnibus account facilities available to international investors	X	X		
Dealing Landscape				
Brokerage—sufficient competition to ensure high-quality broker services	X	X	X	
Liquidity—sufficient broad market liquidity to support sizeable global investment	X	X	X	
Transaction costs—implicit and explicit costs to be reasonable and competitive	X	X	X	

TABLE 2.2 Continued

Market and Regulatory Environment	Developed	Advanced Emerging	Secondary Emerging	Frontier
Short sales permitted	X			
Off-exchange transactions permitted	X			
Efficient trading mechanism	X			
Transparency—market depth info/visibility, timely trade reporting system	X	X	X	X
Derivatives				
Developed derivatives market	X			

Source: FTSE International Ltd, author's analyses.

TABLE 2.3 FTSE Emerging Economies

Americas	Europe, Middle East, and Africa	Asia
Advanced Emerging		
Brazil	Czech Republic	Malaysia
Mexico	Hungary	Taiwan
	Poland	Thailand
	South Africa	
	Turkey	
Secondary Emerging		
Chile	Egypt	China
Colombia	Morocco	India
Peru	UAE	Indonesia
		Pakistan
		Philippines
		Russia

Source: FTSE International Ltd, author's analyses.

its external advisory committee of investment professionals, focuses mainly on working with markets that have been placed on the Watch list. The Watch list comprises a set of markets that international investors believe are close to promotion to the next category, or occasionally, demotion from their existing country classification category.

FTSE gives investors a minimum of six months' notice prior to changes being implemented in its indexes as a result of country classification reviews as stated in the published methodology of FTSE.

The FTSE country classification has won the approval of a large section of the investment community and now offers a benchmark for defining market status. There are, however, numerous competing emerging market definitions, classifications, and indexes linked to products or asset allocation models.

The differing methodologies and perspectives can be partly explained by competitive forces. Since index providers are commercial undertakings, differentiation is important to gain users and followers of the various indexes. A large number of fund managers, exchange-traded funds (ETFs), and financial as well as analytical service providers follow indexes and generate income for index providers.

Since the investment community is diverse, different needs and preferences in the market are better served by different index products.

MSCI Emerging Markets Index

One of the most commonly used and prolific index providers is Morgan Stanley Capital International (MSCI). Starting in 1988, MSCI developed the first comprehensive emerging markets index. From covering about 1 percent of global equities, this index now covers about 14 percent of global market capitalization. The index covers over 2,700 securities in 21 markets classified as emerging markets.[5] MSCI has developed its own market classification based on each country's economic development, size, liquidity, and market accessibility, as described in Table 2.4.

The company reviews market classification of all countries regularly in discussion with the investment community. As with all index providers, certain economies are under review and on reclassification are provided with some advance notice to investors.[6]

Resulting from this framework, MSCI recognizes 21 emerging markets, listed in Table 2.5.

MSCI also provides a range of specialized indexes for other emerging economies such as the MSCI Gulf Cooperation Council Index excluding Saudi Arabia, the MSCI Arabian Markets Index excluding Saudi Arabia, and the MSCI China indexes among others.

Dow Jones Emerging Markets

The premier index provider for the US stock market, Dow Jones, today a CME (Chicago Mercantile Exchange) Group company, provides both a

TABLE 2.4 MSCI Classification Framework

Criteria	Frontier	Emerging	Developed
Economic development			
Sustainability of economic development	None	None	GNI per capita 25% above World Bank high income threshold for three consecutive years
Size and Liquidity			
Number of companies meeting the following criteria	2	3	5
Company size (full market cap)	US$505M	US$1010M	US$2020M
Security size (float market cap)	US$35M	US$505M	US$1010M
Security Liquidity	2.5% ATVR	15% ATVR	20% ATVR
Market Accessibility			
Openness to foreign investors	At least some	Significant	Very high
Ease of capital inflows/ outflows	At least some	Significant	Very high
Efficiency of operational framework	Modest	Good and tested	Very high
Stability of institutional framework	Modest	Modest	Very high

Source: MSCI Inc., author's analyses.

TABLE 2.5 MSCI Emerging Markets

Americas	Europe, Middle East, and Africa	Asia
Brazil	Czech Republic	China
Chile	Egypt	India
Colombia	Hungary	Indonesia
Mexico	Morocco	South Korea
Peru	Poland	Malaysia
	Russia	Philippines
	South Africa	Taiwan
	Turkey	Thailand

Source: MSCI Inc., author's analyses.

proprietary country classification system and a number of developing market indexes.

Economies are assessed along three dimensions: (1) market and regulatory structure, (2) trading environment, and (3) operational efficiency, to classify markets into the typical three categories:

- Developed markets are the most accessible to and supportive of foreign investors. Generally, there is high degree of consistency across these markets.
- Emerging markets generally have less accessibility relative to developed markets but demonstrate some level of openness.
- Frontier markets are typically less accessible to foreign investors, exhibit notable limitations in their regulatory and operational environments, and support a smaller investment landscape. Markets tend to be much less robust and in the earlier stages of development.

More specifically, the criteria for classifying countries into developed, emerging, and frontier include metrics and detailed considerations[7] as shown in Table 2.6.

The application of these criteria is not strictly rule based and classifications will be considered in conjunction with market sentiment.

Each year, classifications are reviewed in midyear and communicated to the public in fall. A minimum of six months' notice is given to the market for any reclassification.

In case of extraordinary events, a reclassification may occur with a minimum of 90 days' notice prior to implementation.

The application of these criteria results in the list of the 21 countries shown in Table 2.7.

Bloomberg Emerging Market Ranking

Earlier this year, Bloomberg published a developing markets ranking that combines a set of indicators and closely mirrors the indexes discussed.[8] The separation of emerging and frontier is kept, but all countries present in the FTSE Frontier 50, FTSE Emerging Market, MSCI Frontier Market, MSCI Emerging Markets, S&P Frontier Broad Market, or the S&P Emerging Broad Market indexes are considered.

In terms of data and methodology, Bloomberg uses multiple sources and indexes including the IMF, the Heritage Economic Freedom, the World's Bank Ease of Doing Business, Transparency's International Corruption perceptions, Bloomberg financial market data, local currency volatility, World Bank demographics, and World Bank energy import data. Forecast

TABLE 2.6 DJ/CME Market Classification

Country Assessment Metrics	Detailed Metrics	Main Considerations
Market & Regulatory Structure	Market Environment	Foreign ownership limits
	Regulatory Framework	Treatment of foreign investors
		Capital flow considerations
		Foreign exchange market
		Investment landscape
		Foreign investor registration process
		Active regulatory bodies
Trading Environment	Market Infrastructure	Transaction costs
	Trading Environment	Trading platforms
		Short selling and stock lending
		Derivatives markets
		DR availability
Operational Efficiency	Clearing and Settlement	Settlement cycle
	Operational Environment	Settlement methods
		Central registry and depository
		Custodian bank services

Source: CME Group Index Services LLC, author's analyses.

TABLE 2.7 DJ/CME Emerging Markets

Americas	Europe	Middle East/Africa	Asia
Brazil	Czech Republic	Egypt	Indonesia
Chile	Hungary	South Africa	India
Colombia	Poland	Morocco	China
Mexico	Russia		Malaysia
Peru	Turkey		South Korea
			Philippines
			Taiwan
			Thailand

Source: CME Group Index Services LLC, author's analyses.

TABLE 2.8 Bloomberg Emerging Markets

Americas	Europe	Middle East/Africa	Asia
Peru (3)	Poland (6)	Turkey (7)	China (1)
Chile (4)	Czech Republic (10)	South Africa (13)	Thailand (2)
Colombia (12)	Hungary (11)		Malaysia (5)
Mexico (14)			Russia (8)
			Indonesia (9)
			India (15)

Source: Bloomberg, Bloomberg Markets, March 2012.

macroeconomic data was considered for the period 2012 to 2016. The scoring gave the best performing country maximum points and the lowest performing country zero points. Points were then summed as the final score.

The resulting ranking of the most attractive developing markets—emerging and frontier—is no different in the selection of markets since it is based on the traditional index constituents but somewhat different and more specific in the ranking than the traditional list we started with.

They select the 15 most promising emerging markets (with rank in bracket) as listed in Table 2.8.

Noteworthy is the absence of Brazil and the relatively lower score for India, Russia and Indonesia.

Three factors published, namely the stock price earnings (P/E) ratio as of December 31, 2011, the local currency volatility for the past three years (standard deviation of daily price changes) and inflation rate provide an excellent numeric return score for investors, called the adjusted price index. This index is a simple discounted P/E ratio of the main stock market by the inflation rate and local currency volatility.

BlackRock

The largest asset manager globally with about US$3.5 trillion under management and US$7 trillion under advisory services, does not apparently define or qualify emerging markets through a published methodology but manages multiple emerging market funds. Based on their holdings as of August 2011,[9] they were invested in those emerging markets enumerated in Table 2.9.

iShares/BlackRock

A different and narrower selection of emerging economies is made by the industry-leading iShares® ETFs—part of the BlackRock Group, who are a dominant force in global exchange-traded funds (ETFs). They claim that around 43 percent of the world's total ETF assets under management are invested in iShares funds.[10] Almost all their emerging markets ETFs are linked to either the MSCI or the S&P emerging markets index. Their recent selection of 11 emerging markets can be seen in Table 2.10.

However, for selected industry sectors they adopt a different approach. For their S&P emerging markets index linked infrastructure fund, their objective is to track the performance of the 30 largest listed companies in the infrastructure industry in emerging markets.

Lipper/Thomson Reuters

Another approach to a definition of emerging markets is taken by Lipper, a leading investment analysis service provider. In order to group funds into similar categories, emerging markets are defined as follows:

- Markets that are not an MSCI developed market (equities).
- Securities issuers domiciled in countries whose sovereign foreign fixed income securities are not rated investment grade by either S&P or Moody, or that are not members of the OECD.

TABLE 2.9 BlackRock Emerging Markets Invested

Americas	Europe	Middle East/Africa	Asia
Brazil	Czech Republic	South Africa	Indonesia
Chile	Poland		India
Mexico	Russia		China
	Turkey		Malaysia
			South Korea
			Philippines
			Taiwan
			Thailand

Source: BlackRock, author's analyses.

TABLE 2.10 iShares Emerging Markets

Americas	Europe	Middle East/Africa	Asia
Brazil	Czech Republic	Egypt	Indonesia
Chile	Russia		China
Mexico	Turkey		Malaysia
			South Korea

Source: iShares, author's analyses.

This approach groups all economies outside developed ones into one category of emerging markets. While avoiding many of the selection issues, it hardly provides any guideline for investors.

In addition to traditional index providers, a number or product and service providers adopt different approaches to selecting emerging markets.

Rising Star

A research report by Rising Star AG[11] documents an emerging market attractiveness compass based on the Global Venture Capital and Private Equity Country Attractiveness Index by the IESE Business School, University of Navarra. Using different weightings, they create attractiveness assessments by region and not by country.

Key attractiveness factors used with examples of specific data are:

- Economic strength—production, inflation, unemployment.
- Stage of development of capital markets—size, number of companies, liquidity.
- Taxation.
- Investor protection and governance—transparency, shareholder rights, rule of law.
- Human resources and social structure—labor market, corruption, education, employment conditions.
- Company development—innovation, administrative barriers, infrastructure.

As a result of applying these criteria, each of the key regions achieves a rating on a scale of 0–100 as seen in Figure 2.1.

The rating shows a marked difference between regions—Asia is clearly in the lead with 74 percent while Africa lags. Latin America and Eastern Europe are similar and are about at 61 to 63 percent of the way.

The qualitative assessment of each region by Rising Star is detailed in Table 2.11.

Overall, the report concludes that since Latin America and Africa depend strongly on Asia as well as on advanced economies and Eastern Europe depends largely on a weakening EU, the rational investor will prefer Asia as the investment destination.

The pull effect of Asian economic success on resource-based economies outside Asia is a derivative of Asian growth. Therefore, Latin America and Africa, although resource rich, lag the prospects of Asia.

Latin America has a strong local economy compared to Africa and offers investors a rather homogenous framework. At the same time, capital

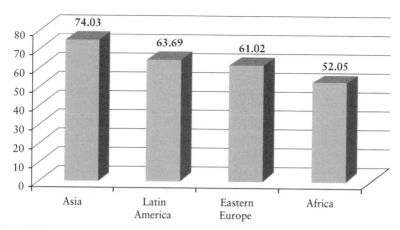

FIGURE 2.1 Regional Attractiveness, Scale of 1–100 (best)
Source: Rising Star AG Research, 2011.

markets are more developed. Therefore, Latin America is ranked second in attractiveness. Eastern Europe and Africa equally offer attractive investment opportunities, but rather on an opportunistic basis.

HSBC Emerging Markets Index

HSBC takes a rather novel approach to evaluating emerging markets and compiling its quarterly index. The HSBC Emerging Markets Index (HSBC EMI) is not based on stock market performance but on microeconomic market sentiment, namely expectations and results of businesses. This makes the index very different but appealing as a measure for change in economic outlook based on the real economy.

Importantly, HSBC, with its well over 150 years of experience in emerging markets, includes 16 emerging economies in its index. Outside the notorious BRIC countries (Brazil, Russia, India, China), Asian countries dominate followed by the Middle East, as depicted in Table 2.12.

The index itself is interesting and described as follows:[12]

> *The HSBC Emerging Market Index (EMI) is a weighted composite indicator derived from the National Purchasing Managers' Index*™ *(PMI*™*) surveys in the selected emerging markets. These surveys collectively track business conditions in over 5,800 reporting companies.*
>
> *National Purchasing Managers' Index*™ *(PMI*™*) surveys on which the EMI is based have become the most widely watched*

TABLE 2.11 Emerging Markets Regional Assessment

Strengths	Weaknesses	Opportunities	Threats	Outlook
Asia				
■ Large, dynamic market ■ Low cost production and high tech industries ■ Ample resources and educated labor	■ Administrative inefficiencies ■ Export dependent ■ Lower corporate governance standards ■ Dependent on local networks	■ Companies look at partners for growth and management skills ■ Midmarket and domestic consumption growing rapidly ■ Fragmented sectors with consolidation potential ■ Large education expenditures with R&D opportunities	■ Subject to natural disasters ■ Gaps in infrastructure (equally an opportunity) ■ Cultural, religious, and other social differences can cause unrest ■ Unrest in China with global implications	■ Progress with respect to transparency and company governance ■ Continued export orientation of production industries ■ Increased comparative advantages on production costs ■ Capital flow restrictions gradually reduced
Latin America				
■ Strong economic activity and high resource reserves ■ Selected mature production companies ■ Strong tax incentives	■ Under-developed capital markets ■ Corporate governance weak ■ Still dependent on economic developments of other countries	■ Protection of investors improving ■ Strong resource sector generates income to improve infrastructure	■ Corruption and crime rate ■ Environmental damage through reckless resource exploitation	■ Differing development paths, disadvantage of countries with populist regimes ■ Growing middle class a strong base for production industries

■ Domestic consumption rising sharply ■ Domestic funding sources well developed		■ Improvement in corporate governance and investor protection increases attractiveness ■ Large appetite for infrastructure investments	■ Growing incomes reduce corruption and crime rate

Africa

■ Economic growth positive ■ Increased stability and rational public governance ■ Increased confidence of investors and openness to investors	■ Great discrepancies in culture, language, and legal systems ■ Level of transactions low outside Nigeria and South Africa ■ Few specialists for private equity investments	■ High investment demand for infrastructure and resource extraction ■ Underdeveloped banking and payment systems ■ Differing level of development	■ Due to its resource dependency, Africa's economic development lags global economic developments ■ Political developments in North Africa could lead to changes and increased attractiveness in other countries ■ Capital inflow largely dependent on global economic outlook ■ Depends on resource income and thus on other emerging markets growth ■ Economic diversification delayed due to emphasis on resource extraction ■ Political risks, transparency, and rule of law still weak

(Continued)

TABLE 2.11 Continued

Strengths	Weaknesses	Opportunities	Threats	Outlook
Eastern Europe				
▪ Attractive tax incentives	▪ Some economies still affected by financial crisis	▪ Privatizations to come	▪ Need to overcome financial crisis	▪ Attractive incentives for companies
▪ Strongly diversified economies due to proximity to Western Europe	▪ Economic growth largely dependent on Western Europe growth	▪ Good investment regulations	▪ Increased political instability through extreme groups	▪ Even with mixed economic outlook, interesting opportunities for investors
▪ Location of many production and service centers for developed corporations	▪ Underdeveloped capital markets	▪ Private public partnership opportunities in infrastructure		
▪ Relatively stable economies	▪ Aversion to non-European investors	▪ EU subsidies for projects		
	▪ Infrastructure still in need of upgrading	▪ Emerging corporate governance		

Source: Rising Star AG Research, 2011, author's analyses.

TABLE 2.12 HSBC Emerging Markets

Americas	Europe	Middle East/Africa	Asia
Brazil	Poland	South Africa	Russia
Mexico	Czech Republic	Israel	India
		Turkey	China
		UAE	South Korea
		Saudi Arabia	Taiwan
			Hong Kong
			Singapore

Source: HSBC, author's analyses.

business surveys in the world, with an unmatched reputation for accurately anticipating official data. The survey data are collected using identical methods in all countries, with survey panels stratified geographically and by international Standard Industrial Classification (ISIC) group, based on GDP contributions.

Survey responses reflect the change, if any, in the current month compared to the previous month based on data collected mid-month. For each of the indicators a 'diffusion' index is produced, which reflects the percentage of positive responses plus a half of those responding "the same." Diffusion indices have the properties of leading indicators and are convenient summary measures showing the prevailing direction of change. An index reading above 50 indicates an overall increase in that variable, below an overall decrease. All data is seasonally adjusted.

Data collected at the national level for manufacturing and services are then weighted together according to relative contributions to national or regional GDP to produce indicators at the national whole economy or aggregate emerging market level.

Goldman Sachs—Growth Environment Scores

Jim O'Neill, the creator of the acronym BRIC (Brazil, Russia, India, and China) and N-11 (Next 11) outlines in his book[13] on growth economies of tomorrow, a measurement of growth prospects for developing economies called the Growth Environment Score (GES).

The GES takes several general macroeconomic factors into account as well as a number of microeconomic measures, as adapted in Table 2.13.

This measurement approach considers many of the key factors that make an economy attractive to its people and therefore to investors. In

TABLE 2.13   Growth Environment Scores

Macroeconomic Variables	Inflation
	Government deficit
	Investment spending
	External debt
	Degree of openness
Microeconomic Variables	Use of mobile telephones
	Use of the Internet
	Use of computers
	Life expectancy
	Education
	Rule of law
	Corruption
	Stability of government

Source: Adapted from O'Neill, The Growth Map.

particular, measures of the texture of an economy such as openness of the economy, the rule of law, corruption, and the makeup of its population (such as education and life expectancy) provide a very good guide to investors. The measures on technology usage go more to connectivity and thus cultural change the economy and its people are likely to undergo.

Morgan Stanley—Emerging Market Universe

The head of Morgan Stanley Investment Management (MSIM)—Emerging Markets Equities, Ruchir Sharma, lists in his book, *Breakout Nations,* his list of emerging markets as adapted in Table 2.14.

The list includes many of the usual suspects, but equally some of the smaller economies with high potential. It excludes a number of markets considered emerging by others, notably all the GCC (Gulf Cooperation Council) economies.

STOXX—Emerging Markets Index

Equally this year, STOXX, the provider of global index concepts (part of Deutsche Börse AG and SIX Group AG), introduced a market classification model to group countries included in the STOXX universe into developed and emerging markets. At the same time a STOXX Emerging Markets Total Market Index was announced.[14]

The classification model relies on a rules-based methodology to exclude subjective decisions from the process. The model is based on a three-step approach applying five screening criteria for which publicly available data from the International Monetary Fund (IMF), the World Bank, and PricewaterhouseCoopers (PwC) is used.

From the universe of 65 STOXX index countries, advanced economies are extracted based on the IMF country classification and based on World Bank data of US$15 billion in stock market capitalization and US$15 billion in trading volume. Three-year averages are used. Finally free currency convertibility and no restrictions on capital flows are required, both data sourced from PricewaterhouseCoopers. Countries that fail any one of these criteria are assigned emerging market status.

Emerging markets are selected from the remaining nondeveloped countries that have US$15 billion in stock market capitalization and US$15 billion in trading volume. These countries are classified as emerging markets as in Table 2.15.

TABLE 2.14 MSIM Emerging Markets

Americas	Europe	Middle East/Africa	Asia
Brazil	Czech Republic	Egypt	China
Chile	Hungary	Morocco	India
Colombia	Poland	South Africa	Indonesia
Mexico	Russia		South Korea
Peru	Turkey		Malaysia
			Philippines
			Taiwan
			Thailand

Source: Adapted from Sharma, *Breakout Nations.*

TABLE 2.15 STOXX Emerging Markets

Americas	Europe	Middle East/Africa	Asia
Brazil	Hungary	Egypt	China
Chile	Poland	Morocco	India
Colombia	Russia	South Africa	Indonesia
Mexico	Turkey		Malaysia
			Pakistan
			Philippines
			South Korea
			Taiwan
			Thailand

Source: STOXX Limited, website.

Given the rules-based approach and the data source, the resulting list of emerging economies looks almost identical to that of several other index providers. The emphasis remains on Asia and stock market volumes.

FRONTIER MARKET CATEGORIZATIONS

When the IFC analyzed its Emerging Markets Database, it became clear that a number of economies had markets for tradable securities but lacked other criteria required to be considered an emerging market. These economies were usefully grouped into a pre-emerging market category. Mainly, these frontier economies were too small, insufficiently regulated, too early stage growth or economically too immature to be considered an emerging market both from an economic and an investment perspective. The term *frontier markets* was thus created to describe this subset of markets that did not fall into the category of emerging markets but had a formal stock market with publicly tradable securities.

This broad set of economies that have a regulated stock market but are not emerging economies amount to roughly one third of the world's economies by number. However, these economies are not equal in terms of size, regulation, market access, liquidity, capital controls, quality of information, or other critical investment factors. Therefore, as the term frontier market was picked up by the investment community at large, further refinement and classification was required. Most of the public equity investment community, emerging markets debt investors, and indeed some of the private equity players, were looking for a distinct delineation and categorization into acceptable (investable) and less acceptable frontier markets. In addition, a benchmark was needed so that passive investors that benchmark themselves against an index would have a point of reference.

The original categorization by the IFC of countries with small stock markets into a class of frontier markets gave the professional investment community a form of a new asset class that would engender the development of tools and benchmarks by external service providers. Thereby, markets previously inaccessible for investment by a large part of the asset management industry due to a lack of analytical services and benchmarks would be researched, indexed, and eventually become investable. This would benefit first and foremost passive (index) investment managers with very large global funds under management. The resulting income from capital flows and ancillary business, not to mention the long-term prospects of frontier economies, would create an exciting subset for the asset management industry. After all, frontier economies are pre-emerging economies and no diversified investment portfolio can really afford to ignore emerging markets or the likely winners of the future.

Frontier markets in the sense of small, unknown but rapidly growing economies have always been surrounded by a mystique and a fascination— the pioneer instinct in many of us. While emerging markets were defined and made a household name by a number of World Bank, IFC, Asian Development Bank, and other multilateral and academic studies, unknown and poorly understood small economies and stock markets of the world had no supporting industry.

Most investors fully appreciate increased risks in these markets, yet they are equally fascinated by potentially higher returns. Frontier markets seemingly promise to deliver both in abundance. Moreover, frontier markets look largely uncorrelated to developed markets and thus have all the hallmarks of a justifiable portfolio diversification.

The country classification by FTSE and the continued search for higher returns and new portfolio diversification led to numerous developments within the index and analytical support industry with respect to frontier markets. FTSE, S&P, and MSCI, Barra to name some leaders, launched investable frontier market indexes.

S&P

In August 2007, S&P launched the S&P/IFCG Extended Frontier 150 Index, which included companies from the S&P Emerging Markets Database that are not included in S&P's investable emerging markets indexes. A few months later, in October 2007, it rolled out a subset of that index, the S&P Select Frontier Index.

The investable S&P Select Frontier index covers 40 of the largest and most liquid stocks from countries that have smaller economies or less developed capital markets than traditional emerging markets and are, therefore, excluded from most emerging market benchmarks and investment funds. The index is designed to meet the increasingly sophisticated needs of global investors seeking to expand into markets with the potential for similar or greater returns than in better known emerging markets.[15]

S&P chose a slightly different methodology by deriving the universe of possible stocks from the S&P Emerging Markets Database (EMDB) rather than relying on the FTSE Country Classification. The criteria for index inclusion are as follows:

- Universe: All listed companies from those markets in the S&P EMBD that are not included in the S&P/IFCI are eligible. Large and liquid companies from non-EMDB markets are also screened. Local listings of stocks from countries that may present significant problems for a foreign investor are excluded. However, companies with ADR/GDR are eligible.

- Market Capitalization: Companies must have at least US$100 million in float-adjusted market capitalization as of the data reference prior to the semiannual index reconstitution.
- Domicile: All markets are included except those that lack Reuters real-time pricing, have high foreign investment restrictions or high capital gains taxes, have low overall market liquidity, or have limited currency markets or high foreign portfolio investment risk.
- Liquidity: Constituents must have a minimum average daily value traded of US$1 million for the preceding six months as of the data reference prior to the semiannual index reconstitution and at least 15 trading days over each of the previous six months prior to rebalancing. In case of multiple listings, the listing with the largest liquidity is selected.
- Public Float Available to Foreign Investors: If a stock has foreign investment restrictions, then it is considered for inclusion only if its foreign investment limit has not been reached.

The resulting investment portfolio covers companies listed in 13 countries (one GDR), of which Georgia, Kazakhstan (GDR), Kuwait, and Panama are not considered frontier markets by FTSE and Colombia, Pakistan, and the UAE are classified as secondary emerging markets by FTSE.[16]

Standard & Poor's also produces the S&P/IFC Global Frontier Markets index that tracks 270 companies and provides monthly returns of equity markets with less liquid stocks.

FTSE

The FTSE Frontier 50 Index is FTSE's first index to be created from an eligible universe of 25 new frontier markets. They are screened using FTSE's established country classification methodology that assesses markets against the size requirements, basic governance, and market infrastructure elements required by international institutional investors. The new index is calculated in real time and is designed to be used as the basis for financial products such as ETFs, mutual funds, and derivative products.

The universe for this index covers the 25 markets in Table 2.16, which have been identified by applying five criteria from FTSE's renowned country classification criteria.

TABLE 2.16 FTSE Frontier Markets

Americas	Europe	Middle East/Africa	Asia
Argentina	Bulgaria	Bahrain	Bangladesh
	Croatia	Botswana	Sri Lanka
	Cyprus	Cote d'Ivoire	Vietnam
	Estonia	Jordan	
	Lithuania	Kenya	
	Macedonia	Mauritius	
	Malta	Nigeria	
	Romania	Oman	
	Serbia	Qatar	
	Slovakia	Tunisia	
	Slovenia		

Source: FTSE International Ltd, author's analyses.

The index tracks the performance of the 50 most liquid stocks from the eligible universe of new frontier markets based on the following criteria:

- There must be a formal and independent stock market authority that actively monitors the market.
- There should be no objection to or significant restrictions or penalties applied on the repatriation of capital and income.
- Transparency: There should be market depth information, visibility, and a timely trade reporting process and a requirement of international price dissemination.
- Settlement: There should be a rare incidence of failed trades.
- The clearing and settlement period should be shorter than $T + 7$ (and greater than $T + 1$).

Markets must also meet a minimum country-free float-size requirement of US$750 million.[17]

MSCI

Morgan Stanley Capital International (MSCI) also developed a regional Frontier Market Index that includes 25 frontier countries somewhat dissimilar to the FTSE country classification and a further seven stand-alone frontier market indexes. Inclusion of a country is based on investability requirements within each market. Selected are large, mid, and small cap representations. They cover approximately 98 percent of the investable equity universe across all frontier market countries. The MSCI Frontier Markets Index is a free float-adjusted market capitalization index that is designed to measure equity market performance of frontier markets.

The emphasis is on the Middle East/Africa and Eastern Europe (see Table 2.17).

In addition to these comprehensive frontier market indexes, there are more specialized indexes that are focused on frontier markets.

Stand-alone frontier market country indexes are: Bosnia-Herzegovina, Botswana, Ghana, Saudi Arabia, Trinidad and Tobago, Zimbabwe, and Jamaica. The addition of these country indexes to the MSCI Frontier Markets Index was under consideration as of the end of May 2011.[18]

Morgan Stanley—Frontier Market Universe

Morgan Stanley Investment Management (MSIM) considers the quite exhaustive list of frontier economies in Table 2.18.

Bloomberg Emerging Market Ranking

In its market ranking, Bloomberg selects the top 15 most promising frontier markets (with rank in parentheses), as shown in Table 2.19.

The frontier market selection shows quite a different picture from other classifications. Essentially, the key players in formerly Eastern Europe, the oil-rich countries of the Middle East, and selected Central Asian and African markets make the cut for most attractive frontier economies. This represents a varied and thoughtful selection of markets.

TABLE 2.17 MSCI Frontier Markets

Americas	Europe	Middle East/Africa	Asia
Argentina	Bulgaria	Bahrain	Bangladesh
	Croatia	Jordan	Kazakhstan
	Estonia	Kenya	Pakistan
	Lithuania	Kuwait	Sri Lanka
	Romania	Lebanon	Vietnam
	Serbia	Mauritius	
	Slovenia	Nigeria	
		Oman	
		Qatar	
		Tunisia	
		UAE	

Source: MSCI Inc., author's analyses.

TABLE 2.18 MSIM Frontier Markets

Americas	Europe	Middle East/Africa	Asia
Argentina	Bulgaria	Bahrain	Bangladesh
Ecuador	Croatia	Jordan	Kazakhstan
Panama	Estonia	Kuwait	Pakistan
Jamaica	Latvia	Lebanon	Sri Lanka
Trinidad and Tobago	Lithuania	Oman	Vietnam
	Romania	Qatar	
	Serbia	Saudi Arabia	
	Slovenia	UAE	
	Ukraine	Botswana	
		Ghana	
		Kenya	
		Mauritius	
		Namibia	
		Nigeria	
		Tunisia	

Source: Adapted from Sharma, *Breakout Nations*.

TABLE 2.19 Bloomberg Frontier Markets

Americas	Europe	Middle East/Africa	Asia
	Bulgaria (3)	United Arab Emirates (2)	Vietnam (1)
	Romania (4)	Kuwait (5)	Kazakhstan (6)
	Serbia (8)	Qatar (7)	Ukraine (15)
	Croatia (13)	Bahrain (9)	
		Tunisia (10)	
		Botswana (11)	
		Oman (12)	
		Kenya (14)	

Source: Bloomberg, Bloomberg Markets, March 2012.

NASDAQ OMX

The NASDAQ OMX Middle East North Africa Market Index is designed to track the performance of the most liquid and largest stocks of companies located in North African and Middle Eastern countries. The countries included in the index have less-developed capital markets and smaller economies than the traditional emerging stock markets.

The index[19] currently includes securities from Egypt, Morocco, Kuwait, Lebanon, Oman, Jordan, Bahrain, Qatar, and the United Arab Emirates (UAE), making it effectively a regional frontier market index.

Bank of New York Mellon

This index tracks the performance of depositary receipts, in ADR or GDR form, that trade on the London Stock Exchange, New York Stock Exchange, NYSE, Amex, and NASDAQ stock market of companies from countries that are defined as the frontier market. The Index Provider defines frontier market countries based on an evaluation of gross domestic product growth, per capita income growth, experienced and expected inflation rates, privatization of infrastructure, and social inequalities.

The index covers some 42 countries, including some outliers such as Malawi and Papua New Guinea.

CONCLUSION

There is hardly any consensus on what constitutes an emerging or a frontier market. Equally, there are numerous definitions and analytical approaches, as illustrated, on classifying such economies. Overall, some 50 to 60 economies qualify as either emerging or frontier markets with significant consequences for capital flows. Implications of these classifications and issues are reviewed in the following chapters.

NOTES

1. www.sp-indexdata.com.
2. Standard and Poor's Global Equity Indices Methodology.
3. Marc de Luise, "What Are Frontier Markets?," *Journal of Indexes* (September–October 2008).
4. FTSE Global Equity Index Series Country Classification documents, www.ftse.com/indices.
5. www.msci.com/resources.
6. MSCI Emerging Market Index documentation, www.msci.com/indices.
7. Dow Jones Indexes literature, www.djindexes.com.
8. Bloomberg Rankings, network release, 8 February 2012, published by Bloomberg Markets, March 2012.
9. BlackRock, annual audited accounts, announcements.
10. www.ishares.com.

11. Rising Star AG, Switzerland, "Investments in Emerging Markets—Short Term Opportunity or Secular Theme?" (2011).
12. HSBC, www.hsbc.com/1/2/emergingmarketsindex.
13. Jim O'Neill, *The Growth Map: Economic Opportunity in the BRICs and Beyond* (New York: Portfolio, Penguin Group, 2012).
14. S&P documentation, www.indices.standardandpoors.com.
15. S&P Select Frontier index documentation, www.indices.standardand poors.com.
16. FTSE Frontier 50 documentation, www.ftse.com/indices.
17. MSCI Inc., Frontier Market Index documentation, www.msci.com/products/indices.
18. www.etfdb.com.
19. Press release, "STOXX introduces market classification model and emerging market index," www.stoxx.com, March 27, 2012.

CHAPTER 3

Considerations on Emerging and Frontier Market Classifications

The selection of methodologies, index composition, and country assessments shows considerable consistency in coming to a definition of what constitutes an emerging and thus investable market.

The leading analytics firms have a similar methodology and therefore arrive at similar results. A couple of countries, namely Pakistan, South Korea, Turkey, and the UAE are not uniformly considered emerging markets and some have recently reclassified other countries. Some countries in one emerging market index equally feature in frontier market indexes, so that there is some overlap between emerging and frontier economies.

Product and specialized index providers tend to focus on a narrower selection that better fits their investment objectives. Overall, there is increasing congruence on the definition of an emerging market and investors have a rather solid benchmark to track relative investment performance. With this congruence also comes increased reliability on emerging market indexes and an equal need for competitive index providers to proliferate specialized and country-based indexes. This trend is driven by both the passive and active investment industry that needs to have performance benchmarks. This benchmark provides an important service for those specialized asset managers.

Satisfaction with some of the index providers is not high. A study summarized in this book[1] suggests that a good part of asset managers have issues with equity indexes although indexes are relatively widely used in all asset classes.

The common set of emerging markets looks increasingly similar to developed markets, although their stock market is generally smaller and their securities market infrastructure generally less developed. The boundaries are becoming blurred and in a short period of time some emerging markets will be hardly distinguishable from developed markets by the standards of the investment community. In fact, some of the European developed markets may find it hard to compete with the most advanced emerging markets. The prevailing perception on emerging markets of increased volatility and risk, limited liquidity, and partially restricted foreign investor access is likely to vanish in the foreseeable future.

By contrast, the list of frontier market indexes is not congruent even with a partial selection of providers. The conclusion from this review is that, although a widely published and largely accepted methodology to classify developing (emerging and frontier) markets exists (FTSE), there is hardly any consensus on which country should be considered a frontier market.

The main consensus of the investment community is that a country with low to middle income and a stock market that meets certain minimum size, liquidity, and transaction requirements for foreign investors, can be considered a frontier market. This market becomes partially investable as a consequence. This alone has allowed several major index providers to come up with more than 50 different countries that fit the respective index provider standards.

There is, of course, a vested interest of listed companies in frontier markets to be included since it generates investment flows and transactions in their shares. Index providers or their clients may have a preference for individual companies from new markets that only become investable for a large number of asset managers if the country is included in the index. This may explain why certain indexes include certain economies while others exclude the very same economies.

Invariably some, if not most, of the criteria for being considered a frontier economy are qualitative. This leaves room for judgment and, as a result, different assessments. Therefore, the variance in categorizing frontier markets by index providers should be seen as the consequence of differing judgment calls. It allows a diverse number of funds and investors to pursue diverse investments and have some benchmark to be measured against.

The overall approach and diversity of results summarized in Table 3.1 does, however, lead to a number of consequences and raises some important issues.

CONSEQUENCES OF CLASSIFICATIONS

The consequences of market (country) classifications are similar to a rating. With the significant and rising interest in developing (emerging and frontier) markets from an investment point of view and the consequential creation of indexes, funds, ETFs, and other tradable instruments, the inclusion or exclusion of a country from a particular category has significant impact on capital flows. In particular, the dominant index providers such as the MSCI

TABLE 3.1 Comparative Selection of Frontier Markets

FTSE Frontier 50	MSCI Frontier Market	S&P Select Frontier	S&P IFC Global Frontier	BNY Mellon New Frontier DR
Argentina	Argentina			
Bahrain	Bahrain	Bahrain		Bahrain
Bangladesh	Bangladesh		Bangladesh	Bangladesh
Botswana			Botswana	
Bulgaria	Bulgaria		Bulgaria	Bulgaria
				Chile
		Colombia		Colombia
Cote d'Ivoire			Cote d'Ivoire	
Croatia	Croatia	Croatia	Croatia	Croatia
Cyprus		Cyprus		
				Czech Republic
			Ecuador	Ecuador
				Egypt
Estonia	Estonia		Estonia	Estonia
		Georgia		Georgia
			Ghana	Ghana
			Jamaica	Jamaica
Jordan	Jordan	Jordan		Jordan
	Kazakhstan	Kazakhstan	Kazakhstan	Kazakhstan
Kenya	Kenya		Kenya	Kenya
	Kuwait			Kuwait
			Latvia	Latvia
	Lebanon		Lebanon	Lebanon
Lithuania	Lithuania		Lithuania	Lithuania
Macedonia				
				Malawi
Malta				
Mauritius	Mauritius		Mauritius	Mauritius
				Morocco
			Namibia	
Nigeria	Nigeria	Nigeria		Nigeria
Oman	Oman	Oman		Oman
	Pakistan	Pakistan		Pakistan
		Panama	Panama	Panama
				Papua New Guinea
				Peru
				Poland
Qatar	Qatar			Qatar
Romania	Romania	Romania	Romania	Romania

(Continued)

TABLE 3.1   Continued

FTSE Frontier 50	MSCI Frontier Market	S&P Select Frontier	S&P IFC Global Frontier	BNY Mellon New Frontier DR
Serbia	Serbia			
Slovakia			Slovakia	Slovakia
Slovenia	Slovenia		Slovenia	Slovenia
Sri Lanka	Sri Lanka			Sri Lanka
			Trinidad and Tobago	Trinidad and Tobago
Tunisia	Tunisia		Tunisia	Tunisia
	Ukraine		Ukraine	Ukraine
	UAE	UAE		UAE
Vietnam	Vietnam	Vietnam	Vietnam	Vietnam
				Zimbabwe
25	24	14	24	41

MSCI Country Indexes
Bosnia-Herzegowina
Botswana
Ghana
Zimbabwe
Jamaica
Saudi Arabia
Trinidad and Tobago
7

Emerging market index and others, have taken on a much wider significance. Countries now seek inclusion or upgrades and consider such reclassifications as a sign of approval.

Surely this was not the main intention of country classifications. At the outset, as described, they were simply intended to be categories to group economies of similar economic development or growth trajectory. They were largely a macroeconomic descriptor and as such they serve an analytical purpose. This how the IMF, the World Bank, and the IFC use these categorizations in their statistics and many of us use these statistics to compare, for example, the developed world with the rest of the world or with economies that have certain attributes, such as high growth rates or an established stock market. Country classifications as originated by the global multilateral finance organization were not designed to influence capital flows.

The investment community, largely those that invest in listed securities only, require some form of approval that the markets on which such securities are traded also meet a minimum set of requirements. To this effect the creation of stock market classifications by external service providers is a legitimate and useful instrument to allow the investment community to trade in these securities supported by factual knowledge on barriers and limitations of these trading markets and general transparency requirements for listed securities. That is a critical value added to investors.

The community should equally consider a rating of all stock exchanges (as transaction platform and not as investment) to formalize the process. The World Federation of Exchanges (WFE) formerly FIBV (*Fédération Internationale des Bourses Valeurs*/International Federation of Stock Exchanges) could well act as a catalyst. Rating a stock exchange is quite different than classifying a country.

At the same time, there is unquestionable need for a multitude of indexes to evaluate markets, compare performance, take investment decisions, benchmark or replicate asset class returns, or establish asset allocations. Indexes are used for many ancillary purposes and it is hardly imaginable to analyze global investment and capital flows, develop asset allocations, or develop investment products without access to such indexes. These indexes and their analytical support are invaluable to the investment community and the base for most investment analytical tools.

The growing importance of indexes as a measure of performance, however, may have overshot this objective by becoming the investment guide for large capital. While accepting inherent limitations in any aggregation— this applies equally to developed markets—the bucket of developing markets has its own and very special characteristics. The constituents of any emerging market group, however selected, have at times widely different growth rates, short-term outlook, and widely different issues to deal with. Most countries are subject to significant political and contagion risk, as we have seen in the Arab Spring, and every country election of a new government can mean a significant change in the country's texture.

When sizable global investment capital replicates or approximates for example the MSCI or the S&P emerging market indexes, then any change of constituents in these indexes has immediate consequences for capital flows. Any inclusion or upgrade has immediate positive capital flows and any exclusion a negative consequence. Membership of any leading emerging markets index has therefore consequences well beyond simply providing a solid and much needed base for analytics.

As such country (market) classifications straddle uncomfortably sovereign ratings, issuer ratings and potential stock market ratings as exhibited in Figure 3.1.

In a perfect world, a country's economic potential, current financial or monetary situation, and fiscal management should be fully incorporated into a country's rating and not its classification. This is largely the case and sovereign ratings enjoy great support and respect in the community.

S&P, for example, scores countries on five major factors and related subjects:[2]

1. Political—institutional effectiveness, stability.
2. Economic—structure and growth prospects.
3. External—liquidity and international investment position.
4. Fiscal—performance and flexibility as well as debt burden.
5. Monetary—flexibility and resilience of financial system and capital markets.

Without going into the complexities and intricacies of sovereign ratings, it suffices to say that by and large country ratings by major players, say S&P

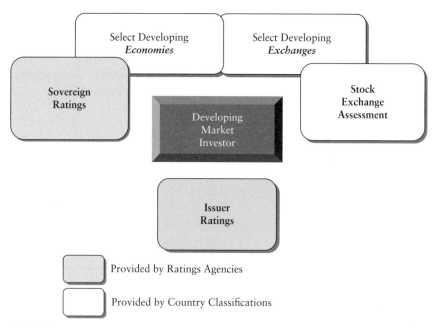

FIGURE 3.1 Ratings and Classification Framework

and Moody's, are quite similar and solidly grounded in analytics. Capital markets take note of ratings and price accordingly, although markets tend to adjust prices faster and thus there is often a gap between the ratings-normal interest and the effective rate a government has to pay or a particular security may yield. Looking at the large number of sovereign ratings changes in early 2012, it became quite clear that the dominant ratings agencies are increasingly on the ball.

At the same time, a very large number of issuers are rated. Moody's, for example, rates more than 12,000 corporate issuers, more than 25,000 public finance issuers, and more than 106,000 structured finance issuers in more than 110 countries.[3] This includes some 130 exchanges and clearinghouses. Thus, from an independent ratings point of view, ratings agencies largely fulfill their role. Clearly, the vast majority of ratings is for issuers in developed economies or for very large companies in developing economies because of the cost and effort involved.

This leaves a gap that country classifications try to fulfill. Arguably, country classifications in their current application focus predominantly on the stock exchange and within the exchange on the tradability of shares for foreign investors. This would be fine if the country classification would not have such signaling effects that do not reflect the opportunity at hand.

When comparing sovereign ratings across country classification categories, anomalies are evident. Clearly, AAA status is restricted to developed economies. Emerging economies cannot aspire to an AAA rating at this stage. Even the emirate of Abu Dhabi, arguably one of the richest economies globally with quasi-unlimited wealth accumulation potential, only receives a AA rating. However, even without the AAA rating, commonly accepted emerging and frontier economies taken together look a lot higher rated than the non–AAA-rated developed economies (see Figure 3.2).

Emerging and frontier economies together (namely developing economies with a reasonable stock market) look like the "middle class" of the world, and that is exactly what they are. The top 10 developing economies look increasingly higher rated than the bottom 10 developed economies. In a few years the top 10 developing markets will be rated like many developed economies today. Already, since the downgrade, Austria, France, New Zealand, and the United States(!) with AA+ are only a fraction (an important plus sign) ahead of developing economies such as Chile, Qatar, or the Czech Republic. Greece, Italy, and Spain sit squarely on the same average rating as a frontier economy.

This leaves some questions about what exactly defines a developing economy from a macroeconomic or sovereign rating perspective. For emerging bond investors this is surely one of the key factors. For equity investors, sovereign ratings are arguably only one aspect in the investment decision making.

Looking at the much-coveted but seemingly artificial separation (save for stock markets) between emerging and frontier economies, it becomes obvious that there is hardly any difference. In fact, frontier economies look stronger from their sovereign ratings than the higher category of emerging markets (see Figure 3.3).

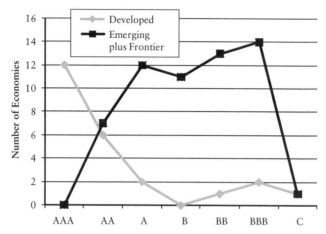

FIGURE 3.2 Sovereign Local Currency Ratings (S&P)—All Markets Classified by Main Index Providers

Source: S&P Ratings data, end of 2011, author's analyses.

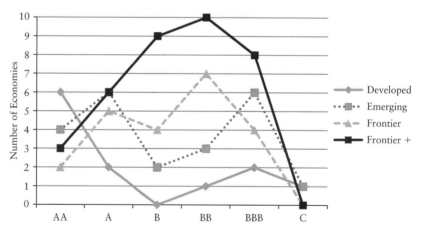

FIGURE 3.3 Sovereign Local Currency Ratings (S&P)—All Classified Markets (excluding all AAA ratings)

Source: S&P ratings data, end of 2011, author's analyses.

As the basis for this comparison, we took the FTSE classification. The frontier + category includes markets considered frontier markets by some index providers and where an S&P or Moody's country rating exists, which is not always the case.

If you assigned a linear score to each rating (with all its deficiencies), say 6 for AAA and 0 for CCC, then the difference in the mean or the average between emerging and frontier markets based on their ratings is very small, as depicted in Figure 3.4. This also raises the question of why a distinction of such importance to capital flows can be based on such small difference.

We may therefore conclude that country classifications and the adjudication of emerging or frontier market status is not a reflection of the macroeconomic conditions but more an assessment of stock market and foreign investor conditions. As a consequence, all markets and companies on such markets that do not have a regulated or formal stock exchange that meets certain other formal criteria are excluded. However, the prevailing selection includes markets that by other standards such as economic freedom or rule of law should not be included in the same category.

Since a large part of the asset management and investment community follows either a passive or an indexed investment approach, the exclusion of certain attractive markets and the inclusion of certain relatively unattractive markets has a significant redirecting effect on foreign investment capital flows. If, for example, Mongolia or Lao PDR is the best-performing stock market, it is almost impossible for investors with managed assets to participate because these markets are not graded. Their results are also not included in the

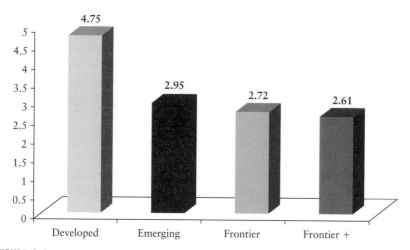

FIGURE 3.4 Average Rating on a Linear Scale (AAA = 6, CCC = 0)
Source: S&P ratings data, end of 2011, author's analyses.

benchmark index. The investment success of developing markets as measured by global indexes does not properly reflect the performance of these markets.

Such markets then remain reserved for specialists, direct investment and active, alternative, or contrarian investment managers. This is surely not the purpose of grading economies by mainstream players and index providers. It effectively and wrongly influences the freedom of capital markets.

If these failings are the case, then the investment community would seem better off with having a country rating by traditional ratings agencies and a separate stock market rating (including stock market framework conditions for foreign investors). This would take the sting out of the country classification and make these assessments what they really are, namely assessments of the environment and conduciveness to foreign investment in listed equities.

If we had separate assessments of the country (sovereign ratings) and the stock market, the investment community could focus on the essence of investing, namely, selecting stocks and companies with attractive potential while accepting country and stock market limitations. These limitations should define the required risk premium required but not shape stock selection. Investors would not be conditioned to put some allocation into a country that happens to make the cut for being an emerging or frontier economy in order to replicate the index or benchmark their performance.

This would hand back responsibility for asset allocation to the asset manager, where it belongs. Even for passive asset managers, if some developing market indexes cover a much wider range of markets, true performance of developing markets would be established. Then index or benchmark providers can segregate markets into developing economies with a solid and deep stock market and those with a fledgling stock market, or select any other combination that suits their investor demand. This would achieve an objective benchmark and allow investors to properly separate attractive countries, attractive trading markets, and attractive stocks.

With this information basis, the decision model for picking stocks would follow a different trade-off matrix and reflect in our view much more clearly the true nature and inherent risks of developing economies.

It is this very dilemma between very conducive overall opportunities, for example, resource endowment in the Republic of Mongolia and possibly the opposite regarding the stock market/access for foreign investors. Today, with generalized country assessments, the Republic of Mongolia does not make any category, nor does Lao PDR. Both led the stock market performance league table for much of 2011 (see Figure 3.5).

The trade-off between attractive economies or attractive companies and attractive trading markets is at the heart of selecting developing markets for investing. A better and independent assessment of the two key decision factors would be along the matrix in Figure 3.6.

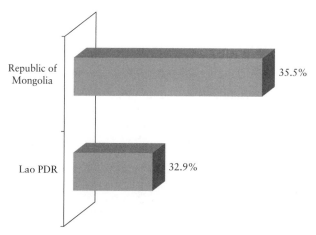

FIGURE 3.5 Top Performing Stock Markets, First Half 2011
Source: Bloomberg, author's calculations.

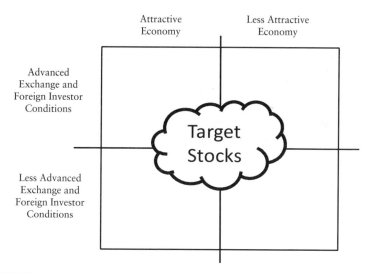

FIGURE 3.6 Investment Attractiveness Trade-Off Matrix

The investment community and their service providers are not doing the investor a favor by treating developing (both emerging and frontier) economies as more or less exotic animals well before any stock selection takes place. In fact, as we demonstrated, several developing economies can hardly be distinguished from developed economies except for size and some stock market attributes. One of these attributes is short selling or stock borrowing, but we have to ask ourselves whether short selling is such a critical feature for the investor when an index can be short sold or other hedging instruments are available.

Let us separate the economy from the stock market and both of these from possibly a few very attractive companies in these markets. Then we do not encourage the investment community to restrict itself to a few countries that made the cut and we avoid the continuous lobbying of those countries that did not make the cut. This cat and mouse game basically leaves the investor in the cold.

ISSUES WITH CLASSIFICATIONS

There are a number of specific issues inherent in the classification systems outlined—not for all proponents, but in general. They can be grouped into three themes:

1. Lack of differentiation between the concept of investable markets (attractive economies) and investable securities in less-developed stock markets.
2. Bias of the investment community and investment service community for large and liquid stock markets and well accepted or understood economies.
3. Moral hazard implications of country classifications and resulting indexes as a measure of the performance.

The issues raised serve to highlight the dilemma that country classifications and related indexes have created.

Lack of Differentiation between Investable Economies and Investable Securities

Investment is all about selecting the best security, not the best stock market infrastructure. Ideally we have both but when we are not operating in developed economies, there is always a trade-off. Surely a minimum of securities market requirements must prevail to trade a security with confidence, but the attractive stock remains the first port of call.

As a consequence, there must be both necessary and sufficient conditions fulfilled to qualify a market as emerging or frontier or nonexistent. The dominant approaches today emphasize as a necessary and largely sufficient condition a stock market with adequate infrastructure, size, turnover, liquidity, and macroeconomic performance/framework. This leaves a lot wanting.

If in a developing market there are perhaps five stocks listed that are relatively very large, partly from privatizations and partly from genuine IPOs, and the stock market was created with the advice or equity participation of experienced consultants and market operators, then, everything else being equal, such an economy would make the cut to be a frontier or possibly emerging economy. The category does not matter in this hypothetical example.

Typically, in most developing economies this would include counters from telecommunications, banking, utilities, possibly trading, conglomerates, property, airlines, and resources. They tend to be the first bigger companies, were often government-owned, and can be sold off or be motivated to list on the new stock exchange. They also carry good public support because they are household names in these economies.

If country classifications include such a market in their indexes, then all asset managers tend to follow suit and have a very small universe to pick from. Everybody picks the relatively best ones. If we all pick the same or similar stock we all get the same returns and carry the same risks. But we did not pick the stock because of its inherent attractiveness, we picked the stock because the country with limited stock choices is included in the index and we wish to replicate the index. If we look at the holdings of emerging markets fund managers, they often hold positions the same securities because they are essentially a must—best in class. This causes high concentration risks since any change in the index leads a number of players to move in concert. On a good day that is fine but on a bad day that compounds the problem. This may also explain the growing convergence of price earnings multiples between developed and developing markets when there is hardly any justification based on a proper risk adjustment.

The fundamental tenet of asset management, to pick the best stocks, no longer works at its best because we artificially restricted the universe of choices. The specific investment seems to matter less than framework conditions. In a broad market, we may choose from a great variety of securities and still be able to benchmark ourselves against this very market index. In a narrow market we can only benchmark ourselves against the regional or sector or category index and suffer from limited choices.

Thus we need to broaden the horizon and not constrain the universe. We should define all markets or economies with a minimum of tradable securities and a minimum of stock market attributes as our base to make choices—not assign emerging or frontier or unclassified status to each country. We should differentiate more clearly between more and less solid trading environments but not at the cost of ignoring the underlying business or economic structures. This would reduce the concentration risk of current developing market investors and probably reduce volatility in emerging markets.

We simply need to accept that some or probably all developing markets simply cannot take more than a certain level of investment. If we broaden our horizon, we may alleviate the problem. Time will further alleviate the issue of narrowness through new offerings but not to the degree desired. Thus we have to accept limits on what developing markets can absorb at reasonable prices. After all, it took developed economies several decades to get to the depth of today—already developing markets are catching up at about five times the pace.[4]

Bias toward Large and Accepted Stock Markets

Many resource-based, rapidly growing, and potentially attractive investment regions or countries without a stock exchange or without a qualifying stock exchange remain outside the current definition of a frontier market. They include most prominently economies in Africa, parts of Central America, and the Caribbean, the Pacific, and many of the smaller economies globally. Moreover, the requirement of a qualifying stock exchange excludes a number of potentially attractive investment destinations that do not have stock exchanges at all, although their numbers are dwindling.

Today there exist some 220 to 230 distinct economies globally. How many independent markets or economies are recognized is largely a political issue. Well over 100 of them have stock exchanges or participate in a joint stock exchange. In March 2011, the FTSE Global Equity Index System classified 48 of the existing 100-plus stock markets as developed or emerging. Most other classification providers are not much different. Up to 50 other economies with a stock market are considered frontier economies by at least one provider, but in general the consensus is that frontier economies number around 30 to 35.

This leaves a number of economies with exchanges that do not meet the standard for frontier market classification by the dominant classifications and some 100 economies that are not classified at all for investment purposes. Even when accounting for regional exchanges such as in West Africa, there remain a number of largely ignored countries, to the detriment of investors.

Economies with stock exchanges such as Bhutan, Zambia, Libya, Rwanda, Algeria, Cambodia (very recently), and Lao PDR (a joint effort with the Korean market) are off the frontier market list. Economies like Angola and Syria without any stock exchange (yet), are equally not qualified as frontier markets. Even when they open their markets, as in the case of Cambodia with the help of the Korean stock market operator and therefore based on developed market standards, it will take a long time before they meet size or liquidity requirements. Yet the first few companies may well prove to be adequately large and attractive investments, as demonstrated recently.

Focusing on size negates some of the fundamental characteristics of developing markets: small but highly attractive.

With the current definition that only economies with many equity and other tradable securities on formal exchanges are considered, economies with a fragmented economic structure, say a dominance of SMEs (small medium sized enterprises), can never aspire to becoming a classified market. Such economies may well start a market—partly because the classification system makes them second-rate citizens without a market—but may fail to sport sizable listings. Such markets do not qualify under the current definition of frontier markets and would thus be considered pioneer markets or least-developed markets. That does not do justice to the attractiveness of investing in such a market that may well have a small but decently organized and governed exchange. To access these markets there are multiple avenues: smaller country funds, investment companies, private but securitized debt transactions, public partnership projects, property related structures, and depository receipts, or, occasionally, foreign listings. Without a country recognition and inclusion in some index, it is hard for mainstream asset managers to invest.

Many economies develop securitized debt markets ahead of deep equity markets simply because the financial system needs to funded, refinanced, and managed by the central bank or regulator. This requires debt instruments that can be traded and may have good liquidity. Public finance, international multilateral finance, and private-public partnerships (PPP) are all possible avenues to participate in a developing economy without requiring a large stock market. Without country recognition this becomes more problematic.

We therefore need a better and much wider definition and categorization, if necessary, for developing markets in addition to the clear leaders such as BRIC (Brazil Russia, India, China), Mexico, South Korea, or the Next 11 or the CIVETS. This definition needs to include markets heretofore not considered investable and markets with heretofore wanting stock markets.

The Dilemma of Country Classifications

Emphasizing current investor perceptions and creating analytical and index tools for such markets only leads to a self-fulfilling prophecy and to the exclusion of interesting other markets. As indicated earlier, there is hardly any economic difference between emerging and frontier markets but there is an implied or actual difference in the quality of the stock exchange and there is a fundamental difference between a graded market and the others.

The dilemma occurs when an asset manager makes a decision about stock selection on the basis of country classification by third-party information providers. Essentially this creates a moral hazard situation whereby moral hazard is seen as a special case of information asymmetry. Since classifications are pretty rigid, the fundamental choice of market is taken on the basis of lesser information.

The implied moral hazard of country classifications is twofold: first, the vested interest of economies to be included in classifications, that is to meet as closely as possible and feasible in their own culture the requirements of becoming an emerging or frontier economy. This would lead to their inclusion in many indexes and unlock new capital flows. Thus economies effectively determine the outcome by making the necessary adjustments and putting some public assets on the market. Typically most countries will have a major bank, certainly utilities and telecoms, probably an airline, and one or two flagship companies they can influence. Then there are a couple of amendments to liberalize the regime for foreign investors without giving away all the toys. In combination, this would get them close to becoming an accepted member of the frontier or emerging market club without providing a real base for companies in the economy to motor away and grow for the long term.

In fact, a number of transition economies, in particular smaller ones, have done exactly that, possibly to their detriment.[5] They include countries with mandatory listings after mass privatizations and mandatory listings of minority packages during privatizations. Many of these economies may be better off allying themselves with global markets or importing stock market services. Since, however, membership and capital flows depend on having a stock market, every economy is forcing market development even if a domestic market is difficult to develop for most. For Baltic states, for example, the proximity to and possible aspiring membership in the European Union would suggest that going it alone, with limited domestic supply of companies outside privatizations and a few public companies, is not the optimal approach. Nevertheless, they cannot aspire to becoming a frontier economy without. That is not in the investor's interest—it would be better to buy a Latvian company listed in London with its leading trading infrastructure than to deal with an emerging Latvian exchange. Latvia, however, would be sidelined. It is also not in the interest of the country because the complexities of developing and managing a modern stock exchange, calling for cooperation or outsourcing. Thus costs may well exceed benefits and there are alternative, electronic, or joint venture means to having a securities market for limited and smaller domestic companies.

COUNTRY OR INDUSTRY DOMINANCE?

There is an argument that in fact in many emerging economies, industries are more important than the country economy. For example, Mongolia is dominated by attractive resource industries, several Middle Eastern economies by oil, and Norway equity markets by a dominant energy industry. Conversely, about half of the automotive market capitalization is in Japan. Thus, the relative importance of industry and country assessment needs to be considered.

MCSI conducted research and reviewed previous studies in an excellent report.[6] The conclusions of this report were: "We have investigated the relative strengths of industries versus countries in the global equity markets. We considered three regions: (1) a 48-country global model comprising both developed and emerging markets, (2) a 24-country model for emerging markets, and (3) a 16-country model for developed Europe. In emerging markets, we found that countries consistently dominated industries since 1994. In developed Europe, industries have strongly dominated countries since 1999. Globally, the result is more balanced, with industries dominating for some periods and countries dominating in others. We also studied market capitalization dependencies in the relative strength of industries versus countries. We found that for small-cap stocks, industry effects become relatively weaker, whereas country effects retain their full strength."

The continued evaluation of country economies as a base for establishing investable markets seems to hold for emerging economies. Regardless of the dominance and attractiveness of selected industries, country parameters still seem to matter more.

In this virtuous circle the fundamental objective of the investor gets lost: finding the best possible company in any market with acceptable trading conditions. It is questionable whether many markets remain that have less than a minimum level of trading conditions. Since markets are increasingly competitive and most developing markets have joint ventures and cooperation agreements with leading stock market operators, hardly any stock markets exists that lack the basics. Some aspects may be wanting but the basics are there.

Since most assets under external management cannot invest in markets not covered by an index or by some analytics, country assessments of developing markets with limited stock selection become the decision model when they should be analytical support.

The second aspect of the moral hazard problem is the herding effect. If an economy migrates to become an emerging/frontier club member, all investors with asset allocations to developing economies—and most of them should have such an asset allocation—get corralled into a few markets where by the virtue of increased investment, prices and volumes tend to rise. Most if not all emerging market investors will hold or have held Gazprom, Petrobras, ICBC or Bank of China, or Reliance Industries, to name a few, to meet their BRIC quota and because these companies have by far the largest market capitalization. Hence, the share is more active and prices are driven by foreign allocations. While there is some liquidity, exiting a relatively sizable position by a foreign investor can be daunting, private transactions excluded, regardless of the analyzed depth of the market, since local players are better informed and like to take advantage of foreign investors. This means that in any event a long-term holding strategy as opposed to active trading becomes the dominant strategy and mitigates the issue of liquidity.

Under a long-term investment strategy, the investor wants to be sure that the underlying assets are adequately valued and perform well. Here we reach boundaries in most developing economies. The underlying asset is invariably not properly valued, accountants do not apply the same standards, contracts do not meet the same level of rigor, and connected transactions are prevalent. Investors rely very heavily on public financial information. International accounting firms claim to apply the same standards or the same IFRS throughout the world but anyone who has analyzed some of the audited balance sheets in developing economies knows that this is simply not the case. This is the flip side of the information asymmetry that does not exist in developed economies to the same degree, recent scandals and extreme cases of fraud excepted. Therefore, as leading investors point out,[7] there is really no substitute for visiting a company, validating some of the key areas, and undertaking substantial due diligence on the company's corporate governance. However, under a stringent onsite due diligence and long-term investment strategy, the quality of a stock exchange above a certain minimum becomes secondary. Either way, the dominance of stock market criteria only serves short-term traders. They are different than investors.

The number of "stuck" investors with sizeable stakes, many of them severely overvalued, is far larger than those moving into and out of developing market investments as dictated by their own investment policy. Blaming market liquidity is a popular explanation. Reluctance to invest in developing markets is a widespread consequence. The perception of high risk and illiquidity is compounded, but not for the right reasons or for properly researched fundamentals.

The root cause is the investment framework—stock exchange, foreign investor conditions, trading environment—propagated by country classifications for investors and followed by a large part of the investment community. As long as a developing economy can arbitrage these classification requirements and meet some criteria to the satisfaction of the analysts, it becomes a member of the classification club. The investor, certainly the passive investor, has a tendency to follow suit. We thereby create seemingly successful markets but in reality create a self-fulfilling process or augment the returns of local businesses and shareholders. That is not the purpose of developing markets investments for diversification and performance management, though.

A POTENTIAL LEAP IN CLASSIFICATIONS

The first Inclusive Wealth Report[8] by the joint initiative of several United Nations agencies, attempts to quantify all capital aspects of an economy—human, production, and natural resources—and proposes a wealth measure or stock metrics to establish sustainability as opposed to the income or flow measure of GDP and forecasts thereof. Although in its early stages, the concept is intriguing and could result in the addition of a much more relevant aspect of an economy's true prospects.

While many of the national assets measured fall into the category of environmental sustainability, overall they form a comprehensive picture of the development path of an economy. The key variables used are listed in Table 3.2.

The first assessment and quantification of some twenty economies starts with the premise that the wealth of a nation is the social worth of an economy's assets: reproducible capital, human capital, knowledge, natural capital, population, institutions, and time. Although measurements are fraught with uncertainties and quantification issues, this approach quite comprehensively addresses many of the shortcomings in current classifications. Measuring the growth and sustainability of a nation's wealth could present a very solid foundation for making investor decisions. If we complement such wealth assessment with practical investment aspects such as rule of law, governance, and conditions for doing business, we are moving towards a very clear distinction between economies with a future and those in decline.

This would significantly influence country classification of today based on GDP, stock market size/attributes, or other purely macroeconomic aggregates. Countries depleting their resources of any kind would be classified differently than economies that are growing or building their resource base.

The report concludes that if states with an inclusive wealth per capita annual growth rate less than their GDP per capita annual growth rate want to sustain high GDP growth rates for the long term, increased (inclusive)

TABLE 3.2 Key Variables of the Inclusive Wealth Report

Key Variables	Subcategories	Examples of data
Human Capital		Population
		Mortality
		Employment
		Education
Produced Capital		Investments
		Depreciation
		Assets
		Productivity
Natural Capital	Fossil fuels	Reserves
	Minerals	Production
	Forest Resources	Prices
	Agricultural land	
	Fisheries	
Health Capital		Age
		Value of life
Adjustments	Total factor productivity	
	Carbon damages	
	Oil capital gains	

Source: Inclusive Wealth Report 2012.

investment will be required. Ultimately the policy response of such declining nations would be a watershed decision criterion for long-term investors.

Countries assessed in the first report include: the United States, Japan, Germany, the United Kingdom, France, China, Canada, India, Russia, Norway, Indonesia, South Africa, Portugal, Iran, Venezuela, Singapore, Saudi Arabia, Nigeria, and Nicaragua. This covers economies with more than 75 percent of global GNI (gross national income).

Key findings of the report are worth further consideration:[9]

- Seventy percent of countries assessed show a positive inclusive wealth per capita growth indicating sustainability.
- High population growth rates in 25 percent of the countries assessed indicate the unsustainability of their economic development.
- Nineteen out of 20 economies experienced a decline in natural capital.
- Six countries assessed also show a decline in inclusive wealth driven by resource depletion. The report states that in almost all countries, potential gains in renewable resources were not enough to compensate for the depletion of exhaustible stocks.
- The majority of countries saw an increase in manufactured wealth and all countries improved on human capital.

In simple terms, we are largely depleting natural resources and compensating with more manufacturing and human development. Most relevant is the finding that 25 percent of countries that have positive GDP and Human Development Index (HDI) trends (typically attractive investment destinations), were found to have negative inclusive wealth development. Thus one may conclude that income flows of GDP can be a short-term measure while national assets and their trends can be a long-term measure of an economy's outlook. This would clearly separate exploitative short-term economies from long-term attractive economies.

It is further interesting to note that the average consumption- and production-based resource depletion is very significant in high-income economies (above US$12,276 per capita GNI) to the tune of US$300 billion plus per year and much lower in upper-middle, lower-middle, and low-income economies (US$50–150 billion). All else being equal this may well suggest that high-income economies are rapidly depleting their national assets. This supports the argument that the competitiveness of high-income economies is declining at the expense of upper-middle and lower-middle–income economies.

Ignoring the many issues and complexities with measuring the assets of a nation, initial findings strongly support the notion of a global sea change in economic attractiveness from developed economies towards developing economies. As we argue from different angles, investors are well advised to look for sustainable economies rather than bandit economies. An inclusive wealth indicator may prove very usable but is still some steps away from being accepted. Investors today thus have to make way with other comparable measures.

INDEXING AND PASSIVE INVESTMENT: THE ASIAN INVESTOR PERSPECTIVE

Noël Amenc, Felix Goltz, Padmanaban Narasimhan, Masayoshi Mukai, and Lin Tang[10]

Indexation continues to play an important role in global asset allocation. Total worldwide assets under internal indexed management rose from $4.8 trillion to $6.0 trillion as of June 30, 2011, a 25 percent increase from one year earlier (Olsen 2011). In view of the growing volume in assets under management in passive indexing strategies, a great many index providers have emerged worldwide; not only the organizations specializing in the index service but also stock exchanges as well as investment banks. Each provider has created or is creating a host of indexes representing a full complement of asset classes, as well as asset class segments.

In the history of indexes, country-based capitalization-weighted indexes have proved to be the most popular indexes for both equity and bond markets. Such indexes are often used as a bellwether for the economy, as they are supposed to represent market trends. Today, a growing demand for indexes as investment vehicles has led to innovations including sector, style, and size-based indexes that provide exposures to specific risk factors.

As the choice of an index is a crucial step in both asset allocation and performance measurements, it is useful to investigate index use and perceptions about indexes. In fact, relatively little is known about the views of potential users of indexes in the Asia Pacific region. The EDHEC-Risk Asia Indexing Survey 2011 is the first comprehensive survey of Asian investment professionals that aims to analyze the current uses of and opinions on stock and bond indexes. It is our hope that this survey will provide unique insight into the users' perspective of the index industry.

The survey was conducted during April and May of 2011, and received a total of 127 responses. The respondents provided a balanced picture of the Asia Pacific asset management industry and include asset managers, institutional asset owners, investment consultants, and private wealth managers of different size categories. While we have included Japan in the survey, responses from Japan are relatively low at 4 percent of total respondents. Thus the survey mainly represents respondents from Asia Pacific excluding Japan, and in particular the major asset management centers of Australia, Hong Kong, and Singapore, which each account for roughly 20 percent of overall respondents.

The objective of this essay is to summarize the key findings of the study. It captures only the most important themes, and further results can be found in the complete survey document (see the EDHEC-Risk Asia Indexing Survey, EDHEC-Risk Institute [2012]). We first provide a look at the perception that Asia Pacific investors have of different asset classes. We then turn to an overview of survey results concerning equity indexes. Our focus on equity indexes is driven by the fact that this is the asset class where indexes are most commonly used among Asian investors.[11]

Respondents' Usage and Perception of Standard Market Indexes

We first provide an overview of overall usage rates and satisfaction rates of index users across indexes for different asset classes. Note that these results relate to the indexes themselves, rather than to investable products that would track such indexes. Table 3.3 provides an overview of these results.

Overall, our findings suggest that index use is relatively widespread in equity indexes but much lower for bond indexes. While almost 90 percent of

TABLE 3.3   Summary of Usage and Satisfaction with Indexes by Asset Classes*

Issue	Equity	Government Bond	Corporate Bond
If you invest in this asset class, have you used indexes for these investments?	88.5%	51.5%	40.8%
Are you satisfied with the index products you have used in each asset class?†	71.1%	49.2%	59.8%

*Percentages shown in this table have been normalized by excluding the nonresponse for each question.
†Percentages shown in this row are obtained by those who have used indexes for their investment in the respective asset class.

equity investors who respond to our survey use equity indexes, only about 50 percent of government bond investors use indexes for this asset class, and the usage rate is lower for corporate bond indexes. The satisfaction rate for indexes is moderate for equity, at about 71 percent. For bond indexes, the satisfaction rate is even lower (49.2 percent for government bond indexes and 59.8 percent for corporate bond indexes).

The results show that while indexes are relatively widely used in all asset classes, satisfaction rates are moderate. A potential explanation for this is that despite obvious advantages such as liquidity, transparency, and cost efficiency when implemented as investments, standard indexes also come with a number of issues. The recent literature has cited several issues with indexes. With our unique sample of investment management practitioners from Asia-Pacific, we had the opportunity to verify whether these points are indeed shared by practitioners. Also, given that we cover not only equity indexes but also bond indexes in our survey, we are able to assess which issues are most pronounced according to the view of practitioners for indexes in each asset class. These practitioner views may also be useful feedback for index providers who are looking at developing improvements over the currently available indexes.

The standard market indexes in equity and bond markets have been capitalization weighted and debt weighted indexes. For equity indexes, research has raised the issues of overinvestment in the overpriced stocks (Hsu 2006), and concentration in a few large stocks (Tabner 2007 and Malevergne et al. 2009), which leads to relatively poor diversification. In the case of bond indexes some of the issues observed are similar to equity indexes, like the so-called Bums Problem. This problem refers to the fact that issuers with a large amount of debt outstanding account for a relatively large fraction of the total debt market. It has thus been argued that bond indexes that are debt weighted may have a tendency to be overinvested in rather risky assets. We can see that this problem bears some resemblance to the problem of overinvestment in overpriced stocks as in the case of equity indexes. However, other issues are different from equity indexes and unique to bond indexes. Such commonly cited issues are the pricing difficulties (Elton and Green 1998) and unstable duration or credit risk exposures (Siegel 2003, Benning 2006, and Campani and Goltz 2011), for example. When considering the problems pointed out in the existing literature, it thus appears that challenges when constructing indexes differ across asset classes.

Our survey assesses the importance of such issues to index users. Table 3.4 shows the important issues that respondents have across different asset classes. All these issues listed in the table have received a high importance ranking by the average respondent to our survey (importance level of at least 1.95[*] on a scale from −1 to 3).

The findings of our survey make it clear that the issues investors see with existing indexes differ across asset classes. Equity investors fear overinvestment in overpriced stocks and insufficient diversification/size biases due to concentration of the indexes in a small number of often highly correlated stocks. Fixed-income investors, by contrast, are more likely to be concerned by duration stability and liquidity of the indexes. These results suggest that

TABLE 3.4   Important Issues Associated with Indexes by Asset Class

	Equity Indexes	Government Bond Indexes	Corporate Bond Indexes
Important issues associated with indexes	■ Overinvestment in overpriced stocks ■ Poor diversification ■ Sector and size biases ■ Lack of economic representation	■ Difficult to invest/ replicate ■ Instability of duration ■ Inconsistent security selection rules and nonsystematic pricing	■ Overinvestment in more risky companies ■ Lack of liquidity ■ Unreliable credit exposure

[*]The rating is based on a conversion to a score for the scaled responses: −1 (not important), 0 ("I don't know"), and 1 (slightly important) to 3 (very important), excluding nonresponse.

investors in a given asset class need indexes that provide solutions to problems that are different from those faced by investments in other asset classes. Overall, our results imply that a potential path for index providers in terms of future development may be to think about index construction methods that are specific to a given asset class rather than trying to apply a given index construction principle to various different asset classes without considering the specific issues at hand.

Defining the Index Universe: Indexes for Subsegments of a Broader Universe

Within a given investment universe (such as "Asian equity"), investors have different ways of defining the relevant subcategories, if any. This question is of practical importance as it will guide implementation through the respective indexes, such as broad indexes, country indexes, sector indexes, and so on. Perhaps more important, the choice of subcategories will determine how investors exploit the diversification opportunities within the universe. In the academic literature, the definition of breakdowns into subcategories or basis assets has received a fair amount of attention as tests of asset pricing models may depend on how the categories are chosen (see Lewellen et al. 2010 or Ahn et al. 2009). In investment management, results of asset allocation studies may depend in a similar manner on how subsegments are formed. For example, there is a regular discussion on whether sectors, styles, or countries are more relevant ways of forming subsegments of global or regional equity universes (e.g., Hamelink et al. 2001, Ferreira 2006, Errunza et al. 1999). In particular, research assesses whether diversification effects are stronger within the universe for certain segmentation approaches. Our survey allows us to assess which segmentations investors prefer. It is also interesting to assess which segmentation approaches are preferred across different geographic investment universes. For instance, one might expect that segmentation approaches could differ between equity portfolios covering relatively homogenous countries (such as a European equity portfolio) and universes covering more heterogeneous countries (such as an Asia equity portfolio).

In order to assess which equity index categorization (segmented equity indexes based on style, size, sector, country, etc.) is more relevant according to the views of practitioners, we first asked investors to rank the importance of various kinds of equity indexes that correspond to different segmentation approaches.

Table 3.5 shows the overall importance of broad indexes as well as various segmentations. The results are reported in terms of scores, where an

TABLE 3.5   Importance of Equity Indexes to the Portfolio Construction Process

	Regional or Worldwide Indexes	Country Indexes	Sector Indexes	Size-Segment Indexes	Style Indexes (Value/ Growth)	Factor-Based Equity Indexes
Average score	2.28	2.2	1.78	1.39	1.30	1.02
% not important at all	4.4	5.2	11.2	14.9	18.3	24.3
% important and very important	85.0	81.9	67.2	52.5	49.6	40.0

increasing score* signals increasing importance. The results show that broad indexes (regional or worldwide indexes and to a lesser extent country indexes) are much more important than segmented indexes (sector, size, style segment indexes). It is also clear from Table 3.5 that among the ways of forming subsegments, sector indexes are seen as more important than size, style, and factor indexes.

Table 3.5 depicts the average scores received by breakdown. For each breakdown, respondents rate them as one of the categories—very important, important, slightly important, I don't know. Based on this scaled response we compute a score. A higher score indicates a more important breakdown.** Aggregated score of all respondents is reported.

With a perspective on overall preference of equity indexes among investors, we asked the investors how they would like to handle the segmentation of their universe when using equity indexes in different geographic universes. The basic idea is that it is possible that different geographic investment universes lead to different segmentations. For each investment universe, we asked the respondents to choose their top three segmentation approaches, indicating the importance of each (i.e. from one to three). The results are reported in terms of scores in Table 3.6, where an increasing score

---

*The respondents were asked to choose three options for breakdown, and rank them in their preferred order of importance. If a particular choice was selected as the most preferred it was given a score of 3. The second preferred choice of breakdown was set to 2, and the third preferred is set to 1. The score for other choices of breakdown is set to zero.

**Conversion from scaled response to score is done so that very important $= 3$, important $= 2$, slightly important $= 1$, I do not know $= 0$, not important $= -1$.

TABLE 3.6 Importance of using Indexes by Type

Segmentation Approach → Geographic Universe ↓	Using a Broad Market Index	Using Sector Indexes	Using Size-Based Indexes	Using Style-Based Indexes	Separate Indexes for Emerging and Developed	Individual Country Indexes	Regional Indexes
Investment in local country	N/A	1.28	1.28	.49	N/A	2.42	N/A
Investment in Asia except Japan	2.11	.80	.46	.37	.79	1.06	N/A
Investment in Asia	2.00	.69	.53	.39	.99	1.05	N/A
Investment focus that is oriented worldwide	1.91	.76	.42	.32	.89	.66	.67
Investment within Europe	2.05	1.03	.62	.40	.66	.92	N/A

signals increasing importance of a particular choice. The results show that there exists a significant difference when comparing the importance of using a sector breakdown to the importance of using a style breakdown. Within all investment universes, a sector definition is more important than a style definition. This can potentially be explained by the fact that Asian investors still adhere to a tradition based on fundamental analysis, which tends to specialize in sectors. Styles, which are a more common notion in countries with a strong focus on multimanagement and for manager selection (such as the United Kingdom and the United States) are not widely used in Asia.

Table 3.6 indicates the average scores received by breakdown. For each investment universe set, respondents were asked to choose their top three preferred choices of breakdown and rank them. This rank is converted to a score, and the higher the score received the more preferred is that choice of breakdown in that investment universe set. Note that broad market index is N/A in the first row because the individual country index is the broad market index. Regional indexes were not provided as an option in the first three and the fifth cases. Hence they are N/A. EM/DM represents emerging/developed market indexes.

We also perform statistical tests on the results above to see whether differences are statistically significant. Two types of statistical tests are performed. The first type of test looks at differences of practices across geographic universes, that is, we assess whether the type of breakdown used may depend on the investment universe. For example, we assess whether a sector breakdown is more important in an Asian investment universe than it is in a European investment universe, or, perhaps more precisely, we test whether this difference is statistically significant. The second type of test assesses practices within a given geographic universe. It assesses whether the difference of importance of certain types of breakdowns within a given universe is statistically significant. For example, we test whether the greater importance of sector indexes is indeed significant within a given universe.

Table 3.7 captures the key results from the significance tests concerning differences between geographic universes. Here we present results for only those comparisons, where not only a test is possible (similar breakdowns exist between the investment universe sets), but the test results are also significant. We note from Figure 3.6 that the choice of distinction between sector and emerging versus developed markets is high between European and Asian investment universes. Specifically, Figure 3.6 captures the most pronounced difference, which is between Investments in Europe and Investments in Asia. The results show that in the Asian investment universe, using a breakdown by development stage of the market is more important than in the European investment universe. Using sector indexes for the Asian universe is less important than it is within a European equity universe, as shown in Figure 3.6. Both differences between these two regions are highly significant with a p-value of less than 1 percent.

In the second part of the statistical tests, as mentioned, we hold the investment universe constant and assess whether within a given universe, a particular type of breakdown is more important than another. Specifically, we compare the relative importance of three types of breakdown: (1) sector index versus style indexes, (2) sector versus country indexes, and (3) country versus broad market indexes. Table 3.7 summarizes the results from this analysis. The results reported in Table 3.7 lead to three findings of significant

TABLE 3.7 Importance by Region of Index Breakdown

Type of Breakdown	In Asia	In Europe	P-Value of Difference
Importance of using breakdown by emerging/ developed market	0.99	0.66	<0.01
Importance of using sector indexes	0.69	1.03	<0.01

differences between different types of breakdowns. The first panel shows that the higher importance of sector breakdowns compared to style breakdowns (which is apparent from the results in Table 3.6) is statistically significant in all geographic universes. The second panel shows that a country breakdown is significantly more important than a sector breakdown in a regional Asian universe. Note that the difference of importance between country and sector breakdowns is insignificant within the other investment universes but this is not shown in Table 3.8, which only reports statistically significant results. The implication of this result is that product providers who wish to provide useful tools for Asian investors concerning their investments in the Asian region likely need to pay more attention to

TABLE 3.8 Importance of Indexes by Investment Universe

Panel 1	Breakdown by Sector versus Breakdown by Style		
Investment Universe	Importance of Using Breakdown by Sector	Importance of Using Breakdown by Style	P-Value of Difference
Local country	1.28	0.49	<.01
Asia except Japan	0.8	0.37	<.01
Asia	0.69	0.39	0.018
Worldwide	0.76	0.32	<.01
Europe	1.03	0.4	<.01

Panel 2	Breakdown by Sector versus Breakdown by Country		
Investment Universe	Importance of Using Breakdown by Sector	Importance of Using Breakdown by Country	P-Value of Difference
Asia	0.69	1.05	<.01

Panel 3	Breakdown by Country versus Using Broad Market Index without Further Breakdown		
Investment Universe	Importance of Using Breakdown by Country	Importance of Using Broad Market Index without Further Breakdown	P-Value of Difference
Asia except Japan	1.06	2.11	<.01
Asia	1.05	2	<.01
Worldwide	0.66	1.91	<.01
Europe	0.92	2.05	<.01

developing country indexes than to developing sector indexes. Panel 3 shows that the higher importance of broad market indexes compared to country breakdowns (which was apparent in Table 3.6) is statistically significant in all geographic universes.

The main findings of this assessment are thus: (1) a predominance of sector breakdowns compared to style breakdowns, and (2) a predominance of using a single broad index for a given geographic universe rather than a country breakdown, and (3) with an Asian investment universe, country breakdowns tend, nevertheless, to be more important and in particular are more important than sector breakdowns. While the second finding may be justified by the fact that cross-country diversification effects have tended to decrease over time (e.g., Errunza et al. 1999, Bakaert and Harvey 2000), the first finding is clearly surprising. In fact, there is a consensus in both academia (see Fama and French 1993) and practice (as shown by the widespread use of multifactor models such as Barra) that style factors such as value and size have strong explanatory power for expected returns. Despite this evidence on the importance of style factors, investors tend to attach relatively little value to taking into account style classifications when breaking down their investment universe and hence when defining their asset allocation. We have summarized some main findings of our survey concerning usage rates, satisfaction, and perceived issues with indexes, and the preferences Asian investors have when defining and breaking down their beta.

CONCLUSION

Country classifications have created a range of secondary world citizens without an adequate base, to the detriment of the investing community and these countries as well. As investors we fail to understand why to follow some classification system that was developed for economic analyses but not to guide capital flows. The prevailing classification system has developed a misguided life of its own.

Most issues raised by country classifications—we have ignored all technical data and information issues, another moral hazard problem as seen with government information in many countries—can be addressed by classifying markets according to their economic attributes, freedoms, rule of law, and less so based on their trading environment.

For this we need to better understand the drivers of economic performance and competitiveness as well as the drivers of the economic structure. In essence we need to better understand the nature of developing markets and what differentiates the good ones from the less good ones without considering the capital market at all.

The conclusion from the indexing review of Asian investors is twofold. Firstly, usage of indexes is much higher in equities than in fixed income asset classes among Asian investors. Likewise, the satisfaction rates with indexes are lower for bond indexes when compared with equity indexes. This could be attributed to specific issues with bond indexes, such as difficulty in investing and replication and risk/reward properties of these indexes (such as instability of duration and a tendency to overweight high debt entities).

Secondly, for portfolio construction in equities, Asian investors regard indexes that allow a geographic approach (global, regional, and country indexes) as much more important than indexes allowing for other segmentations. Looking at other ways to segment the universe, sector breakdowns appear to be those most relevant for investors and clearly more important than style and size based breakdowns. However, there are some differences in preferred segmentation depending on the investment universe. For example, segmentation by emerging and developed markets is more important for an Asian investment universe than for a European investment universe while segmentation by sector is more important for the European investment universe of Asian investors.

NOTES

1. Noel Amenc, Felix Goltz, et al. EDHEC Risk Indexing Survey, EDHEC Risk Institute, (prepublication flyer, for summary see Part 2) (2012).
2. S&P Country Rating Framework, Sovereign Government Rating Methodologies and Assumptions, Standard & Poor's literature.
3. www.moodys.com.
4. Karen Ward, "The World in 2050," *HSBC Global Research* (January 2011).
5. Stijn Claessens, Someon Djankov, and Daniela Klinebiel, "Stock Markets in Transition Economies," The World Bank, Financial Sector Discussion Paper No. 5, Washington, DC (2000).
6. Jose Menchero and Andrei Morozov, "The Relative Strength of Industry and Country factors in Global Equity Markets," *MSCI Research Insight* (April 2011).
7. Marc Mobius, *The Little Book on Emerging Markets* (Hoboken, NJ: Wiley, 2012).
8. UNU-IDHP and UNEP, Inclusive Wealth Report 2012, Measuring Progress towards Sustainability, Cambridge: Cambridge University Press, 2012.
9. Ibid., key findings, p. xxix.
10. We would like to thank Amundi ETF for their support for the EDHEC-Risk Asia Indexing Survey.
11. As confirmed by the results of our survey.

CHAPTER 4

Alternatives on Selecting Investable Developing Economies

To qualify developing economies for investors in a different way, we should focus primarily on those economic framework conditions that matter most to investors. In this respect the most critical factors include:

- The rule of law: contracts, property, justice/corruption.
- Regulatory effectiveness: licenses, ownership, taxes.
- Economic openness: trade, investment, capital flows.

If these elements are predominantly positive or are developing in the right direction, then we suggest a market has primary attraction to foreign investors. For the lack of a better term, we may call these factors *essential economic freedoms*. The ability to finance and contract under reasonable government regulations is the hallmark of an economy that is investable. Only then should we concern ourselves with entry and exit of such investments or purchase and sale of listed stocks.

Thus as a second condition, the quality (e.g., regulations, liquidity, transparency) of formal or informal capital markets to buy and sell securities in such prima facie attractive markets must meet certain standards. At what level such standards are acceptable to an investor should be largely determined by the investors themselves but the quality of the existing securities trading environment should be objectively assessed by a third party.

The variety and quality of listed or traded securities should matter less to qualify a market; after all, this is the skill and decision of the investor. Any particular security is not better because five other possibly unattractive securities are listed, and no single security should be excluded simply because the market is small or has certain restrictions that still may be acceptable to any one investor. Every specific investment in its trading environment needs to stand up on its own.

Thus, if we find attractive (relatively open) markets that sport a trading environment of some reliability and we have at least one investable (attractive) security, we have a market that should be investable, included in an index—adequately weighted and properly researched using other analytical tools provided by service providers to allow asset managers that replicate, follow, or benchmark themselves against indexes, ratings, or even classifications, to invest. Today and in the absence of recognition of many worthwhile economies this would not be possible, to the detriment of investors.

From a global perspective, at the end of 2010, an estimated US$80 trillion of conventional assets were under third-party management. Alternative assets add about another US$10 trillion.[1] This excludes estimated private wealth with another US$43 trillion, some of which will be included in conventional assets under management. Other estimates put the industry for assets under professional management for a fee in 2010 at around US$56 trillion.[2] This industry grows at 5 to 15 percent per year, excluding years of financial meltdown, and requires growing investment destinations.

A good share of assets under management involves some form of passive management. We define passive management as a method of managing assets whereby the asset managers holds the majority of securities in largely the same weightings in those markets, regions, sectors, or other indexes that they have chosen to invest in and benchmark against. Thereby, they reduce trading frequency and rely on superior asset allocation to achieve overall performance.

While many asset managers claim to seek superior returns by deploying active management, they in fact are largely passive. They are largely passive because they do make discretionary reallocation and weighting decisions but not to the extent of an active manager. This emphasis on passive management stands to reason for principal and practical reasons.[3] There are reams of academic and empirical research and common logic (the sum of all returns is given so that at least some active managers must underperform) to demonstrate that only a few active managers regularly outperform any market.

The trend toward passive investing (TheCityUK and BCG reports) is growing strongly. Multiplying index funds, rapidly developing ETFs, and similar instruments are often passively managed. Maybe more equity and even bond funds are becoming more passively managed. More than half of equity funds managed by third parties outside alternative investments qualify as rather passively managed.

However, the corollary of all styles of asset management is the need to have benchmarks in a variety of forms. They should cover global equity markets without making choices for investors; they should cover different aspects such as regional, country market, or sector indexes. If country classifications seemingly exclude many equity markets, then the asset management industry outside alternative products is artificially constrained.

INVESTOR FACTORS OF IMPORTANCE

We therefore need to consider a different way of looking at selecting investable economies that align investor interests even more than current classifications with all their weaknesses. In line with the need to have some quantifiable basis, we consider some of the most relevant reports in two categories: principal indicators and sector indicators.

Principal Indicators

- The "Index of Economic Freedom" by The Heritage Foundation.[4]
- The "World Competitiveness Reports" by the World Economic Forum.[5]
- The "Doing Business" Index by the International Bank for Reconstruction and Development/The World Bank.[6]
- The "Worldwide Governance Indicators" by the World Bank Group.[7]

Sector Indicators

- The "Global Financial Centers" report by The City of London and the Y/Zen Group.[8]
- The "Global Manufacturing Competitiveness Index" by Deloitte and the US Council on Competitiveness.[9]

These reports have in common that they take a much wider perspective on the current position, competitiveness, and therefore outlook of an economy. They focus more on the underlying texture of the market and less on stock market development or trading infrastructure. This better reflects the true nature of developing economies and should in the long term lead to better investment results than a trading opportunity perspective based on the stock market.

A number of other rankings and global assessments merit attention. The Human Development Index by the United Nations Development program is useful to assess average educational attainment, life expectancy, and average wealth. The Environmental Performance Index published by Yale University is a good indicator of the potential of a market on the basis that environmental responsibility translates into positive economic development. Indicators on natural resource endowment and agricultural production would be another helpful tool. It is, however, not the accumulation of country rankings that will provide the answer but a clear selection of the most pertinent success factors.

In applying the various reports and rankings, we exclude the traditionally advanced economies that are members of the Organisation for Economic Co-operation and Development (OECD). The original charter of the OECD states that "the economically more advanced nations should cooperate in assisting to the best of their ability the countries in process of economic development."[10] Only advanced economies (those considered advanced) were initially admitted to the OECD although today, membership in the OECD is no longer restricted to developed economies but includes advanced emerging economies (OECD statement) that fulfill a number of demanding policy requirements. All current 34 members of the OECD are classified as developed or advanced emerging economies by market participants. The current list of OECD members is depicted in Table 4.1 and emerging markets are highlighted.

We only discuss developing markets that are not OECD members in further consideration and evaluation unless some overall analysis requires their inclusion.

TABLE 4.1   OECD Membership

Americas	Europe	Asia	Australia
Canada	Austria	Japan	Australia
Chile	Belgium	South Korea	New Zealand
Mexico	Czech Republic		
United States	Denmark		
	Estonia		
	Finland		
	France		
	Germany		
	Greece		
	Hungary		
	Iceland		
	Ireland		
	Italy		
	Luxembourg		
	Netherlands		
	Norway		
	Poland		
	Portugal		
	Slovak Republic		
	Slovenia		
	Spain		
	Sweden		
	Switzerland		
	Turkey		
	United Kingdom		

Source: OECD website.

ESSENTIAL ECONOMIC FREEDOMS

The "Index of Economic Freedom" published by the Heritage Foundation and the *Wall Street Journal* quantifies and scores 10 factors that determine in their view economic freedom in any one economy. The 10 factors are:

Rule of law
1. Property rights—private rights, judiciary, effectiveness.
2. Freedom from corruption—government and black market practices.
Limited government
3. Fiscal freedom—tax rate and tax burden.
4. Government spending—government expenditure to GDP.
Regulatory efficiency
5. Business freedom—start, open, close a business.
6. Labor freedom—wages, termination procedures and costs, other barriers.
7. Monetary freedom—price stability and price controls.
Open markets
8. Trade freedom—tariff and non-tariff barriers to imports and exports.
9. Investment freedom—flow of capital.
10. Financial freedom—banking efficiency, government intervention and ownership.

While arguably some of these factors imply some debatable philosophical judgment on what is best for an economy, they do reflect in many elements necessities for an investor. If all these factors score highly, we have indeed a very attractive market to invest in.

"The Heritage Foundation Report" scored 184 countries at midyear 2011. At regional aggregate level, North America was clearly in the lead followed by Europe. South and Central America, the Middle East, and North Africa as well as Asia Pacific were moderately lower and Sub-Saharan Africa was the laggard. This result in Figure 4.1 is not very surprising and rather intuitive.

Most notable at the aggregate level is that regions outside North America and Europe, by definition almost all of them developing economies, are not far behind. If it were not mainly for the rule of law scores, there would be hardly any difference between the regions. Differences of 10 to 15 percent between developed and developing economies are not a reason not to invest.

This seems to support the point made that in fact the rule of law matters critically in assessing the attractiveness of a developing economy. "The Heritage Report" noted: "The independence, transparency, and effectiveness

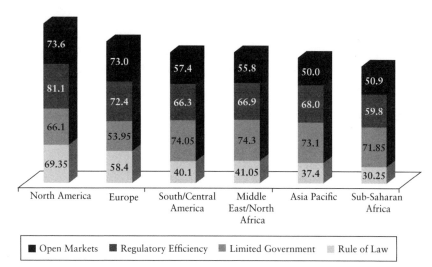

FIGURE 4.1   Economic Freedom 2012 by Region on a Scale of 0 to 100 (best)

Note: In terms of comparative assessment, scores of 80 to 100 indicate truly free economies and scores of 70 to 79.9 mostly free economies. Scores above 60 are termed moderately free economies. A score below 60 is considered mostly not free and such a score should eliminate an economy from the perspective of attractiveness.

Source: Heritage Foundation, author's analyses.

of the judicial system have proved to be key determinants of a country's prospects for long-term economic growth."

Equally notable is that in terms of limited government, that is, fiscal freedom and government spending, developing economies outside Europe and the United States, have better scores. This shows the overreliance of developed economies on debt and budget deficits while many developing economies adopt more prudent fiscal policies. "The Heritage Report" indicates a decline in economic freedom through excessive debt raising, taxation, and regulation and thus both the United States and Europe lost some ground in 2010/2011.

The most concerning aspect surely is the overall low score on rule of law. This factor includes property rights and the absence of corruption. While some improvement with respect to land property (land registries, title issuance, etc.), contract law, and court system is taking place, the overall score is the lowest for nearly all developing economies. It stands globally just about at an average of 40 percent of the possible score against 69 percent and 58 percent for North America and Europe respectively. The top economies score 90 percent. Some degree of an informal economy can be accepted for developing economies but the size of the gap should be a worrisome factor for an investor that is largely ignored in current country classifications.

In open markets, business freedom, that is, the ability, effort, and time to start a business in the legally prescribed form, scores uniformly high as does trade freedom. Investment freedom, or the freedom of capital flows, remains in the aggregate in the moderately restricted category.

We can therefore conclude that globally, much effort is devoted to liberalizing business in most countries but that barriers in terms of rule of law and foreign capital flows lag considerably. This raises a number of fundamental questions for foreign investors in general. By ignoring the lack of rule of law and thereby potentially corruption as well as bandit approaches to conducting business, foreign investors may not only sail perilously close to the wind but may also support a system that does not benefit the investor to the degree deserved. In case of adverse developments, these factors come home forcefully.

To arrive at a different selection of attractive developing economies, we must look at countries individually. If we accept the scalar assessment that with a score above 60 the specific freedom element is positive and below 60 the factor is negative, then in aggregate and on average, developing economies have mainly two areas to work on: open markets (some improvement) and rule of law (much improvement). That is the very essence of the nature of developing markets outlined earlier.

From an investor's point of view and within the parameters of the Heritage Index, we propose that the rule of law, business freedom, and investment freedom are most significant to investors. Government involvement, labor freedom, and other factors are important but investors may assume that good management does overcome such restrictions. Otherwise they hardly have a worthwhile business proposition at all. Without adequate legal framework or the ability to enter and exit the business with few restrictions, foreign investment becomes very high risk and largely unattractive. At this stage, stock markets play an important role. They do mitigate or even overcome investment flow barriers because in general investment into/out of the stock market is regulated in a more conducive way than international capital flows for local businesses.

As a consequence, we could accept a below average score on investment freedom if a decent stock market exists; let us say we accept a score of 40 or above. We can also lower the rule of law requirements to a score of 50 to meet inherent development deficiencies of developing markets and accept that some balancing factor is provided by an organized informal system or a variant of a sponsorship system. We also need to take into account that certain negative factors in the assessment are only applicable to certain situations and requirements.

On business freedom, we maintain that the market must be at least moderately free or have a score of 60 or above. These minimum scores are applied to all markets that are considered emerging or frontier by major players.

Looking at the country scores individually, we find a host of economies that score very well, but a number of markets considered emerging or frontier fail. We then look at a subset of those that narrowly fail in any one category. Only thereafter do stock market considerations in each of these economies come to the forefront. We maintain that this is the sequence that best aligns investor interests with overall market assessment.

Countries are scored in Figure 4.2 on rule of law, business freedom, and investment freedom for those countries that meet our minimum scores.

Of the 15 countries selected, we find a number of usual markets but we also find a number of small economies and some unusual candidates. Most importantly, some of the biggest and highly invested developing markets considered in general to be advanced emerging do not make the cut. In fact, all the BRIC (Brazil, Russia, India, and China) or even the BRIIC (+Indonesia) economies fail one or more requirements.

Noteworthy about the BRIIC economies is that uniformly, they fail on rule of law and investment freedom (free capital flows), as shown in Figure 4.3. The latter is generally overcome by the investment community but the former raises warning signals.

In addition, commonly applauded investment destinations such as Argentina, Bulgaria, Croatia, Kuwait, Malaysia, Mexico, Pakistan, Peru, Philippines, Romania, Saudi Arabia, Slovak Republic, South Africa, Thailand, Turkey, UAE, and Vietnam, to name the most significant ones, fall outside the first grid, although some very narrowly.

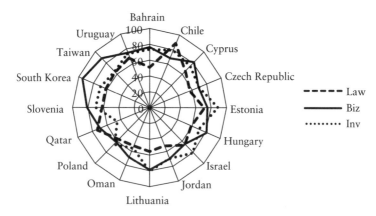

FIGURE 4.2 Investable Economies: Economic Freedoms—Primary
Source: Heritage Foundation, author's analyses.

We may widen the net to adjust for economies that may not meet certain formal criteria but otherwise score very highly. This second set of emerging economies fails narrowly on any one criterion. The standards applied in Figure 4.4 are: at least close to a score of 40 on rule of law, score of 60 on business freedom, and at least 35 on investment freedom. We allow a much lower score on investment freedom because in general more liberal rules apply to stock market or foreign direct investments than for an economy as a whole.

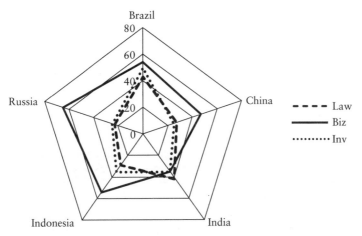

FIGURE 4.3 BRIIC Economies: Economic Freedoms
Source: Heritage Foundation, author's analyses.

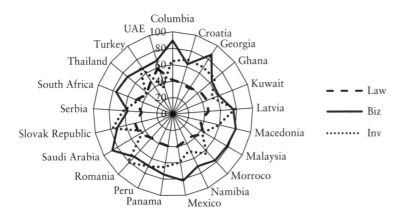

FIGURE 4.4 Investable Economies: Economic Freedoms—Additional
Source: Heritage Foundation, author's analyses.

A good example is the UAE, where onshore investment requires majority local shareholding but free zones allow sole foreign ownership and stock market investments have more benign rules. The score, however, heavily takes into account onshore restrictions.

The secondary group of 21 economies still excludes the BRIIC countries but now covers most of the markets commonly considered interesting.

Any form of index that includes qualitative factors is not a science but rather an art. It is, however, useful to remember that the application of multiple screens increases the likelihood of accurate results and as such a decade-long time series on important investor factors should not be ignored. The Heritage Economic Freedom Indicators are somewhat at odds with prevailing country classifications, but are certainly well grounded.

GLOBAL COMPETITIVENESS

The World Economic Forum publishes yearly the coveted Global Competitiveness Index. In the latest publication, 142 economies are scored. The World Economic Forum report is based quantitatively on 12 pillars of competitiveness and qualitatively on supporting assessments by market participants. The 12 pillars of competitiveness of the World Economic Forum are in summary:

1. Institutions: legal and administrative framework between individuals, firms, and government.
2. Infrastructure: transport and communications.
3. Macroeconomic development: stability, inflation, and public finances.
4. Health and primary education: health services and schooling.
5. Higher education and training: secondary and tertiary education and staff training.
6. Goods market efficiency: supply and demand conditions; competition.
7. Labor market efficiency: flexibility and incentives.
8. Financial market development: banking, capital markets, financial services.
9. Technological readiness: adoption and enhancement of technologies.
10. Market size: domestic and trade markets.
11. Business sophistication: suppliers, branding and marketing, distribution, and production processes.
12. Innovation: R&D and intellectual property.

In applying these factors, the report finds three types of economies: factor driven economies that are dominated by pillars 1 through 4, efficiency driven economies that are weighted heavily on pillars 5 through 10, and innovation driven economies that are strongest in pillars 11 and 12. These stages of development relate in general to GDP per capita thresholds of up to US$2,000 (factor driven), up to US$9,000 (efficiency driven), and above US $9,000 for innovation driven markets. Between each category there are transition categories to account for economies that are developing toward a higher level of competitiveness.

It is more than reasonable to assume that the competitiveness of an economy translates into both growth and economic success. This would be borne out intuitively by an average score across regions. Regional averages cannot be more than an indication, as they are distorted by the top performers.

We eliminate the top 10 most competitive economies: Switzerland, Singapore, Sweden, Finland, the United States, Germany, Netherlands, Denmark, Japan, and the United Kingdom. The rankings by region in Figure 4.5 do not change materially.

More important, however, are individual country scores and competitiveness factors. We therefore cross-reference the primary list of investable nations from the Heritage Economic Freedom Index with the World Competitiveness report.

We postulate that primary investable economies must be in the top half of the world's assessed (142) most competitive economies. This proves to be true. In fact, for bigger economies, except for Armenia and Botswana, all markets selected as primary from the Heritage Index are in the top half, most of them in the top third of global competitiveness.

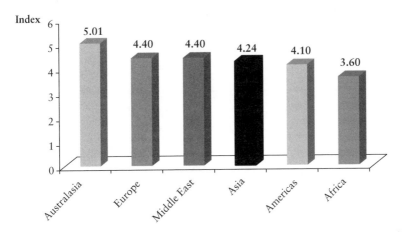

FIGURE 4.5　World Economic Forum: Global Competitiveness—Average by Region
Source: WEF, "Global Competitiveness Report," author's analyses.

From the secondary list, only Croatia, Georgia, Ghana, Macedonia, Namibia, and Romania are not in the top half of global competitiveness. It is interesting to note three European economies in the second half of competitive nations globally.

Again, the BRIIC countries (Brazil, Russia, India, Indonesia, and China) do not fare as well as the general hype would suggest. Their global competitiveness rankings, except for China, are mostly in the lower first half of economies. Their specific ranks in the 2011/12 report were:

- China: 26
- Indonesia: 46
- Brazil: 53
- India: 54
- Russia: 66

This raises the question of whether a large population and large stock market alone are sufficient to create an attractive investment destination.

The competitiveness report lends a lot of support to a selection based on basic economic freedoms and framework conditions outside capital markets. Equally, the commentary and analyses of the World Economic Forum strongly suggest that liberalizing economic reforms adds to the competitiveness of an economy. And so it should be for investors. Long-term investors should be interested in the competitiveness of an economy before evaluating the prospects of specific companies therein.

It seems unlikely that companies outside monopolistic undertakings in banking, telecoms, utilities, natural resources, and infrastructure can stem the tide and succeed in an economy that is overall not competitive.

DOING BUSINESS

The World Bank publishes a "Doing Business Report" that essentially measures the degree of business regulation and the ease with which a business can be started, expanded, operated, and closed. The assessment is based on laws and regulations as well as costs.

The evaluation criteria applied in the report include several important criteria shown in Table 4.2.

The report collects data from 183 economies and is very comprehensive in its coverage. To be an attractive destination, we postulate that such economies must be in the top half of economies in terms of ease of doing business.

TABLE 4.2 Doing Business Criteria

Start-Up	Expansion	Operations	Insolvency
Starting a business	Registering property	Dealing with construction permits	Resolving insolvency
	Getting credit	Getting electricity	
	Protecting investors	Paying taxes	
	Enforcing contracts	Trading across borders	
		Employing workers	

Source: World Bank, "Doing Business Report," author's analyses.

The BRIIC nations again look very weak. Except for China, that sits exactly in the middle of the rankings (rank 91 out of 183), Brazil, Indonesia, Russia, and India rank between 120 and 132. This should not inspire investors.

Initial selections from the Freedom Index hold up well. Except for Jordan and Costa Rica, all primary investable markets rank in the first half, most in the first quarter of countries assessed. In other words, nearly all economies that score highly on economic freedom also make the top third/half in terms of competitiveness and ease of doing business.

The second group of economies ranks equally as expected. Except for Morocco (just at the halfway mark), all additional economies considered attractive due to their freedom rank are in the top half of ease of doing business and, with the exceptions noted earlier, also in the top half of global competitiveness. These findings are very consistent with the postulated relationship by the Heritage Foundation that economic freedom increases economic competitiveness.

The ease of doing business aspect applies to all potential investments: small and large, public and private. Every company needs to expand, manage its operations efficiently, and be able to open and close businesses with some degree of ease.

GOVERNANCE INDICATORS

The World Bank also researches and publishes a global governance assessment of some 213 economies and countries. While both methodology and results are not uncontested they do provide a very valuable benchmark to assess the quality of the regulatory and administrative reality of any given economy.

The "Worldwide Governance Indicators" report constructs aggregate indicators of six broad dimensions of governance:

1. Voice and accountability
2. Political stability and absence of violence/terrorism
3. Government effectiveness
4. Regulatory quality
5. Rule of law
6. Control of corruption

The six aggregate indicators are based on 30 underlying data sources reporting the perceptions of governance of a large number of survey respondents and expert assessments worldwide.[11] Details of the approach and aggregation method can be found in their research paper.[12]

When looking at all economies (including all OECD economies), it becomes evident again that less than half of economies worldwide meet 50 percent of potential scores. A somewhat sad world we live in. The scores displayed in Figure 4.6 are the percentile ranks among all countries, ranging from 0 (lowest) to 100 (highest). This mitigates absolute (mis)judgments that are inherent in independent country scores.

Exactly 100 economies out of 213 make the cut at 50 percent and this includes 34 OECD members that by definition or membership access require a high score on the aspect of public governance. Without OECD economies (only one OECD economy scores below 50 percent, namely Mexico), only just half of world economies rank in relative terms above 50 percent. Whether this is an indictment of prevailing attitudes to governance is a

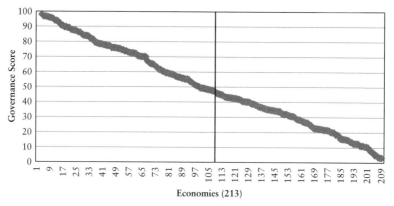

FIGURE 4.6   World Bank: Governance Indicators Worldwide, 2010
Source: World Bank, The Worldwide Governance Indicators, 2011 Update.

different and much more complex subject. The situation should be of much concern to the risk conscious investor.

The consideration of governance is not futile for the investor. We compare 83 stock markets and their market capitalization—this excludes very few stock markets—with the countries' average governance indicators ranking (Figure 4.7).

There is a positive relationship (trend line in the graph) between higher levels of governance and the growth or size of the stock market. Without going into a futile discussion about cause and effect, it stands to reason that larger markets require more governance, therefore governments seek a higher level of governance, and at the same time larger capital flows induce higher levels of corporate and public governance. Governance and stock market size have a positively compounding relationship.

In other words, if it is big enough, the environment tends to be better regulated and, conversely, to become big enough, the environment has to be somewhat stable. If this applies to developed economies, we would suggest it also applies with some time lag to emerging markets, as Figure 4.7 suggests.

The more disturbing factors are that, for example for BRIC, only Brazil meets the 50 percent hurdle. All others fail, in the case of Russia starkly.

Furthermore, there is a limited number of sizable emerging markets stock exchanges operating in an environment of good governance. Outside the BRIC markets, all over US$1 trillion in stock market capitalization, some 19 markets exceed US$100 billion market capitalization. They are: Chile, Colombia, Indonesia, Israel, Kuwait, Malaysia, Mexico, Philippines, Poland, Qatar, Taiwan, Thailand, Turkey, Saudi, Singapore, South Africa, South Korea, and the United Arab Emirates, of which only Indonesia, Colombia,

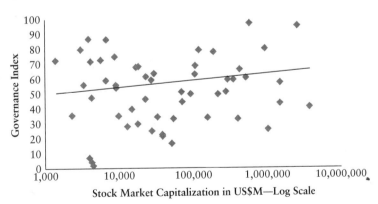

FIGURE 4.7 World Bank Governance Indicators, 2010, and Stock Market Capitalization, May 2011 (log scale) in US$ million

Source: World Bank, The Worldwide Governance Indicators, 2011 Update, Bloomberg.

Mexico, and the Philippines have below average rankings. This demonstrates the relatively small universe of large and investable emerging markets based on a range of governance factors.

If, therefore, emerging markets investors are primarily seeking a solid governance base, they have to consider markets smaller than US$100 billion in market capitalization.

FINANCIAL CENTERS RANKING

For investors, deep financial markets beyond a stock market matter. They matter in terms of transaction capabilities but also in terms of investment opportunities since financial services companies regularly account for a large share of market capitalization and liquidity.

The Global Financial Centers Index provides an independent perspective on the competitiveness of existing and emerging financial centers.

The report looks at five overarching areas of competitiveness (with examples of data collected) for 75 different locations included in the rankings:

1. People: intellectual capital, education, HR development, lifestyle.
2. Business environment: ease of doing business, corruption perception, tax rates, economic freedom, banking, risks.
3. Infrastructure: office occupancy costs, real estate, city/airport infrastructure.
4. Market access: capital access, securitization, stock market capitalization, value/volume of shares/bonds/options traded, credit ranking.
5. General competitiveness: global competitiveness index, FDI flows, innovation, cost of living, retail price index, trade fairs.

The ratings and rankings are calculated using a factor assessment model that combines the listed factors with a financial center assessment based on questionnaires. 1.690 financial services professionals provided input into the questionnaire to add experience and real life quality to the data collected.[13]

The attraction of the financial center index is that capital markets are prominent in the scores and thus the element of well-functioning markets is retained. At the same time, important data such as the Heritage Economic Freedom Index and the World Economic Forum Global Competitiveness Index are equally included. The drawback, of course, is that only a limited number of cities are assessed and not the attractiveness of an entire market to investors.

The resulting ranking categorizes cities into a matrix of geographic reach and stage of development. All advanced economies and offshore centers, typically islands or segregated jurisdictions, are excluded in the results of the GFC 7 survey 2012, in Table 4.3. The scores correlate relatively well with overall competitiveness indexes, indicating that economies or markets that succeed in competitive markets also have competitive financial centers. Also interesting to note is that emerging markets score the highest improvements in this year's report.

Major issues raised by questionnaire respondents include overregulation, taxation, and ease of doing business in the business environment category. Quality and availability of staff as well as labor market flexibility were the main "people" concerns; infrastructure weaknesses, fear of recession, and dilution of clustering of professionals and institutions' competitiveness were concerns in the other categories.

GLOBAL MANUFACTURING COMPETITIVENESS

In the same vein as financial services, manufacturing prowess should equally be considered. The Deloitte-US Council on Competitiveness report looks at 10 drivers of manufacturing competitiveness that reflect both government

TABLE 4.3 Financial Centers Ranking

	Broad and Deep	Relatively Broad	Relatively Deep	Emerging
Global				Beijing
				Dubai
				Moscow
				Shanghai
Transnational		Seoul	Bahrain	Bangkok
			Shenzhen	Kuala
			Taipei	Lumpur
				Mumbai
Local	Johannesburg	Mexico City	Bahamas	Budapest
		Sao Paolo	Buenos Aires	Istanbul
		Warsaw	Jakarta	Prague
			Malta	Riyadh
			Manila	St Petersburg
			Mauritius	Tallinn
			Qatar	
			Rio de Janeiro	

Source: The Global Financial Centers, City of London and Y/Zen Group.

and market forces; the relative importance ranking by respondents is scored from 1 low to10 high:

1. Talent driven innovation (9.22)
2. Cost of labor and materials (7.67)
3. Energy costs and policies (7.31)
4. Supplier network (5.91)
5. Local business dynamics (4.01)
6. Economic, trade, financial, and tax systems (7.26)
7. Quality of physical infrastructure (7.15)
8. Government investments in manufacturing and innovation (6.62)
9. Legal and regulatory system (6.48)
10. Quality and availability of health care systems (1.81)

The index is based on a survey of more than 400 executives asked to rank 26 countries (or add a country) and responses were standardized for potential country and cultural bias as well as for company size and geographic experience.[14] The ranking includes current competitiveness and competitiveness in five years.

The results in Table 4.4 show the developing economies and the dominance of B(R)IC economies. Excluding developed markets and Singapore, the results show the strong and growing position of emerging economies in manufacturing.

TABLE 4.4   Manufacturing Competitiveness Ranking, 2010 through 2015

Rank	Country	Current Score	5-Year Score	5-Year Rank
1	China	10.00	10.00	1
2	India	8.15	9.01	2
3	Republic of Korea	6.79	6.53	3
5	Brazil	5.41	6.32	4
7	Mexico	4.84	4.84	6
10	Poland	4.49	4.52	9
11	Czech Republic	4.38	3.95	12
12	Thailand	4.17	4.53	10
20	Russia	2.58	3.47	14
22	South Africa	2.28	2.52	19
25	Argentina	1.03	1.53	24
26	Saudi Arabia	1.00	1.32	25

Source: The Global Manufacturing Competitiveness Index, Deloitte, US Council on Competitiveness.

The role of developing economies is evident. Except for the United States (rank 4 and in five years rank 5), Japan (rank 6 and in five years rank 7), Germany (rank 8 and in five years rank 8) and Singapore (rank 9 and in five years rank 11), the top 10 are all developing economies and China is far ahead. Only India can aspire to catch up somewhat up over the coming decade.

The survey was tested for issues and concerns of respondents. Asian respondents rate future government investments in manufacturing and innovation as very important to their continued development while European respondents rate legal and regulatory and quality of infrastructure higher in importance to sustain their competitiveness. Otherwise, results are fairly consistent.

Looking at critical factors for continued success, the difference in Asian and European responses is indicative of the unfettered strength of emerging economies and the weakness of advanced economies' governments to foster the manufacturing sector. Just from this ranking and assessment, it seems unlikely that emerging economies will lose their advantage anywhere in the foreseeable future.

STOCK MARKET ASPECTS

Having developed a long list of candidates, a necessary condition for defining investable markets is to establish the existence of a stock market of some significance. Without some attractive listings, some level of turnover, and some adequate trading environment, there is hardly an immediate opportunity to participate in these economies. Such economies are better suited and served by private equity that then can be grouped into country/regional funds or investment vehicles to be listed.

Members (54 exchanges) or reporting associates of the World Federation of Stock Exchanges each show between 20 and 1,000 company listings. Not all markets have an independent trading environment—for example, Estonia and Lithuania are grouped among others under NASDAQ-OMX—and some economies have more than one market. Not all stock exchanges report regularly or publish on their web sites a number of listed companies, market capitalization, or annual turnover.

The need for a consistent stock market rating and comparable market data is evident. Without such data, investors rely on third parties to estimate or research such data. Investors should be able to get aggregate stock exchange information in the same way than they should get company information.

In terms of resulting markets that can be considered investable, subject to review of stock exchange processes, we find a number of smaller markets that should not be ignored. While the BRIIC markets plus Mexico, Pakistan, and a few others have deficiencies but are comparatively large in market size and have large companies listed, the universe of developing countries should be first and foremost assessed on the basis of economic conduciveness and second only on the size of the stock exchange.

Overall, we suggest that some 27 developing economies outside the BRIICs and OECD member countries are worth considering based on economic freedoms and competitiveness—factors directly correlated to economic success and therefore stock market growth. Among them there will be the coming high-performing markets (Table 4.5). The underlying selection factors suggest that most of the highly performing markets of the future over a longer

TABLE 4.5 Primary and Secondary Investable Economies Based on Economic Freedoms and Additions (47 countries)

	Americas	Europe	Middle East North Africa	Asia	Africa
Non-OECD/ Non-BRIIC	Colombia (E)	Croatia (F)	Bahrain (F)	Georgia	Ghana
	Panama	Cyprus	Israel	Malaysia (E)	Namibia
	Peru (E)	Latvia	Jordan (F)	Taiwan (E)	South Africa
	Uruguay	Lithuania (F)	Kuwait (F)	Thailand (E)	
		Macedonia	Oman (F)		
		Romania (F)	Morocco (E)		
		Serbia (F)	Qatar (F)		
			Saudi Arabia		
			UAE (F)		
Additions	Argentina (F)	Bulgaria (F)		Pakistan (F)	
		Slovak Republic		Philippines (E)	
				Vietnam (F)	
OECD	Chile (E)	Czech Republic (E)		South Korea (E)	
	Mexico (E)	Estonia (F)			
		Hungary (E)			
		Poland (E)			
		Slovenia (F)			
		Turkey (E)			
BRIIC	Brazil (E)	Russia (E)		China (E)	
				India (E)	
				Indonesia (E)	

Note: MSCI index countries are marked as follows: (E) emerging market, (F) frontier market.

period will come from these markets. There are a number of very small other markets that deserve the attention of small cap managers, such as Malta, Mauritius, Ghana, or Costa Rica, but they remain specialties.

In addition, the BRIIC markets and economic freedom outliers such as Argentina, Pakistan, or Vietnam and others (Table 4.5) should be included even if they do not meet all criteria since they have already attracted a large share of foreign capital.

For the rational investor, it is now a matter of getting comfortable with the trading environment (stock market), the size, liquidity, and rules or the lack thereof, as well as selecting specific stocks. The universe of investable developing markets is much wider than the current classifications suggest.

CONCLUSION

Looking at different measurements of economic development or progress yields interesting results. Economic freedom, overall competitiveness, doing business, governance, financial centers, and manufacturing are factors often outside traditional macroeconomic analyses, yet of great importance to assess an investment destination. Assessing the investment destination is one of the first steps in making investment decisions.

Interestingly, BRIC economies do not fare particularly well but a number of other economies show promise. This would suggest that investors need to look beyond traditional measures, as do several of the analytical service providers to select the most attractive investment destinations with long-term potential.

NOTES

1. "Fund Management," The City UK Research Centre (October 2011).
2. BCG, "Global Asset Management 2011, Building on Success, The Boston Consulting Group" (2011).
3. See, e.g., William F. Sharpe, "The Arithmetic of Active Management," *The Financial Analysts' Journal* 47, no. 1 (Jan/Feb 1991), Bogle, John C., *The Clash of Cultures: Investment vs. Speculation* (Hoboken, NJ: John Wiley & Sons, 2012).
4. 2012 Index of Economic Freedom (Washington/New York: The Heritage Foundation and Dow Jones & Co Inc., 2012).
5. Klaus Schwab, The Global Competitiveness Report 2011/2012 (Geneva: World Economic Forum, 2011).
6. "Doing Business" Washington: The International Bank for Reconstruction and Development/The World Bank, 2012).
7. The Worldwide Governance Indicators, The World Bank, 2011 update, www .govindicators.org.

8. Global Financial Centers Index (GFCI) (London: The City of London and Z/ Yen Group, 2012).

9. Deloitte and US Council on Competitiveness—2010 Global Manufacturing Competitiveness Index; © Deloitte Touche Tohmatsu, June 2010.

10. OECD, convention text, www/oecd.org.

11. www.govindicators.org.

12. Daniel Kaufmann, Aart Kray, and Massimo Mastruzzi, "The Worldwide Governance Indicators: A Summary of Methodology, Data and Analytical Issues," World Bank Policy Research Report, Working Paper no. 5430 (Washington, 2011).

13. www.cityoflondon.gov.uk/gfci.

14. GMCI, methodology explanation to index, www.deloitte.com/globalcompet itiveness.

CHAPTER 5

Private Equity Flows as a Lead Indicator

Another indicator to consider is the private equity industry and their selection of markets. Private equity (PE) can be simply defined as active investing. In other words, private equity is the combination of capital under freely negotiated contracts with active contributions to the investment company at strategic, management, or operational level. By contrast, investing in public equities is generally standardized. That means there are no tailored contracts and no additional shareholder contributions to the company. Buyouts, takeovers, and majority acquisitions may have hallmarks of private equity but within defined parameters that are given by prevailing shareholder rights, the stock market, and the existing company constitution.

Because private equity allows for negotiated contracts and active management participation, private equity can by definition invest in more markets. First, there is no requirement of an active and broad stock market or for a minimum level of stock market regulations and second, framework conditions are of less relevance because most barriers can be overcome by contract and structuring. Contracts and investment structures can change a company's constitution, avoid restrictive company law or foreign investment laws, and make extensive use of offshore jurisdictions more conducive to the investment objective, the shareholder agreement, or any security for the investment.

This contribution looks at the theoretical argument and considers the long-standing International Finance Corporation (IFC)[1] experience in support of the argument.

PRIVATE EQUITY FLOWS: THE NEXT WAVE OF INVESTABLE MARKETS

Private equity investors look primarily at target investment companies and appropriate capital structures and secondarily at local framework (market) conditions. Public equity is quite the opposite. Public market investors seemingly look first at stock market standards and then at the most attractive companies within. The analyses of market selections and market classifications argue that due to a restrictive perspective with essentially three classes of markets (emerging, frontier, and unclassified), many worthwhile investment opportunities at company level are excluded because overall market conditions do not meet the required standards.

Since private equity investors have more markets to choose from but are return maximizers, the question arises whether cumulative and unrelated private equity flows have any predictive value with respect to the rise or advent of investable markets that should be considered on a broader scale. For the purpose of this discussion, we shall define investable markets as markets with a stock exchange that has a minimum level of regulations, size, and liquidity, and listed companies from several economic sectors. It also includes exchanges that have just started. Essentially, this is relevant for markets outside the MSCI Emerging Markets Index but covers most frontier markets and those markets yet unclassified but with exchanges.

From the outset there are two logic arguments why the lead function of private equity should hold true:

1. Private equity enhances the governance and performance of companies and therefore provides good candidates for stock markets.
2. Private equity requires ongoing investment opportunities and exits and therefore generates two-way liquidity in company shares.

Both factors are a necessary albeit not sufficient condition for rapid growth of any developing stock market.

Private equity flows to emerging markets changed considerably over the past decade.[2] First, the relative proportion of flows to emerging or developing markets is rising (see Figure 5.1). Emerging markets exclude the United States, Western Europe, Japan, and Australia/New Zealand.

Second, private equity flows within emerging markets have experienced a reversal of flows over the past decade (see Figures 5.2 and 5.3). From a relative dominance of Latin America in 2002, flows changed to a relative dominance of Emerging Asia.

Essentially, from 2003 onward, the private equity industry took aim at two elements of the BRIC (Brazil, Russia, India, China) opportunity and refocused investments toward emerging Asia, mainly China and India, and away from Latin America and Russia/Central Eastern Europe (CEE).

This is confirmed by a detailed review of private equity flows among the BRIC economies. China and India are dwarfing flows to Brazil and Russia (see Figure 5.4).

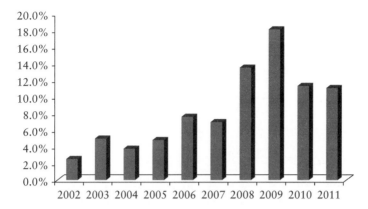

FIGURE 5.1   Emerging Markets PE Flows as Percent of Total PE Flows
Source: EMPEA Industry Statistics, 2011, author's analyses.

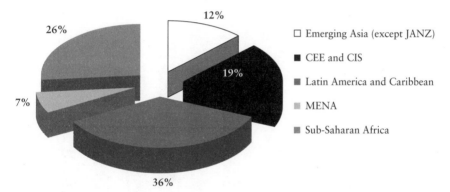

FIGURE 5.2   Emerging Markets PE Investments by Region, 2002
Source: EMPEA Industry Statistics, 2011, author's analyses.

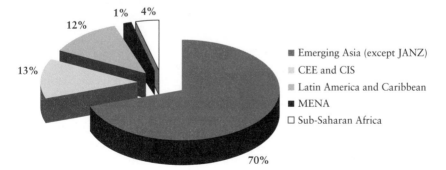

FIGURE 5.3   Emerging Markets PE Investments by Region, 2011
Source: EMPEA Industry Statistics, 2011, author's analyses.

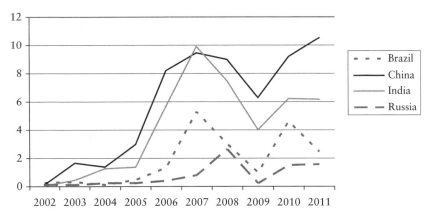

FIGURE 5.4   Private Equity Flows to BRIC 2002 to 2011 in US$B
Source: EMPEA Industry Statistics, 2011, author's analyses.

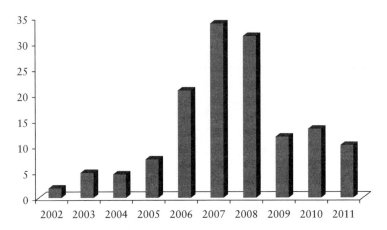

FIGURE 5.5   Emerging Asia Excluding China and India—PE Investments 2002 through 2012 in US$B
Source: EMPEA Industry Statistics, 2011, author's analyses.

Private equity has turned to emerging Asia. However, the dominant recipients, China and to a lesser degree India, mask the relevance of multiple other emerging Asian investment destinations for private equity (see Figure 5.5).

Clearly the sheer dominance of China and India overshadows other emerging Asia investment destinations, but volumes excluding China and India remain significant and were well above US$30B during the bumper years prior to the financial crisis.

Looking at all emerging Asia countries in detail, we see newcomers and prospective high flyers (Table 5.1). It must be noted that at country level,

TABLE 5.1 Emerging Asia (excluding China and India) Reported Private Equity Transactions by Country, 2008 to 2011

Country	2008	Total Capital Invested (US$m)			Totals
		2009	2010	2011	
South Korea	4,114.0	1,714.0	591.0	469.3	6,888.3
Indonesia	1,570.0	734.0	892.0	670.0	3,866.0
Singapore	1,158.0	966.0	395.0	253.6	2,772.6
Malaysia	2,253.0	4.0	31.0	5.6	2,293.6
Taiwan	1,236.0	37.0	218.0	4.0	1,495.0
Philippines	728.0	10.0	158.0	126.0	1,022.0
Vietnam	285.0	82.0	10.0	450.4	827.4
Mongolia	300.0	15.0	11.0	10.5	336.5
Thailand	90.0		65.0		155.0
Papua New Guinea	1.0	–	57.0		58.0
Bangladesh	51.0	–	–		51.0
Sri Lanka	7.0	–	–	20.0	27.0
Cambodia	–	6.0	5.0	1.0	12.0
Laos	–	–	–	3.4	3.4

Source: EMPEA Industry Statistics, 2011, author's analyses.

these statistics are most certainly incomplete because they rely on reported transactions. Not all fund managers or private equity investors report investments, and based on anecdotal evidence the true value is probably double if not more as private transactions with prominent individuals are a significant pool of development capital in frontier and unclassified markets. Therefore numbers are understated, but the reported direction makes for interesting observations.

Following the usual suspects at the top of the list, markets like the Philippines, Vietnam, Mongolia, Bangladesh, Sri Lanka, Cambodia (recent stock market), and Laos (new stock market) make their appearance. Emerging Asia numbers are understated as a matter of fact. For example, Mongolia, Cambodia, and Thailand attract many investments that are not reported. Although these markets collectively only amount to slightly over 13 percent of all Emerging Asia private equity flows, they could be a lead indicator.

The same conclusion applies to CEE and the Commonwealth of Independent States (CIS) (Table 5.2).

While a number of markets are already included in the MSCI Index or are advanced emerging markets (FTSE), a good number of markets remain unnoticed by most investors.

Equally, other regions such as Latin America and the Caribbean sport some interesting investment destinations (Table 5.3).

TABLE 5.2 CEE and CIS (excluding Russia) Reported Private Equity Transactions by Country, 2008 to 2011

Country	2008	Total Capital Invested (US$m) 2009	2010	2011	Totals
Turkey	2,364.0	481.0	66.0	764.5	3,675.5
Czech Republic		1,522.0	185.0	1.4	1,708.4
Poland	410.0	45.0	343.0	681.7	1,479.7
Ukraine	541.0	38.0	80.0	35.0	694.0
Bulgaria		334.0	105.0	19.4	458.4
Croatia	205.0	196.0		5.0	406.0
Hungary		11.0	42.0	306.1	359.1
Romania	117.0	185.0	26.0	19.0	347.0
Slovenia	44.0	168.0			212.0
Kazakhstan	15.0	70.0		50.0	135.0
Lithuania		52.0		2.7	54.7
Estonia		4.0	13.0	1.0	18.0
Moldova			15.0		15.0
Slovakia				7.6	7.6
Cyprus				6.0	6.0
Georgia			5.0		5.0
Latvia			2.0	2.2	4.2

Source: EMPEA Industry Statistics, 2011, author's analyses.

TABLE 5.3 Latin America and the Caribbean (excluding Brazil) Reported Private Equity Transactions by Country, 2008 to 2011

Country	2008	Total Capital Invested (US$m) 2009	2010	2011	Totals
Chile	929.0	40.4	298.4	3.0	1,270.8
Colombia	123.0	9.6	612.0	376.3	1,120.9
Argentina	85.0	150.6	525.0	89.0	849.6
Mexico	455.0	67.0	149.6	127.7	799.3
Peru	88.0	7.0	2.0	–	97.0
Trinidad and Tobago	50.0		18.8		68.8
Jamaica			33.7		33.7
Honduras				33.5	33.5
Cayman Islands		30.0			30.0
Dominican Republic		12.0			12.0
Uruguay		1.0		10.5	11.5
Costa Rica		10.8	0.5		11.3

Source: EMPEA Industry Statistics, 2011, author's analyses.

Outside Chile, Colombia, Argentina, and Mexico, most economies are not commonplace investment destinations. Yet investment in these other minor economies already amounts to some 7 percent of total private equity investment in the LATAM and Caribbean region.

The Middle East North Africa region (MENA) (Table 5.4), although small overall, sports another array of markets often overlooked. Egypt and the United Arab Emirates are clearly attractive investment destinations, although the Arab Spring will constrain further growth in Egypt and some other affected markets.

Finally, the African continent is growing as a private equity investment destination (Table 5.5). Multiple countries are attracting private equity investment indicative of future investment growth in public markets. Many of these markets have fledgling or developing stock markets that could provide one of the opportunities going forward.

Overall, private equity flows show appreciable activity in some 60 markets outside the emerging markets of the MSCI index. These markets are not considered mainstream or even frontier markets by many index, research, and analysis providers.

The outlook and future strategies for Asia-Pacific articulated by private equity investors[3] confirms an upcoming change of emphasis and shows a

TABLE 5.4 Middle East Reported Private Equity Transactions by Country 2008 to 2011

| Country | Total Capital Invested (US$m) | | | | |
	2008	2009	2010	2011	Totals
Egypt	2,263.0	1,290.0	6.0	125.0	3,684.0
UAE	216.0	188.0	676.0		1,080.0
Pakistan	109.0	361.0			470.0
Jordan	329.0			93.0	422.0
Saudi Arabia	76.0	200.0	22.0	75.0	373.0
Bahrain	231.0	26.0		75.0	332.0
Morocco	53.0	64.0			117.0
Sudan		19.0	70.0		89.0
Oman	40.0	27.0			67.0
Tunisia	47.0	3.0			50.0
Kuwait		25.0	20.0		45.0
Lebanon	6.0			13.5	19.5
Algeria		11.0			11.0
Palestina				3.7	3.7

Source: EMPEA Industry Statistics, 2011, author's analyses.

TABLE 5.5 Sub-Saharan Africa Reported Private Equity Transactions by Country, 2008 to 2011

Country	2008	Total Capital Invested (US$m)			
		2009	2010	2011	Totals
Nigeria	165.0	368.0	188.0	121.0	842.0
Kenya	217.0	138.0	50.0	99.4	504.4
Ghana	300.0	15.0	20.0	10.9	345.9
Cote d'Ivoire	30.0	98.0		14.0	142.0
Togo	28		89		117.0
Madagascar				100.0	100.0
Uganda	51.0		7.0	2.2	60.2
Mauritania	28.0			8.0	36.0
Zimbabwe		6.0	15.0	10.3	31.3
Djibouti	30.0				30.0
Liberia	20.0				20.0
Botswana			15.0		15.0
Malawi				10.0	10.0
Mauritius		10.0			10.0
Sierra Leone				10.0	10.0
Benin			4.0		4.0

Source: EMPEA Industry Statistics, 2011, author's analyses.

remarkable appetite for new opportunities, as shown in Figure 5.6, away from the past mainstream markets of China, Hong Kong, and India.

For Asia-Pacific, this means that several economies considered today frontier or unclassified are attracting the interest of private equity investors. Other regions may show a similar picture of moving cautiously away from traditional markets.

PRIVATE EQUITY AS LEAD INDICATOR

If private equity investors have adequate confidence in managing and exiting investments in these markets with above US$100M in aggregate investment over the past four years, other investment should follow suit.

To establish whether existing or future private equity investment is a lead indicator would require either to establish causality, which in the best of a fully researched world with complete information would be a stretch, or to show some correlation between private equity investment flows and general market size or growth. To develop the argument of causality exceeds the scope of this book. This subject is reserved for academic studies

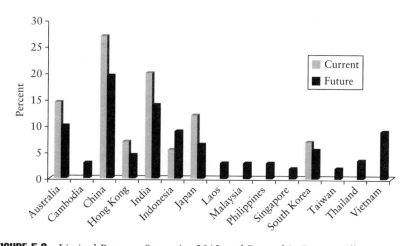

FIGURE 5.6 Limited Partners Strategies 2012 and Beyond in Percent Allocation
Source: PEI Surveys, 2012, author's analyses.

and deserves further attention but will require long and well established data series.

However, some correlation can be established. To this effect, we differentiate between MSCI Emerging and Frontier markets and others; we also segregate economies by the volume of private equity investment received (above and below US$100 million) over the period 2008–2011. The US$100 million delineation is arbitrary but seems indicative of serious investment flows.

For each of these groups of economies, we review the ratio of private equity to public equity market capitalization and control this ratio by the level of market capitalization to GDP.

Of the MSCI emerging economies attracting more than US$100 million in private equity, almost all have a private equity to market capitalization ratio of below 1 percent. The exceptions are the Czech Republic, India, Turkey, and Hungary. These exceptions can be explained by the level of stock market development. In each of these markets, stock market capitalization as a percentage of GDP (in purchasing power parity) is below 40 percent, indicating a relatively less developed stock market as do those markets highlighted in Figure 5.7.

For emerging markets (excluding MSCI Emerging Markets) that received in excess of US$100 million in private equity investments over the period 2008 to 2011, the ratio of private equity to stock market capitalization tends to be in the range of 1 to 2.5 percent and above. The majority of

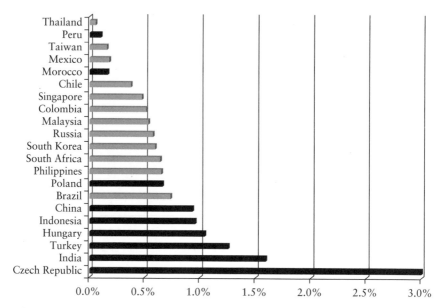

FIGURE 5.7   Ratio of Private Equity Investments 2008–2011 to Stock Market Capitalization—MSCI Emerging Markets Index Constituents above US$100 million private equity flows

Note: Excludes Egypt due to irregular stock market developments following the Arab Spring; market capitalization is generally as of May 2011.
Source: EMPEA, Bloomberg, Everest Capital, author's analyses.

these economies also have a ratio of stock market capitalization to GDP (in purchasing power parity) of well below 40 percent, except for the major Arab states (see Figure 5.8).

Saudi Arabia is a major exception with very low private equity. This can be explained by prevailing barriers to private equity for foreign investors and the lack of reporting of private transactions locally.

While recognizing the deficiencies of available data and the selection of time lines, we can conclude that we are faced with two distinct groups of emerging markets within our chosen parameters:

1. MSCI Emerging Market constituents have generally below 1 percent ratio of private equity to public equity save for those markets with relatively less developed stock exchanges.
2. Other markets have generally a ratio of 1 to 2.5 percent private equity to public equity and some markets well above, such as Mongolia (resource investments), Ghana, Bulgaria, and Kenya.

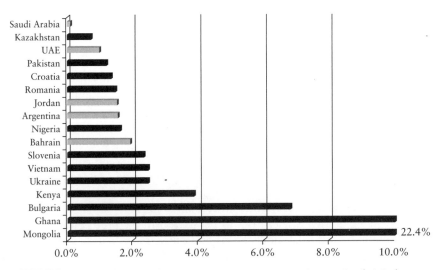

FIGURE 5.8   Ratio of Private Equity Investments 2008 to 2011 to Stock Market Capitalization (economies above US$100M private equity investments excluding MSCI Emerging market constituents)

Note: Excludes Côte d'Ivoire and Togo (regional exchange with several other West African markets), and Madagascar (no exchange); market capitalization is generally as of May 2011.

Source: EMPEA, Bloomberg, Everest Capital, author's analyses.

If we assume that equity investment is driven by the attractiveness of the investment destination and the opportunities afforded, there is no apparent reason why private equity investors would value one market so much above public equity investors.

Leaving distortions on reported private equity aside, the obvious explanation for the difference in relative private equity investment is that private equity investors are ahead of public markets and subsequent MSCI inclusion and/or the MSCI inclusion fosters faster public market development. Either way, private equity looks ahead by maybe two to five years, because private equity is less constrained by stock market governance issues.

It is very difficult to test the hypothesis with the most advanced markets because the by far leading private equity markets of the United States and Western Europe are dominated by mega deals and buyouts. These transactions do not allow for a proper comparison of developed market private equity flows to market capitalization.

We therefore conclude that if economies with established private equity investment flows (above US$100M between 2008 and 2011) also have a low stock market to GDP ratio, then such stock markets are likely to expand faster than others.

The lead function of private equity seems logical for three reasons:

1. Private equity creates companies that are market listing candidates and private equity requires exits and will use initial public offerings (IPOs) where possible and economically attractive. They therefore contribute to the supply side, which drives market capitalization.
2. Private equity with serious sums is only advisable if a minimum of investment framework conditions are met. Thus some conditions for wider scale investment already exist and private equity contributes to the further development of the legal framework and to adjustments to stock exchange governance where still wanting.
3. Private equity lends itself well to being transformed into public equity through the listing of funds, ETFs, and other tradable instruments both on local and offshore markets. Thus, private equity investment has the potential to spur a staged public equity opportunity open to passive and public equity investors before the local stock market necessarily has to meet all desirable requirements.

There is a second hypothesis to be considered. If market capitalization is comparatively small in proportion to GDP (at PPP), continued and high GDP growth will foster growing and successful companies and requires more corporate funding. Equity is a major solution in particular in times of restrictive banking conditions.

We may therefore assume that rapid economic growth goes generally together with stock market development, albeit with a time lag—the time investors need to appreciate that economic growth is stable, investment conditions are attractive, and sizable transactions are possible.

For public equity markets to grow, more companies need to list or prices need to increase. Since prices are somewhat constrained by company growth and comparable price earnings, more companies need to come to market to increase market capitalization in a meaningful way.

Private equity fosters the supply side to stock markets and supports existing stock market investments and IPOs. This leads to increased supply and volumes on the stock markets. Thus market capitalization is likely to increase if and when private equity starts to play a bigger role in economies with a lower relative importance of the stock market to the overall economy.

We have two asymmetries that suggest some form of forthcoming stock market growth:

1. The relative importance of private to public equity—relatively stronger private equity flows are at the forefront of stronger public equity flows.
2. The relative importance of public equity to the economy—strong economic growth with strong private equity flows eventually leads to stronger public equity flows.

We therefore look for markets that have more than 1 percent private equity flows to public equity (provided private equity is in sizable amounts) (point 1) and high-growth markets with relatively low market capitalization to GDP but high private equity (point 2).

If we divide markets with at least US$100M private equity into those above 1 percent private to public equity and into markets below 40 percent market capitalization to GDP, we find an interesting mix of economies not generally considered the next winners by many investors (Figure 5.9).

Based on our observation, the non-MSCI markets of Jordan, UAE, Bahrain, Croatia, Pakistan, Argentina, Romania, Nigeria, Vietnam, Ukraine, and Kenya are poised to expand their stock markets over the coming years.

Kazakhstan and Saudi Arabia (KSA) do not fully meet the attractiveness criteria, but deserve further attention. Both markets have very specific issues to deal with—rule of law and barriers to investment.

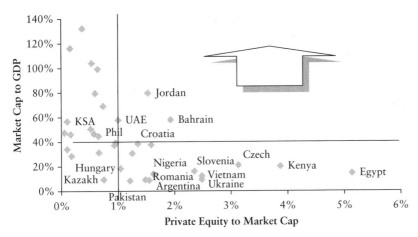

FIGURE 5.9   MSCI Emerging Markets and Frontier Markets with over US$100M in Private Equity, 2008 to 2011

Source: EMPEA, Bloomberg, Everest Capital, author's analyses.

We should also not ignore those economies with a lower level of private equity investment. There are numerous reasons why reported private equity flows understate the true private investment volume. In most if not all developing economies, the first port of call for equity and risk funding is friends and family, as well as prominent (ruling) family members as well as the national diaspora. The most successful or promising companies in developing economies do not always invite foreign private equity investors. There are good reasons for funding preferences between equity and debt and between independent and connected equity. In many cases private equity acts dysfunctionally and has a poor reputation.

Because of these issues with private equity, we cannot be solely guided by reported private equity flows. We may thus include countries in our selection with a lower level of reported private equity.

Related private equity cannot be easily measured. Several publications have tried to establish sources of funds in Asia. For example, in 1988 early studies[4] show the dominance of Chinese family capitalism across Southeast Asia and the connectivity of family owned business groups. This has persisted and was only disturbed by the various financial crises. Yet in Thailand,[5] a review of the capital structure for 384 listed companies in 2004 well after the Asian crisis shows that 290 companies (75 percent plus) still had 61 to 80 percent+ shares held by the top 10 shareholders. A further review of the type of ownership of 419 listed firms in 2006 shows that 211 or 50 percent were fully or partly family owned. Related or connected transactions are not reported as private equity. In these environments, private equity from third parties is also not as attractive. This could well explain a low private equity role in many frontier economies. Paucity of data prevents a country by country review and estimate of true private investment flows.

We therefore review all countries with both low private equity (not desirable but possibly understated) and low stock market development as secondary candidates (see Figure 5.10).

All these markets attracted US$10 million to US$99 million of private equity investments over the past four years and are therefore of interest to at least some investors.

They should develop into bigger investment destinations for public equity over the coming years. A judgment call is required to determine exactly which markets are at the forefront. Let us assume that US$50 million or thereabouts in third party and reported private equity is a minimum benchmark. This gives us another five non-MSCI markets to consider, namely Trinidad, Oman, Lithuania, Bangladesh, and Tunisia. However, Kuwait, Jamaica, Zimbabwe, Sri Lanka, Lebanon, and Estonia are not far off the mark.

Going further down the ladder we find serious watch candidates in Figure 5.11.

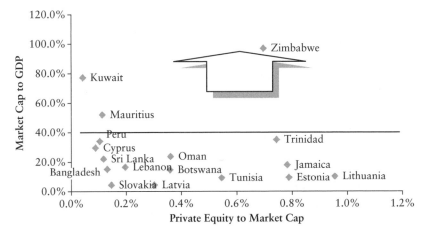

FIGURE 5.10 Frontier and Unclassified Markets with under US$100M in Private Equity, 2008 to 2011

Source: EMPEA, Bloomberg, Everest Capital, author's analyses.

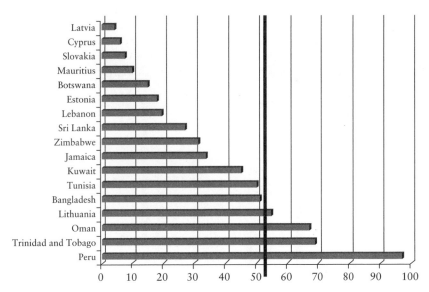

FIGURE 5.11 Frontier and Unclassified Markets by Private Equity Investments Made between 2008 and 2011 (in US$M)

Source: EMPEA, Bloomberg, Everest Capital, author's analyses.

The argument that private equity is a lead indicator does not mean that the opposite is equally true. The lack or absence of private equity does not mean that stock markets are not worth investing in or could not become the next growth wave. It simply says that other indicators must be used.

Private equity is a very powerful and immensely relevant pioneer in investing in new markets and should not be ignored as major selection criteria for public equity investors. In fact, in some economies private equity is a necessary precursor because either the stock market is really small or does not yet exist, such as in Cambodia. With growing investment interest, stock markets develop and the leading role of private equity remains for a period of time. Then size and diversity of the stock market makes private equity a separate business. Until then, however, private and public equity are complementary and should benefit from each other.

EMERGING MARKETS PRIVATE EQUITY IN PRACTICE

The number of countries that are suited to private equity has increased noticeably. As an indicative measure, the Economic Freedom Index of the Heritage Foundation can be taken. In 2012 alone, the scores of 75 economies improved, of which 73 are considered developing or emerging countries. Over the past two decades, the number of mostly free countries has almost doubled and so has the number of countries that are moderately free.

With some concessions, there are today around 90 markets that can be considered investable for private equity from an overall perspective (see Figure 5.12). That is about half of all economies globally.

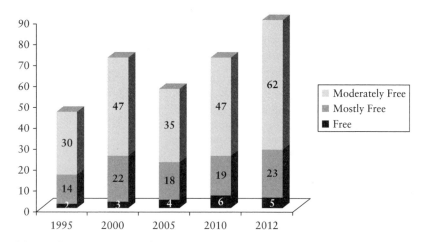

FIGURE 5.12 Number of Countries and Level of Freedom (1995–2012)
Source: The Heritage Foundation, 2012, author's analyses.

The opportunity is therefore larger than generally recognized. Specifically for private equity, the number of markets that meet the basic criteria for successful private investment is growing. For private equity to succeed, principal framework conditions fall into two categories:

1. Enabling conditions primarily with respect to the overall business framework, most importantly:
   - Rule of law (property rights and freedom of corruption).
   - Open markets (trade, investment, and business freedom).
2. Business conditions relating to the market opportunity, primarily:
   - Attractive businesses in which to invest.
   - Ownership structures that allow for influence over the business.

Enabling Conditions

With respect to enabling conditions, the rule of law is most certainly the toughest criteria to fulfill. By the very nature of an emerging market, the rule of law criterion suffers from two major deficiencies: First, while generally and increasingly solid and well-reasoned laws are enacted, the implementation of these laws depends on an efficient court system. This in turn depends on well-educated and experienced judges, prosecutors, and advocates or arbitrators. Unfortunately, the development of human resources does not keep pace with economic development. It takes years if not decades to bring human resources to the level of education and experience required. Thus in most emerging economies economic success is far ahead of public legal administration and the courts. Private equity investors can protect themselves to some extent against this deficiency through intelligent corporate and financial contracting.

Second, in all emerging economies there is a tendency to have a gray or informal economy that invariably engenders some form of irregularity. This behavior pattern ranges from business facilitation to outright malfeasance. More often than not, corrupt practices serve to overcome stumbling blocks or deficient processes rather than perverting the course of public administration. It represents a form of tax on doing business and in many cases this tax is indirectly legalized. Another aspect is transfer payments and the taking of commissions for business introductions or simply executing a transaction. This practice is often a matter of public knowledge and pride, although in our world such commissions would not fall under appropriate rewards for arm's-length transactions.

Variations are endless. One of the fine examples of commissions was the recapitalization of Barclays Bank PLC after the financial crisis. Two members of the ruling families of the United Arab Emirates and Qatar, also respectively top government officials and executives, brokered the capital contributions of the equivalent of sovereign funds and received several hundred millions of pounds of commissions in their private offshore accounts,[6] all properly and publicly documented in the prospectus to shareholders of Barclays Bank PLC and voted on by shareholders.

As a consequence, some concessions need to be made on the rule of law because weaknesses are inherent in the nature of any emerging economy. Various indexes can be taken to measure progress on the rule of law criterion. The Heritage Freedom Index, for example, scores rule of law and includes the Transparency International corruption perception index. When excluding advanced OECD economies, over 30 countries achieve a 50 percent or higher score for rule of law and some 34 other countries achieve 35 percent or better. With a 50 percent score, economies are on par with advanced OECD countries such as Italy for property rights and on par with countries like South Korea for freedom from corruption.

On the criterion of open markets, most economies (globally more than 125) score 70 percent or better on the aspect of trade freedom. Clearly, globalization has caused widespread trade liberalization. Trade barriers are generally not a restriction for private equity.

The two other aspects of open markets are investment and business freedom. Investment freedom measures the national treatment of foreign investors, land ownership and sectoral restrictions, foreign exchange and capital controls as well as expropriation incidents; 28 emerging markets score 70 percent or better for investment freedom and 51 markets score above 60 percent.

Business freedom is the quantitative measure of the ability to start, operate, and close a business and represents the overall burden of regulation as well as the efficiency of government in the regulatory process. Thirty-five markets score above 70 percent and 30 markets above 60 percent, as seen in Figure 5.13. Equally in this aspect many economies have made significant progress.

Overall, some 60 to 70 emerging economies meet the basic qualifications for private equity investment regardless of the existence of a stock market. Almost all the economies will also have a stock market and thus be investable in general, but the stock market may be narrow, illiquid, or fail to meet governance standards.

Potential destinations for private equity cover about one third of the world.

Business Conditions

Three trends have increased both the number of businesses and the ability to acquire influence:

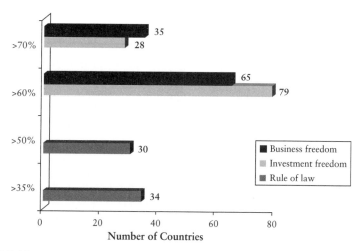

FIGURE 5.13   Number of Countries and Business Freedom
Source: The Heritage Foundation, 2012, author's analyses.

1. The move to market based economies since the 1990s is increasing entrepreneurial activity and the number of businesses with interest in private equity (PE).
2. The opening of trade and capital flows since 2000 increases both opportunities to expand and competitive pressure, leading to more business owners seeking third party capital as a solution.
3. The close identification of family status and wealth with direct owner-ship of a company reduces as portfolio wealth becomes an option and is seen to work, reducing reluctance to allow third party equity.

Measures of conditions for private business have improved across a wide range of emerging markets since the 1990s, leading to an increase in the number of companies of interest to private equity. The scale of improvements in private business conditions in emerging markets is signif-icant (see Figure 5.14). Developed markets seem to be moving in the other direction.

Emerging markets have opened their trade and capital accounts since 2000, increasing opportunities to both expand and compete in domestic markets. This creates situations where the sale of equity with influence over the business is seen as desirable by owners in order to attract the capital or the skills necessary to expand, compete, or increase focus on the core business by the sale of non-core businesses.

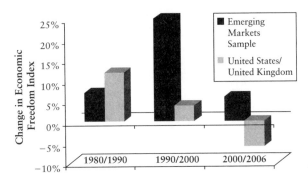

FIGURE 5.14 Change in Economic Freedom of the World Index

Source: Fraser Institute, Economic Freedom of the World Index (EFW), author's analyses.

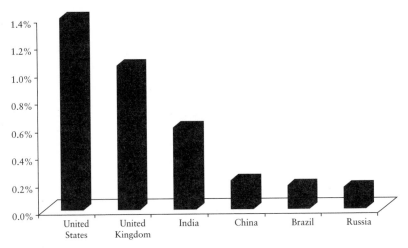

FIGURE 5.15 Private Equity Investment as Percent of GDP 2008

Source: EMPEA, author's analyses.

The Opportunity

Even in the BRICs (Brazil, Russia, India, and China), private equity funds as a percentage of GDP are low compared to the United States and the United Kingdom, indicating much room for growth (see Figure 5.15).

When further considering restrictions and capital constraints of the local banking systems as indicated by the comparatively low financial freedom scores of many emerging markets, private equity has a true role to fill in augmenting the entrepreneur's ability to meet domestic market demand and exploit regional export or contract manufacturing opportunities.

Overwhelmingly, domestic expansion is the target for companies taking private equity investment (see Figure 5.16).

Domestic and to some extent regional expansion provides vastly superior returns compared to focusing internationally (see Figure 5.17). Domestic opportunities in emerging markets are growing much faster than those in global markets with arguably less competitive rivalry. Familiarity and proximity reduce transaction costs. The average annual revenue growth rate in sample private equity investee companies is a staggering average of 37.8 percent (across 527 companies in IFC invested funds with a holding period of at least one year) and job creation achieves an average growth rate of 22.3 percent (412 invested firms).

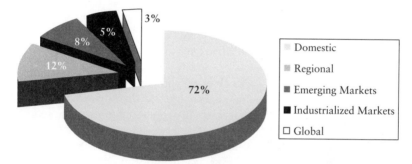

FIGURE 5.16   Private Equity Target Market Focus
Source: IFC, 833 companies.

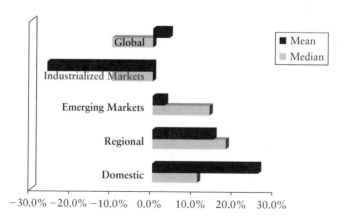

FIGURE 5.17   Private Equity Returns by Market Focus
Source: IFC, 300 companies fully exited.

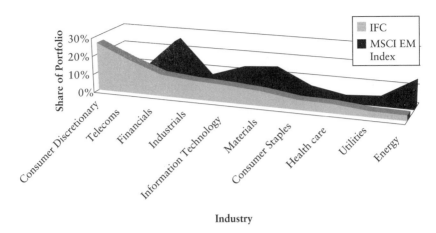

Industry

FIGURE 5.18   Industry Exposure IFC Private Equity—MSCI EM Index
Source: IFC investee companies within IFC backed funds, 2000 and later.

This stellar performance is achieved with an average debt to equity ratio of 0.74. To replicate similar benchmarks in advanced economies would be hardly possible across such a broad spectrum of companies and industry sectors.

Private equity funds back more consumer oriented businesses and demonstrate a very different structure than public market investments, as indicated by the MSCI Frontier Index weight (see Figure 5.18). The continued argument made, namely that emerging economies are getting more self-sufficient and are increasingly providing a sustainable domestic consumer base, is well recognized by private equity investors.

While the performance and opportunity for private equity in emerging markets seems underestimated, risks in emerging market private equity seem overestimated.

Risks

Many investors see minority positions in private equity as an additional risk and drag on the return. Experience to date suggests otherwise (see Figure 5.19). Minority positions performed well in all forms of exit, indicating that risks associated with minority positions can be managed effectively. They also performed well in terms of exit values.

Another often cited risk factor that does not bear out is the notion that emerging market private equity tends to be in smaller companies that are inherently riskier and less attractive. Experience suggests that while smaller deals are riskier, they are not inherently unattractive provided investments

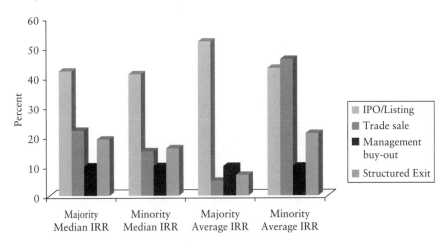

FIGURE 5.19 Median and Average IRR (Internal Rate of Return) at Exit—Minority and Majority Stakes

Source: IFC, 61 exits from majority positions and 251 from minority positions.

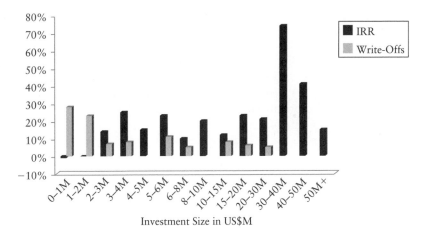

FIGURE 5.20 Median IRR and Write-offs by Investment Size

Source: IFC, 313 exits for IRR analysis and 323 exits for write-off analysis.

are adequately managed to minimize write-offs that are higher for smaller transactions. Mean returns are in fact higher for smaller deals than for medium deals, as shown in Figure 5.20.

Many critics argue that exits are not available. IFC private equity investments made 325 exits in emerging markets through a variety of channels, as shown in Figure 5.21.

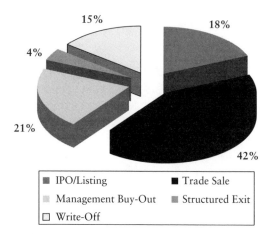

FIGURE 5.21 Exits and Channels
Source: IFC, 325 exits.

While IPOs did provide the highest returns with an average return of just above 40 percent, trade sales did very well and achieved on average in excess of 30 percent IRR. MBOs and structured exits were in the low to middle teens. The average holding period was 4.9 years.

Finally, in the IFC experience it does not take longer to exit the typical private equity J-curve in emerging markets. Comparing all IFC funds by vintage year with IFC private equity funds by the same vintage year does not show any noticeable differences.

CONCLUSION

Private equity in emerging markets has great potential as more and more economies reach the stage where they provide the necessary conditions for private investment. The role is to foster the development of high growth companies even if they are smaller. In this respect, private equity has a lead function for capital market development.

There are a number of attractive markets hereto not adequately considered based on strong private equity flows and stock market growth opportunity (Figure 5.22). Private equity invested companies tend to focus on domestic and regional markets for high returns, which provides for

	MSCI Economies	Non-MSCI
PE above US$100 million	• UAE • Bahrain • Croatia • Pakistan • Argentina • Romania • Vietnam	• Nigeria • Ukraine • Kenya
PE below US$100 million	• *Kuwait* • *Estonia*	• Trinidad • Oman • Lithuania • Bangladesh • Tunisia • *Jamaica* • *Zimbabwe* • *Sri Lanka* • *Lebanon*

FIGURE 5.22   Potential Stock Market Winners

Note: primary economies in bold, secondary economies in italic.

attractive exits. This strategy also supports the stabilization of local companies and makes them attractive to a wider investor community.

Risks need to be managed but with lower leverage, private equity investee firms also present lower risks during times of stress.

NOTES

1. Special thanks to David Wilton, head of private equity investments, IFC, for providing the data and supporting material /presentations as well as his profound insights.
2. Emerging Markets Private Equity Association—EMPEA, Industry Statistics, 2011 (published March 15, 2012).
3. Private Equity International, PEI Surveys, Asia-Pacific Private Equity Review (March 2012).
4. Yoshihara Kunio, *The Rise of Ersatz Capitalism in South East Asia* (Singapore: Oxford University Press, 1988).
5. Pasuk Phongpaichit and Chris Baker, *Thai Capital: After the 1997 Crisis* (Silkworm Books: Chiang Mai, Thailand, 2008).
6. Barclays Bank PLC prospectus and notifications to investors.

CHAPTER 6

A Different Selection of Investable Markets

We argue that a rigid classification into emerging and frontier economies largely based on stock market attributes is not a valid approach to selecting developing markets for investment. This may be an excellent guide for short-term traders, but not for investors. Below one year holding is speculative, one to three years is cash management, and above three years is investing. If we adopt these time parameters, investing in developing markets does not primarily depend on the stock market attributes or ease of trading in the short term. It depends on the longer-term outlook of an economy and more importantly on the longer-term prospects of a specific company or investment.

We argue that stock markets should be rated, not as listed companies, but as to their quality of trading environment for local and foreign investors. That would take care of the issue of trading environment. It would also take the exchange requirements out of the equation and focus investors on selecting specific investments and the analytical service providers on classifying markets according to their true economic potential.

The BRIC opportunity is a case in point. Except for the developed economies of the United States, the United Kingdom, Australia, France, Germany, Japan, and Switzerland and the economy of Hong Kong (significantly attributable to China), they are by far the largest stock markets. The size of the stock market could well be the consequence of the foreign investor BRIC focus and consequential capital flows. Nobody can argue the economic prowess of China and to a lesser degree India—they will dominate manufacturing and certain services for decades to come. However, the economies of Brazil and more so Russia do not figure in the same league other than by size and resources. On many scores of competitiveness, governance, or financial depth they simply do not match other emerging markets.

Size of stock market should not constitute the primary selection criterion for all investors. Asset managers with large sums to invest necessarily need to look for the largest absorption capacity but they do so at their peril and need to recognize that they become a driver of the market as opposed to simply an investor.

The BRIC economies (Brazil, Russia, India, and China) are also a good example for the flawed application of country classifications. These markets are overappreciated when compared to their performance in the categories of rule of law, investment or business freedom, or global competitiveness. BRIC economies should not have a very special place because they cover a third of the world population or because China and India dominate certain sectors. They are clearly dominant developing markets, but not necessarily more attractive than a number of other economies.

There is no right or wrong answer for selection criteria of the most attractive or promising developing markets once the size argument becomes secondary. And there should be no wrong and no right answer. We cannot predict the future, and the event risk in emerging economies is significantly higher than in developed markets. More recently, in the United States and very recently in Europe, this tenet that event risk is higher in developing economies seems to be in question. We are, however, looking at one of several decades' events in these markets; in emerging markets smaller events matter as much. Every government change, every economic policy reversal, and every change in conditions among neighboring or buyer economies can have significant consequences. Stock market volatility is not the right indicator since foreign capital compounds or even unlocks price volatility.

The responsibility of the asset manager or investor is in essence to select the most promising markets based on preferred economic attributes and then pick the right stocks. No country classification dominated by stock market or even macroeconomic evaluations can discharge this responsibility. Country classifications can only increase the moral hazard issue and foster an environment of window dressing by countries vying for membership in a coveted classification for increased capital flows. This does hardly anything to the attractiveness of companies or securities.

The rational investor will always prefer a lower risk investment within same return opportunities or a higher return investment with the same risk. The BRIC hype as a group seems to be a higher risk investment for higher returns. That is not a rational investment choice when alternatives—either same level of risk or same level of expected return—exist. Excess liquidity is not a valid base for making poor and concentrated investment decisions. Of course, the herding consequence of hype (in the worst-case scenario they generate euphoria or bubbles) masks the poor choices because capital flows sustain increases in market prices.

There seems hardly any reason why any investor would want to invest in an economy that operates as a bandit economy or on the fringes of governance. This is abundantly clear to the private equity investor who seeks contract and offshore solutions to insulate investments in high risk countries. The private equity investor takes willingly the risk of adverse framework conditions to achieve a superior return through active management and guidance of the investment company as well as protected corporate finance structures.

Yet across all private equity investments there is a 42 percent probability of failure (partial or total loss of the investment).[1] Even if the failure probability is only about 30 or 21 percent for funds respectively buyout funds, the prevalence of high risk is part of the choice of the private equity investor. The largest and most experienced emerging market private equity investor, IFC, attests to this with its published performance and loss figures.[2] Private equity makes an active and conscious trade–off decision between higher risk and higher returns that the stock market investor typically does not accept.

This is not the case with public equity since the element of active contribution and contractual protection is generally missing. If public equity investors allocate investments based on classifications that in turn are based mainly on stock market attributes, the underlying risk factors are ignored. The underlying risk factor is not only the company itself, which may well be properly managed, but the less than desirable framework conditions in which the company has to prosper. Therefore, public equity investors who value stock market attributes and some confidence in a proper purchase and exit process (with some degree of information and transparency) accept a level of risk not dissimilar to private equity investors. In a country with limited rule of law and high levels of corruption, no investment in which the investor has little or no influence, performs as well as it should or as can be expected from analyses. It is a fallacy to assume that because the stock market and foreign capital flows are somewhat benign, companies listed on the market operate in a transparent and orderly fashion. They do not and cannot if the environment is primarily informal. In Rome, do as the Romans.

More conceptually, every natural or artificial system eliminates system enemies and fosters system supporters. Otherwise the system gradually collapses. In economies with weak governance there is no choice but to accept the rules of market leaders and unwillingly become a bandit.

In any given country, investors therefore take the same framework risks but can deploy different tools to manage the risk. Private equity investors can influence and manage many more inherent risk aspects, but public equity investors can generally only sell if the investment does not develop according to plan. Thus the private equity investor has a higher probability of the same return than the public equity investor given the same risks. Therefore, the rational investor will not (not only) invest in public equity in a bandit economy where private equity alternatives exist.

As a consequence, the public equity investor must include as the primary market selection factor a higher level of governance to compensate for the lack of risk management tools. At a higher level of governance, the public equity investment with its advantages of transparency and requirements offers a true, lower risk alternative and the rational investor will select the low risk option given a similar level of expected returns.

This does not seem to be the case to date since the lion's share of the emerging public equity investment goes into economies that are at the fringe of bandit economies simply measured by the governance indicators, the World Economic Forum indexes, the corruption index, or any other related measure. From a rational point of view, such investment is misguided. That does not mean that it cannot be sustained for years with a few ups and downs or that improving governance may solve the problem but the systematic risk remains higher than investors seem to factor into their assessments.

We suggest that some or many of the BRIC investments fall into that category. Not all sectors and not all industries and certainly not all companies across these economies have the same risk profile, but the systematic risk applies to all. To ignore this and to ignore solid governance base in which solid companies can prosper, is foolish.

Since we postulate that the relevant nature of developing economies lies in their degree of informality of economic interaction and dispute resolution, we consider governance or the rule of law, investment freedom and business freedom as the main indicator of investor attractiveness. These factors can be augmented by various global competitiveness aspects. Together they ultimately determine the success of a company and thus the return to the investor. They are the sufficient condition. Stock market attributes and size are a necessary but not sufficient condition.

The excess liquidity argument (essentially, size requirement) and transactional predictability is well taken. However, our proposed approach to evaluating and selecting emerging markets for investment only negates the size and classification arguments as the primary drivers or selection criteria.

We suggest one way of combining the size (stock market) and quality (governance) issues. This is a process and not a static list. There is no value in creating a list of currently attractive economies since this can change rapidly. Developing countries are prone to major shocks that can wreak havoc on a vulnerable economy.

The universe is composed of 86 stock exchanges in excess of US$1 billion or the vast majority of exchanges. Against each country we match the average of the World Bank governance indicators as the primary axis and define three workable universes based on two cutoff points: The stock market must have at least US$10 billion in market capitalization and governance must exceed 50 percent of global ranking (see Figure 6.1).

Only the newer and less advanced members of the OECD are considered. They number nine and only Mexico does not meet the governance standard. Their combined market capitalization is just above 4 percent of global market capitalization. South Korea is by far the most prominent market; Mexico is second.

The category of targets includes many well established emerging markets of today and amounts to over 15 percent of global market capitalization. BRIC economies, except Brazil, are not included in this category. Hong Kong, Brazil, and Taiwan dominate.

The next prospects are similar in size, about 14 percent of global market capitalization and include China, India, and Russia. They, Russia in particular, need to develop their economic structure and governance to be considered main targets. That holds regardless of their global economic role. China is again a major exception because some of the indicators are much higher for key agglomerations of Beijing, Shanghai, and South China. Thus the urban and core industrial part of China probably makes the cut of 50 percent governance. The same argument could be applied to India and its core economic regions. It applies less so to Russia and Indonesia.

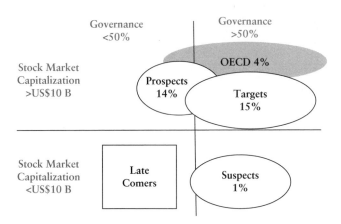

FIGURE 6.1 Market Capitalization (May 2011) and Governance Indicators 2010—Share of Global Stock Market Capitalization in Percent

Source: IMF, Worldwide Governance Indicators, author's analyses.

Future markets are much smaller, less than 1 percent of global market capitalization, but they can grow into decent sized markets given that their economic structure is largely developed with high to very high governance rankings. They may suit smaller or specialized asset managers and include: Malta, Cyprus, Barbados, Mauritius, Lithuania, Latvia, Botswana, Bulgaria, Ghana, Tunisia, and Trinidad. Their stock market capitalization range from US$1.3 billion to just under US$10 billion.

This categorization is dynamic and results in the country categories based on current data.

Overall about one third of world market capitalization is addressed (Table 6.1). However, these economies represent well more than half of

TABLE 6.1   Market Selection: Governance and Market Capitalization (by size of market, May 2011)

OECD "New" Economies	Targets	Prospects
4.2% of World—9 markets	15.3% of World—19 markets	14.0% of World—18 markets
Mixed	>US$10B Mkt Cap, >50% Governance	>US$10B Mkt Cap, <50% Governance
Chile	Hong Kong	China
Czech Republic	Brazil	India
Estonia	Taiwan	Russia
Hungary	Singapore	Indonesia
Mexico	South Africa	Colombia
Poland	Malaysia	Philippines
Slovak Republic	Saudi Arabia	Peru
Slovenia	Turkey	Egypt
South Korea	Thailand	Argentina
	Israel	Nigeria
	Qatar	Bangladesh
	UAE	Pakistan
	Kuwait	Vietnam
	Morocco	Ukraine
	Oman	Sri Lanka
	Bahrain	Kazakhstan
	Croatia	Swaziland
	Jordan	Kenya
	Romania	

Note: MSCI emerging and frontier as well as advanced markets in italic.

world market capitalization outside the United States, Japan, and the United Kingdom.

It is interesting to note that target markets based on a combination of reasonable stock market size (excluding all float and liquidity considerations) include all GCC (Gulf Cooperation Council) countries. These countries have decent legal systems and orderly economic processes that are continuously improving due to their resource incomes. Several are just considered frontier today. Their markets are mostly above US$100 billion; the exceptions are Oman and Bahrain.

The path for countries to join the target or prospect list is to improve governance and administrative systems rather than upgrading the stock market and leaving companies to fight on their own in a less than organized or structured economy. Investments in bandit economies are more speculative and higher risk than investments in solid economies, regardless of the growth rate, GDP capita improvement, resource endowment, or a host of other exciting macroeconomic data. Taking a higher risk needs to be rewarded and returns then must be commensurate. To date they are not. We all invest in about the same markets and the same major stocks and we all get about the same returns that do not compensate for the risks. Looking at structural fundamentals can diversify such a portfolio and position us for the future that is bound to happen along the lines of a dominance of a group-variety of emerging markets.

This, we argue, serves the investor better and certainly achieves better results over the long term.

In this context we must therefore accept the route of investing in smaller markets because it will take decades before several new emerging markets are anywhere near a size that allows them to compete with the big markets of today. By then, a good part of the potential performance will already be unlocked.

NOTES

1. Tom Weidig and Pierre-Yves Mathonet, *The Risk Profile of Private Equity* (Luxembourg, 2004) (across 5,000 investments); Thomas Meyer and Pierre Yves Mathonet, *Beyond the J-Curve* (West Sussex: John Wiley & Sons, 2005).
2. www.Ifc.org.

Two

The Investment Case for Developing Markets

In Part Two we offer different perspectives on why developing markets will become a mainstream asset class and why opportunities as well as pitfalls are abundant. It is not only the relative size of population and superior economic growth rates that unlock investor interest. Undoubtedly, the sheer size and growth of major emerging markets is overwhelming; however, specific opportunities in regions, countries and even at individual company level deserve as much attention. They are often neglected.

A backdrop on the growing importance of developing economies relative to developed economies sets the scene. The question to address is the likely permanence or stability of this trend and the resulting opportunities.

The future importance of developing economies is highlighted by the contrast of some of the woes of developed economies with the increasing advantages of developing economies. The resulting opportunity lies squarely in new markets and developed nations may have lost ground for good. This view, argued by a fund management company, illustrates a number of compelling reasons for investment in developing economies or markets. It suggests that current opportunities are but a first stage of the coming sea change across the world: Investments will increasingly divert to developing economies in line with the capacity to absorb larger capital flows and in line with the institutional development of emerging markets. Investing in the more advanced developing markets today is by no means a pioneering activity anymore.

It also sheds light on the issues developed markets face in retaining some of their economic leadership positions. A reversal of economic dependence and political power from developed to developing countries is on the horizon and investors are well advised to gear up for this opportunity.

A case for the poorer cousin of emerging markets, frontier markets, is made on the bases of their economic potential. The advantages of frontier markets—faster growth, young growing population, strong macroeconomics, and attractive market fundamentals—provide a powerful long-term investment theme. Not the type of investment for everyone, but a growing ingredient in a broad based and performance seeking investor portfolio. Even if at country level a number of issues and challenges remain, grouping these countries into subcontinents or regions can provide much required diversification. The economic role and position of major regions result in the conclusion that Asia is likely to provide the majority of winning countries.

Sub-Saharan Africa has been in the wider discussion for some time now, mainly because of humanitarian considerations and possibly political considerations but increasingly as an investment destination. We look at a region that has long been considered borderline investable by commercial investors as opposed to politically motivated investment such as from China, South Korea, or Middle East economies. The case for African investment, excluding South Africa and North Africa, is strong and slowly global attention is turning to Africa. Despite all its shortcomings, this continent has its fair share of opportunities to offer.

Southeast Asia with its very sizeable populations and a number of performing markets must be seen in a wider context. Several countries around the Mekong, for example, have recently started their stock markets and several others are investing in upgrading their capital markets. Next to China and India, Southeast Asia has consistently figured among the most important destinations for developing market capital. The case is made that a portfolio of country investments is very attractive and is likely to become an important balance to the mega investments in China and India. The diversity of these Southeast Asian nations augurs well to create a regional network of significance well outside ASEAN. Regional country networks and support cascades, also termed the *flying geese pattern* by the economist Akamatsu,[1] reinforce growth. As a stepping-stone for investors, a regional perspective and diversified approach is one strong solution to the selection challenge.

The prodigious wealth accumulation of hydrocarbon-rich Middle Eastern countries, in particular the GCC, and some North African economies contrasts with the lower speed of development of some of their neighbors and the Levant economies. This regional grouping sports some very traditional approaches and investment needs to follow a different route. The soft side of doing business in MENA is illuminating as to culture and prevailing values. Capital markets in Middle East-North Africa (MENA) are less well developed in comparison to outward investments but joint opportunities for investors are abundant. This region is gaining speed given the pace of development demonstrated in the past few decades.

As a country case study, Oman is an economy that has a long tradition of trade between East and West. Its economy has developed stably and its stock market is well established. Looking at framework conditions for foreign investors and foreign investment, the country is making great strides to attract foreign businesses. The stock market should grow over time. Of the GCC economies, Oman is likely one of the lesser noticed but equally attractive economies long term.

From humble beginnings, the UAE has become a major outward investor and sports the cosmopolitan agglomeration, Dubai, at world-class levels. Infrastructure is first rate and businesses have a very conducive environment for development. The potential for a sizable capital market is latent even if cultural considerations may delay the full unlocking of its potential. The case of the UAE is also used to demonstrate that atypical development does not necessarily determine the prospects of the capital market for foreign investors.

NOTE

1. K. Akamatsu et al., "A historical pattern of economic growth in developing countries," *Journal of Developing Economies* 1, no. 1 (March–August, 1962): 3–25.

CHAPTER 7

Emerging Markets Investments— Short Term or Secular Theme

Josuah Rechtsteiner and Tobias Weinert

Rising Star AG
(translated from German and edited by Gordian Gaeta)

Emerging markets, led by the BRICs (Brazil, Russia, India, and China) are increasingly at the forefront of the media, typically on the subject of economic growth, resource endowment, and increasing exploitation of their growing political clout.

Yet, today there remains a valid debate about the permanence of the rise of emerging economies. Are we witnessing a fundamental shift in the global economic landscape or a short-term development? This issue is of fundamental importance to investors.

The present study comes to 10 straightforward conclusions to address the question of the stability of the rise of emerging economies and direction of future investments:

Stability

1. Industrial nations are avoiding necessary economic restructuring at all costs. This will limit their growth prospects and freedom of action for some time to come.
2. Low public debt and high reserves in emerging markets are a major competitive advantage for emerging economies.
3. Developing economies possess almost unlimited natural resources as well as other abundant production factors.
4. While developed economies are reducing their investment in education, emerging economies are investing in the innovation of tomorrow.

5. The contribution of developed economies to the economic progress of emerging markets will decline progressively.

Direction

6. Various financial crises have demonstrated that equity is the safest form of investment.
7. There is demand for IPOs on emerging market stock exchanges and no lack of capital.
8. Alpha results will be based on business and management performance, not leverage.
9. Private equity leads investment in the most attractive industries and companies.
10. Personal relationships are an essential value added for business management.

The financial crisis has helped clarify a number of macroeconomic challenges faced by industrial and emerging economies. Thus we study the current situation of industrialized economies to better understand the future of emerging economies.

For investors, it is important to assess the current starting position of global economies to establish whether the current trend toward emerging markets is short term or structural. To this effect, we will analyze the state of affairs in advanced economies and contrast these with developments and prevailing framework conditions in emerging markets. We subsequently develop an attractiveness ranking by geographical region (see Part One, Chapter 2).

THE CONFOUNDED STATE OF INDUSTRIAL NATIONS

No consideration of emerging markets is complete without differentiating between developed economies and emerging markets. Since the latest financial crisis, emerging markets have developed so independently that their growth actually supports the recovery of developed economies. Some emerging markets are creating employment in developed economies through direct investment and some emerging markets are creditors to developed nations. Emerging markets survived the financial crisis well and retain the strong competitive advantages that will allow them to grow sustainably and reduce the gap between them and developed economies. Their political influence may be increasing. Moreover, emerging markets include the majority of the global population that aspires to be economically independent.

All developed economies were seriously affected by the financial crisis. Public debt is rising and growth is moderate with little prospect of improvement. The consumer remains cautious and freedom of governments is restricted.

In 2008, the United States started an unprecedented set of economic measures and regulatory changes to the financial sector. The purpose of these economic measures was to support those economic sectors that were most affected by the recession. The regulatory changes were aimed at restoring the necessary liquidity to the financial system. At the same time, these measures sought to prevent the US consumer with "bad" home mortgages from becoming insolvent. In the meantime, these measures have partially expired.

The result has been a positive effect on preferred sectors, since for every US dollar spent by government, GDP increases by US$0.7.[1] (By comparison, tax reductions of US$1.00 increase GDP on average by US$3.00.)

Measures to stabilize the financial system were rather half-hearted. While the World Bank and the IMF imposed rigorous conditions during the previous crises, the US measures sought to avoid any medium-term unpleasant consequences. The liquidity provided served primarily to improve the balance sheet situation of banks. Credit expansion has not taken place for either corporations or consumers. Past crises demonstrate that it will take a couple of years before debt reduction is completed and sustained growth returns, as shown in Figure 7.1.

As a consequence, the IMF assumes a slow recovery in the United States. The main reason lies in the central role of the US consumers. Their

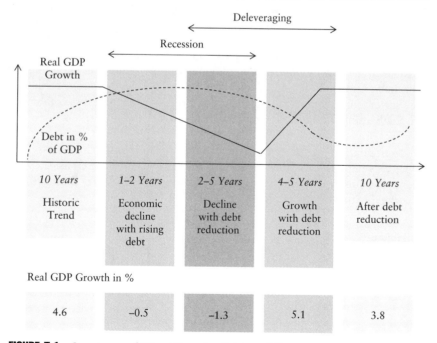

FIGURE 7.1 Structure and Time Line of a Crisis and Recovery
Source: McKinsey Global Institute, January 2010, Rising Star Research.

confidence is undermined by the crisis and employment conditions have not improved. The difference between potential and actual production remains significant. Low capacity utilization prevents employment recovery. Moreover, debt reduction has not taken place. The decline of real estate values predominantly affected low income households that typically consume the majority of their disposable income.

The key question now is how the United States can balance short-term measures to support recovery with medium-term credit rating. Government intervention needs to be reduced without endangering recovery, while all market participants must reduce their debt burden to strengthen the financial system.

The European Union is also recovering slowly. In particular, public debt concerns of individual member states impaired recovery before it got fully under way. Reforms to the pension and social security systems are urgently required, as is increased efficiency of administration. Equally in Europe, unprecedented rescue measures for the financial sector and selected member states have been taken. This has, however, reduced the credibility of the common currency and restricted fiscal freedom of governments.

Germany finds itself in a relatively strong position as exports are increasing, although traditional trade partners are growing slowly. The current export boom is largely due to emerging markets that require quality capital goods. This may not be sustainable since trade with these economies is relatively low when compared to Germany's traditional trade partners.

France, however, suffers from low consumption due to high unemployment. The IMF posits that economic support programs expired too soon. Italy, Greece, Portugal, Ireland, and Spain face more serious problems. They suffer from a significant deficiency in terms of competiveness combined with high public debt. They are constrained to reform markets without affecting private consumption. The most important subject in Europe is the consolidation of the government budgets and long-term ability to service existing public debt. Only countries less affected by the crisis, such as Poland, or countries with strong private and public balance sheets, such as Turkey, can progress relatively unscathed.

Key Issues

Several key issues are similar across industrial nations. The financial crisis would have caused unimaginable consequences for the economy, society, and politics of developed economies had it not been for government stimulus programs and rescue packages. The crisis was the consequence of wrong incentives and global misjudgment. A more dramatic restructuring, such as those in the late 1990s and early 2000s in several emerging markets, could have cleansed the global financial system, but economic, social, and societal risks and costs were unpredictable. Decision makers therefore focused on fighting symptoms to allow the system to recover. Instead of a dramatic and painful one-time restructuring, a path of gradual change was chosen. As the problems arose primarily from debt, the only effective solution is sustained debt reduction. This applies to all market participants, consumers and companies, and public corporations from municipalities to the federal government. Reduction of debt requires that we spend less then we generate in revenue. We therefore must save. Since the revenue bases of the state and corporations depend on continued consumption and investment, it would not be wise to reduce expenditures. To generate the necessary means to reduce debt, incomes or revenues must increase. Ultimately therefore, economic growth is required to afford and balance the fight against the symptoms while steadily improving the financial system.

The difficulty lies in generating solid economic growth without incurring new debt. Growth is generated through domestic demand as well as the export of goods and services. Countries are therefore dependent on domestic demand and demand for exported goods and services.

In addition to the difficulty of generating new income to reduce debt, the management of existing debt is getting more complex since financial markets associate distinctly higher risks with some of the developed nations. As a consequence, credit terms worsen and further reduce freedom of action of governments.

We need to critically review the general competitiveness of industrial nations.

Global Trade

Exports of developed nations have changed significantly during the last decade. Figure 7.2 shows exports by region and destination in 2009.

It is noticeable that regions such as Europe, North America, and Asia primarily trade among themselves. Latin America, the Middle East, and Africa have more diversified trade partners. What does the high proportion of intraregional trade mean? The obvious conclusion is that regions with important intraregional trade are less dependent on diversified exports. While this may seem an advantage, deeper analyses reveal a double-edged sword. Trade statistics are often used for or against the de-coupling theory. As such, a decoupling trend was argued by some based on the increased intraregional trade in Asia leading to a reduced dependency of Asian economies on developed nations. This seems to stand to reason. However, it remains to be seen whether this is an advantage and whether decreasing trade diversification also reduces risks. In the past 10 years, emerging markets such as the BRICs generated strong economic growth and continued growth is generally expected. It is therefore beneficial for Asian economies, and other fast growing economies, to strengthen intraregional trade.

Less dynamic regions such as the United States and Europe seek to increase trade with dynamic regions such as the BRICs. In fact, developed economies have steadily increased their exports to the BRIC economies. Nevertheless, these exports declined as a proportion of intraregional trade.

Developed economies are therefore becoming more dependent both on the BRIC markets and domestic and regional consumers. The reduction of trade as a percentage of GDP for Latin America and Asia (Figure 7.3) is a

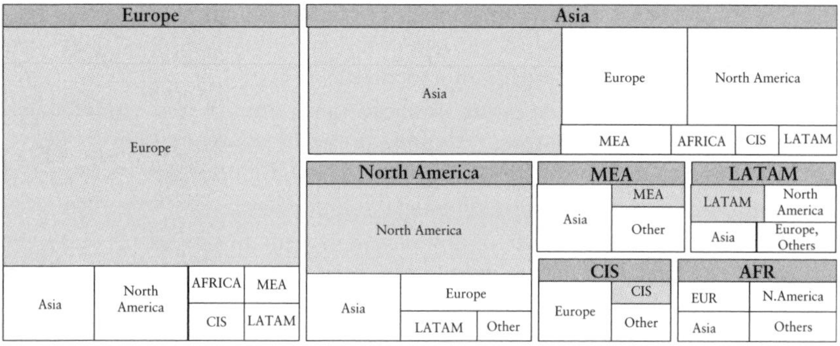

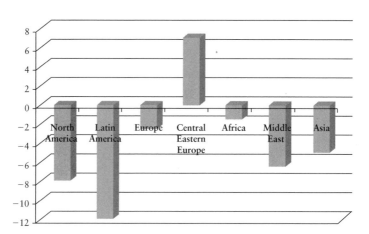

FIGURE 7.2 Exports and Destinations by region, 2009
Source: International Trade Statistics 2010, WTO, Rising Star research.

FIGURE 7.3 Export Share of GDP in Percent Change, 1999 to 2009
Source: World Trade Organization, International Trade Statistics 2000–2010, WTO, Rising Star research.

positive development, as it demonstrates the increasing importance of local consumption in driving economic growth. One could argue a regional coupling of dependency. This regional cluster trend is reinforced by rising transportation costs. At a market price of US$100 per barrel for oil, transport cost between the United States and Asia are equivalent to a 10 percent import duty, a considerable hindrance to trade.

Self-Generated Growth

Future economic growth of developed nations therefore depends primarily on domestic demand by consumers and corporations. In turn their demand depends on their disposable incomes and outlook. The outlook determines the saving rates and credit demand and thus total capital of an economy for consumption and investment. In the past decade credit demand was high, and between 2000 and 2009 households considerably increased their indebtedness, except in Germany and Japan. In the United States, Canada, the United Kingdom, and Spain private debt in 2009 exceeded 80 percent of GDP. Japan, Germany, France, and Italy household debt for 2009 was between 40 and 70 percent of GDP. The financial crisis increased the uncertainty of consumers. A report by The Boston Consulting Group (BCG) in 2010 concluded that the slower the economic growth and the higher the private indebtedness, the lower the confidence in the future. This seems compelling since existing loans have to be serviced first. Any consumer reticence slows recovery. Although the lessons learned from the financial crisis should instill some financial discipline in households, debt reduction has not yet started and consumers in developed economies only plan to reduce their consumption.

According to BCG, 85 percent of all consumers plan to either maintain or reduce their consumption expenditure while more than 80 percent of consumers seek cost-effective substitution products. This does not augur well for producers of high cost, high quality goods. The contribution of private households to the GDP of developed nations could decline significantly if financial discipline of private households increases along with higher savings and lower cost consumer goods. Employers are the determining factor for private households, as they create employment opportunities and decide salary increases. Yet, the ability of companies in this respect is constrained by low capacity utilization and financial stress.

OECD statistics in Figure 7.4 show a decline in average weekly working hours for full time employees between 2000 and 2009.

Although these numbers hardly predict future employment levels, they suggest a rather sobering employment demand.

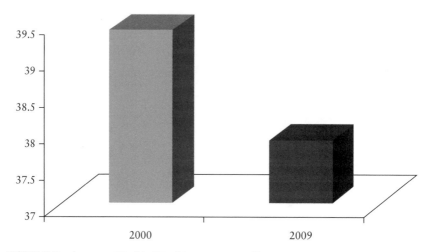

FIGURE 7.4   Average Weekly Working Hours, Full–Time, 2000 to 2009, in Selected Industrialized Nations
Source: OECD, January 2010, Rising Star research.

The financial situation of corporations is not dissimilar to the situation of private households. The debt burden has increased, except for Japan. Debt of non-financial corporations in all major global economies is particularly high: In the United Kingdom, France, and Spain corporate debt exceeds 100 percent of GDP. Corporations are exploiting low interest rates to reduce their cost of debt capital. Loan requirements by banks are getting stricter so that corporations must adopt more financial discipline to be able to refinance or restructure their debt burden. The objective of increasing liquidity of the financial system in order to motivate banks to increase lending to businesses has failed. Monetary aggregates in the United States show that liquidity stays with the banks. Then again, it may not be wise to address a financial crisis with new borrowing.

During the recession following the financial crisis, government tried to support the most critical sectors of the economy. The idea was to gain time until consumption regains its strength. How purposeful such policy is and whether government can afford such a policy remains an important yet unanswered question. First, current government action has dramatically increased public debt. The result has been historically unprecedented rescue programs to prevent the collapse of public finances in weaker Euro economies. Interest tends to rise to compensate capital providers for the increased risk interest rates have. Yet interest rates remain at very low levels. There are more market asymmetries.

Risk premiums for public debt of some developed nations are at the same level as those for some emerging economies that have significantly lower credit ratings. Factors outside pure default probabilities seem to determine the pricing, but ultimately only the trade-off between interest payments and default risk matters. The market typically corrects the current asymmetry, which should lead to either a revaluation of the creditworthiness of emerging markets or a devaluation of the creditworthiness of certain developed economies. The latter would lead to increased interest payments and a substantial burden on government budgets. As a consequence, any increase in interest rates is fiercely resisted in Europe. Proposals by the Euro Group to issue Euro-wide Union bonds to include all member states with collective liability would reduce the interest cost for the weakest economies at the expense of the strongest economies such as Germany.

The ability of government to remedy the symptoms of the crisis and return to business as usual is limited. The effectiveness of public economic stimulus packages on the GDP has been increasingly the subject of academic studies.[3] Harvard professors Barrow and Redlick suggest that the multiplicator of public consumption on the GDP trends toward 1 only in an environment of high unemployment but remains between 0 and 1 otherwise. This contradicts the statement of the Obama administration, which claims a multiplicator of 1.5 for its measures. Results by US economist Ramey are similar: The multiplicator of public expenditure ranges between 0.6 and 1.1 times GDP. The reason for the limited impact of public consumption lies in the decision making. Government consumption is an inefficient political decision process and not based on actual market demand.

The capital deployed by government for its stimulus packages reduces the capital available to households and corporations. While stimulus packages are an expensive luxury, they compensate for significantly lower household and corporate consumption due to prevailing uncertainties. This strongly cyclical behavior reinforces economic cycles and may lead to excessive stock exchange movements. The true cost of public measures is already felt both in the United States and Europe. Governments need to reduce expenditures; a fiscal crisis is on the horizon. Public consumption must be reduced and refinanced through tax increases. Both have negative effects on economic growth.

Thus, since the financial crisis, economic growth of industrial nations depends increasingly on the success of emerging markets that determine global economic growth.

Competitiveness under Review

Globalization stands for all efforts that contribute to the free flow of goods, capital, and other production factors across the globe. Initial advocates of globalization, multinationals and multilaterals from advanced economies, praised the advantages of better access to production means and reduction of market entry barriers in emerging economies. Others argued globalization as a means of poverty reduction. While there has been limited success in poverty reduction during the first decade of globalization, several emerging markets faced severe financial crises in the 1990s due to errors in opening their markets.[4] The tide has turned and following the last financial crisis, developing economies emerged stronger than industrial nations from their crises and the lessons learned.

More and more goods and natural resources originate from countries that were asked to lower market access barriers for our goods. The resulting growth dynamic creates technology competencies that compete with those of developed nations. The idea of China as "extended production facility" has long been applicable to other emerging economies that are less advanced. Global trade flows thus are increasingly from emerging economies toward industrialized economies.

Globalization increases competitive rivalry. Where do industrialized nations stand? Growth of industrial nations depends on their competitiveness not only with their exports but also in their domestic consumption. After all, consumers will choose imported goods for better prices or even for higher quality.

The competiveness of a nation depends on several factors: In principle, these are the availability of production factors, the competency of the domestic industries, and strength of domestic consumer demand. The latter reduces dependency on foreign trade. Equally, administrative barriers and taxation affect competiveness. These factors have changed considerably over the past 10 years and we shall review the current state of affairs.

Availability of Production Factors

Recent experience in the Western high-tech industry related to China's export restrictions for rare minerals as well as the scarcity of qualified professionals in Germany demonstrates the importance of production factors for economic growth. Emerging markets cover 73 percent of global land and about 81 percent of global population. This suggests that emerging markets also cover the majority of global natural resources and global working population. In fact, reserves of natural resources in emerging markets significantly exceed those of industrial nations (see Figure 7.5).

The value of these resources, on which the growth of emerging markets depends heavily, has also increased dramatically.

About 1.2 percent of the population in China owns a car, while in Germany ownership is 50 percent. It is not hard to imagine the long-term consequences of vehicle registration in China with respect to the demand for gasoline once China catches up to developed economy standards. Demand for natural resources will further increase and consequently their prices. This will lead to distribution effects between industrial nations and emerging markets and between emerging markets themselves. The distribution effect between emerging market themselves is difficult to estimate. However, the collective competitive advantage of emerging markets with respect to natural resources is evident. The consequential dependence of industrial nations is evident well beyond the oil crisis of 1973.

Table 7.1 shows the value index of different natural resources that underscore the growing advantages of emerging markets.

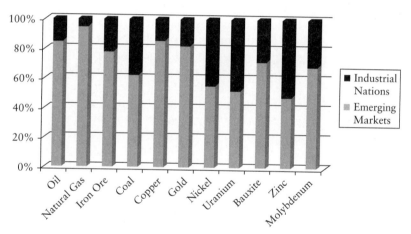

FIGURE 7.5 Distribution of Global Natural Resources
Source: Fidelity International, Rising Star research.

TABLE 7.1 Natural Resources Price Changes, 2000–2010

Agriculture	+46.02%
Metals	+379.77%
Energy	+106.95%

Source: Rogers International Commodity Sub-Index Total Return, Rising Star AG research.

Scarcity and the strategic necessity of natural resources has led to multiple, often armed, conflicts. It is interesting to note how China is securing global access to natural resources without conflict. Developing mutually beneficial relationships is a specialty of China's natural resource policy. Expensive armed conflicts have been avoided while their political influence has grown. The shift in political power toward emerging markets will be discussed later.

In the past, high-technology nations such as Japan and Germany with few natural resources were able to compensate for their disadvantage through a qualified workforce and high performance in research and development. Product complexity and production processes require specialized skills. In particular, Asian emerging markets were not considered a threat in the 1990s due to the perceived gap in specialized skills. Since then, Western multi-nationals have exported specialized skills to China. One of the key virtues of the Chinese leadership was to combine market entrance and profit opportunity of Western companies with a transfer of skills. At the same time, the education system expanded greatly. Today China alone generates more university grad-uates than all major industrial nations combined. Critics claim that only half of these are actually well educated, but even half would be a significant factor. China, Brazil, and Russia together graduate 10 million students each year. The most important industrial nations combined achieved about 4 million gradu-ates. This is less than half and it is only a question of time until universities in emerging markets provide the same quality of education that industrial nations provide. The reduction of education budgets of industrial nations caused by the present fiscal crisis will further compound this discrepancy.

China is the pioneer in education among emerging markets, at least by measurable standards. The OECD Pisa 2009 study demonstrates China's lead, although only Shanghai was included, as shown in Figure 7.6.

Even more indicative are patent registration by various nations at the World Intellectual Property Organization (WIPO). Patent registrations are somewhat indicative of usable research output. Notably China ranked third in number of patent applications for each of the years 2006–2009 and the high growth rate of China's patent registration is indicative of a grow-ing innovation capability. Russia and India still have some way to go. Looking at patent registration dynamically, major industrial nations such as Germany, the United States, and the United Kingdom, show a declining rate of registration while China is quite the opposite. The catch up with respect to human capital is in full swing. Since patent registrations are the outcome of several years of research these numbers reflect the educational progress of several years. This trend could strengthen over coming years.

Already today we note that, for example, German imports of research and development services has strongly increased. A prominent example is the recent decoding of the genomes of the EHEC virus by Chinese researchers at

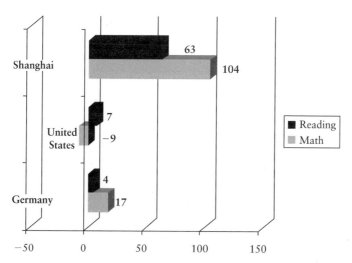

FIGURE 7.6 Pisa Results Relative to OECD Average Scores
Source: OECD Pisa 2009, Rising Star research.

the Beijing Genomics Institute, one of the leading institutes. They have the most advanced equipment and technologies, so the genomes could be decoded in three days. In Europe and with older equipment, this would have taken up to two weeks.

Research and development imports from China increased more than fourfold over the period 2004 to 2008 and equivalent imports from India more than threefold (see Figure 7.7). In addition, China exports more research and development services to the European Union than the European Union exports to China. These numbers demonstrate that the production factor human capital has dramatically improved in emerging economy.

In the same way, productivity of the workforce improved rapidly in emerging markets. While work productivity in Europe increased by 1 percent yearly between 2000 and 2008, work productivity in Brazil, China, and India rose on average by 7.7 percent a year. Also in Africa where productivity is steadily rising, work productivity increased by 2.8 percent per annum over the same period. This increase in productivity somewhat mitigates the effects of labor cost increases and thus contributes to the attractiveness of human capital in emerging economies. Human capital compounds the competitive advantage of emerging economies over established industrial nations.

Industrial nations have lost their leadership in the area of manufacturing competiveness, as evidenced by the Deloitte Index of Global Competitiveness in Manufacturing (Table 7.2).

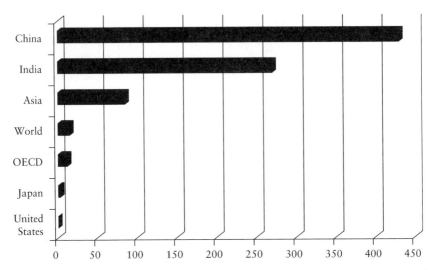

FIGURE 7.7   German Imports of R&D Services in Percent Change, 2004 to 2008
Source: DB Research, Eurostats, Rising Star research.

Consumer Developments

Strong domestic consumption strengthens economies and provides resilience against weak export performance. Local consumption of industrial nations suffers increasingly from demographic trends—the birth rate of industrial nations is on average 1.7 children per couple, as opposed to 3.3 children in emerging markets. The consumer basis of industrial nations tends to decrease long term. Projected annual population growth rates in Europe and the United States for the coming five years are 0.03 percent to 0.9 percent. After 2015, Europe will start to shrink. At the same time, projected real GDP growth rates for industrial nations until 2015 are 2 to 3 percent per annum. Per capita growth of real GDP is weak. Any private debt reduction or moderate tax increase will thus noticeably reduce future private domestic consumption.

Equally relevant for the assessment of consumption development is the expected change in income structure. Couples with tertiary education have fewer children and have them later in life. Thus the main population growth happens in segments with lower education. Academic studies demonstrate that the life income of children heavily depends on levels of education and net worth of their parents. This suggests a further concentration of net worth and income within the population. Employment with low qualifications will tend to migrate abroad, much as in the past the automotive supplier industry

TABLE 7.2 Manufacturing Competitiveness—Current and 5 Years Out

Rank	Country	Current Score	5-Year Score	5-Year Rank
1	China	10.00	10.00	1
2	India	8.15	9.01	2
3	Republic of Korea	6.79	6.53	3
4	United States	5.84	5.38	5
5	Brazil	5.41	6.32	4
6	Japan	5.11	4.74	7
7	Mexico	4.84	4.84	6
8	Germany	4.80	4.53	8
9	Singapore	4.69	4.52	11
10	Poland	4.49	4.52	9
11	Czech Republic	4.38	3.95	12
12	Thailand	4.17	4.53	10
13	Canada	4.11	3.71	13
14	Switzerland	3.07	2.62	18
15	Australia	3.07	3.40	15
16	Netherlands	2.9	2.63	17
17	United Kingdom	2.82	2.51	20
18	Ireland	2.78	2.43	21
19	Spain	2.67	2.63	16
20	Russia	2.58	3.47	14
21	Italy	2.42	2.37	22
22	South Africa	2.28	2.52	19
23	France	1.70	1.92	23
24	Belgium	1.18	1.00	26
25	Argentina	1.03	1.53	24
26	Saudi Arabia	1.00	1.32	25

Source: Deloitte and US Council on Competitiveness, 2010 Global Manufacturing Competitiveness Index, Deloitte Touche Tohmatsu, 2010.

migrated to Eastern Europe. Already today the proportion of under-skilled labor seeking employment for more than six months exceeds 60 percent.

Emerging markets increasingly diversify their economic and industrial structure. This increases their relative advantage over developed economies and attracts low qualification employment. We can therefore also expect a reduction of income and net worth in lower income segments of developed economies. Although this part of society consumes little, they reduce the consumption potential of other households through the social transfer payments they receive. Social payments today already amount to 32 percent of the German federal budget. The proportion of social payments will increase because the balance of social transfer receivers or payees to employees or payors increases. This increases public financing requirements.

Since we require a qualified labor force, we hire increasingly from emerging economies. After a few years, these imported laborers then return as specialists to their home countries. The foreseeable democratic development is therefore not conducive to the growth of domestic consumption. Although not all economies have a similarly wide social system as Germany (covering essentially the entire population and multiple conditions of individuals, e.g. unemployment, disability, family care, etc.), the structural demographic issue is widespread. Not only are baby boomers in the United States reaching retirement age, they saved little and consumed much. As soon as income drops, consumption will decline considerably. We can therefore expect negative domestic growth in consumption.

This is particularly important for the United States, as its economy depends to almost 80 percent on domestic consumption. Such dependency was sometimes an advantage in comparison to economies like Germany's that are more exposed to global economy developments. In 2007, the average indebtedness of US households already stood at 138 percent of income. Since 2000, private consumption has been on average 77.3 percent of GDP. If, therefore, domestic consumption declines by 1 percent, GDP growth declines by 0.77 percent. Clearly, this also depends on the development of disposable household income, but the impact of reducing consumer debt as opposed to consuming is evident particularly in light of the increase in consumer debt in the past decade by more than 30 percent above its long-term trend (see Figure 7.8).

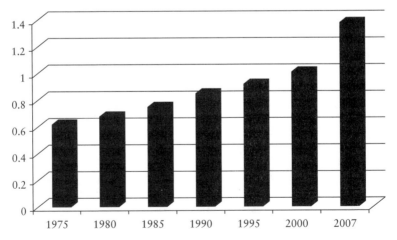

FIGURE 7.8   US Private Debt in Multiple of Income

Source: Federal Reserve, McKinsey Global Institute analyses, Rising Star research.

The way back could be tough for a consumer dependent economy such as the United States. The continuously declining savings rate over the past 30 years contributed actively to economic growth. Therefore, continued growth in consumer credit is critical. A capital restructuring of companies, households, and the federal government could rapidly result in several years of depression.

Financial Crisis Uncovers Vulnerabilities

The financial crisis was more than a wake-up call. It went to the heart of financing growth of industrial nations. Consumers, companies, and the government got into the habit of living beyond their means at the expense of the future. The foundation of our economy is becoming increasingly fragile while the time span between consumption enjoyment and future falling off the cliff is getting close to zero. Through measures that either provide liquidity or open rescue parachutes, we were able to extend the time frame. Experience suggests that the distance between renewed alarm signals and conceding defeat is shortening until it turns hectic again and we regret not having acted earlier. Many of us face this dilemma in our daily lives. A transfer of this experience to high-level decisions only happens rarely. Several countries and economies are now under severe pressure and must assess under pressure desirable and necessary measures and the real availability of freedom of action.

Public debt of the G7 economies has reached proportions not seen since the end of World War II. It was not the crisis itself but our behavior over several decades prior that led us to this situation. Growth weaknesses have been compensated for by new public debt while in phases of high growth public debt was not reduced. We now need a serious change of tack to stabilize the fiscal position of economies and prevent further deterioration. The continued aging of the population will increase the cost of health care and retirement. To reduce public debt we must therefore first absorb cost increases. This represents a definitive challenge. Current growth in Germany is fragile, as it primarily based on exports. Few resources are left for countercyclical measures. Several countries are experiencing financial difficulties that also increase interest costs for other nations.

To avoid a fiscal crisis, governments need to increase their incomes and reduce their costs by both restricting private households and corporations. However, according to a study by Ernst & Young (see Figure 7.9), industry decision makers are asking for more stimulus measures to improve economic growth prospects.

Most of the measures primarily asked for will increase government expenditure. Yet none of the highly indebted European countries can really

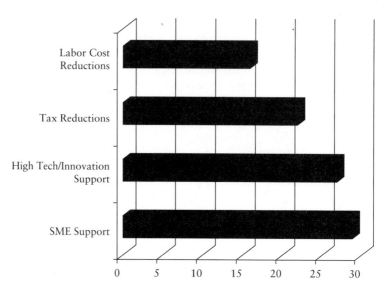

FIGURE 7.9 Top Four Measures to Stimulate the European Economy in Percent

Source: Ernst & Young, 2010 European Attractiveness Survey, Rising Star research.

afford such growth stimulus since countries either require surplus budgets or high economic growth to keep indebtedness in check. It is assumed that the most highly indebted countries will depend on strict fiscal discipline until 2020. Strict fiscal discipline is a barrier to stimulus measures. This recurring dilemma has cost many central banks their independence from politics. As long as interest rates are low, the government can refinance its debt. The required fiscal discipline is the difference between cost of interest and cost of growth. In times of low interest, less economic growth is required; respectively, with some economic growth less fiscal discipline is required. This explains the inherent interest of governments in keeping interest low.

If interest does not compensate the market adequately for the risk taken, sovereign spreads, the insurance costs for government securities such as credit default swaps, increase. Looking at default insurance for five-year government securities over the past 16 months, very significant differences are evident. Interest should therefore be much higher to eliminate the need for insurance. To avoid an unrealistic deleveraging at the moment, monetary aggregates are expanding. However, experience suggests that expansive monetary policy leads to a rise in interest rates to combat inherent inflationary pressures. To date inflation is under control but interest should adjust to the risk incurred while controlling inflation due to expansive monetary policy. As long as this does not happen, we have a market asymmetry that reduces the value of the currency. If interest rates subsequently increase, a devaluation of the currency is expected. This affects primarily the currencies of industrial nations, especially the US dollar and the euro.

Central banks and governments of highly indebted industrial nations then are challenged to implement a mix of fiscal discipline, increase public income, and expend stimulus for the economy. Any two of these goals can be achieved, but all three together are vastly more complex. The rebalancing of public budgets will also require corporations and households to scale back growth, with negative consequences for government finances.

CHANGE IN GLOBAL POWER BALANCE

For some time it has been recognized that the voting structure of multilateral organizations such as the IMF or the G8 does not properly reflect the global economic power structure. Until recently, large economies such as China and India only had a spectator role; smaller economies in Asia and Africa often no role at all. More recently, there has been a call for giving emerging markets a wider role in multilateral organizations to better reflect realities of global markets.

The G20 meeting in January 2008 made a start in recognizing economic realities. Since then the IMF has reformed voting arrangements to give emerging economies a higher weight. Since 2009, emerging economies are also members of the Financial Stability Forum. Also, the voting rights of countries such as China have been dramatically increased since 2010. In the meantime, China has the third largest number of votes at the World Bank. Emerging economies play a critical role not only with respect to capital markets; it is hard to imagine any meaningful dialogue or result in meetings on climate change or environmental protection without the participation of China, India, and Brazil.

This change in the architecture of global power emphasizes the shift toward emerging economies. Key emerging economies are rightly more prominent, based on their fundamental role.

Minor emerging economies still have a long way to go before their voices are heard. There are, however, encouraging signs. In April 2009, the then British Prime Minister Gordon Brown invited several government representatives from Africa and Asia as observers. Even though they were not allowed to participate directly, this represented a major improvement over those meetings where they were not even present.

The reason to give poorer emerging markets a more prominent voice in multilateral organizations is both humanitarian and economic. Thus a variant of G30 has been proposed. Proponents argued that the world is simply too small to exacerbate the division into rich and poor. The credibility of multilateral organizations is also at stake: As long as organizations such as the Security Council of the United Nations do not represent India or Africa, they can hardly be considered democratic forums.

The greatest challenges of globalization, such as climate change, nuclear technologies and weapons, natural resources and energy security, poverty, and social inequality, require the collaboration of all international actors. To progress in these areas for the years to come, emerging economies need to fortify their position in global multilateral organizations.

Until now, the global political arena was dominated by economic Darwinism and capital power. Every step now means a shift in balance. This will positively affect societal and economic developments in emerging markets. A stronger representation of emerging economies is welcome because the global economy gains stability. The redistribution of economic power and capital has been ongoing for decades. This is particularly evident by the country of origin of the wealthiest 100 individuals. In 2000, 90 percent of the wealthiest individuals came from industrialized nations. Only 10 years later, their share was only 64 percent. More than a third of the wealthiest individuals originate from emerging economies. This roughly represents the share of emerging economies in global GDP.

The substantial change in power structures under way will require time to fully materialize but it is clear in which direction it will unfold. In 2020, the share of emerging economies in global GDP will be around 50 percent and that could merely be a stopover. Implications for global power and voting redistribution are far-reaching and we may well witness a new world order in which emerging economies will rise to become equal partners at the level of industrial nations.

The Rise and Fall of Superpowers

While professional historians prefer to see the past as unique events and distance themselves from commenting on patterns in the past, Professor Paul Kennedy, Yale University, took on the challenge of describing patterns in the past that are relevant today, in particular to be considered by political decision makers. In his book *The Rise and Fall of the Great Powers*, he postulates a thesis on why nations rise and fall and provides as evidence a rather undisputed history of Europe and the great powers between 1500 and 2000 and the subsequent confrontation of superpowers.

The principle of his thesis states that the more power a nation acquires, the higher the public expenditure to maintain such power. The ability to maintain a conflict with a nation of similar size or a coalition of nations is inseparably linked to economic performance. At the peak of their military power, most states are already in an economic decline. The United States is no exception to this rule. Power can only be secured through a fine balance between economic net worth and military expenditure. In the process of decline, nations invariably shift their emphasis from economic performance to military expenditure. Spain, the Netherlands, France, and Great Britain did exactly that. After the Soviet Union, the United States may be on the same path.

The pattern of excessive expansion and decline is clearly visible in Spain in the sixteenth century. To maintain power, a combination of excessive public debt and inflation would have brought the country to its knees if not for its main rival, France, being in even worse condition. But by the seventeenth century, France introduced a new system of bureaucracy and military administration that brought its considerable economic resources to bear. Only a combination of all other European powers was able to avoid the dominance of France over the continent. France itself then expanded beyond its means and was soon unable to sustain the costs of its military participation, which led to insolvency and fueled the French Revolution.

France's main opponent was Great Britain, whose claim to power was economically based rather than military. During the eighteenth century, a virtuous circle was created: The network of trade partners generated funding and loans that were necessary to finance the navy to protect shipments, further expand the trade network, and impede competing trade. At the same time, Great Britain was able to raise the capital necessary to fund technological progress that ensured its leadership for a good part of the nineteenth century. Toward the end of the nineteenth century, Great Britain needed to devote increasing resources to its navy; after various extended war operations, only a massive increase in private and public debt and the liquidation of profitable overseas assets prevented a collapse of public finance. In the early twentieth century it required the support of the United States to allow the Allied troops to successfully end World War I. Thereafter, Great Britain declined steadily since it was unable to sustain the levels of expenditure necessary to maintain control and defense of its vast overseas empire.

The German Empire was doomed by its leaders and political structure, although Germany dominated the continent economically and politically toward the end of the nineteenth century. Waging two disastrous wars in the twentieth century in which a hopeless confrontation with the United States and later with the Soviet Union was initiated, Germany was unable to translate its economic performance into political leadership.

The United States emerged as the global leader from the two wars and its economy was greatly stimulated by them, although like other nations in the past, the United States benefited from little competition for leadership. During its global leadership, the United States took on very significant commitments. Since the recovery of Europe and Japan and the rise of emerging economies such as China, Brazil, India, and Russia, the United States is gradually moving toward being *primus inter pares*, or first among equals. Like other nations, the United States failed to create a domestic taxation system that would generate the huge resources required to fund military developments. Instead it turned to foreign markets. This is only sustainable because other superpowers are not in a much better position.

Dr. Kennedy's postulations are more than 25 years old, but nothing much has changed in the overall context of global developments. It cannot be contested that we live in a multipolar world under the political leadership of the United States. It remains to be seen whether today's leaders are doomed for decline or if the world can engineer a system or power oligopoly.

EMERGING MARKETS ON THE GROWTH PATH

Economic growth in emerging markets and resulting opportunities for investors are a long-term and core investment subject, and not only since the financial crisis, since for more than 30 years now emerging markets have consistently achieved a higher share of global GDP than developed economies (see Figure 7.10).

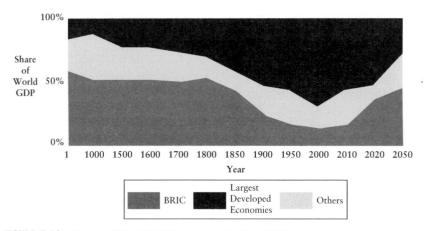

FIGURE 7.10   Share of World GDP—Year 1 (AD)—2050

Source: IWF 2001, Goldman Sachs GE CSR 4, 2009, Angus Maddison, Rising Star research.

What has changed is the approach by investors and the available choices of attractive investment opportunities. High growth rates of emerging economies have proliferated. While 30 years ago the emphasis was on Asia and Tiger economies, today a broadly diversified set of dynamically growing economies exists with different structures and at different stages of development. Globalization has reduced barriers to trade and led to the liberalization of markets. This new freedom challenges the governments and management of companies of emerging markets and leads to many errors in judgment, culminating in the emerging market crisis at the end of the 1990s.

The knowledge gained from this experience is evidenced by the resilience of emerging economies during the financial crisis. As risks in emerging markets are decreasing, investments in emerging markets are no longer speculative. Rather they migrated from a specialty to a mainstream counterweight to industrial nation investments. The role of emerging markets in the portfolio of professional investors is nothing but a mirror image of the role of emerging markets as growth leaders of the world economy. For the investor it is critical to understand the driving framework conditions of emerging markets and how permanent these developments are.

Driving Framework Conditions

The basis for long-term growth in emerging markets is multifaceted. This has advantages and disadvantages for the decision process of investors in emerging economies. This complexity should be seen as a positive aspect but it requires skills to fully master the subject. The reward of such preoccupation is the recognition that growth and development of emerging markets is a forgone conclusion and solidly grounded in the variety of observable fundamentals.

Political Frameworks for Growth   The base for the rise of emerging markets is the liberalization of trade and financial markets as well as the creation of functioning legal systems to secure property rights. Although freedom of goods and capital flows has not been completed yet, great progress is being achieved. Some reticence can be explained by the painful experience at the end of 1990s. During that period, capital markets were opened fairly rapidly at the instigation of industrialized nations without being fully prepared for the ensuing responsibility and national interests. Mistakes were made that are partly attributable to the pressure of industrial nations. Resulting crises are forgotten but the knowledge gained allowed emerging economies to remain largely unscathed by the recent financial crisis.

Emerging markets today prefer a model that fits their specific needs and allows for gradual adaptation rather than following the model of industrialized nations. This is very positive for investors, as risks are better mitigated. In the course of this liberalization a number of regional trade agreements and treaties were concluded that allow a frictionless exchange of goods and capital within a region in adaptation of the model of the European Union Customs Union. Equally in this arena, the reduction of tariffs and duties is gradual to allow for domestic adjustment. Reduction of bureaucracy in trade increases trade velocity and increases intraregional trade profits. The potential of AFTA, for example, is by no means fully exploited since many measures are planned but not implemented. They include standardizations in documentation and reduction of tariffs, infrastructure improvements, and even very long-term plans such as a common currency along the lines of the euro.

Emerging markets will not repeat the mistakes made by model industrial nations. In this respect, the European Union plays a pioneer function that demonstrates much room for improvement. Equally outside AFTA, developments are under way. The regional economies of Africa and Latin America have objectives similar to those of AFTA. Each planned simplification of trade will increase trade profits and increase the efficiency of regional markets. The governments of emerging markets are successfully working on increasing market efficiency by targeting a reduction of red tape and reforming the legal systems.

China demonstrates beyond doubt that democracy is not a requirement for economic success. Many of the political decisions faced by emerging markets to be competitive in the global landscape extend over several election periods so that continuity and independence from the next election may be an advantage.

The Harvard economist Dani Rodrik postulated the Impossibility Theorem in connection with globalization.[5] The theorem argues that of the three desirable goals—globally integrated economy, national sovereignty, and democratic legitimization—only two of these goals can be accomplished at any one point in time. In Europe we have come to realize that in the course of the euro crisis, we have to accept some loss of national sovereignty in order not to make concessions on matters of democratic legitimation and integration of the European economies. The leadership of China does not claim democratic legitimation and can therefore achieve the goals of globally integrated economy and national sovereignty. Although not uncontested, the political system of China seems to give the country a competitive advantage that fosters economic growth. By contrast in Europe, rather right-wing parties are getting stronger, probably in support of the national sovereignty agenda.

Financial Situation In general, emerging markets have healthier budgets and higher reserves than industrial nations. As a consequence they enjoy wider freedom of action to engender economic growth. At present, growth is excessive and stimulus programs are being curtailed all around. It was during the financial crisis that emerging economies for the first time were able to institute countercyclical measures. Given the success of these measures, emerging economies can now reduce growth investments and amortize the cost of their stimulus measures. If emerging economies succeed in amortizing their stimulus packages, they will be a good step ahead of industrialized nations. Industrial nations never recovered the investment or reduced the debt caused by countercyclical measures in subsequent high growth phases.

Industrial production of emerging economies has not only recovered to pre-crisis levels but regained a position exactly on the long-term trend and well ahead of industrial nations that are still 15 percent below their long-term trend and even below pre-crisis levels. Stimulus packages in emerging economies can therefore be reduced without endangering growth, and thus avoid any overheating of the economy. This situation seems unjust from the perspective of industrial nations because emerging markets can amply afford stimulus packages but do not require them anymore. Industrial nations require further stimulus packages but cannot afford them. The diverging trend of growth paths will therefore continue and it is less surprising that emerging economies increasingly step into the strong role of creditors. Liabilities of industrialized nations to emerging markets are increasing. This opens new avenues of influence and market development. News of emerging markets companies buying competitors in North America or Europe are plentiful as is news of financial aid packages for stressed euro countries. This would have been unthinkable only a short time ago.

The overwhelming difference in financial strength between industrialized economies and emerging markets is demonstrated by their respective reserves. Since about five years ago, emerging markets have been holding the majority of currency reserves, today about 65 percent. The distribution is exactly the opposite of the distribution in GDP. In proportion to their GDP, emerging markets have more than three times the fire power for growth stimulus, fiscal expansion, and currency support measures.

Moreover, levels of public debt are comparatively low for emerging markets (see Figure 7.11). Very few of the emerging economies would have a problem meeting the Maastricht debt limitations. In fact, those who used their reserves most are among the euro countries. Even in 2010, still during the phase of stimulus measures, growth in new public debt of emerging markets was –2.8 percent.[6] On average, 80 percent of all emerging market debt is held by nationals. Another advantage of emerging markets is the

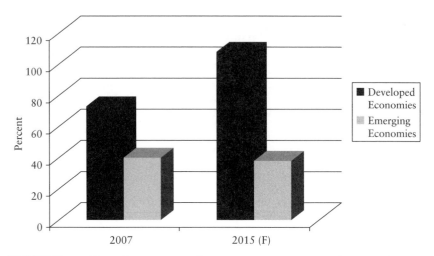

FIGURE 7.11   Public Debt as Percent of GDP—Pre-crisis (2007) and Projected (2015)
Source: IMF WEO update 2010, Rising Star research.

relatively low rate of taxation and the relatively low base of taxpayers. There is therefore room for significant revenue improvement. Since social transfers are much lower than for industrial nations, governments face less financial pressure. This is caused on the one side by demographic developments but equally by easier access to finance by emerging economies driven by higher ratings and the reduction in interest burden.

Some countries such as Brazil, Costa Rica, Peru, Panama, or Morocco experienced a ratings upgrade to investment grade in the midst of the financial crisis. Since the crisis, there have been six ratings upgrades for every one ratings downgrade of emerging economies.

Availability of Production Factors   As outlined earlier, emerging markets hold the majority of global production factors, be they capital, human resources, or natural resources. China, by far the largest emerging market, requires large quantities of natural resources both for domestic use and for export production to the great benefit of Africa and Latin America. These regions, except, for example, Brazil, are not as far advanced in manufacturing as some Asian and Eastern European economies. Natural resources constitute a form of monopoly for those economies that are endowed with the resources. Capital is mobile and will migrate to attractive investment locations. Human capital requires longer gestation periods. In this respect the increased education expenses of emerging economies in the past 5 to 10 years will prove an advantage over the coming 10 to 20 years. Overall, emerging markets possess all production factors necessary for their own growth. Accordingly, trade relationships of the future will tend to improve to the benefit of emerging markets.

Demographic Trends The population of emerging markets is very young. The median age of emerging markets is 28.1 years while the median age of industrialized nations is 39.9 years. A comparison of the population age structure between industrialized nations and key emerging markets (China, India, and Brazil) reveals one major difference: The population of emerging markets decreases with increasing age groups; they form a true pyramid, while in industrialized nations the population of age groups above and below the median decreases. This means that in emerging markets those in retirement are compensated by a sufficient number of economically active individuals. Retirement systems of emerging markets, insofar as they exist, are faced with considerably less pressure than those of industrialized nations. For the latter, the numeric relationship between pensioners and economically active individuals is getting worse as the baby boomer generation is nearing retirement age. Social transfers will therefore certainly increase for industrialized nations and further reduce disposable income.

At the same time, this demographic trend reduces the previous quasi monopoly of industrialized nations with respect to human capital. Regardless of the quality of education, industrial nations will have a smaller qualified work force in absolute numbers. Mobile employment seekers from emerging economies will benefit from this gap in human resources. They may have the opportunity to gain experience in industrialized nations and transfer acquired competencies to their home countries. The competitive position of industrialized nations is therefore hardly sustainable at the current level.

The consumers in emerging markets will not have to worry for some time to come about high social transfer payments. Governments of emerging markets have recognized that they have to invest in education to provide a growing part of the population access to the emerging middle class. From their perspective, it seems the best way to counteract inflation caused by a lack of qualified workforce and potential social unrest due to the inequality of income distribution. The young generation receives a better education than their parents did and can aspire to higher incomes. Local consumption is therefore set to rise. This trend is augmented by increasing urbanization. The transformation of economies toward services and manufacturing creates employment in agglomerations and cities. These agglomerations create efficient markets for employment, goods, and services. In aggregate, the middle class of emerging economies (annual income of US$3,000 to $30,000) will double within six years and count almost 1 billion individuals by 2022 (see Figure 7.12).

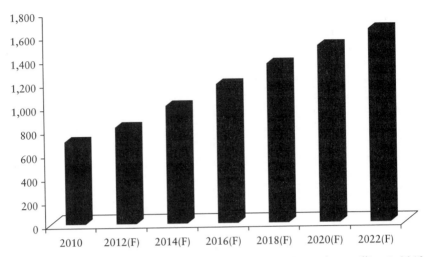

FIGURE 7.12 Aggregate Middle Class—China, India, and Brazil (in millions), 2010 to 2022

Source: Goldman Sachs Global Economics, Commodities and Strategy Research, BRICs monthly, March 2010, Rising Star research.

This group is equivalent to several billions of US dollars in consumer demand and will make the emerging markets middle class by far the largest consumer group. The middle class of emerging markets alone will be larger than the population of all industrialized nations combined. The equivalent developments in industrialized nations are rather static and, due to the small number, of little relevance. Once a growing number of individuals enters the middle class, the average per capita GDP rises. This promulgates such countries into the middle income class of economies. The income distribution on a global scale is getting more equitable. The number of middle income economies will double in the coming decades. The expansion of the middle class flattens the Lorenz curve, the income distribution within an economy. Already today, India has a smaller Gini coefficient than the United States (*CIA World Fact Book,* 2011). Increasing demand for all kinds of goods increases demand for natural resources. This will foster the rise of emerging markets that hold most of the world's natural resources.

GLOBAL REDISTRIBUTION HAS ONLY STARTED

Globalization and the consequent rise of emerging economies are often considered a gigantic redistribution process. This is not necessarily wrong, but polarized. Over centuries, pressure from the North-South asymmetry increased. Through liberalization of goods and capital flows, the pressure is being rebalanced. This adjustment process will continue until a balance is restored. It is the nature of this process that emerging markets will benefit primarily from these developments while industrialized nations should urgently rethink and adjust their business models. There is the danger of a gradual loss of economic and political influence with consequential income loss and social changes.

As we know, China toppled the United States as the largest manufacturer in 2010, a position the United States had held since 1895. The reclaiming of the top spot closes a 500-year circle, according to historian Paul Allen. Even this event is only a stopover. Nicolas Craft, long-term economic trend expert from the University of Warwick, considers the change so fundamental that it will not change again in the foreseeable future. The rise of emerging markets, here the example of China, has historic dimensions far beyond several multiyear economic cycles.

We need to ask ourselves which forces govern this redistribution process that is changing our customary economic and political landscape. Assuming that there is no superior order for global distribution equality and that no predestined global economic structure exists, change must be driven by past decisions and resulting dynamics over several decades. We will review individual changes that make up in sum recent economic history.

Following the Stolper-Samuelson theorem on trade, under a framework of increased international trade, production factors of one country are in higher demand and achieve better prices if they are plentiful in comparison to those of other countries. For a leading industrialized nation such as Germany, these factors would be capital and a quality work force. The only production factor that industrialized nations have in excess, when compared to emerging economies, is knowledge. In the past, emerging markets only had excess low cost labor and natural resources. Natural resources probably even generated monopoly gains for the exporting economy. The fundamental dynamic of producing low cost goods with low cost labor in emerging markets started increased demand for low cost goods from Asian manufacturers and was probably at the origin of the prevailing dynamic. Through manufacturing plants investment was attracted. Over time, the economy started to diversify and education improved. As a consequence, these regions were able to attract international companies that reinforced transfer benefits. Good examples from the past are the Asian Tiger economies that started with low cost manufacturing and now sport some of the leading high-tech corporations. Of course, employment for low cost goods migrated to other economies.

A similar development can be observed globally with emerging markets, albeit with regional specialties. China took over the low cost status from

Taiwan and is developing further. To date, the quality of Chinese goods has reached a relatively high level according to a study by the ECB and improves continuously (Pula & Santabarbara, 2011). This undermines the current advantage of industrialized nations and fosters employment in rural parts of China and in other emerging markets in Africa, Asia, and Latin America. Countries like Vietnam and Cambodia are already considered extended production facilities of China since labor costs are lower than they are in China. China itself invests heavily in education to avoid any shortage of qualified workers. This policy is not only based on farsightedness; investment in education is part of a long-term plan to fight inflation because continued education and a larger workforce can mitigate demand side pressure on labor cost. The availability of a qualified workforce causes a further diversification of the economy and promotes research and development. Increasingly complex products can be made in China. Already today, China increasingly attracts capital and know-how from industrialized nations. Thus China creates for itself the opportunity to extract monopolistic profits from human capital. The next and the following generation of Chinese will be far better educated. Education investments have long amortization periods but are an essential requirement for economic progress. Germany already imports R&D services from China, a potential alarm signal.

Increase in qualifications and further diversification of the economic structure in advanced emerging economies creates new competitive advantages. Competitive positions are continuously changing. The Stolper-Samuelson theorem also stipulates that for relatively scarce factors such as low cost labor in Germany, conditions worsen with increasing trade. The theory offers an explanation of the fact that in the past one and a half decades about 3 million jobs with social security were lost in Germany while at the same time long-term unemployed have a comparatively low level of qualification. These jobs are now in emerging economies from which we import our products. Competition over the advantages of qualified labor is in full swing. The effect of Chinese imports on the employment situation has also occupied academia. In a recent US economic report, the term *China Syndrome* was coined. It describes the displacement of low income labor domestically and the consequential cost through social payment transfers from the disadvantaged domestic work force. It is assumed that the negative effects of social transfer payments at least compensate for the advantages of lower cost consumption.

Since transport costs tend to increase, regional trade is on the rise. If a product from Europe is always 10 to 20 percent more expensive than one from a neighboring country, imports from the neighboring country will be preferred. Since over time increasingly more complex products are manufactured by a better qualified work force in emerging economies, the advantages based on knowledge by industrialized economies is decreasing. The availability of goods in regional trade areas such as Latin America, Africa, and Asia is growing. To save transport costs and to support other regional economies for strategic reasons, products from industrialized nations will gradually lose market share. This means that industrialized nations will find it increasingly difficult to participate in the growth of emerging economies through exports. Either industrialized nations develop new business models based on knowledge or the progress of emerging economies will contribute less and less to the growth of industrialized nations. That is the new form of decoupling. Growth in emerging markets is already decoupled from industrialized nations.

In all emerging economies the middle class is growing rapidly. Domestic consumption is already solid in several markets and will increase over the coming years. In China alone, according to Société Générale, the French bank, the middle class will grow by 200 million individuals by 2015. The question that remains is how much industrialized nations can benefit from the rise of emerging economies. If growth of industrialized nations gets separated from the material growth dynamic of emerging economies, countries such as Germany would suffer. In 2010, China replaced the United States as the primary non-European export destination of Germany. Without exports to emerging economies, Germany would be in worse economic shape, similar to other European economies. As a preventive measure, industry is fostering production facilities in emerging economies. Thereby produced goods can better succeed in regional trade areas. This compounds the redistribution. As in the past, the relocation of manufacturing facilities, for example to China, has helped create know-how and supported the further diversification of the receiving economy. Some companies could move completely to an emerging economy if Europe becomes only one of many distribution markets. Industrialized nations are under increasing competitive pressure. These developments will, according to the Stolper-Samuelson theorem, further reduce employment and thereby further burden our social system.

CONCLUSION

The change described has been ongoing for several decades and will continue for several decades. The BRIC economies share of global GDP will more than double from 2010 to 2020. From the perspective of investors with interest in solid net worth creation, emerging markets are not a trend, or just hype. For a number of years, emerging markets have been part of institutional portfolios, and increasingly private investors are considering emerging markets. Portfolio diversification and yield management are the main benefits.

NOTES

1. V. De Ruby and J. Debnam, "Does Government Spending Stimulate Economies?," Mercatus on Policy No. 77, George Mason University (July 2011).
2. J. Rubin and B. Tal, "Will Soaring Transport Costs Reverse Globalization?" StratEco, CIBC World Markets Inc. (May 2008).
3. V. A. Ramey, "Identifying Government Spending Shocks: It's All in the Timing," NBER Working Paper No. 15464 (October 2009); R. Barro and C. J. Redlick, "Macroeconomic Effects from Government Purchases and Taxes," NBER Working Paper No. 15369 (September 2009).
4. J. E. Stiglitz, *Globalization and Its Discontent* (New York: W.W. Norton & Company, 2002).
5. Dani Rodik, "The Inescapable Trilemma of the World Economy" (June 2007), www.rodrik.typepad.com.
6. JP Morgan, "EM Moves into the Mainstream as an Asset Class," JPM Emerging Markets Research (October 2010).

CHAPTER 8

A Case for Frontier Markets

Tord Stallvik
Everest Capital

The frontier markets classification includes some of the fastest growing, most populated, and least integrated economies in the world and, importantly, some of the most undervalued equity markets.

Recent economic development and implementation of investor-friendly policies in many of these countries has helped to begin integrating them into the global economy and has led to increased depth and liquidity in their stock markets.

However, frontier markets continue to be under-researched and are structurally underweighted by institutional investors, making these markets inefficient and undervalued. This offers astute active investors the opportunity to earn attractive, less-correlated returns.

In this chapter, we outline the key drivers of the frontier markets opportunity set and argue that combining a top-down and bottom-up approach to identifying and capturing key investment themes in frontier markets can produce attractive, low-correlation investment returns.

Frontier markets represent a large opportunity virtually ignored by the global investment community. In 2010, frontier markets accounted for 15 percent of global GDP (PPP-adjusted) but represented some 3 percent of current global market capitalization and less than 1 percent of the MSCI All Country World Index (see Figure 8.1).

Frontier markets combine a very attractive set of development factors that justify further analyses and consideration.

- **Faster Growth.** Frontier markets represent a much larger percentage of global GDP than their market capitalizations would imply, and they are experiencing significantly faster growth than most mainstream emerging

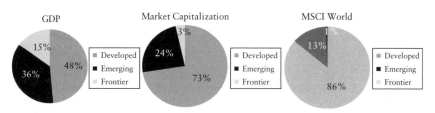

FIGURE 8.1 Frontier Market Representation Globally
Source: IMF, Bloomberg, MSCI.

and developed markets. Indeed, 39 of the 45 fastest-growing economies in the world are frontier markets. Of the remaining six, none is a developed market.

- **Favorable Demographics.** Frontier markets have young, often large and growing, populations compared with the rest of the world. Over 37 percent of the world's 15- to 34-year-olds live in frontier markets. Large, young populations are among the key drivers for long-term economic growth.

- **Strong Macroeconomic Fundamentals and Healthy Balance Sheets.** Frontier markets generally have healthy macroeconomic foundations, including shrinking current account deficits (and, in many cases, surpluses). In addition, governments, companies, and households are typically less indebted than those in developed markets. Macroeconomic stability attracts greater foreign direct investment.

- **Integration with the Global Economy.** While frontier markets have suffered from historical underdevelopment, they are poised to benefit from integration with the global economy. Frontier markets governments have been keen to embrace free enterprise in an effort to attract foreign capital. As a result, modern technology and communication infrastructures are being constructed at an accelerated pace. In addition, education and travel are on the rise, helping to further integrate frontier economies with the rest of the world.

- **Attractive Market Valuations.** Despite these advantages, frontier markets still trade at attractive valuations. At a multiple of only 9.3x 2012 estimated earnings, frontier markets are undervalued, trading at a discount to both emerging markets (10.3x earnings) and developed markets (11.5x earnings) despite higher returns on equity, higher dividend yields, and higher overall growth prospects.

- **Inefficient Markets.** One reason frontier markets trade at a discount despite their attractive fundamentals is that these markets are inefficient. Of the over 2,500 frontier market companies in Everest Capital's universe, we estimate that fewer than 20 percent are covered by global sell-side investment research firms. Equities in frontier markets are under-researched and under-owned, offering an attractive entry point into a long-term growth story for investors utilizing managers with in-house global frontier markets research capabilities and the infrastructure and relationships in place to access these markets.

- **Low Correlation to Other Markets.** Finally, frontier markets offer the diversification benefit of low correlation to other markets. Frontier markets tend to have low correlation to developed and mainstream emerging markets, and to each other. Since the launch of the MSCI Frontier Markets Index in June 2002, frontier markets' correlation to developed markets is only 0.35, while emerging markets have had a 0.84 correlation to developed markets.

These advantages of frontier markets provide a compelling long-term investment opportunity set. In order to capture these opportunities, Everest Capital uses a top-down approach to identify attractive investment themes within our expanded frontier markets universe. We then employ fundamental, bottom-up, on-the-ground research and take advantage of inefficiencies in local company and market information to best express these themes.

NEW, YET FAMILIAR TERRITORY

The term *frontier markets* was coined in 1992 by the World Bank's International Finance Corporation (IFC) to describe the smaller, less liquid, "emerging" emerging markets. In the ensuing 19 years, these economies have become among the fastest growing in the world. The path of development of current mainstream emerging markets[1] over the past two decades provides a road map for today's frontier markets to become the next emerging growth story.

The Evolution of Today's Mainstream Emerging Markets Provides a Roadmap

In the late twentieth century, emerging markets experienced a decade of reforms during which policy makers abandoned fixed exchange rates, adopted inflation targeting, increased foreign exchange reserves, and dramatically reduced external debt. Nearly the entire stock of Brady bonds[2] were retired by 2006, and many emerging markets today are net creditors.

The share of global GDP of all emerging markets, on a purchasing power parity (PPP) adjusted basis, increased from 40 percent in 2000 to 51 percent in 2010. Emerging markets' share of global trade increased sharply as well, from 43 to 55 percent, highlighting their integration into the global marketplace. The emerging markets consumer class has grown in step with GDP and trade, currently accounting for 44 percent of global household consumption compared to 26 percent for the United States.[3]

Indeed, as argued in our white paper, "The End of Emerging Markets?,"[4] emerging markets have emerged. The long-held assumption that mainstream emerging markets are different than developed markets no longer holds: The fundamental distinctions between the sizes of their economies and financial markets, as well as corporate governance and government policies, have blurred. We concluded that the world will increasingly be shaped by the rapid growth of these economies, providing the impetus for greater investor allocations to emerging markets.

Several markets that were frontier in the 1990s, such as India, South Africa, and Russia, are now mainstream emerging markets.[5] We believe that today's frontier markets are poised to follow a growth and development trajectory similar to that which these and other former frontier markets experienced over the past 20 years. Indeed, with access to technology and information, today's frontier markets will likely emerge even faster than did their predecessors.

Our Expanded Frontier Markets Universe

Traditional frontier markets indexes, typically comprising only 25 to 35 countries, do not capture the full frontier markets investable universe. At Everest Capital, we have what we believe is a better definition of the frontier markets universe that currently includes 65 countries (see Figure 8.2). In addition to the 26 members of the MSCI Frontier Markets Index, we incorporate in our universe the smallest, often ignored members of the MSCI Emerging Markets Index (the seven "forgotten" emerging markets that each constitutes less than 1 percent of the index, such as the Philippines and Colombia). We found that these latter countries, although considered emerging by MSCI, have more similarities with frontier markets than with traditional emerging markets. We also include 32 other markets that are typically not included in passive frontier market indexes, but which fit the definition of a frontier market and to which we have access (such as Iraq and Rwanda).

Drawing from Experience

Everest Capital has been an active global investor over the past 21 years and has experienced the realignment of the global economy firsthand, investing through numerous market cycles across the spectrum of frontier, emerging, and developed markets. Since 1990, Everest Capital has invested in 95 countries, including 65 emerging and frontier markets. This unique perspective

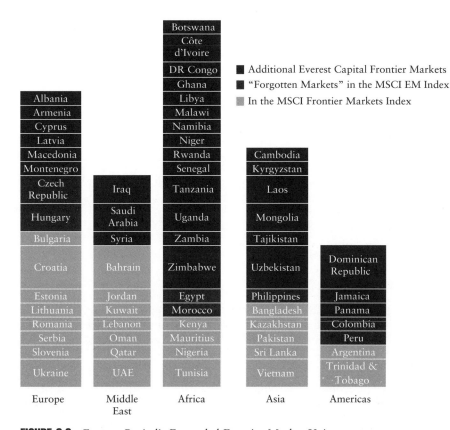

FIGURE 8.2 Everest Capital's Expanded Frontier Market Universe

and experience reinforces our belief that many of the attributes of mainstream emerging markets seen over the past 20 years will recur in the smaller and faster-growing frontier markets of today.

While we continue to believe that mainstream emerging markets are an excellent place to invest for growth relative to developed markets, frontier markets can serve as an attractive addition to an existing emerging markets allocation. Figure 8.2 shows the expanded universe of frontier markets.

KEY DRIVERS OF THE FRONTIER MARKETS OPPORTUNITY SET

Developed markets were the first to achieve economic prosperity, followed by the mainstream emerging markets of today. By our count, these classifications account for less than one quarter of the world's 184 countries for which the IMF keeps statistics. But many of the remaining countries have the same prospects for economic development as today's mainstream emerging markets had when they were in a similarly underdeveloped economic state two decades ago.

From a top-down perspective, we believe that many of the 65 countries in our frontier markets universe are poised to benefit from:

- Faster growth.
- Favorable demographics.
- Strong macroeconomic fundamentals and healthy balance sheets.
- Integration with the global economy.
- Attractive market valuations.
- Inefficient markets.
- Low correlation to other markets.

Faster Growth

Frontier markets as a whole are experiencing significantly faster economic growth than developed and mainstream emerging markets. Indeed, 39 of the 45 fastest growing economies in the world over the next five years, according to the IMF, fall within our frontier markets universe.

Of the remaining six, none is a developed market. Thirty nine of the 45 fastest growing economies through 2015 are frontier markets (see Figure 8.3).

In 1990, although having comparatively insignificant purchasing power in the world, China had one of the world's highest projected growth rates. By 2010, China had a per capita GDP (PPP) of $7,519, an increase of over 840 percent from two decades earlier.[6] Over this same period, the mainstream emerging markets average per capita GDP rose to 39 percent of the developed markets average from 28 percent, similar to frontier markets' current 30 percent of the developed markets average. Excluding the richer GCC (Gulf Cooperation Council) countries,[7] frontier markets are at only 22 percent of the developed markets average (see Figure 8.4).

In the past 20 years, China and India combined have increased their share of world GDP (PPP) 160 percent, from 7.5 to 19.5 percent.[8] Other countries that emerged along with India and China over the past 20 years had differing competitive advantages in the global economy (e.g., ample natural resources) but the same end result: economic growth and greater accumulation of wealth over time.

Today's frontier markets have the advantage of mimicking the development path of mainstream emerging markets where, when certain factors are aligned, the shift from an economically insignificant economy to a

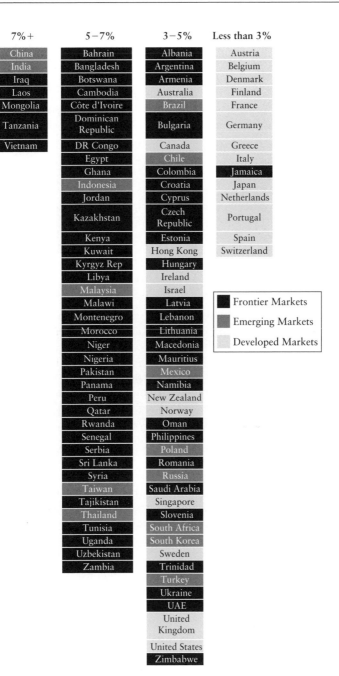

7%+	5–7%	3–5%	Less than 3%
China	Bahrain	Albania	Austria
India	Bangladesh	Argentina	Belgium
Iraq	Botswana	Armenia	Denmark
Laos	Cambodia	Australia	Finland
Mongolia	Côte d'Ivoire	Brazil	France
Tanzania	Dominican Republic	Bulgaria	Germany
Vietnam	DR Congo	Canada	Greece
	Egypt	Chile	Italy
	Ghana	Colombia	Jamaica
	Indonesia	Croatia	Japan
	Jordan	Cyprus	Netherlands
	Kazakhstan	Czech Republic	Portugal
	Kenya	Estonia	Spain
	Kuwait	Hong Kong	Switzerland
	Kyrgyz Rep	Hungary	
	Libya	Ireland	
	Malaysia	Israel	
	Malawi	Latvia	■ Frontier Markets
	Montenegro	Lebanon	■ Emerging Markets
	Morocco	Lithuania	□ Developed Markets
	Niger	Macedonia	
	Nigeria	Mauritius	
	Pakistan	Mexico	
	Panama	Namibia	
	Peru	New Zealand	
	Qatar	Norway	
	Rwanda	Oman	
	Senegal	Philippines	
	Serbia	Poland	
	Sri Lanka	Romania	
	Syria	Russia	
	Taiwan	Saudi Arabia	
	Tajikistan	Singapore	
	Thailand	Slovenia	
	Tunisia	South Africa	
	Uganda	South Korea	
	Uzbekistan	Sweden	
	Zambia	Trinidad	
		Turkey	
		Ukraine	
		UAE	
		United Kingdom	
		United States	
		Zimbabwe	

FIGURE 8.3   Estimated GDP (PPP) CAGR 2011 to 2015
Source: World Bank data, author's analyses.

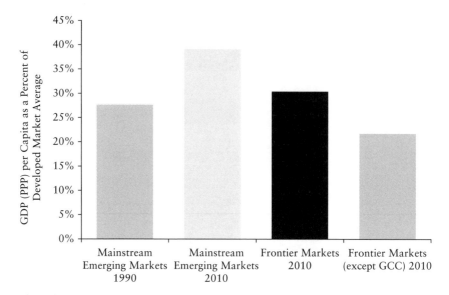

FIGURE 8.4   Economic Growth Produces Wealth over Time

Source: World Bank data; GCC includes Bahrain, Kuwait, Oman, Qatar, Saudi Arabia, and the United Arab Emirates; author's analyses.

significant global market participant happened quite rapidly. From our on-the-ground experience, we know that countries like Bangladesh, Vietnam, and many in Eastern Europe are looking to the lessons learned from their successful neighbors India, China, and Western Europe, respectively.

Favorable Demographics

Demographics play a large part in the potential economic success of a country. Not only do large and youthful countries have an economically attractive labor base for foreign investment, but youthful populations grow into consumers in subsequent years.

Today's frontier markets have large, young populations, providing a demographic dividend in the coming years that we expect will promote increased foreign investment, employment, and consumption, which all lead to higher relative economic growth rates. Of the 20 most populous nations in the world today, 9 are frontier markets and only 3 are developed markets.

Today 9 of the 20 largest populations are frontier markets (see Figure 8.5).

In 2010, frontier markets accounted for 39 percent of the world's 15- to 24-year-olds and 36 percent of the world's 25- to 34-year-olds, making frontier market populations as large in these age groups as China and India combined.

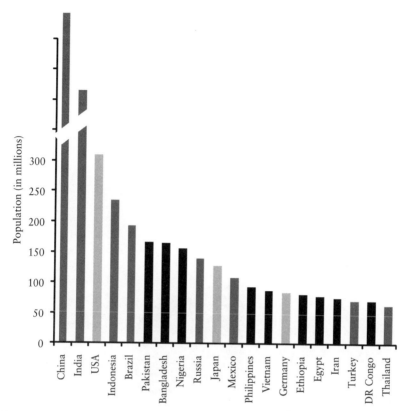

FIGURE 8.5   Countries by Population 2010
Source: IMF, 2010, author's analyses.

Large portions of the world's young people are in frontier markets (see Figure 8.6).

Today's large, youthful populations in frontier markets are positioned to become tomorrow's producers and consumers, driving economic growth higher than in the aging developed markets for years to come.

Shrinking current account deficits, lower overall external debt, and growing foreign direct investment all contribute to the increasing stability and growth of frontier economies.

Shrinking Current Account Deficits

Frontier markets on average have shrinking current account deficits, projected by 2015 to nearly match G7 current account deficits, which are growing larger as a percent of GDP.

(A) 15–24 Years Old

Total Population 1.22 Billion

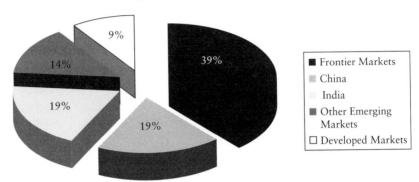

(B) 25–34 Years Old

Total Population 1.07 Billion

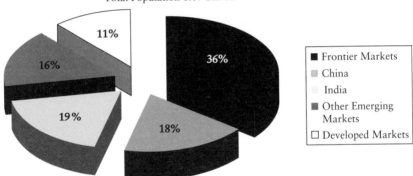

FIGURE 8.6   Young Population in 2010
Source: United Nations, World Population prospects, 2010, author's analyses.

Current account deficits are shrinking in frontier markets, growing in G7 (see Figure 8.7).

Lower Debt Levels

The macroeconomic foundations of frontier economies as a whole are not tainted with the large debt levels of developed economies. Developed markets have the largest per capita external debt levels in the world, at an average of 73 percent of GDP, versus frontier markets' average of 44 percent (see Figure 8.8).

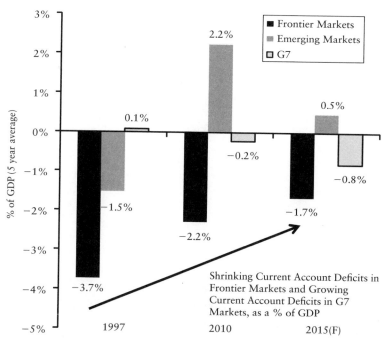

FIGURE 8.7 Current Account Deficits 1997 to 2015(F)

Source: IMF, author's analyses.

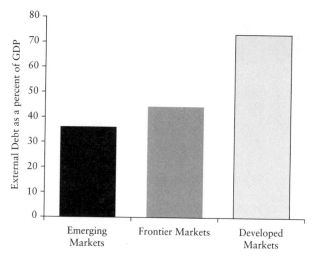

FIGURE 8.8 Average External Debt to GDP

Source: CIA, *The World Factbook*, 2010, author's analyses.

Further, low domestic credit penetration signals tremendous potential for consumption growth in the years ahead (see Figure 8.9).

Increased Foreign Direct Investment

The low levels of debt and concomitant interest expense of frontier markets create greater domestic economic stability. These cleaner balance sheets also attract greater foreign investment. While historically underdeveloped, frontier markets have begun attracting foreign direct investment (FDI) at levels similar to those of emerging markets about 20 years ago. Over the ensuing two decades, FDI into mainstream emerging markets increased more than 13 times (see Figure 8.10), as foreign investors sought to capture the growth opportunities in these markets.

Integration with the Global Economy

While the demographic and other macroeconomic advantages of frontier markets will lead to economic growth, the integration of these economies into a globalized world will be a crucial factor in attracting foreign investors.

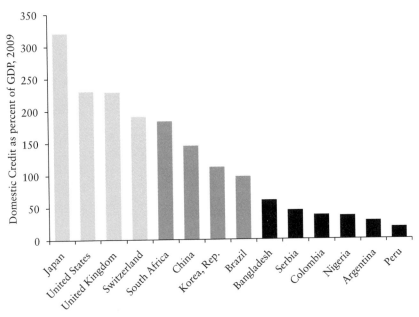

FIGURE 8.9   Domestic Credit Provided by the Banking Sector, as Percent of GDP

Source: The World Bank, author's analyses.

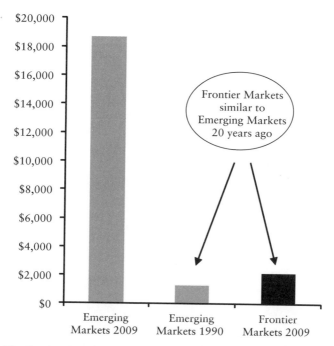

FIGURE 8.10 Foreign Direct Investment, Net Inflows (million current US$)
Source: World Bank, author's analyses.

Frontier economies are able to integrate into the global economy more rapidly than did today's emerging markets due to the availability of increasingly powerful technology, access to education at home and abroad, and transfers of knowledge and capital by expatriates.

The Benefits of Technology

Technology adoption by an economy has several benefits. It gives people a means for accessing local and world events, accelerating the rate at which local citizens become global citizens. It provides a solid communication network that can be a strong selling point to FDI providers. And communication infrastructures, comprised primarily of mobile phone and Internet technology, offer frontier market producers and consumers an accelerated entrée into the global marketplace.

Frontier markets today have technology penetration rates similar to those of mainstream emerging markets. As Internet, mobile phone, and computer technologies become more cost efficient, they become more accessible to poorer countries. This phenomenon is enabling today's frontier market economies to progress at a much faster pace than in the past. As a result, frontier markets have Internet penetration rates similar to developed markets in 1999, which tripled over the following decade (see Figure 8.11).

We expect a similar or faster trend in frontier markets in the coming decade.

Since most frontier and many emerging markets did not have the wealth to participate in the land-line telecom build-outs of the twentieth century, they were able to skip a generation of technology and implement the more efficient cellular technology that is available today at a relatively low cost. As a result, when traveling through several frontier markets in the past few years, we have noticed that the locals rely completely on their cellular phones for personal and business communication. Most are also able to run e-mail and connect to the Internet via their low cost cellular devices. Indeed, frontier markets on average have mobile phone penetration rates nearly as high as mainstream emerging markets, and both are catching up to developed markets (see Figure 8.12).

Instead of building on legacy technologies, frontier markets are able to skip generations and use today's most efficient technologies, which were

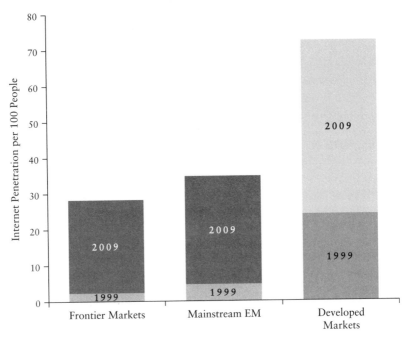

FIGURE 8.11   Internet Penetration of Frontier Markets Is Only Years behind Developed Markets

Source: World Bank data, author's analyses.

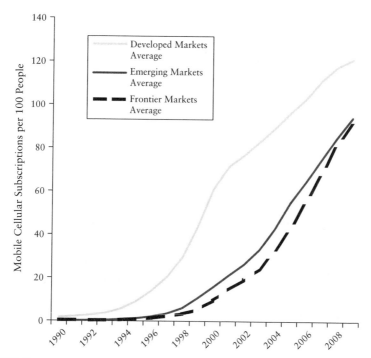

FIGURE 8.12 Frontier Markets Mobile Penetration Nearly Equals Mainstream Emerging Markets

Source: World Bank data, 2010, author's analyses.

underwritten by decades of research and development by developed economies. This has enabled frontier markets to close the mobile phone penetration gap with developed economies and create a robust communication infrastructure to support their future growth.

The Benefits of Education

Education helps countries integrate their populations into the globalized world, sustain growth and development over the long term, and stay competitive and innovative in the global marketplace. Higher educational attainment not only helps to attract foreign investment but is also a catalyst for domestic technological innovation and creation of new industries and businesses.

Increasing literacy rates is a crucial first step in achieving higher educational development. Frontier markets are experiencing increases in primary education enrollments, which in turn promote higher literacy rates.

As students increase their educational attainment, many look to continue their education at overseas institutions that are often in developed markets. Economic and business management skills, among others, are learned by frontier markets students in developed nations and are then brought back to their native countries.

This trend can have two positive effects. First, students often bring back the skills learned overseas to their native country where they will start businesses of their own. These future leaders add significant value as they create local jobs and provide accelerated development to their home economies.

Second, if a student secures a job and earns a living in a developed country, remittances back to his or her native country can become a source of capital into the local economy.

Attractive Market Valuations

In addition to their top-down advantages, frontier markets have advantages that make them attractive from a bottom-up perspective as well. Current market valuations and fundamentals are compelling: Many publicly listed companies in frontier markets are considerably undervalued given their strong balance sheets and economic growth potential.

Looking at current valuation metrics, frontier markets are undervalued relative to developed and emerging markets on a price-to-earnings (P/E), price-to-book (P/B) and dividend yield basis, despite higher returns on equity (see Table 8.1).

Holding these ratios constant, prices will rise as earnings and book values grow. Over time, we expect these ratios to expand as well, further boosting prices.

Inefficient Markets

Despite frontier markets' large share of global GDP, strong top-down economic foundations, and attractive fundamentals, their equities are under-owned by institutional investors (who are still overweight developed

TABLE 8.1 Financial Returns by Markets 2010 and 2011

	P/E	P/B	Dividend 2010	ROE 2011
Frontier Markets	11.2x	9.3x	1.5x	3.8%	17.1%
Emerging Markets	11.5x	10.3x	1.8x	2.9%	15.6%
Developed Markets	12.4x	11.5x	1.6x	2.7%	13.5%

Source: Bloomberg, based on MSCI Frontier Index, MC+SCI EM Index and MSCI World, author's analyses.

markets) and under-followed by the equity analyst community. We estimate that fewer than 20 percent of the over 2,500 listed equities in Everest Capital's frontier markets universe are covered by global sell-side investment research firms, leaving those investors without on-the-ground research capabilities at a distinct disadvantage.

The market capitalization-to-GDP ratio quantifies the size of a market in relation to the size of its economic activity. As economic output increases, so does market size and liquidity. In countries like Brazil and India, for example, market capitalization-to-GDP ratios increased from about 10 percent in 1989 to over 70 percent by 2009. Today, many frontier markets' market capitalization-to-GDP ratios are at low starting points similar to those of mainstream emerging markets two decades ago.

Many frontier markets are at the same market capitalization to GDP starting points as mainstream emerging markets two decades ago (see Figure 8.13).

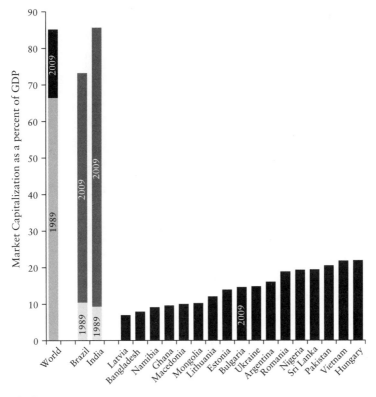

FIGURE 8.13 Market Capitalization as Percent of GDP, 2009

Source: World Bank, author's analyses.

As these economies grow, their market capitalizations as a percent of GDP should expand, producing a multiplier effect on their equity markets. Notwithstanding their attractiveness, fund flows into frontier markets are a small fraction of mainstream emerging markets flows, albeit growing substantially on a percentage basis.

Frontier market flows are dwarfed by emerging markets flows (see Figure 8.14).

Low Correlation to Other Markets

The benefit of portfolio diversification (i.e., the reduction of risk) is often considered the only free lunch in the investment world. However, risk is reduced only to the extent diversified portfolio assets are not correlated to each other. Investing in two assets with a correlation of 1.0 provides no diversification benefit.

Because they have low correlation to developed and emerging markets as well as to each other, frontier markets can provide significant diversification benefits to a portfolio. In contrast, the mainstream emerging markets have significantly higher correlation to each other.

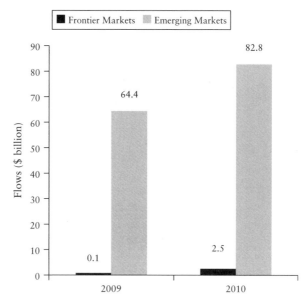

FIGURE 8.14   Fund Flows, 2009 and 2010

Source: EPFR, UBS, author's analyses.

Frontier markets are less correlated to developed and emerging markets (see Figure 8.15).

Individual frontier markets are less correlated to each other (0.16 on average) than are individual emerging markets (see Figure 8.16).

RISKS TO INVESTING IN FRONTIER MARKETS

Investing in frontier markets is not without risks. We address five of the more commonly cited risks here.

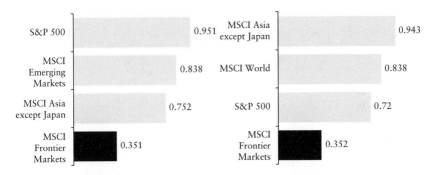

FIGURE 8.15 Market Index Correlations

Source: Bloomberg, correlations of weekly returns June 2002–April 2011, author's analyses.

	Russia	India	China	Indonesia	Korea	Malaysia	Mexico	South Africa	Turkey	
	0.62	0.52	0.57	0.47	0.62	0.45	0.76	0.72	0.56	Brazil
		0.52	0.47	0.38	0.56	0.42	0.64	0.69	0.52	Russia
			0.62	0.52	0.59	0.56	0.55	0.59	0.45	India
				0.53	0.67	0.61	0.57	0.62	0.48	China
Colombia	0.00				0.50	0.54	0.46	0.42	0.33	Indonesia
Egypt	−0.05	0.42				0.57	0.64	0.64	0.50	Korea
Nigeria	0.07	0.05	0.09				0.47	0.49	0.38	Malaysia
Pakistan	0.01	0.13	0.18	0.08				0.74	0.57	Mexico
Qatar	0.11	0.15	0.26	0.03	0.11				0.60	South Africa
South Arabia	0.00	0.23	0.33	0.01	0.09	0.23				
Serbia	0.07	0.31	0.32	0.19	0.11	0.29	0.20			
Ukraine	0.00	0.31	0.32	0.14	0.12	0.22	0.19	0.42		
Vietnam	−0.01	0.17	0.19	0.11	0.04	0.20	0.19	0.29	0.28	
	Bangladesh	Colombia	Egypt	Nigeria	Pakistan	Qatar	South Arabia	Serbia	Ukraine	

FIGURE 8.16 Country Market Correlations

Source: Bloomberg, correlations of weekly returns June 2002–April 2011, author's analyses.

Market Illiquidity

With a few exceptions, frontier markets are less liquid than developed or mainstream emerging markets. Illiquidity risks can range from negative price impacts on trades of size on single securities, to complete market shutdowns, as was the case during the Egyptian uprising in early 2011. These risks cannot be hedged but can be mitigated through country and company diversification. At Everest Capital, we typically invest in 25 to 30 frontier markets at any given time. Frontier market volumes, and thus liquidity, are generally increasing.

Inflation

Maintaining low inflation levels during periods of high growth can be difficult. While inflation in frontier markets has been more moderate recently, inflation will need to be analyzed and monitored carefully on a country by country basis.

Inflation in frontier markets is moderate now (see Figure 8.17).

Political Risk

As frontier markets endeavor to integrate themselves into the global economy, the political environment is improving. However, while the majority of

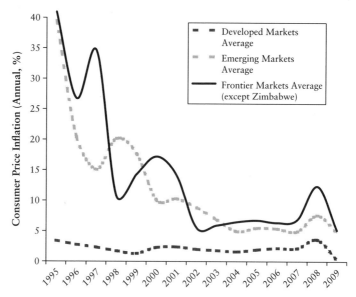

FIGURE 8.17   Inflation by Market Groups, 1995 to 2009
Source: World Bank, author's analyses.

frontier markets are generally facing a positive trend of advancement, political crises can and do erupt. In many cases the negative pressures may be pure noise and rather short-lived; in other cases, the political risk is much greater and value destroying (e.g., Egypt, Ivory Coast, and Zimbabwe). Many of these markets have a non-democratic form of government, so an investor does bear the risk of unfavorable government action toward its investment. These political events can have a damaging impact on the equities of the affected country and, by association, its neighbors.

From a portfolio construction standpoint, one of the greatest attributes of frontier markets is the low correlations that these markets have to each other. This highlights the importance of being global rather than regional as well as being invested in more countries rather than fewer. The best portfolio hedge against political risk is country diversification.

Corruption and Investor Protection

To many, frontier markets represent the Wild West of investing. However, frontier markets on average are perceived to be less corrupt than today's BRIC markets (see Figure 8.18) and have garnered improving investor protection ratings that nearly match BRIC levels (see Figure 8.19).

As growth in developed markets slows, global investors are allocating more capital to emerging markets in an effort to capture their larger relative

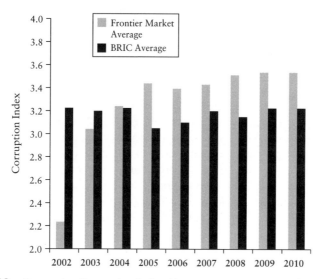

FIGURE 8.18 Corruption Perception Index (0 = most corrupt, 10 = least corrupt)
Source: Transparency International, author's analyses.

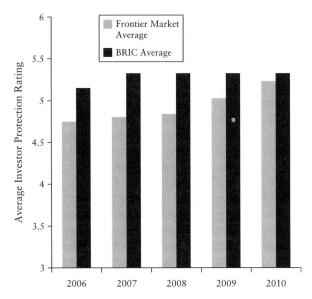

FIGURE 8.19 Strength of Investor Protection (0 = riskiest, 10 = safest)
Source: World Bank.

growth opportunities. If concerns of corruption or lack of investor protection are not a fundamental deterrent to investing in today's most popular emerging markets (i.e., the BRICs), they should pose no greater deterrent to investing in a diversified portfolio of frontier markets.

Systemic Risk Events That Stem from Developed Markets

Although they do offer a significant diversification opportunity, frontier markets—like all other markets—are not immune to increased correlation with other markets during global systemic risk shocks. Global economic and financial integration can provide growth and development opportunities for frontier markets, but integration can also mean the economic problems of one economy or region becomes a problem for others.

Although the MSCI Frontier Markets Index has shown lower correlation than other indexes to developed and emerging markets since its inception in 2002, there was a sharp increase in correlations during the 2008–2009 financial crisis (see Figure 8.20).

However, Everest Capital's frontier markets universe is more diversified than the MSCI Frontier Markets Index, and adding these countries to an investor's portfolio may result in even lower volatility.

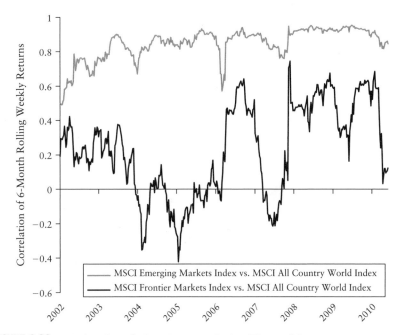

FIGURE 8.20   Market Correlations Increase during Times of Stress
Source: Bloomberg, author's analyses.

CONCLUSION

The advantages of frontier markets—faster growth; young, growing populations; strong macroeconomic foundations; accelerated integration with the global economy; and attractive market fundamentals—provide a compelling long-term investment opportunity. Our experience with investing in the now-mainstream emerging markets over the past two decades has taught us that investing in today's less developed economies, with similar growth potential and mispriced assets, may be rewarding over the long term.

We believe an allocation to frontier markets can serve as an attractive, complementary investment opportunity to an existing global or emerging markets portfolio, and that a top-down thematic and bottom-up fundamental investing approach applied to an intelligently expanded frontier markets universe is the best framework for taking advantage of this compelling growth story, which is still in its early stages.

NOTES

1. Defined as those countries representing 1 percent or more of the MSCI Emerging Market Index.
2. US dollar-denominated bonds, named after US Treasury Secretary Nicholas Brady, issued in the 1980s to replace defaulted bank loans to emerging market sovereign borrowers.
3. World Bank data (2009).
4. November 2009.
5. These countries entered the MSCI Emerging Markets Index in 1994, 1995, and 1997, respectively.
6. World Bank data.
7. Bahrain, Kuwait, Oman, Qatar, Saudi Arabia, and the United Arab Emirates.
8. IMF data.

CHAPTER 9

Subcontinents: Sub-Saharan Africa and Southeast Asia

Two of the most promising and popular developing regions are sub-Saharan Africa and Southeast Asia. Both hold great promise—they each have some very populous countries, a few tigers in the making, and abundant resources. Their capital markets may be generally immature but they are developing rapidly. They probably represent the most imminent group of economies that will gain in importance for investors.

THE INVESTMENT CASE FOR AFRICA

Fungai Tarirah
Momentum Investments

Having long drawn the fancy of traders, hunters, miners, and arms dealers from across seas, the continent's charms are finally getting to work on one last set of unbelievers—portfolio investors. Fast shedding titles such as the "dark continent" and the "third world," Africa's rolling plains, fertile soils, winding rivers, abundant ore reserves, and marketplaces have attracted those who seek to participate in the continent's vast wealth. After a number of false starts, portfolio investors are back among those jostling for elbow space at the tables brimming with Africa's wares.

Indeed, African success stories have ensured their places in the history books, stories of companies having prospered where none could be fathomed to do so. Mobile phone operators went into countries without reliable electricity supply, retailers spread to areas with no distribution networks to speak of, and manufacturing businesses settled in places where only game farmers and construction companies saw prospects. Such intrepid undertakings belonged once to pioneer operators who boldly went where sometimes the locals feared to tread and bring development, earn profit, and even establish lasting institutions. In contrast, portfolio investors have been slow and seemingly quite afraid to venture into many countries across the continent.

Approaching the opportunity of Africa with a slightly less conventional view and searching out opportunities in some of the continent's less glamorous locations, reveals many a gem. Apparently all is not 401(k) scams in the heart of Nigeria, but also confectionery businesses that have worked out amazing distribution networks to get their product to customers across the country as often as three times a week. Kenya not only holds some of the world's most famous safari trails but also the continent's largest, best-run, and only listed advertising company. And some way toward the Indian Ocean, set against palm trees and sandy beaches with some of the finest resorts on the planet, is a brewery making a remarkable and award-winning lager and exporting to many destinations across the world. Indeed, significant changes in governance practices and economic stewardship across the continent have improved transparency and openness, bettered operating environments for businesses, and allowed international participants better access to investments.

For investors in search of diversification, African exposure offers a compelling diversification, as well as alpha and beta opportunity sets. Many investors are not currently prepared to commit the time and effort to understand Africa and the upside of higher and sustained returns in this investment space.

By way of illustration, the large global private equity firm, the Carlyle Group, is currently achieving 4 percent per annum S&P500 returns versus developed market private equity returns of 8 percent, emerging market private equity of 10 percent, and African private equity of 25 percent. While these excess returns will no doubt diminish with increased investment, this is unlikely to happen in the next three to five years. This makes African exposure a compelling option for any portfolio.

Over the past decade significant progress has been recorded with respect to the political and economic environments found in many African markets. There have been strong shifts toward democracy and accountability, as most recently reflected in the Arab Spring in North Africa.

Economic progress due to better governance, stable policies, rising commodity prices, debt relief, and improved targeting of aid have also boosted business climates. In addition to rising commodity prices and lower external debt servicing claims, African economies are also very open. Openness ratios of above 60 percent of GDP and international trade agreements mainly with Europe, North America, and Asia have boosted foreign exchange exports earnings and improved endogenous tax bases for government finances. Africa has thus become much less reliant on foreign aid flows to balance their external and fiscal books.

Governance has improved in both the public and private sectors in ways that are unrecognizable to those who lived in or dealt with African counterparts in the 1980s and early 1990s. Anticorruption commissions have become the norm as parliaments require more oversight of government, albeit with a wide spectrum of success to date. Headline ministries such as finance, foreign affairs, and the presidency are where most progress can be seen. The same can also be said of central banks, some of which are beginning, probably prematurely, to consider best-practice policies like inflation targeting.

Equally, the private sectors continue to grow very rapidly in many of our target markets. In fact, we would argue that this is the most unsung and unknown aspect about Africa's economic revival as indigenous companies have been at the forefront of economic change and progress. Much of this has been as a result of improvements in corporate governance as firms have internationalized to gain greater market access and to secure diversified sources of capital to fund their rapid growth needs, as African societies have become more connected to world trends.

In spite of the global financial crisis, economic growth has continued to outpace the rest of the world and remained in positive territory across the sub-Saharan region (see Figure 9.1).

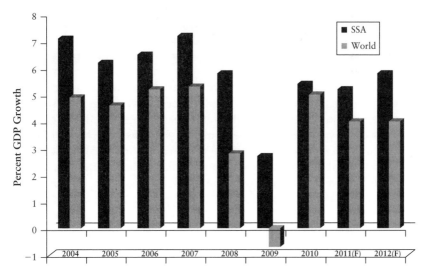

FIGURE 9.1 Real GDP Growth in Sub-Saharan Africa (SSA) and the World
Source: IMF, MAM Africa.

As a result of almost two decades of growth, African countries have started to gain a reputation for continuity. This is most evident in the burgeoning middle classes and repeated improvements in health and education metrics, albeit off a very low base and challenged by still high population growth. Indeed, off a base of political and macroeconomic continuity, the emergence of viable external sectors adds to Africa's most powerful investment case: its demographics.

Much is made of the misery of overpopulation in Africa—famine, disease, and wars, for example—but this is increasingly to live in the past rather than the future. To the extent that slowing population growth is derived from rapid urbanization, better health levels, and improving education standards, particularly among women, Africa could enter the "take–off" sweet spot for economies. The still-plentiful labor supply becomes more differentiated to provide the necessary skills and middle class earnings potential that creates diversification, including financial deepening, and drives the rapid growth of Africa's economies. A thriving indigenous middle class that looks ever more outward will also be the best bulwark against any threat of a return to bad government. Nigeria, Ghana, Kenya, and Zambia are four excellent examples of where we see these exact dynamics playing out. Other countries are likely to follow their lead.

Investment Dynamics

A starting point for framing terms of investment is set by the rating agencies. As more African sovereigns and, increasingly, corporations have sought foreign debt issuance, they have acquired ratings from the major agencies. I summarize Fitch's rating in Table 9.1, chosen because this agency has the most comprehensive listing of ratings.

One important way in which governments have sought to anchor perceptions of better government is to implement investor-friendly policies. To be sure, the jury is still out on this score, as the possibility for backsliding into transitional political economies is always there. Even so, the turning tide is reflected in foreign direct investment (FDI) that more than doubled in the past decade to about US$15 billion per annum. Much of this has been in the oil & gas sector and other capital-intensive commodity extraction industries. A recent example of this is Vale's purchase of meaningful Congolese copper assets. This in itself will likely improve hitherto appalling corporate governance in the DRC. Yet, if our investment view of the potential evolution of Africa's economies is directionally correct, such FDI will follow the same pattern as elsewhere: away from over-loved foreign exchange earning export sectors to under-loved domestic demand sectors, often in the form of M&A buyouts of successful indigenous companies.

TABLE 9.1 Ratings of Selected Countries

Country	Rating	Outlook	Drivers	Rating Agency
Botswana	A	Stable	Well-managed public debt	Fitch
Cameroon	B	Stable	Improvement in public finances but constrained by weak economic growth	Fitch
Egypt	BB+	Stable	Negligible external debt	Fitch
Ghana	B+	Stable to Negative	High inflation & rising current deficit	Fitch
Kenya	B+	Stable	Improved public finance & external debt ratios	Fitch
Morocco	BBB-	Stable	Stable public finances & growing economy	Fitch
Mozambique	B	Positive	Strong economic export growth & decline in public debt	Fitch
Namibia	BBB	Positive	Expansion of uranium sector, improving external balance sheet	Fitch
Nigeria	BB-	Stable	Savings of oil windfalls reducing government debt	Fitch
Tunisia	BBB	Stable	Declining external debt reliance	Fitch
Uganda	B	Positive	Macroeconomic prudence	Fitch
South Africa	BBB+	Negative	Increasing public debt & weakening current account deficit	Fitch

Source: Fitch, author's analyses.

For example, Heineken recently announced a 68 percent capacity expansion of their beer interests in Nigeria, investing in excess of US$600 million in the project.

The single largest constraint to African development, and the most lasting legacy of capital stripping that was the hallmark of Africa's bad governance days, is the chronic lack of investment in infrastructure of all kinds, but most notably roads, energy, and urban housing. There is no reason why these backlogs cannot be addressed, provided that investment conditions, especially sufficiently attractive rates of return, are offered to investors. This is reflected in the returns enjoyed by Vodafone through Safaricom or MTN through its Nigeria operations (dwarfing their South

Africa home base). And Mo Ibrahim is still one of Africa's richest self-made billionaires following the sale of his cell phone pioneering company Celtel to Zain (now owned by Bharti Airtel). There have also been unexpected technological spinoffs from these successes, notably Safaricom, which has become a world leader in mobile money transfer services and banking.

For us, the prospect of public-private partnerships (PPPs) working to solve the physical infrastructure backlog may be better than elsewhere, partly because governments have fewer options, and partly because local populations do not put up with endless environmental or NIMBY (not in my backyard) protests that stymie these funding structures and operational agreements elsewhere. Africans just want better roads, and the sooner the better. One recent example of a PPP success is RMB's funding of the Lekki Expressway toll road, which has revolutionized parts of otherwise gridlock-wracked Lagos. Another is the construction of Tatu City on the outskirts of Nairobi, which will involve a mixed use of residential and commercial development. This project is being developed in conjunction with the complete overhaul, refurbishment, and expansion of Jomo Kenyatta International Airport, unquestionably East Africa's hub. When completed, it will be larger than Johannesburg's O.R. Tambo International Airport.

Correlations of African Markets to South Africa

Correlations of African markets to South Africa and indeed global markets continue to be low, which offers a worthy diversification opportunity for international investors. This is illustrated in Table 9.2, which considers the relationships on a weekly basis over a five-year period from September 2006 to 2011.

Fast-Paced Economic Growth

Consensus forecasts agree that 7 of the 10 fastest growing economies in the world over the coming five years are in Africa, with many of them achieving 7 percent GDP growth rates or more. This means doubling every 10 years. This opportunity can be unlocked by participating in Africa-domiciled assets. Table 9.3 shows actual and forecast GDP growth rates from 2001 through to 2015F of the world's fastest growing economies.

Africa's economic growth expectations over the next four years in comparison to Asian economies underscore the opportunity (see Figure 9.2). While the Asian economic growth potential seems to be considered universally as a global locomotive, core African economies have quietly overtaken Asia on this metric.

TABLE 9.2 Correlations between Africa and Other Asset Classes—Correlations of Weekly USD Returns across Markets for 5 Years

	MSCI Africa	JSE	MSCI Frontier	MSCI Emerging	MSCI World	S&P 500	Morocco	Egypt	Nigeria	Kenya	Brazil
MSCI Africa	1										
JSE	0.2461	1									
MSCI Frontier	0.5786	0.3410	1								
MSCI Emerging	0.3706	0.7982	0.4596	1							
MSCI World	0.3331	0.7793	0.4597	0.7845	1						
S&P 500	0.2386	0.6847	0.3946	0.7731	0.9550	1					
Morocco	0.4804	0.2643	0.2747	0.3594	0.3345	0.2229	1				
Egypt	0.1515	-0.0962	0.0601	-0.0410	-0.0435	-0.0286	0.0367	1			
Nigeria	0.6349	0.0121	0.3936	0.0345	0.0404	0.0165	0.1819	0.0367	1		
Kenya	0.3626	0.1562	0.2667	0.2803	0.2448	0.1937	0.2099	0.1819	0.0526	1	
Brazil	0.3069	0.7776	0.3963	0.8986	0.8663	0.7986	0.3562	-0.0233	0.0111		1

Source: Bloomberg, MAM Africa, author's analyses.

TABLE 9.3   World's Ten Fastest Growing Economies—Annual Average GDP growth in Percent

2001–2010(E)		2011(F)–2015(F)	
Angola	11.1	China	9.5
China	10.5	India	8.2
Myanmar	10.3	Ethiopia	8.1
Nigeria	8.9	Mozambique	7.7
Ethiopia	8.4	Tanzania	7.2
Kazakhstan	8.2	Vietnam	7.2
Chad	7.9	Congo	7.0
Mozambique	7.9	Ghana	7.0
Cambodia	7.7	Zambia	6.9
Rwanda	7.6	Nigeria	6.8

Source: Data from *The Economist* magazine, various issues, author's analyses.

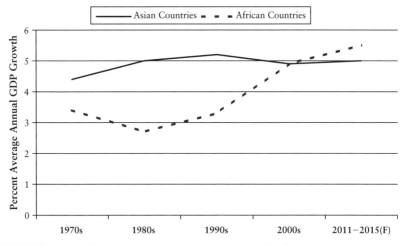

FIGURE 9.2   Annual Average GDP Growth—Asian and African Countries

Source: Data from *The Economist* magazine, various issues.

Urbanization

Africa's young urbanizing populations should underpin sustained long-term demand growth for consumer products. While growth comes from a very low base, the investment opportunity is in the quantum of growth, not the size of the base. Moreover, an investor who addresses these opportunities

TABLE 9.4 Selected Multinationals' Contribution to Profit Expected from Africa and Forecast Growth in Earnings from Africa

Company	2010 Earnings from Africa	3-Year Annual Growth in Africa Earnings (forecast)
Nestle	3%	18%
Heineken	20%	14%
PZ Cussons	42%	15%

Source: Company filings, MAM Africa.

early, will continue to accrete first mover advantages until the continent as an asset class becomes more discovered. Many African countries currently sport fast growing youthful populations that are beginning to add millions to the labor force every year, generating increasing spending power.

One good example is in Kenya where less than 40 percent of the population was estimated living in urban areas in 2009. This number is expected to swell to 50 percent by 2030. With population growth being forecast in the region of 2.4 percent per annum, this will result in some additional 15.5 million people in the country's urban areas over the coming 18 years, effectively doubling the current urban population. (By comparison, South Africa's midyear population estimates in 2011 put Gauteng, the country's most populous province, at 11.3 million.)

With GDP growth likely to be driven more by services and manufacturing and less by agriculture, GDP per capita is expected to rise some 34 percent by 2030 from current levels, a move that would deliver significant spending power to urban dwellers and develop a strong market for manufactured and processed goods. This opportunity has already been realized by multinationals operating in Kenya and other African countries, who are allocating more resources to their African businesses in anticipation of an increased return (see Table 9.4).

Investors can also participate in these dynamics by exposure to in-country African listings.

Improving Business Operating Conditions and Economic Stewardship

As African economies have opened and allowed more foreign investment and firms to compete in domestic markets, the quality of corporate governance of indigenous firms has improved. Nowhere is this more apparent than in Nigeria, a country that has historically been associated with high levels of corruption, but where the World Bank's "Doing Business"

TABLE 9.5 "Doing Business" Rankings for Nigeria in 2012 and Process
Effectiveness 2012 versus 2006

Category	2012 Rank	2012 Effectiveness	2006 Effectiveness
Starting a business (**days**)	116	34	43
Registering a property (**days**)	180	180	274
Getting credit (**strength of legal rights**)	78%	90%	70%
Protecting investors (**index rating**)	65	57	57
Enforcing contracts (**days to enforce**)	97	457	730

Source: The World Bank, MAM Africa.

ranking has seen the country's corporate sector improve by leaps and bounds (see Table 9.5).

Nigeria's recently completed election was the fourth consecutive democratic election in a country with a rich history of coups and military intervention.

National debt has been reduced to sustainable levels (partly thanks to debt forgiveness) and maintained, as can be seen in Figure 9.3. Further, the country successfully issued a Eurobond: US$500 million at 7 percent that was 2.5 times oversubscribed, largely by international investors, highlighting their optimism about Nigerian progress. Figure 9.3 illustrates the reduction of the long term debt-to-GDP levels of Nigeria from their peak in the mid-1990s—to levels a number of developed countries may not see for some time to come.

Figure 9.4 shows the increase in net investment flows over 30 years. Flows are rising to appreciable levels, highlighting increased foreign interest in the country due to an improving investment climate.

Currency volatility has fallen as monetary policy has become more effective and foreign currency reserves have been built up to stave off crises, as was demonstrated in the 2008 food/fuel price hikes. (By comparison, over the past three years the ZAR (South African rand) has been 2.7 times more volatile than the naira (Nigerian currency) 2.5 times more volatile than the Brazilian real, and 1.6 times more volatile than the euro. Volumes in the weekly naira auctions at CBN have been in excess of US$200 million.)

Practical Aspects of the Africa Opportunity

Investment products that are available to investors today are typically actively managed by well-trained, dedicated, and focused investment teams, scouring the continent for information and investment opportunities.

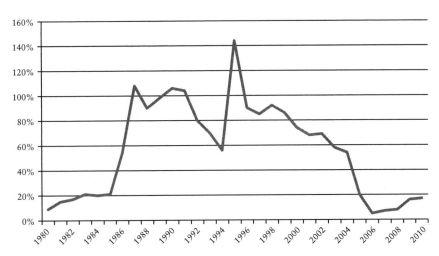

FIGURE 9.3   Nigeria's Declining and Contained Debt-to-GDP Ratio:
A 30-Year History
Source: Nigeria Debt Management Office, MAM Africa.

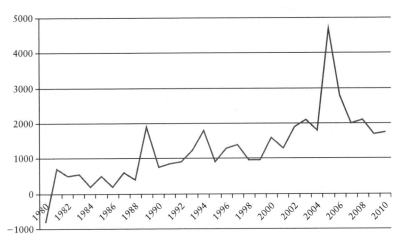

FIGURE 9.4   Net Investment Flows into Nigeria for 30 Years (to 2010)
Source: EIU, IMF, MAM Africa.

The process necessarily involves a busy travel schedule to unlock value from inefficiently priced assets in the continent, regardless of the asset class under consideration, but more so in the case of private equity.

Diligent practitioners will have a process that delves into foreign exchange (FX) and country risk assessments. Creating a framework within which to understand the investment risks faced in Africa by complementing (somewhat) limited rating agency sovereign work with proprietary sovereign risk models is prudent, if not mandatory. This work would be married to FX, equity risk premium (ERP), and discount rate derivations, from which investment teams are able to implement a successful investment process.

Of equal importance would be a keen understanding of actual businesses and projects to be invested in. In the absence of large numbers of buyers and sellers and with high commissions, taxes, and the high cost associated with obtaining public, decision-critical information, many of the asset markets across the continent can comfortably be classified as weak-form efficient. Assets are routinely inappropriately priced and sometimes for long periods. Taking time to understand individual companies, meeting and learning to trust management teams will likely yield positive results. Over the years we at Momentum Asset Management have learnt that "cash is king" and made our choices based on the cash flow that a business or a project can generate on a sustained basis.

SOUTH AND SOUTHEAST ASIA FRONTIERS: OPPORTUNITIES ABUNDANT

Thomas Hugger
Leopard Capital

Every day new research reports and investment recommendations are published internally by investment houses, private banks, and fund managers, and mailed to current and potential investor clients that recognize (finally) that investing in emerging markets generates better returns than investment in developed ones.

This was not always the case. In the 1980s and 1990s, investments in the emerging markets of Asia, Eastern Europe, Latin America, and, last but not least, Africa were generally deemed as "high risk," "speculative," and "volatile." Unfortunately, the typical boom and bust cycles or bubbles in emerging and frontier economies have proven these skeptics somewhat correct. Most notably, the "Tequila Crisis" of 1994 in Mexico; the 1997 Asian financial crisis affecting the then-booming Southeast Asian countries such as Indonesia, Malaysia, South Korea, and Thailand; and the Russian financial crisis in August 1998 were disastrous for financial investors in these markets and wiped out fortunes for local and foreign investors. These and other events that adversely impacted emerging and frontier markets have deterred many foreign investors, both institutional and private, from considering these markets throughout the late 1990s and the last decade.

Instances of investing in these types of markets have revolved around investments in big global companies with relatively large sales in emerging and frontier markets, such as Microsoft, Nestle of Switzerland, and Unilever from the UK/Holland, which are considered by large investment houses better and safer investments in these markets due to their sound financial balance sheets and overall sizes.

However, this mentality has changed drastically over the past 10 years. We believe one of the most important events that altered the skeptical perception vis-à-vis investing in emerging markets was the catching acronym *BRIC*. Used to describe the growing economies of Brazil, Russia, India, and China, the term was cleverly coined by Jim O'Neill in 2001 and particularly well marketed by the US investment house Goldman Sachs to lure foreign investors into new markets. Of course, the (consequential) stellar performances of the stock markets within these four countries (until the 2008 global financial crisis) played a crucial role in their unprecedented economic growth, global notoriety, and enticing even larger numbers of investors. However, even today, almost 11 years since BRIC became commonly known, huge pension funds, family offices, asset allocators, and private banks in North America and Europe are just starting to think about allocating their first and often small BRIC exposure in their global (or sometimes even mainly domestic) equity portfolios.

This has been our experience when communicating with chief investment officers and other senior investment officers at family offices and pension funds in Western Europe throughout the first quarter of 2012. After many such conversations, the question arises: To what degree will stock markets in emerging countries be impacted once global investment giants finally decide to allocate and deploy more significant capital to these markets? When these investors finally invest, will these countries still be emerging, or will they have already evolved into developed economies?

After the overwhelming success of BRIC, Goldman Sachs and Jim O'Neill went on to create another term, *The Next Eleven* or *N-11*, indicating what they believed to be the new emerging markets of the next decade. N-11 helped further increase the awareness of international investors regarding South and Southeast Asian markets: Bangladesh, Indonesia, Pakistan, Philippines, South Korea, and Vietnam are all a part of N-11. The mad rush into Vietnamese stocks in 2006 and 2007 (the Ho Chi Minh Index gained 201.4 percent over this period) can be partially blamed on the countries' affiliation with N-11.

In spite of their success, these markets still play second fiddle to the largest financial markets of developed nations. While the marketing blitzes associated with BRIC, N-11, and other up-and-coming economies helped spur economic growth and greater interest within their stock exchanges, the market capitalization within developed markets is still well above that of BRIC, N-11, emerging, and frontier markets taken together (see Table 9.6). Yet, we see a day in the future when the market capitalization in current emerging and frontier markets catches up with the bigger players, such as the

TABLE 9.6 Equity Market Capitalization in USD Million as of March 16, 2012

	Market Cap in US$ M	In % of World	In % of GDP
World	51,844,676	100.00%	82.46%
United States	16,785,101	32.98%	105.82%
Japan	3,803,736	7.34%	72.70%
United Kingdom	3,355,202	6.47%	148.53%
Canada	2,045,863	3.95%	133.56%
France	1,643,132	3.17%	68.70%
Germany	1,495,433	2.88%	45.39%
Australia	1,308,215	2.52%	136.19%
Switzerland	1,170,157	2.26%	229.35%
Taiwan	829,137	1.60%	182.95%
Sweden	567,525	1.09%	130.25%
Spain	555,056	1.07%	44.89%
Singapore	550,431	1.06%	259.08%
Italy	544,674	1.05%	32.25%
		67.44%	
BRIC			
China	3,519,897	6.79%	63.95%
Hong Kong (China)	2,425,865	4.68%	1107.19%
Brazil	1,410,808	2.72%	69.21%
India	1,242,935	2.40%	94.21%
Russia	951,334	1.83%	67.53%
		18.42%	
N-11			
South Korea	1,113,733	2.15%	106.25%
Mexico	463,715	0.89%	47.76%
Turkey	246,878	0.48%	40.85%
Philippines	185,250	0.36%	79.26%
Indonesia	412,494	0.80%	50.48%
Egypt	66,760	0.13%	38.61%
Nigeria	40,512	0.08%	26.44%
Pakistan	38,457	0.07%	22.08%
Vietnam	33,808	0.07%	37.00%
Bangladesh	31,443	0.07%	28.57%
		5.10%	

Source: World Bank/Bloomberg, author's analyses.

United States, the United Kingdom, and Japan. Although the path will not be easy for these economies, economic development trend lines indicate frontier markets are the new emerging economies; emerging economies the next developed economies.

Why Invest in Asia Frontier Markets Today?

Investing today in Asia frontier markets is like investing in China and India 10 to 20 years ago or in Thailand and Indonesia 20 to 30 years ago. At Leopard Capital, we look at countries that are already in the MSCI Frontier Index like Bangladesh, Pakistan, Sri Lanka, and Vietnam, or not yet/soon to be: Bhutan, Cambodia, Laos, Maldives, Mongolia, Myanmar (Burma), Nepal, and Papua New Guinea.

There are numerous reasons for investors from developed countries to start investing (even small amounts) in Asia frontier markets today. Carl Delfeld highlighted some of reasons for investing in these markets on his web page that are discussed in greater detail.[1]

Rapid Growth

"Faster Growth: Faster growth than emerging markets like the BRIC countries (Brazil, Russia, India, China)." With the exception of China, whose average rate of GDP over the past decade grew by over 10 percent, Asian frontier economies fared very well against other BRICs, and in many instances outperformed them (see Figure 9.5). From 2000 to 2010, average GDP growth of Cambodia, Laos, and Vietnam outperformed or equaled that of Brazil, India, and Russia. Sri Lanka and Mongolia outgrew Russia and Brazil. It appears that despite outperforming three out of four BRIC economies, Asian frontier markets have not received their fair share of attention simply because they are not superficially categorized within a single group and provided a pithy name.

Youthful Population

"Young population: 40 percent of the world's 14- to 25-year-olds are in frontier markets, while North America, Europe, and (especially) Japan together make up only 10 percent of this future key consumer and growing middle class group." Lower-income countries with young median ages (within the twenties) generally indicate developing economies with the potential to experience decades of consumer-based economic growth, anchored by a strong, globally competitive workforce. This is key for providing the global economy with cheap labor for its growing demand for

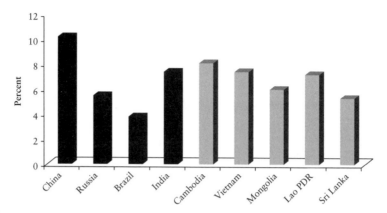

FIGURE 9.5 Average GDP Growth in BRIC and Selected Asian Frontier Economies: 2000 to 2010
Source: World Bank, author's analyses.

manufactured goods, including textiles and electronics. In general, a country's growing middle class is founded on low-wage manufacturing jobs, that in turn create a large domestic consumer base.

In contrast, the populations within some of the largest economies are far older. The United Kingdom, Italy, and Germany, three of the largest economies in the Euro Zone, all have a median age over 40. Japan, whose population is decreasing, has a median age of over 44 years, and an overall decreasing population[2] (see Table 9.7).

Low External Debt as a Percentage of GDP

"Low debt: Frontier markets have, on average, better balance sheets, with only half the debt to GDP of developed markets." Although Asian frontier economies are not highly leveraged compared to developed economies, this does not imply that these markets do not depend on external forces for financing. Asian frontier markets rely heavily on donor aid, financial rescue assistance, and soft loans from allies like Japan, the United States, and the European Union, and supranational institutions like the Asian Development Bank (ADB), the World Bank, and the International Monetary Fund (IMF) (see Table 9.8). These types of assistance provide Asian frontier economies the opportunity to receive financing without entering into burdensome debt.

The reason these countries require such handouts is simple: In many of these countries, the banking systems are either very conservative or simply nonexistent. This can be perceived as both good and bad. Providing loans to small businesses and entrepreneurs can help spur growth in a community

TABLE 9.7 Median Age within Asian Frontier Markets, BRICS, and Selected Developed Economies

Country	Median Age
Bangladesh	23.3
Bhutan	24.8
Cambodia	22.9
Laos	21
Maldives	26.2
Mongolia	26.2
Myanmar	26.9
Nepal	21.6
Papua New Guinea	21.8
Sri Lanka	30.8
Vietnam	27.8
Japan	**44.8**
United Kingdom	**40**
Germany	**44.9**
United States	**36.9**
Russia	**38.7**
India	**26.2**
China	**35.5**

Source: CIA, *The World Factbook*

TABLE 9.8 External Debt as Percent of GDP

Country	External Debt
Bangladesh	23
Bhutan	64
Cambodia	37
Laos	91
Maldives	50
Mongolia	41
Myanmar	17
Nepal	35
Papua New Guinea	16
Sri Lanka	36
Vietnam	32
Japan	**45**
United Kingdom	**400**
Germany	**142**
United States	**99**

Source: World Bank, author's analyses.

and economy. Without a capable banking system, socioeconomic mobility is nearly impossible for a large portion of the global population.

However, limiting the number of loans also helps to limit the eventual number of defaults. We like the fact that companies have a low gearing debt to equity level and never believed in the financial paradigm of the 1990s, the Modigliani-Miller theorem, that the level of leverage on a company's balance sheet does not affect the value of a company. Given similar valuations, we prefer a conservatively financed company to a highly leveraged one.

Globalization

"*Integration with the Global Economy: Cell phones and the Internet have made 'catch up' easier and faster.*" These are not your grandparents' frontier markets. People living in frontier markets, especially Asian ones, are more innovative, entrepreneurial, and tech-savvy than ever before. The ability to do business is now limited only by the capabilities of your phone, computer, and Internet connection. The importance of these technological advances in relation to a developing country and its ability to achieve strong economic growth cannot be disregarded. And the pace is only getting faster and more furious. Perhaps most intriguing, technological advances will enable some lower-income countries to immediately implement third and fourth generation technology while leap frogging some of the older forms. Very few individuals and residences in Lagos, Nigeria have landline telephones. And why should they? The cost of cellular technology has decreased so significantly since its inception that most Nigerians today have no need to take the steps from landline telephone to bulky mobile to sleek smart phone. Most Nigerians simply use their mobile phones to communicate and for their banking transactions.

Market Valuations

"*Attractive market valuations: Cheaper than both emerging and developed markets despite higher profit growth.*" That is one of the fascinating observations we made during recent research. Frontier markets are today priced more attractively than emerging markets (see Table 9.9).

MSCI Inefficient Markets

"*Inefficient markets: offer experienced fund managers opportunities to pounce on bargains.*" During research we came across many undervalued companies. One example is the leading Cambodia entertainment operator Naga Corp., listed on the Hong Kong Stock Exchange. Even after rising

TABLE 9.9 Price Earnings Forecast 12 Months

	Forecast
MSCI World Index	11.6
MSCI Emerging Markets Index	11.4
MSCI Frontier Markets Index	10.3

Source: Factset, author's analyses.

94.9 percent year to date, the stock is trading at an estimated P/E ratio of 9.8 times, with a dividend yield of 6.28 percent. Furthermore, three analysts covering the stock estimate that the company's earnings will grow on average 18 percent in 2012. Naga Corp. also supports the thesis that listings of companies outside of their home stock exchange does not create adequate value for either the investors or the companies in the long run. However, in the short term there are opportunities to exploit. In the many instances, like that of Naga Corp., there was higher liquidity and better investor sentiment in a foreign country.

These scenarios also played out in 2010 and 2011 when companies like Prada, Samsonite, and the aluminum producer Rusal from Russia listed on the Hong Kong Stock Exchange. Not surprisingly, all three companies' performances have been disappointing. Companies feel compelled to list their initial public offerings (IPOs) in foreign countries because of the prospect of higher stock valuations in a different market if investors in that location have a better understanding of a particular sector or industry.

During the Internet bubble Chinese and other Asian Internet companies listed on NASDAQ achieved better valuations for selling shares. However, in the long run, these companies did not experience a particular advantage from launching their IPOs on foreign stock exchanges. Using Naga Corp. as an example, if the stock were listed on the Cambodia Stock Exchange (CSX), it would trade at a much higher valuation since the company is better known to local investors. The first company just listed on the Cambodia Stock Exchange (CSX), Phnom Penh Water Authorities (PPWA) had an indicative pricing P/E of 15.9 times, earnings growth of 11 percent, and a dividend yield of approximately 2 percent. These indicators are all attractive and the local market has a better idea of PPWA's true worth than a foreign market does. This suggests that despite Naga Corp.'s 94.9 percent share price increase in the first few weeks in 2012, it would have been even more attractive and beneficial had it been listed domestically because, in the long run, the local market has a better appreciation of a company's true value.

Why Are Stocks Mispriced?

But why are stocks trading on frontier market stock exchanges so often mispriced? There are several reasons. One of the most important is the lack of research and information on the listed companies. Despite access to the Internet, it is still difficult to access annual financial statements, releases, announcements, and disclosures of the listed companies. Unfortunately, we do not expect investment houses will begin publishing research reports for these stocks anytime soon, as long as they have a relatively small market cap. In addition, the continuing trend to lower brokerage commission rates in developed markets will also deter big investment banks or research houses from covering emerging and frontier market companies trading on stock exchanges.

Another reason for mispriced stocks is that local investors are often not trained in the same methodologies that are used in developed markets to value companies. Recently, our local finance manager and accountant, when asked about the P/E ratio of the recent IPO, responded in a manner indicative of the problem with mispriced stocks. "I am sorry, this is all new for us in Cambodia. We have never heard it before or learned this expression at university." Also very famous are so-called trading floors in countries like Malaysia, South Korea, Thailand, and China where dozens of people, supposedly mainly housewives, meet and talk about stocks and "jockey" a particular stock with the intent of selling that same stock a few hours later for a small profit.

It is obvious that Asian stock markets are more volatile compared to non-Asian exchanges, particularly in South Korea and Vietnam, which implement daily circuit breakers, both limit-up and limit-down. It is not uncommon to see close to one third of all small companies in South Korea or Vietnam trading at these limits for an entire day. Also, the intra-day price fluctuations at most Asian stock exchanges, including Hong Kong, can be enormous.

Lower Portfolio Volatility

"Low correlation to other markets: frontier markets don't move in tandem with emerging or developed markets, offering the potential for lower portfolio volatility."

The big surprise is the fact that most countries observed above are more correlated to the MSCI World Index than to the MSCI Frontier Index. The reason is that almost 60 percent of the countries in the MSCI Frontier Index are located in the Middle East and thus benefit from higher or increasing oil prices. Whereas in countries like Bangladesh and Vietnam, the retail price of gas/petrol is still subsidized and does not impact the overall economy—a practice that can have severe consequences to the household budget and balance of payments. The currency crisis of February 2012 in Bangladesh when commercial banks ran out of US$ for several days, is a warning for both governments and foreign investors.

Another notable observation is that the former East Pakistan, now Bangladesh, has the lowest correlation to the MSCI World and Frontier Index, while the former West Pakistan, now Pakistan, has the highest correlation to both indexes. In general, Table 9.10 shows clearly that the frontier markets are not highly correlated to global indexes, or each other (any number below 50 percent can be considered as lowly correlated).

Table 9.10 also shows the absolute five-year performances in US$ in 11 Asian frontier markets. Despite the negative performances of the MSCI World and MSCI Frontier Indexes, the countries in the table, that is all Asian Frontier Countries, achieved a positive performance during the observation period. Three stock exchanges in particular: Mongolia (+870 percent), Bangladesh (+227 percent) and Sri Lanka (+108 percent) achieved triple digit performances. The big exception is Vietnam. Despite a positive performance in 2007 (+23.3 percent), Vietnam experienced an overall net loss of 63 percent (in US$) over the five-year period (see Figures 9.6, 9.7, and 9.8).

These developments show clearly that country allocation within a frontier markets portfolio is even more important than one that includes solely developed markets. These findings underscore a strict top-down approach to

TABLE 9.10   Correlations Indexes and Asian Economies

	Correlation based on 5 Years of Monthly Returns		5-Year Return
	MSCI World Index	MSCI Frontier Index	
MSCI World Index	100%		−21%
MSCI Frontier Index	86%	100%	−27%
Bangladesh	−18%	−37%	227%
Sri Lanka	4%	−26%	108%
Mongolia	16%	−1%	870%
Indonesia	22%	−4%	211%
India	42%	21%	18%
Philippines	48%	13%	30%
Thailand	50%	23%	52%
Malaysia	56%	25%	34%
Vietnam	78%	61%	−63%
Laos	79%	78%	N/A
Pakistan	88%	79%	2%

Source: Leopard Capital Research, author's analyses.

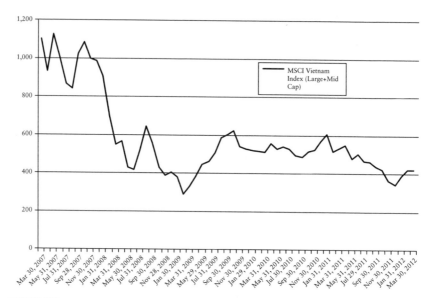

FIGURE 9.6 Five-Year Vietnam Ho Chi Minh Stock Index/VN-Index
Source: Bloomberg, author's analyses.

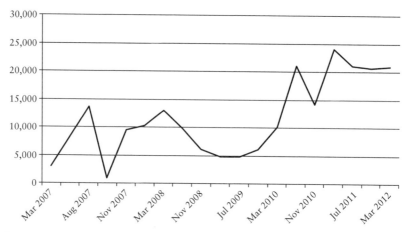

FIGURE 9.7 Five-Year Mongolia Stock Exchange Top 20 Index
Source: Bloomberg, author's analyses.

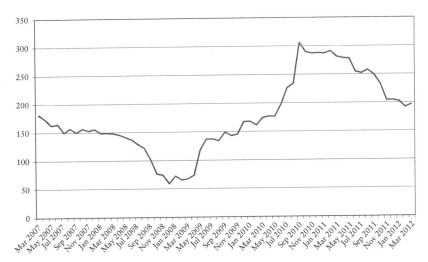

FIGURE 9.8　Five-Year Sri Lanka Colombo Stock Exchange All Share Index
Source: Bloomberg, author's analyses.

avoid making major and disastrous allocation mistakes into markets like Vietnam. Many fund managers today invest according to a fund's benchmark index and they (or the strategy team/asset allocation team) underweight or overweight a currency, country, or asset class accordingly.

Frontier investors and fund managers must realize that forces driving growth within each economy are very different. In Mongolia, the most sparsely populated country in the world (1.76 persons/km^2), the most significant economic driver is the extraction of natural resources like coal, gold, and copper. However, Bangladesh, the most densely populated country in the world,[3] with limited extractive opportunities, will look to capitalize on a different type of natural resource—its large, young, low-cost workforce—as its competitive advantage. In the short to medium term, large labor-intensive industries, such as garment production, will shift from China, particularly Guangdong province, to countries like Bangladesh, Cambodia, India, Pakistan, and Vietnam, which can provide labor at even lower cost than China.

Examples such as these are plentiful throughout Asian frontier countries; agriculture will be the key economic driver for Cambodia, Laos, and Myanmar; minerals and energy for Mongolia, Myanmar, and Papua New Guinea; tourism for Bhutan, Cambodia, Maldives, Myanmar, Nepal, Sri Lanka, and Vietnam; and electricity generation for Laos and Nepal. Asian frontier markets enable investors to diversity assets by investing in different sectors and industries within separate countries, all of which are forecast to generate strong economic growth.

Issues of Concern for Investing in Frontier Markets

While the investment attraction is great, risks and issues in investing in these markets need to be considered carefully.

Frontier Markets Are Vulnerable to Currency Fluctuations Even developed countries like Switzerland, Denmark, and Sweden have faced the problem of sudden and nearly uncontrollable capital inflow. During the height of the Euro/Greece crisis in August 2011, the value of the Swiss franc rose from 1.15 per US$ in June 2010 to as high as 0.7071/US$ on August 9, 2011. Amid the crises, the Swiss franc was regarded by international investors as one of the few safe havens. The sudden and aggressive shift from the euro and the US dollar toward the Swiss franc prompted the Swiss National Bank to take unprecedented actions; they implemented a quasi–peg of the Swiss franc to the euro in order to protect the Swiss export industry from further loss of competitiveness and falling profits.

Currency risk is one of the major concerns when investing in a frontier market and there are many factors that can cause severe fluctuations in currency valuations. During the Asian Crisis of 1997, foreign investors started to withdraw Thai baht, Malaysian ringgit, Indonesian rupiah, and Korean won, and began flooding the exchange markets with those currencies. The crisis was halted only after regional countries employed drastic fiscal policies. The Malaysian premier, Dr. Mahatir Mohammad, tied the ringgit to the US dollar at a rate of 3.80 ringgit/US dollar. Under Financial Secretary Donald Tsang, Hong Kong maintained the HK$-pegged exchange rate system while increasing interest rates to reduce further speculative flows of capital.

The massive capital inflow into Vietnam in 2006 and 2007 caused its currency, the dong, to fluctuate violently. Due to the shortage of investment opportunities and small stock and property markets, an asset bubble quickly ballooned and eventually burst in October 2007, sending the Ho Chi Minh Stock Index from a high of 1110 points to a low of 235 in February 2009 (a loss of 78 percent in local currency). During the same period, the Vietnamese dong decreased in value by 8 percent (from 16,080 dong/USD to 17,480 dong/USD). The dong has continued to lose value and was trading in March 2012 at 20,820 to the US dollar.

The impact of capital and investment inflow in Vietnam was very obvious when we saw ghost construction sites; four-lane roads built to nowhere; and huge billboards announcing the future openings of hotels, shopping malls, and industrial parks, all silent witnesses to the asset bubble of 2006 and 2007. The scene resembled that of Bangkok in the early 2000s when following the 1997 Asian crisis, the city's skyline was littered with half-built skyscrapers, resembling grand monuments to excess capital flows. The worst seems over for Vietnam's economy and the Ho Chi Minh stock market will finally come to life again, as foreign investors have already begun to start investing in the country. It takes about 4 to 5 years for an economy or stock market that experienced massive overinvestments and subsequent currency fluctuations to begin to recover.

Financial Reforms Quickly Follow Financial Crises There are plenty of opportunities for foreign investors after an economy or stock market has faltered. Investors can purchase shares of a good company at a deeply discounted price compared to its overvalued bubble price. Another phenomenon occurs after a stock market falls: reforms. After a steep stock market fall, regulations for foreign investments are softened or even completely abolished. Several examples have occurred in the past few years. Despite opening a stock market in 1961,Taiwan was completely closed to foreign investment until 1991. Following the 1990 market correction in which the TAIEX Index fell 53 percent to 4530.16 points, Taiwan permitted qualified foreign institutional investors (QFIIs) to invest in its stock market.[4] The introduction of QFIIs helped raise the TAIEX Index 1052 percent from 835.12 to 9624.18 points.

Other examples include South Korea, Indonesia, and Thailand, which completely removed or substantially reduced foreign restrictions on stock market investments during or shortly after the 1997 Asian financial crisis. In the early 1990s the foreign limit for any South Korean listed company was only 10 percent and foreign investors were prepared to pay a 100 percent premium for the South Korean blue chip stock Korean Mobile Telecom.

Frontier Markets Are Still Exposed to Exogenous Shocks Statistics prove that stock markets in frontier countries have lowly correlated or even negative correlation with developed market indexes. However, frontier economies are highly exposed to various exogenous factors, including:

- Higher energy and commodities prices
- Foreign investment in- or outflows
- Transportation or production bottlenecks
- Weather/climate
- Politics, wars, strikes
- General status of the world economy

A recent example of a weather/climate shock was the 2011 flooding in Thailand, which caused a halt to industrial production for several weeks in Bangkok's manufacturing districts.

Since many emerging countries are still subsidizing domestic food and gasoline prices, higher commodity and oil prices have a severe impact on the country's trade deficit, foreign reserves, and inflation, resulting in a weaker local currency compared to the US dollar. This year weakness of the Sri Lankan rupee and the Bangladesh taka are certainly a result of the high oil prices and we have already seen violent protests in Sri Lanka since gas prices increased.

Conversely, higher food prices will benefit exporting countries like Thailand, Vietnam, and Cambodia, which are large exporters of rice. These examples show that a top-down asset allocation is extremely important in order to react early to trend shifts that might ultimately alter the investment climate and avoid allocating investments to countries that have major economic problems that will result in weak stock markets. The art of investment, of course, is to detect these problems early and sell the stocks before they start to lose value.

Growth of China and India   Most Asian frontier countries have strong economic and political influence with their smaller neighbors. In many instances, the economic well-being within frontier countries is highly dependent on the sustained economic growth within their larger neighbors. Mongolia, which has just started to explore and extract its enormous coal and copper deposits, will certainly help fuel China's growing economy and thirst for energy resources. This dependency can be both positive and negative. At the moment, Mongolia is among the fastest growing countries in the world and its GDP is forecast to grow by over 15 percent annually over the next three years, attributed in large part to its export of coal and copper to its neighbor, China. However, China's rate of growth is not infinite, and some analysts forecast the days of China's double-digit GDP growth may come to an end. Alarmists speak of a hard landing brought on by an overheated economy. In either case, Mongolia would be remiss to become overly dependent on one country as the sole destination for its exports. The coupling effect holds true for relationships between Mongolia and China, Bangladesh and India, or any other frontier market looking to piggyback off of a larger neighbor's economic growth.

Investing as a Foreigner in Frontier Markets   There are many reasons why foreigners overlook and/or are underinvested in frontier markets. Perhaps the greatest reason is the lack of research and financial information. While many frontier stock markets allow foreigners to buy and sell shares through a qualified broker, in some instances foreigners are not allowed to invest in the stock market. Such is the case within Bhutan and Nepal. However, many of these countries are making inroads toward eventually allowing foreigners to invest in their stock markets and liberalizing their overall foreign investment laws.

An internal study conducted by the Securities Board of Nepal in late 2011 indicated the Nepal Stock Exchange (NEPSE) is not yet mature, professional, and technologically advanced enough to facilitate foreign investment. However, NEPSE is currently implementing a nonresident Nepalese (NRN) fund to enable Nepalese living abroad to invest during a trial period before allowing foreigners.[5]

Foreign investment laws in Myanmar are also undergoing rapid change. Myanmar is currently obtaining technical assistance and training in areas such as foreign exchange controls, finance, and investment law from foreign countries in an attempt to create a more foreign investment friendly climate. A new foreign investment law is expected to pass in 2012. However, until a new law is passed, foreigners who invest in companies in Myanmar through nominees have no legal standing to enforce their rights.[6] A new foreign investment law would ease fears of nationalization of assets and provide an overall framework for foreign investor protection rules and regulations.

Bureaucracy can also be a major hindrance to foreign investors in frontier markets. Investors need to register or obtain a form of trading code, a process that is sometimes extremely cumbersome as it is in Vietnam, and nearly impossible in India, Bangladesh, Cambodia, Mongolia, and Pakistan. These countries all have a similar type of registration process.

In addition, throughout many frontier countries, it is extremely difficult to open a custody account with a bank or a trading account with a broker. We tried to open a trading account with two different local Pakistani brokerage houses. One of them, whose CEO came to the office in Hong Kong, asked for a photocopy of the certificate of incorporation and memorandum of association and two days after his return to Karachi the trading account was opened and the CDS account was set up. Another local broker from Karachi sent us the account opening forms (more than 20 pages) that required all the signatures of the directors and all legal documents be certified by a Pakistani embassy despite being in Hong Kong with no embassy. However, the compliance department insisted that an embassy must certify the documents and signatures.

In other instances, foreign investors are subject to mistreatment. In the most recent incident, the Indian government retroactively levied a tax of over US$2 billion on Vodafone related to their acquisition of an Indian subsidiary in 2007, in spite of the fact that the tax law was not in existence at the time of the buyout nor was the transaction conducted in India. It is not clear what type of effective recourse Vodafone has in the matter at the moment.

Other common policies that disincentivize foreign investment include restrictions regarding repatriation of the currency or capital gains taxes of more than 10 percent in places like Bangladesh, India, and Papua New Guinea, and difficulty in liquidating assets, which is currently hurting foreign investment in the Maldives and Mongolia.

No Sophisticated Financial Instrument Available There are no futures and options exchanges in Southeast Asia outside Bangkok and Singapore. Also, investment banks in Hong Kong, London, and New York only reluctantly offer derivative products (mainly P-Notes) to their prime clients. Hedging the underlying currencies is also only available through non-deliverable forwards (NDF) for a few currencies like the Bangladesh taka and the Pakistan rupee.[7] This may also have its advantages since whenever a country introduced equity futures contracts (like India in June 2000) the country's stock market became more volatile and created opportunities.

Accounting Standards Foreign investors are also deterred from investing in frontier markets due to the lack of internationally recognized accounting standards. With the support of the World Bank and other development partners, many Asian frontier countries have begun to pass accounting laws that require companies to adhere to International Financial Reporting Standards (IFRS). Unfortunately, many of the countries are currently unable to enforce these standards. In many instances, both public and private entities simply do not prepare financial statements that adhere to international standards due to cost and complexity. It is generally recognized that these countries, despite international assistance and the passage of internationally recognized accounting standards, still require greater financial transparency, improved accounting and auditing practices, and stronger enforcement mechanisms to enhance their overall business environment.

However, it should be recognized in light of the Enron and Madoff scandals, that even the best accounting standards do not protect investors from fraud. Therefore, visiting the companies and meeting with the senior executives of the companies you intend to invest in are still an important source of information and should be part of the investment decision/research.

Take the example of BRAC-EPL Securities, today one of the largest brokerage companies in Bangladesh. The first few years were very difficult for the company due to the lack of interest from foreign investors and low stock exchange turnover. However, after negotiations with Bloomberg to add the Dhaka Stock Exchange Index (DSE-Index) onto Bloomberg's Index page, they received many information requests from large institutional investors from all over the world, particularly the United States. Not coincidentally, the DSE-Index moved from 1677.35 points at the end of December 2005 to 8,602.44 points at the end of November 2010.

CONCLUSION

Africa is a continent on the move. With no mountains of sovereign debt and declining state obligations (as a proportion of GDP), many African countries are showing increasing signs of improving governance, better accountability, and more transparency. Extensive commodity riches provide useful underpinnings to economic growth, whose real impetus has become the development of local markets and internally generated demand in many of the countries.

With relatively efficient pricing of assets a patient investor stands to make significant returns over the coming years. But beware of a bumpy ride!

In the same vein, South and Southeast Asian markets hold sizable promise. The story of the Dhaka Stock Exchange could be replaying countless times throughout South and Southeast Asia. The fact remains that one of the biggest deterrents to more foreign investment in these markets is a lack of awareness. Many Asian frontier markets outperformed BRIC over the last decade. More importantly, more of these economies are expected to continue to outpace BRICs growth in the next ten years.

NOTES

1. www.investmentu.com.
2. CIA, *World Factbook*, cia.org.
3. Note: Includes only countries with populations over 10 million.
4. www.twse.com.tw/en/investor/foreign_invest/OCFID_01.php.
5. "Share Market Not Ready for Foreign Investors," *Himalayan Times* (December 21, 2011).
6. "Doing Business in Myanmar," www.myanmarlegalsevices.com (August 2012).
7. Selected currency hedging and derivatives are available in other markets such as the Indian rupee in Dubai.

CHAPTER 10

Regions: Middle East, GCC, Levant, and North Africa

Following the first oil crisis in 1973, the hydrocarbon-rich countries of the Middle East and North Africa (MENA) received a significant boost to their economic development efforts. The oil and gas price development over the past twenty years created very significant capital surpluses in some of these economies. Today, several MENA countries are among the richest nations per capita, the sovereign wealth funds are among the biggest globally, and mega-infrastructure developments and plans are prevalent. Growing economic relationships and interdependence provide for a springboard and opportunity for all MENA nations and thus MENA represents significant regional and country specific opportunities for investors both in private and in public equity and increasingly in debt markets.

However, business in these countries is not always easy and is dominated by cultural and geopolitical considerations. This greatly impacts the status and outlook of their capital markets.

We consider the soft side of the business environment and prevailing business challenges in the region. They determine the attractiveness of investor markets. More specifically, we review Oman as well as the United Arab Emirates (UAE) as case studies of markets that are currently not classified as emerging but have many of the characteristics of a developed market. It is but a question of time until some of these markets will migrate towards advanced emerging, possibly developed market status, and would become more mainstream as investment targets.

THE SOFT SIDE OF BUSINESS IN MENA

Andreas Buelow

MENA, the Middle East and North Africa region, is usually defined to encompass the Arabic speaking countries in North Africa, the Levant as well as those on the Arabian Peninsula. These countries are interesting developing markets, some classified emerging and some frontier, due to their geographic location and their demographic composition as well as the need to develop sustainable economies based on real value creation. At the same time, some of the countries have particularly interesting characteristics for prospective investors, such as the size of their domestic market (e.g., Egypt) or their abundant wealth in natural resources (e.g., the Gulf states) which in turn provides governments with sufficient funds to offer a wide range of incentives to potential investors. Investing in this region brings about specific challenges related to the prevalent cultural and business environment, as is the case for any other developing market.

These challenges provide a natural barrier to entry for some of the less skilled or courageous investors and overall, the above-mentioned factors combine to make the MENA region an attractive investment destination with substantial potential and limited competition. The comments offer a high-level understanding of the important issues any foreign investor needs to keep in mind when doing business there.

The common denominator for grouping specific countries in the MENA region is the common cultural base they share in terms of language, religion, and history. Due to the geographic location and the historic context of the Ottoman Empire, the region has been a crucial business link between Asia, Europe, and Africa throughout the centuries. Within this line of tradition, countries such as the United Arab Emirates have strengthened their position as global logistics hubs for the endless flows of goods and customers between Asia and Europe. At the same time, the Arab countries of North Africa have deep-rooted trading connections to their southern neighbors in sub-Saharan Africa.

Therefore, the countries of the MENA region do not only represent markets in their own right, they also open doors to other attractive or potentially attractive developing markets. However, the MENA region is not legally one single market, unlike for example China or India, and the legalities of doing business throughout the region are complex and require a well-thought-out structure to access the full potential of the region.

Many if not all countries of the MENA region show a demographic composition where a high and increasing percentage of the population is young. Some estimate that, for example in Egypt and Saudi Arabia, about 50 percent of the population is younger than 25 years. This immediately translates into a burning need for the creation of substantial employment opportunities for the young generation. Adding further fuel to this fire is the fact that many of the young generation are fairly well educated and are looking for challenging and well-paid jobs. The sheer size of the demographic development also means that even the richest of countries, such as Saudi Arabia, will not be able to continue compensating the demographic development with the creation of government sector employment; the problem is just getting far too big. Therefore, the demographic development in the MENA region provides a very tangible need for the economic development of the countries in this region.

Also, the economic basis of many countries in the Middle East and North Africa has been mostly trade for many centuries. It only changed to natural resources over the course of the past 70 years. Trading posts along the main trading routes, many of which led through the MENA region in the past, were crucial for supplies in the days when trade relied on sailing ships and caravans to bring goods from Asia to Europe and vice versa. The small margins made at these trading posts were sufficient to sustain the modest standards of living of the relatively small populations there.

The discovery of oil and gas resources changed this dynamic suddenly as huge wealth was becoming available from exporting these natural resources. This triggered the aforementioned demographic development as well as the development of a modern infrastructure that starts to absorb substantial portions of the otherwise unproductive wealth creation from natural resources in a bid to transform the short-term wealth into a base for a long-term sustainable economy.

Along these lines, many countries have embarked on programs to diversify their economic base away from natural resources, for example by developing manufacturing industries or by creating the framework for knowledge based economies. All these steps are accompanied by financial as well as non-monetary incentives for foreign investors to induce foreign direct investments. In other words, the existing and emerging opportunities are further enhanced by governmental support for utilizing them.

These arguments make a case for the attractiveness of the MENA region as a destination for emerging market investments. The main driver is the need for economic development to provide jobs and to ensure that created jobs remain sustainable in the long-term economy, in addition to the attractive geographic location. Even though they are not a legally integrated market, common language, culture, and history bind the MENA region essentially as one market. Goods and services that are being sold successfully in one market can be exported into other markets using the same sales approach. In the case of the countries of the Gulf Cooperation Council (GCC), which is composed of Bahrain, Kuwait, Oman, Qatar, the United Arab Emirates, and Saudi Arabia, exports are further facilitated because these countries have implemented a fairly strong customs and economic union which allows for easy exports from one member country to another. This large and common market allows any investor to select a suitable country as home base in order to maximize initial market potential as well as government support in a bid to reduce the overall risk of the investment.

This strategy has been used by industrial investors, that is, companies that expand into the MENA region within the context of their international growth strategy. Some German companies, for example, have recently established after-sales operations including limited manufacturing of spare parts in the Kingdom of Bahrain to cater to the Gulf region. Another example is global insurance companies who have pursued a hub strategy, basing themselves in one country and subsequently branching out to other countries in the MENA region to minimize overall capital requirements for their operations in the region. All these approaches require careful due diligence to assess issues such as legal implications, import and export duties between countries of the MENA region, and many other points, in particular when looking at countries outside the GCC. Of course, to the investor, the question of the home base is more a question of foreign ownership regulations, international accessibility of the chosen location, and proximity to the investment targets to maximize control.

Just as any other emerging market, the MENA region holds its own specific challenges for international investors. The three most important points, those most antithetical to the Western business approach, in the Arabian cultural context are the meaning of time, the role of personal relationships with local partners, and the fact that connections are often more important than the letter of the law.

To start with the meaning of time: There is somewhat of a relaxed attitude on the matter of punctuality, be it for meetings or project milestones. While this is less of an issue in countries with strong cultural or historic ties to Europe, such as Tunisia or Lebanon, it certainly requires much patience from an investor who is used to Western business practices. Investors who have to rely on a local partner for their investment or who wish to financially involve a local partner in their investment project, for example for co-funding, need to be aware that decision-making processes will take substantial amounts of time and meetings, despite the fact that the local contact will always be very optimistic that the decision is about to be taken.

In the case of companies, this has to do with their highly hierarchical setup where all decisions must be approved by the top echelons; in the case of private individuals or families, decisions are usually taken after extensive consultation with family members in order to ensure the buy-in of everyone who is affected by the decision in question. It is clear that in this environment, planning also retains a lower priority and adjustments to structures or time lines of projects or investments are frequent. There is also a link to religion, which strongly permeates all Arab societies, and the concept of God's willingness (*insha'allah*). Looking at this from a different viewpoint, however, shows that professional foreign investors can add value above and beyond the investment itself by transferring skills and process knowledge, and such transfers are highly welcome in the drive to modernize the economies.

The importance of personal relationships in the Arabian world cannot be overestimated, as they have been the basis of successful business dealings between the often far-apart countries over the centuries when communication was slow and arduous. Suffice to say that the payment method of using checks was invented by Arab traders in the Middle Ages in order to facilitate trade, for example between Cordoba in Spain and Damascus in Syria. These days as in the past, the importance of trust and a personal relationship between business partners is deeply engrained in individuals from the Arab world. They usually will spend significant amounts of time to get to know potential business partners and to build a personal relationship well before engaging in meaningful business. However, once mutual trust has been established and a sustainable personal relationship has been built, business will develop rapidly as a result of having cemented the personal relationship.

In developing business, the Arab partner of an investor or businessman will use his connections, or *wasta*, to the benefit of the partnership combined with the reputation and skill of the foreign business partner. It is important to notice that such connections are often much more important than any written agreements. A powerful partner will be able to get special permission to do this or that, simply on the basis of his own personal relationships that have often been developing over generations between different families. Unfortunately, it is ex ante very often much less clear how powerful a potential business partner truly is. This demonstrates the particular importance of doing due diligence on potential business partners in the Arab world, who are often introduced by referral through gatekeepers, people who have a standing agreement with local businessmen to introduce potential foreign investors and business partners to them.

The challenge is to identify early the truly valuable local partner and to avoid the partner who talks but will not deliver, in order to save time and money in relationships that do not bring about business, even though they result in many interesting conversations over coffee. Of course, a track record of successful partnerships in the past is an important indicator in this regard. Other quintessential items when doing due diligence on a potential partner include background checks with international chambers of commerce, a review of local and regional press, and other means of gathering information on the successful execution of projects. A subtle look at the photo gallery in the office of a potential business partner will often reveal the extent to which the individual has particular contacts in the political establishment of his/her own country or experience abroad.

Ignoring the softer aspects of conducting business in the Middle East causes frustration and ultimately defeats many worthwhile investments. With some appreciation of the inherent culture, this region deservedly ranks among the more promising investment destinations in the coming decade.

INVESTOR MARKETS IN MENA, GCC, NORTH AFRICA, AND LEVANT

Many economies in MENA benefit from significant natural resources. The resulting higher share of foreign direct investment and the growing national income allowed farsighted governments to provide conditions for exceptional growth and development, resulting in several economies of the highest standard. Most of the successful economies invest heavily in domestic physical stock; they create favorable framework conditions and infrastructure for private businesses and enterprises to grow. These economies, by definition, find a way to open their economy to external capital and labor flows without endangering their national cohesion and identity.

The less successful economies and economies with no resource incomes foster large government-related or cosponsored enterprises largely in asset based industries. They devote fewer resources to building conditions for private business growth. They are less open economies and retain a number of protective and restrictive conditions on external capital and labor flows.

In addition to economic strategies, labor market conditions divide the region. Several of the MENA economies, mostly the GCC countries, have relatively small indigenous populations and depend on major, low-cost labor imports. The extensive import of low cost labor allowed the building of sizable physical stock at relatively low cost. It also led to a construction boom and real estate bubble. However, the resulting infrastructure in the GCC economies, for example, is well ahead of general economic development.

Other economies provide high public employment, public investment, and subsidies as well as projects to satisfy a large, indigenous workforce. Both labor importers and public employers in their own way created a protective umbrella for the local population. Labor-importing countries created a wage premium for nationals[1] and to some extent for entrepreneurs while labor-abundant countries allow dominance, possibly a wage premium, through public and sponsored employment.[2]

Work-seeking young people and women cannot be absorbed by either continued infrastructure projects or public employment. Widespread unemployment among youth and women in MENA countries is the consequence (see Figure 10.1). Unemployment or lack of prospects for employment among lower-skilled labor was one of the reasons for the Arab Spring.

In economies with flexible labor markets, unemployment tends to be higher among better-educated nationals and low among laborers. The growing segment of well-educated nationals and women find it increasingly hard to compete with imported labor that often accepts lower wages. In economies with more rigid labor markets, unemployment tends to be higher within the unskilled workforce and women, partly driven by cultural considerations.

As a transitional strategy both approaches may have their validity but the demographic structure of almost all MENA countries presents a major challenge. The average median age across all MENA countries is 25, well below other regions (see Figure 10.2).

The OECD MENA Investment program estimates that in order to maintain current employment levels, 25 million jobs will need to be created over the coming decade. The World Bank even suggests that the region will need to create at least 50 million jobs to maintain social and political stability.[3]

In effect, both labor market strategies reduce skills competition. The motivation for the local workforce is to join local business leaders, aspire to participate in the leadership of local organizations or be the sponsors or partners of foreign businesses in countries where labor and skills imports are relatively free. Alternatively in countries with an abundant local workforce, locals join public or government/ruling/leading families related enterprises or participate in public employment programs.

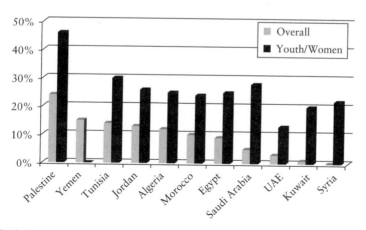

FIGURE 10.1   Overall and Youth/Women Unemployment—MENA
Source: The Arab World Competitiveness Report 2011–2012, author's analyses.

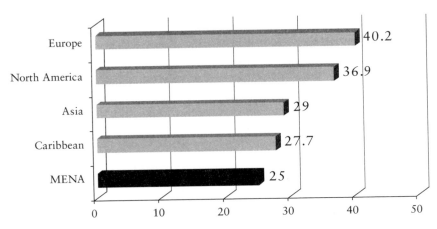

FIGURE 10.2   Average Median Age
Source: The Arab World Competitiveness Report 2011–2012, International Financial Reporting Standards.

Either way, the development of private enterprise, the only sustainable job creation engine of the economy, suffers greatly. Employment growth in the public sector or in the government/ruling family related sector is limited. The solution to the unemployment issue lies in fostering private businesses. In this respect, MENA countries, in particular those with less open economies, lag considerably.

Entrepreneurship is limited in many MENA economies. The World Bank Group Entrepreneurship Survey shows that firm density, that is, the number of new limited companies per 1,000 working population, is a fraction of that in developed and emerging economies (see Figure 10.3).

Entrepreneurial activity is both more cumbersome due to a regulatory burden and seen as less attractive as compared to public/ruling family related jobs with prestige and some employment security. The low female participation rate and cultural barriers also contribute to a lower entrepreneurial activity.

MENA Business Issues

Business flows generally precede capital flows. As a consequence, business barriers have a significant effect on capital flows and thus attractiveness of markets to investors. The most open business environments generate the most attractive companies and provide both public and private investment opportunities. To assess the outlook of the numerous stock exchanges in the MENA region, we need to consider prevailing business environments as well as restrictions and barriers.

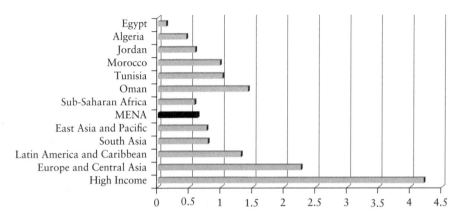

FIGURE 10.3 Firm Entry Density by Region
Source: The Arab World Competitiveness Report 2011–2012, International Financial Reporting Standards.

The MENA region can be divided into three subgroups: GCC, North Africa, and Levant. The major countries in each subgroup earn mixed rankings in their global competitive position and with respect to ease of doing business, as depicted in Table 10.1.

Clearly, GCC economies lead the rankings in MENA. The most consistently ranked economy is the UAE, followed by Qatar and Bahrain. Outside the GCC, Tunisia and Jordan come closest at around the level of Kuwait but remain a sizeable step behind the leaders.

Still, GCC economies sport significant barriers to business. Although different from country to country, they are predominantly in the areas of:

- Company ownership restrictions (onshore)
- Agency laws
- Real estate ownership
- Visa, residency, and labor rules
- Bureaucracy and legal access
- Insolvency process

Overall, MENA countries are reducing barriers to businesses for both locals and foreigners but many still suffer from restrictive framework conditions (see Figure 10.4).

On average, MENA economies are improving business conditions faster than regulatory ease. The legal institutional framework is still weak.

These general business conditions are of relevance to the market investor. First, many of the businesses listed are government or ruling family

TABLE 10.1   Global Competitiveness Ranking 2011/2012: Ease of Doing Business and Economic Freedom of Key MENA Economies, 2012

Economy	WCI Global Rank	Economic Freedom Rank	Ease of Doing Business Rank	Average Rank
GCC Economies				
Qatar	14	25	36	25.0
Saudi Arabia	17	74	12	37.7
UAE	27	35	33	31.7
Oman	32	47	49	42.7
Kuwait	34	71	67	57.3
Bahrain	37	12	38	29.0
Levant Economies				
Jordan	71	32	96	66.3
Lebanon	89	90	104	94.3
Syria	98	139	134	123.7
North Africa				
Tunisia	40	95	46	60.3
Morocco	73	87	94	84.7
Algeria	87	140	148	125.0
Egypt	94	100	110	101.3

Source: The Arab World Competitiveness Report 2011–2012, author's analyses.

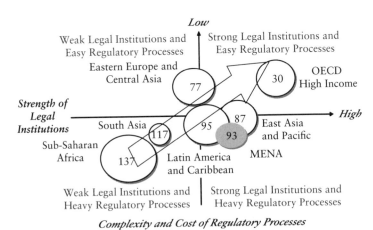

FIGURE 10.4   Legal Institutions and Regulatory Processes by Region, 2012

Source: IBSD/WB, Doing Business 2012, October 2011, author's analyses.

Note: The numbers in the circles Indicate the average ranking; circle size is indicative of the number of economies.

related. Second, the relative lack of entrepreneurship in some countries leaves the supply side of companies to be listed somewhat wanting. Finally, the lack of sound legal access conditions leaves the investor with an increased risk or overreliance on relationships when businesses face disputes or restructuring. Several recent high profile cases attest to this risk.

Given the available wealth and investment appetite, MENA region stock markets, in particular GCC stock markets, should become one of the most attractive future emerging markets. Economic growth (see Table 10.2), even taking into account the Arab Spring and slowdown of developed economies on which the region somewhat depends, is projected to be consistently high, except for Egypt, and rising resource prices should ensure increased revenues for most of the MENA economies, as well as the freedom to make necessary investments.

Most forecasts by financial institutions and regional research houses put growth at 1 to 2 percentage points higher for most economies. Resource prices could add another 1 percentage point of growth. Necessary conditions are the continued development of institutional framework conditions, increased legal certainty, and investment in human resources.

Some of the MENA economies, in particular the Levant economies and some North African economies, face specific challenges that may reduce overall attractiveness of their stock markets until their domestic economy and private business orientation gets into full swing. They also tend to have smaller stock markets and attract less foreign investment.

TABLE 10.2   IMF September 2011 Growth Forecast for 2012

Algeria	3.3
Bahrain	3.6
Egypt	1.8
Jordan	2.9
Kuwait	4.5
Lebanon	3.5
Morocco	4.6
Oman	3.6
Qatar	6.0
Saudi Arabia	3.6
Syria	1.5
Tunisia	3.9
UAE	3.8

Source: The Arab World Competitiveness Report 2011–2012, author's analyses.

MENA Stock Markets

Capital markets in general, covering banking, debt, and equity markets together, are relatively less developed in MENA than in other regions (see Figure 10.5).

MENA capital markets are most dependent on bank loans and utilize bonds least compared to other regions.[4] Equity markets in MENA as a region are relatively smaller than in other regions. This is despite the fact that GCC exchanges are not much less capitalized in proportion to their GDP than developed economies. Selected other MENA markets also sport high market capitalization to GDP (see Figure 10.6).

However, the liquidity gap between them and other markets is great. This liquidity gap is a function of the type of companies listed—concentrated ownership by government and families—and the nature of the stock market (little free float required) in the GCC and other MENA economies.

Overall, all MENA stock exchanges amount to around US$1trillion stock market capitalization (see Figure 10.7). This is less than 2 percent of global market capitalization but a very credible and important share of 14.3 percent of all stock markets outside developed and BRIC economies. Continued economic growth and development potential makes the MENA region a very attractive capital destination in the coming years.

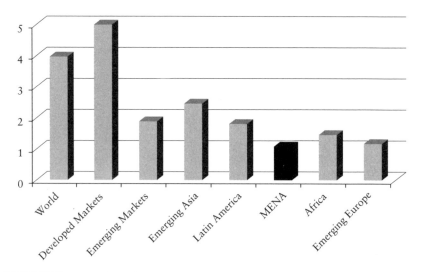

FIGURE 10.5   Capital Markets as Percentage of GDP by Region

Source: IMF, Emirates NBD Research, author's analyses.

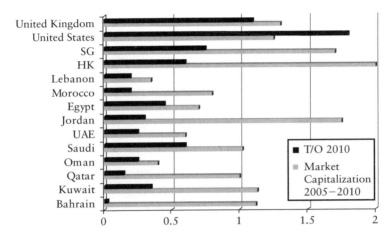

FIGURE 10.6 Capital Markets as Percentage of GDP by Economy

Source: US Census, IMF, Emirates NBD Research, author's analyses.

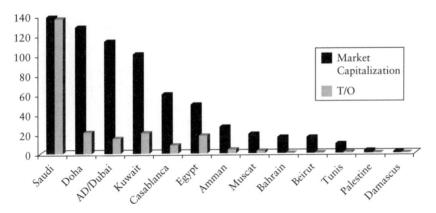

FIGURE 10.7 MENA Stock Markets Capitalization at End of 2011 and Turnover in 2011 (in US$ millions)

Source: Arab Monetary Fund (www.amf.og.ae) and Arab Capital Market Resource Center (www.btflive.net), author's analyses.

The relatively tightly held equity of most companies still represents the major barrier to larger scale foreign investment. As a consequence, liquidity remains a major issue for investors (see Figure 10.8).

For the major economies, the attributes of stock exchanges required to qualify as frontier or emerging economies based on the definitions

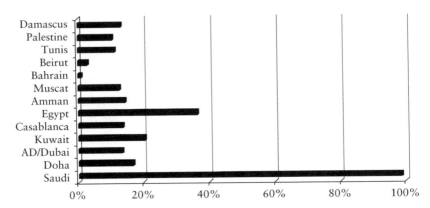

FIGURE 10.8 MENA Stock Market Liquidity Percentages of Market Capitalization at End of 2011 by Individual Market

Source: Arab Monetary Fund (www.amf.og.ae) and Arab Capital Market Resource Center (www.btflive.net), author's analyses.

of major index providers are largely met. They are however not the real issue.

Either current companies allow more float of their shares or new companies need to be listed providing attractive investments with enhanced liquidity. Otherwise, MENA stock markets, while important in their own right, may not fulfill their promise of becoming major investment destinations for foreign and domestic investor capital.

THE CASE OF OMAN: SOLID FOUNDATIONS FOR INVESTMENT

Mohammed Moussallati

The Sultanate of Oman, with a population of over 2.3 million, is the second largest Gulf state, spanning a total area of over 300,000 square kilometers.[5] HM, the Sultan, Qaboos bin Said Al Said, has since coming into power in 1970 overseen political stability, vast infrastructural development, and economic growth.

As an indication of the level of Oman's progress, the United Nations Development Program named Oman in 2010 as the most improved nation during the preceding 40 years among 135 countries worldwide, progress which is not simply attributable to oil and gas earnings, as some might assume.[6]

Recently, Muscat, the capital city of Oman, was voted second best city to visit in 2012. Oman has thus become an attractive major destination for international visitors mainly due to the achievement of immense, almost Dubai-style local development while maintaining very much of a traditional feel.

Recent attractions include the opening in October 2011 of the highly anticipated Royal Opera House in Muscat, equipped with state-of-the-art technology and presenting internationally renowned performers; November 2011 saw Oman's first floating hotel on a ship, named *Veronica*, stationed at Duqm and equipped with luxury entertainment facilities. Such initiatives continue to boost Oman's global profile and play a major part in encouraging tourism and foreign investment, part of His Majesty's key policy to reduce Oman's reliance on oil-related income.

Indeed, fueled by rising oil prices in the international markets and a stable political and economic setting (in comparison to other Arab countries), Oman has seen massive growth and investment by the local government and private sources as well as foreign investment, which is expected to continue. In fact, it is reported that the Omani government had forecasted investment of RO 37.5 billion (approximately US$97.5 billion) for new projects in Oman for the period 2011–2015.[7]

The legal and regulatory system in Oman is also well developed and orientated toward attracting foreign business and the best individual talent from abroad. As lawyers are seeing an increasing number of foreign businesses looking to establish a presence in Oman and accordingly seeking advice on a wide range of matters, such as Omani laws pertaining to foreign investment and public procurement and regulations applicable to specific industry sectors, with the prospect of privatization in industries (such as power, water, electricity, telecommunications, and aviation) being an attractive opportunity to local and international investors. Potential investors are also seeking advice concerning the most suitable structure for their specific needs to engage in business in Oman.

Oman's constitution, issued on November 6, 1996 and titled "The Basic Law of the Sultanate of Oman" ("Constitution"),[8] provides certain key guarantees that are fundamental to the confidence in and development of the Omani economy, including the protected right for individuals to litigate (Article 25), the rule of law and the impartiality of judges (Articles 59 and 61), and the independence of the Omani courts.

The growth in foreign investment into Oman is well documented, driven by the government offering various incentives for foreign investment, including the freedom to repatriate capital and profits and the availability of soft loans with favorable interest for certain investment projects, not to mention a thriving economy. A number of government-established organizations have been formed to facilitate foreign investment, such as the Public Authority for Investment Promotion and Export Development (PAIPED), which renders services such as the provision of investment information, assisting foreign investors to find suitable local partners, and obtaining various government approvals and finance from government and local banks.[9] The free trade agreement signed between Oman and the United States, which took effect at the beginning of 2009, eliminating tariff barriers on all consumer and industrial products, also provides strong incentives and protection for American businesses investing in Oman.

A number of business structures are available for foreign investors seeking to engage in local commerce, including limited liability companies, joint stock companies (the equivalent of public limited companies in other countries), commercial agencies (allowing a local agent to sell, promote and/ or distribute products and/or services of a foreign entity with otherwise no legal presence in Oman) and commercial representative offices (put simply, a marketing branch of a foreign entity, but which cannot contract or engage in sales activity directly). Oman is becoming accustomed to world-renowned brands in its cities. By way of example, Oman's Saud Bahwan Group, with a presence in a diverse range of industries (including oil and gas, property and real estate, travel and tourism, heavy vehicles, industrial and construction equipment, and automotive), holds the agency for leading brands in the automotive sector, including Toyota, Daihatsu, Lexus, Kia, and Ford, and MAN and HINO brands in the heavy vehicles sector. Other popular brands that can be seen in Oman include food chains like McDonald's, KFC, and Nando's, and international hypermarket chains such as Carrefour.

With the priority of the government to diversify and reduce reliance on oil income as the largest sector in the economy, Oman is seeing rapid industrialization and growth in sectors such as tourism, agriculture, fisheries, education, health, and communication. The government encourages industrial production that is export-orientated, resulting in greater local manufacturing of a variety of high-tech products. For example, OCTAL, which is considered to be the largest PET resin manufacturer in the Middle East and the largest integrated PET sheet manufacturer in the world (PET being a highly valued packaging material), has its production facilities in the Omani port city of Salalah. It is reported that approximately 59 percent of Oman's gross domestic product (GDP) is generated outside the oil and gas sector, and this is expected to increase as the government, through its implementation of a series of five-year development plans, continues its policy of encouraging private sector investment into non-oil and non-gas industrial activities.

Other ventures of the Omani government include Oman Brunei Investment Company SAOC (OBIC), a special investment company owned jointly by the governments of Oman and Brunei Darussalam, which invested significantly in Oman. Such foreign and local investment is the cornerstone to greater competitiveness, productivity and quality of service, and advancement in technology.

There is still of course an element of protectionism in favor of locals. For example, the Foreign Capital Investment Law in Oman (Royal Decree No. 102/94) prohibits a non-Omani individual or entity from holding more than 49 percent of the share capital of an Omani commercial company (although experience has shown that in practice it is possible for up to 70 percent of foreign ownership to be authorized). The substantial capital requirements when incorporating commercial companies in Oman (for example, the requisite capital for a limited liability company with foreign shareholding requires capital of not less than RO 150,000, (approximately US$390,000) also provide a safety barrier for local creditors against unscrupulous foreign investors.

Examples include, among others, Oman's membership of the Berne Convention since July 1999 (protection of copyright works), the Madrid Protocol (facilitating the international registration of trademarks), the Paris Convention since July 1999 (protection of industrial property), the Patent Co-operation Treaty since October 2001 (harmonization of patent application process for inventions in contracting states) and the Trademark Law Treaty since October 2007 (harmonization of the trademark application process).

In order to implement the provisions of the relevant international treaties, conventions, and protocols, Oman has enacted local legislation to protect intellectual property rights, including dedicated laws to protect copyrights (Royal Decree No. 65/2008), and geographical indications, industrial designs, industrial property, patents, trade names, trademarks, and trade secrets (Royal Decree No. 67/2008). This comprehensive legal framework provides important recourse for local and foreign entities against abuse or misuse of their valuable intellectual property by unauthorized third parties and a level of comfort which encourages their establishing of a commercial presence in Oman.[10]

In May 2011, the Central Bank of Oman approved the establishment of exclusive Islamic banks and windows (or branches) of existing licensed banks to conduct the business of Islamic banking/finance (in other words, banking which is Shariah-compliant). The expectation is that the move will encourage locals to hold on to their savings and invest in Oman, or to repatriate funds already abroad, as they would no longer need to invest in other countries which offer Islamic banking/finance products, and also to attract foreign investors.

Companies in Oman are able to retain the best local talent and also attract the finest foreign talent from some of the leading educational hubs in the world, including Australia, the United Kingdom, and North America, among others. As employees, the attraction is zero income tax coupled with relatively high salaries, cheaper living costs (for example, subject to daily price fluctuations, gasoline in Oman costs approximately US$0.25 per liter), a warm climate, beautiful wadis, deserts, beaches, and mountains, excellent schools, hospitals, sports facilities, and shopping malls, as well as a friendly local population.

An added comfort for non-Omani individuals working in Oman is the employee-favorable Omani Labor Law (Royal Decree No. 35/03 as amended) and accompanying ministerial regulation. Local cases demonstrate that lawyers have successfully advised a number of aggrieved non-Omanis who, as in any other so-called developed country, are seeking to enforce certain rights against reputable local organizations that are incompliant with the labor law. The Omani courts have shown that, in accordance with the Omani constitution, judgments are compliant with the law, and this provides added reassurance to non-Omanis who leave secure jobs in their home countries to work in Oman.

Rising oil prices in international markets and the stable political and economic setting in Oman coupled with a well-developed legal and regulatory system have attracted significant local and foreign investment (public and private). Oman is becoming less reliant on oil- and gas-related income, in accordance with government policy, and is seeing growth in other sectors such as tourism, agriculture, fisheries, education, health, and communication; in addition, the quality of services, productivity, competitiveness, and advancement in technology continues to improve. This progression is attributable to Oman's ability to attract fine foreign talent and significant investment incentives and protections, including a comprehensive intellectual property framework.

OMAN STOCK MARKET

Oman has a comparatively long history in securities trading. The Muscat Securities Market (MSM) was established by Royal Decree (53/88) in 1988.[11] After 10 years of continuous growth, Oman promulgated the new Capital Market Law in 1998 which separated the exchange, the Muscat Securities Market (MSM) where all listed securities are traded, and the Capital Market Authority (CMA). The Exchange is a government entity, financially and administratively independent from the regulator but subject to CMA supervision.

For a listing on the regular market, companies must have a solid record of profitability. The parallel market has lower requirements and the third market consists of companies facing financial difficulties. Listed companies are from three sectors: banking and investment, services and insurance, and industry.

The MSM index, the MSM 30, includes freely available shares and a 10 percent capping to ensure wider representation of smaller companies. The free float and capping is revised (reset) on a quarterly basis and based on market capitalization, liquidity, and earnings per share. The MSM 30 index comprises three subindexes representing the three sectors (banking and investment, industry, and services insurance). Performance has been mixed (see Figure 10.9).

The trading system from Atos Euronext, France, is highly advanced and ensures the real time provision of data and information to all users. The clearing and settlement system is through a settlement bank (Central Bank) supported by a settlement guarantee fund (SGF).

Incentives for foreign investment in the Oman Capital Market include:

- No tax on capitalist returns or profits.
- No restrictions on capital and profit transfers.
- No restrictions on exchange processes.
- The convertibility of the Omani rial (RO) and fixed exchange rate with US currency.
- Law corporate profit tax.
- Foreign investors can invest in the shares of listed companies or investment funds without prior permission.
- There is independent regulatory and supervisory authority for organizing, monitoring, and supervising Muscat Securities Market to ensure the protection of investors.

Overall, the MSM is an attractive stock market with a market capitalization in end-2011 of around US$21 billion and a turnover of around US$2 billion. Some 22% of turnover or US$440 million is by non-Omanis indicating solid interest by foreign investors.

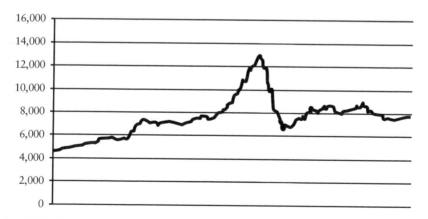

FIGURE 10.9   Muscat Securities Exchange: MSM 30 Index, 2003–2012 (indicative)
Source: Muscat Securities Exchange, Index performance approximated, www.msm.gov.com, author's analyses.

UNITED ARAB EMIRATES: PLENTIFUL BUSINESS AND CAPITAL

The United Arab Emirates (UAE) are a case in point of an economy that successfully addresses the antithesis of the role of the political economy and the success requirements of the private economy. The country excels in both aspects: a strong and often underestimated foundation of the formal economy providing great opportunity for foreign and domestic business, and the often invisible hand of the informal economy that guides much of the commercial activity throughout the country. The UAE has implemented some very advanced solutions to overcoming and mitigating this dilemma that augur very well for rapid progress in international capital markets as and when culturally entrenched impediments are diluted.

Business flows almost always precede capital flows. Selected economies such as Mongolia or for that matter the Emirate of Abu Dhabi with a disproportionate level of natural resource income are an exception. For most economies, entrepreneurs (private or public) drive growth by taking advantage of market inefficiencies and asymmetries to generate profits. They invariably generate and sustain some form of advantage to maintain their gains that competitors cannot match at the time. Whatever the definition of entrepreneurship,[12] businesses require favorable framework conditions to succeed. These framework conditions cover in the most general terms:

- Access to markets, ownership, and influence in dealings.
- Legal framework with freedom and protection.
- Some form or recourse, redress, and dispute resolution.

The UAE has and is providing such conditions to a very large extent. The economic strategy of the UAE has been to deploy its financial resources and legislative powers in creating first world infrastructures, thoughtful legal underpinnings, and living conditions to attract business flows. The result has been a leading position regionally and globally in several sectors, for example aviation, duty free shopping, airport management, entrepot port and port management, logistics, trading with developing and restrictive economies, retailing and tourism, shipping services, and maintenance. Equally the small and medium business sectors operating domestically find a conducive environment to conduct their business.

For foreign businesses, there are hardly any market access restrictions but the UAE maintains controls of ownership. To mitigate this necessary limitation since the local population is only a fraction of total population, free zones and exempted business locations were created. In effect except for solely onshore business, foreign businesses can own and operate under their sole control. Even for onshore business, the sponsorship system allows effective if not legal control by the foreign party. Due to this ownership constraint, the UAE receives lower scores in most global rankings than it would otherwise achieve. This may be formally justified but does not reflect practicalities. Influence of course remains a core matter reserved for locals. While the outstanding hospitality of the country and its inhabitants provides a false sense of importance to foreigners, true influence requires longstanding relationships and is always a derivative of such relationships with locals.

The legal framework is by most standards well equipped to handle the needs of the business community. Certain traditional constraints such as for agencies, immigration, and long-term resident issues as well as bureaucratic impediments or practices exist but are not much different than in many of the advanced emerging or even some developed economies. The corollary of a decent legal system is redress and dispute resolution. In this respect, the UAE has made another stride and allows businesses to choose the jurisdiction of the Dubai International Financial Centre (DIFC) and its courts, a leading court with some of the most prominent international judges adjudicating cases. Moreover, the DIFC has developed an arbitration center together with London that equally provides for professional and well-managed solutions to commercial disputes. This makes Dubai and the UAE unique in terms of enabling business conditions. In all practical aspects the UAE is an advanced emerging market.

At the same time, UAE sovereign wealth funds are among the largest single financial investors globally with an estimated more than US$1 trillion in foreign investments. This outward investment strategy has given the UAE access to global brands, technologies and corporations.

The potential of the UAE of joining the formal ranks of an emerging or advanced emerging economy is evidenced both by its business success and its rapidly developing framework conditions. Similar to Hong Kong, which developed from a "barren rock" (as British envoys in the early 1800s described Hong Kong), the UAE has created an enviable position starting from a traditional trading post and port surrounded by desert to become one of the most attractive cities to live in and transact business.

The reason why international investor acceptance has lagged lies in two factors: One, capital markets are relatively under-developed—the major criteria for becoming an emerging economy—and, two, influence and power, in essence the ability to make things happen and resolve issues, lie squarely with the leading local families and culturally related Arab entrepreneurs from the GCC and the region.

While stock market capitalization to GDP is similar to that of Germany, liquidity and free float is a fraction of Germany or the average developed world. Tradable instruments are limited and although new commodity and currency contracts are being introduced on the commodities exchanges, liquidity remains the core limitation. This liquidity gap is closely related to the strong retention of sole influence by local families. Control (anti-dilution) objectives, modest transparency and disclosure willingness, and the need for external recognition regardless of the substance are some of the barriers to increased global capital flows.

Family and clan issues and relationship histories prevent many rational commercial decisions. There is close to no appetite from leading entrepreneurs to relinquish any form of influence to outside shareholders. This results in some dysfunctional corporate governance and may demotivate international investors.

At the same time, large local entrepreneurs dominate the asset-based industries and invest with very high gearing. High skills businesses are rarely the domain of local families. Local banks also rather support the local asset based businesses very often well beyond prudent bank exposure. Therefore third party equity in more formal markets—private or public—becomes a distant second choice for funding. Debt markets are expensive and only economical for larger issues. Thus the debt market is dominated by sovereigns and government-owned entities. Some disasters with property related finance has not helped the debt market development.

The UAE has the businesses and the capital to develop a strong stock market—leaving aside the detrimental competition between Abu Dhabi and Dubai—if local families are willing to become smaller shareholders in bigger businesses and adopt international corporate governance standards. When this happens, the UAE could be at the forefront of a booming stock market—certainly it could figure among the global fifteen or twenty largest markets in particular if the UAE were to become the springboard for regional economies with less developed infrastructures and lower political stability. It is much a function of cultural and historic impediments that should be decreased by gradual action of the government on the legislative side and the institutions on the market side. Entrenched local protection does not serve international capital markets well and while the potential is there, the choice is entirely up to the ruling family, the administration, and the leading entrepreneurs in the UAE.

CONCLUSION

Overall, the wider MENA region is one of the most attractive investment destinations. Although the region shares a cultural affinity, its components are distinctly different. In particular the GCC economies are well advanced.

As with many other crises, the Arab Spring led all governments to institute reforms and increase their investment programs as well as investing in their people. Most economies and sovereign funds have announced large-scale projects, joint ventures, and development programs that will lead to the continued upgrading of the infrastructure and industry. Liberalization will equally figure on the agenda of many governments. This will, over the coming years, position the core Arab countries as very attractive investment destinations for corporates, possibly private equity.[13]

To become a preferred investor destination, public capital markets need to change. This will require a fundamental shift in corporate and family attitudes and commensurate regulations of the markets. Huge domestic investment alone cannot bring the GCC countries and some of its neighbors to the forefront for public market investors. Investing in the wider MENA region requires a different approach based on the prevalent cultural and business environment. Specifically, the cultural challenges are the meaning of time, the role of relationships with local partners, and often the dominance of connections over the law. This represents a significant opportunity for those with a deeper understanding of the region but also a considerable barrier for the uninitiated.

MENA stock markets are overall relatively small compared to the economic strength and potential of the region. This has to do with the narrowness of the markets and multiple practical rather than legal restrictions for investors. These markets demonstrate well the need to look at markets beyond overall economic growth potential and stock market attributes. At the moment they display a profound lack of liquidity, yet the opportunity available is probably the size of the Russia, Brazil, or India market or even a combination thereof.

Aside from a thriving economy, the government of Oman provides various incentives to entice foreign investment, including the freedom to repatriate capital and profits and the availability of soft loans in designated sectors. Investors have a number of business structures available to engage in commerce in Oman to suit their individual needs and can rely on a comprehensive regime for the protection of their intellectual property. The recent approval of Islamic financing in Oman and the ability for conventional banks to offer Islamic finance products is also expected to attract greater funds into Oman.

The UAE, with its hubs of Abu Dhabi and Dubai, sports an economy, investment position, and fiscal balance that is generally enviable. Overshadowed by reports on the arguably significant financial difficulties of government-related or connected property groups, the performance of major sectors of the economy and investment potential is underrated. If it were not for liquidity constraints and variety of stocks listed, the stock markets of the

UAE could be on the verge of strong performance. As an investment destination, the UAE deserves increasing attention.

NOTES

1. Government of Dubai, Dubai Economic Council, Migration, Labor Markets and Long Term Development Strategy for the UAE, Dubai (2011).
2. Kito de Boer and John M. Turner, "Beyond Oil: Reappraising the Gulf States," *McKinsey Quarterly* (January 2007).
3. The Arab World Competitiveness Report 2011–2012.
4. Tim Fox, Chief Economist Emirates NBD, GCC Economic Overview (October 2011).
5. Ministry of Information, Sultanate of Oman (undated). "Useful Information," www.omanet.om/english
6. Human Development, UNDP (November 4, 2010). "Five Arab Countries among Top Leaders in Long-Term Development Game," http://hdr.undp.org/en
7. Ellatari, L. *Sultanate of Oman—Major Business Sectors.* The Embassy of Switzerland (September 2011), pp. 1–2. Available online: http://www.osec.ch
8. Ministry of Legal Affairs. "The Basic Statute of the State," http://mola.gov.om
9. See, for example: Holdsworth, P. (10 January 2011). "Foreign Direct Investments in Oman Improved by 128 Percent," *Gulf Jobs Market.* Available online: http://news.gulfjobsmarket.com
10. A list of treaties, conventions and protocols to which Oman is a party (including texts) as well as a list of local laws enacted by Oman can be found on the website of the World Intellectual Property Organization (WIPO) at http://www .wipo.int
11. www.msn.gov.com.
12. Joseph A. Schumpeter, *History of Economic Analysis* (New York: Oxford University Press, 1954).
13. Special thanks to Osama Al Rahma, general manager of the Al Fardan Exchange and director of the Al Fardan Group for his continued education and comments on investing in the Arab region.

Pragmatic Investing in Developing and Unclassified Markets

Part Three adds a more practical perspective to the issues identified in the general discussion in Part One of country classifications by analytical service providers and Part Two, which is essentially an advocacy for developing market investing. This part describes on the ground considerations on what constitutes an investable market based on experience and perspectives outside stock market rules.

We start with a comprehensive overview of the true nature of business in China based on decades of experience in that country. Given the size and relative importance of China today and even more so in the future, this review provides investors in both public and private markets a solid foundation on how to approach and evaluate a China investment. It is hard to argue that China can be seen as one country or one economy, yet the overriding culture and business philosophy remains the same throughout China. Dealing effectively with the real China, or the elephant as the metaphor goes, will become increasingly important.

We review markets that are at differing stages of development. One of the more advanced economies of Latin America, Colombia, figures in the league of either the Next 11 or the CIVETS. Infamous for its drug business and crime rate, the country is underestimated from a reform and economic point of view. A review of the economy and some aspects of its markets shows why Colombia is considered one of the front-runners of Latin American opportunities.

Further down the traditional path, we look at one frontier country economy that has abundant resources and progresses despite the moderate level of overall economic development. The Republic of Mongolia does not typically figure on the radar screen of most investors, but the underlying economic potential warrants a closer look. Despite the limited liquidity of the stock market, Mongolia was leading the performance tables for a good part of 2010 and 2011 and is poised to see a broader set of companies coming to the market.

The Republic of Mongolia has been coming onto the radar of investors because of its resource endowment. Multiple large global players are vying for mining and extraction concessions and several companies have sought a listing. Looking at the economy in depth suggests that there may be a real frontier market in the making, albeit some years away.

Haiti, a country struck by tragedy but with committed financial aid exceeding its GDP, could emerge from the ashes in the longer term.

In Asia, we consider three economies that do not make the classification as frontier economy. These economies have tiny and largely illiquid stock markets, two of them less than one year old and with only five listings combined.

Myanmar has been a hot topic since last year when political reforms started. The growing confidence of the international community in a more conducive political system in Myanmar has rekindled interest in the existing but insignificant stock market. The Tokyo Stock Exchange and Daiwa Securities are committed to building and managing a modern infrastructure and there seems no shortage of interesting resource companies and investment opportunities in what is probably the last real frontier economy in Asia of size.

Lao PDR has a stock market with two securities, but globally was among the best-performing market in parts of 2011. The model, namely to establish a joint venture with an experienced market operator, the Korean Exchange, and launch with a leading security, a state-owned utility, and a bank, argues for some consideration despite failing many requirements of current market classifications.

Again in joint venture with the Korean Stock Exchange, the Kingdom of Cambodia sports a number of interesting listing candidates. The first IPO has been heavily oversubscribed and made headlines in terms of immediate performance.

These are markets to watch in the coming few years or for the pioneer investors to participate in, with a very long investment horizon.

Credit markets are the fuel of any economy and the foundation of investment. Developing economies depend on credit markets that function well and Central and Eastern Europe are no exception. A profound analysis of regional credit markets under the umbrella of EU institutions shows the consequences of unfettered expansion in fast-growing economies and economies in transition.

Eastern Europe is an example where rapid direct and market investment has caused a problem for local banks mostly invested by European banks and European investors. Investment flows through or led by commercial banks tend to increase prices and create an asset buzz but they do not provide the equity required for businesses to prosper. Recovery will be hard and long and economies will suffer, most notably the companies and individuals therein.

Many investors have sought to access markets through private, commercial, or industrial property and a review of the various legal conditions across a large number of already popular and emerging economies in Southeast Asia serves as a good reminder that property investments are not always the best way to participate in the growth of an economy. Most economies require advanced legal structures to acquire property and the risks are evident. Many private investors are well served to carefully consider their structures and adjust to the realities when governments will seek to normalize property holdings of foreigners.

On the subject of critical business issues, we emphasize a much overlooked subject, namely responsibility with respect to good governance and avoidance of corruption. Most investors and executives tend to see businesses in their local and regional environment and adjust to requirements on the ground. The international community, however, is increasingly rallying support for a global system of combating inappropriate behavior no matter where it occurs. The review of the UK Bribery Act, while unusual in a book on developing markets, highlights the very essence of international efforts. UK- or US-related companies can no longer rely on the relaxed attitude of local administrations, because they may now face accountability at home. This is a hard call to make in bandit economies that require some flexibility.

The reasoned review of the application of the UK Bribery Act to investments outside the United Kingdom and a comparison to the US legislation provides an excellent backdrop to what should and should not be considered acceptable behavior. Institutional and private investors will need to devote more resources to this issue or risk facing some unpleasant questions or consequences.

One of the critical ingredients in considering, making, or having an investment in developing economies is access to corporate information first and some degree of the reliability of such information second. We often forget that the aggregate information we receive is nothing but the accumulation of lower-level information.

The contribution on information aggregation is a most important subject when assessing company information, research and other external information. Looking at the sources of mistakes and flawed information flows, we must appreciate that not all we receive actually reflects realities. This is the daily challenge of any developing market investor.

From an operating viewpoint, harnessing marketing in less structured economic environments is a critical success factor. Companies need to get their products and services into the market and in many cases we observe very different patterns of marketing success in developing economies. Taking a practical yet relevant look at some of the successes and failures provides a backdrop to some of the pitfalls in bringing foreign products to market or launching domestic products in new markets.

On the subject of practical experience and on the lighter side of developing markets investing, the views of a pioneer investor and respected advisor describe the realities of investing and behavior in developing and bandit economies.

CHAPTER 11

Investments in China

Malcolm Riddell

Riddell Tsang

f you invest in China or a China-related opportunity, you probably find China challenging. But, if China is such a tough place, how come the Chinese are making so much money? One reason: Successful Chinese see the whole China Elephant, and you cannot. Here's what I mean.

SEEING THE WHOLE CHINA ELEPHANT

Consider the Chinese saying: 盲人摸象 "Blind men touch elephant." You probably remember the parable of the blind men and the elephant. A group of blind men heard that in the nearby forest there was an elephant, a beast they had never encountered. So, they hurried into the trees and found the elephant. Each grabbed a part of the elephant and yelled out a description of what he held, believing that that part described the whole elephant.

This parable applies to China investments. We could say that main parts of the China Elephant are:

- The tail, Chinese history, which sometimes wags the Elephant.
- The head, the political system, with the Chinese Communist Party the brains (as in the brains behind the operation).
- The heart, Chinese society/culture.
- The tusks, the Chinese military and its influence on economic and business policy.
- The legs, China's economic, financial, and business activities, and their indicators.

Successful Chinese investors integrate all the parts—the whole China Elephant—into their investment decisions. And that is what you should do, too.

When you find an investment in China (or any frontier or emerging market, for that matter), you apply, by habit or conviction, the approach that worked so well in developed markets: Focus on the economic, financial, and business activities, and their indicators—that is, focus on the legs. But with China, unless you have long experience, you lack the context you naturally have about developed countries. You are just like the blind man in the parable. You grab the China Elephant's legs, and you believe that you understand the whole beast. Next thing you know, you're saying what a tough place China is.

The Whole Elephant: Now You See It . . .

Compare this to investing in developed markets. If you are from a developed country, and you are investing in your own country or another developed country, you probably have—and may not even be aware that you have—a set of internal, integrated assumptions about developed countries that take into account the tusks, tail, head, and heart, as well as the legs. Because of this you can focus on just the economic, financial, and business activities, and their indicators—the legs of the investment—and still predict which way the elephant is going to walk on those legs, how fast, and what might affect its progress. You see the whole elephant.

Let's say, for example, you find a first investment in Germany (and you're not German). In evaluating that investment, you bring along your set of assumptions based on your experience in your own and perhaps other developed countries. You can assume, without much consideration, that Germany has, to name just a few representative factors:

- Politically stability.
- Political leadership elected by popular vote.
- Rule of law and a functioning court system.
- Laws made by an elected body.
- A perhaps ponderous, but not corrupt, independent bureaucracy.
- Generally well-managed major businesses.
- Agreed standards for conducting business that allow for some national differences.
- Reliable data.
- A military that subordinates itself to civilian control and does not meddle in government.

- Shared history, cultural underpinnings, and ways of thinking, deriving from as far back as ancient times (unless, of course, you are a Japanese investor).

Things are different, but manageably different. Your evaluation has a context that allows you to see how the legs connect to the whole German Elephant without really thinking about it. In other words, you see, perhaps just in outline, the whole German elephant.

. . . Now You Don't

Then, you find a first opportunity in China or one influenced by China. This could be:

- Direct China investment: for example, a stake in a company; a Sino-foreign joint venture in China; a purchase of Chinese securities.
- China-related investment: for example, how Chinese demand affects commodities prices; Chinese competition for the purchases of raw materials and foreign companies.
- China-influenced investment: for example, the impact of Chinese trade on the economy of a country in South America; Chinese financing of an infrastructure project in Africa.

Whichever kind the investment is, where will you focus your evaluation? Probably still on the legs. But, if Germany is manageably different, China is just different. And, you know it. So, you may get a lot of opinions to help you understand China better:

- You read about China's currency in the *Wall Street Journal* and *Foreign Affairs*.
- You get research from Goldman Sachs about the impact of China's aging population on long-term growth.
- Your team in Shanghai gives you its views about how much copper China will use in the next three months and why you should go short/long.
- You meet with a vice minister in Beijing who tells you how China's Five Year Plan is going to restructure the Chinese economy by increasing consumption.
- You run into a friend from another firm at the Cathay Pacific Lounge in Hong Kong, and he tells you what's really happening in China's banking sector.

But, these are still opinions about just the legs, and so is your approach. Somehow, though, you might feel that some big things are missing from your evaluation. And you'd be right. You aren't seeing the whole China Elephant. Let me illustrate.

Yesterday, I received an e-mail from an analyst at a hedge fund. He noted that the Chinese Premier had publicly announced a GDP target of 7.5 percent for this year, 2012. He sent along a number of charts he had created that showed a slowdown: monthly air-conditioner production, earth excavator sales, steel production versus GDP, and so on—all well done (within the limits of Chinese data reliability) and useful. Excellent descriptions of the China Elephant's right front leg, the economic indicators. He then asked: What do you predict?

We set a time to meet to talk in detail. But in the meantime, I wrote back briefly the reasons why I believed that China would exceed the stated target:

"First, China likes to exceed expectations. And it usually shoots past its announced target. Under-promise—over-deliver.

"Second, a major factor in local government officials' promotions is strong local GDP. These officials have proven incredibly ingenious and ruthless (as in taking farmers' land with no or little compensation and selling it to developers to fill local coffers and their own pockets) in exceeding Central Government targets, even when the Central Government tries to rein them in."

"Finally, President Hu Jintao leaves office this year. He doesn't want to go out as the guy who ran the Chinese economy into a ditch—some legacy. The government will use its many levers—including easing credit and ramping up investment—to keep GDP acceptably high. And, thus, kick the can down the road."

This added the China elephant's head and the brains inside—the political drivers—to the right front leg. When we meet we will also discuss the tail, a couple of other legs, and maybe one of the tusks. Then, we will tie these together to get a better idea of just which direction this elephant will likely take. In this way, the analyst will, I trust, develop a better analysis based on the whole China elephant, not just on any one or two of its legs. And, that analysis should result in better investment decisions.

CHINA INVESTING, CHINESE-STYLE

Successful Chinese investors make money because they have the same kind of natural internal, integrated assumptions about China that you have about your own country, as well as, but to a lesser degree, other developed countries—they see the whole China elephant. And, that's what you have to begin to do. Without devoting your career to the pursuit, where do you begin?

You might consult books about China business. A lot of the books may counsel you to read things like Confucius' *Analects* and to master the *36 Stratagems*. But telling you to read the *Analects* to understand the Chinese is like telling a Chinese to read the Bible to understand the United States and Europe. Likewise, mastering the *36 Stratagems*, with admonitions such as "loot a burning house" and "toss out a brick to attract a piece of jade," will not give you an advantage—any more than it will for a Chinese to master American commonplaces (the ones I know), such as "walk softly but carry a big stick" or "a bird in the hand is worth two in the bush."

More useful is to look more closely at the parts of the China Elephant themselves:

- History—the tail: how Chinese history influences today's business.
- Politics/policy—the head and the brains: how the Chinese Communist Party runs business from the shadows.
- Economics/finance/business—the legs: how state capitalism controls the China economy and business.
- Society/culture—the heart: how Chinese society and culture affects analysis and getting deals done.
- Military—the tusks: how the Chinese military influences economic and business issues.

If you develop a broad, basic knowledge of these parts, then learn to understand how they work together, you will be able to identify opportunities earlier and evaluate them better than other investors. Here are some thoughts on how each of these parts functions, how each might affect investment in China, and finally how to integrate all the parts to see the whole China Elephant.

History—The Tail: How Chinese History Influences Today's Business

History is the China Elephant's tail, and it sometimes wags the beast. How often do the events of 1840s in your country influence your business decisions today? Not much, I would guess. But, for the Chinese, the 1840s might as well be yesterday.

Chinese educators, the media, and the government (whenever it requires a burst of nationalism) repeat often the history of China's "Century of Humiliation." The "Century" began with China's defeat in 1842 in the First

Opium War, followed by other wars of aggression, and the splitting of China into "Spheres of Influence," all at the hands of Western nations and Japan. The "Century" ended with victory of the Chinese Communist Party. As Mao Zedong proclaimed upon the founding of the People's Republic of China on October 1, 1949, "China has stood up." The Party doesn't let anyone forget this, either.

What does this have to do with business and investment? Here's an example. China long required, albeit informally, that in addition to a foreign company's equity investment, it must also supply its technology for free. Several years ago, when I was negotiating with several Chinese state-owned enterprises (SOEs) on behalf of a western financial services firm to create a new joint venture insurance company, I made a pro forma objection about this practice to my Chinese counter party, the head of a major Chinese financial services group. Urbane and worldly, he smiled and told me that free technology was the "price of admission."

Later, to a senior member of the negotiating team of another Chinese financial services group, who had a Western doctorate in economics and had served as a World Bank economist, I made the same objection. At which point, he turned beet red, and stammered, "You owe China that technology for the Century of Humiliation that you caused." A "Century," by the way, that had ended more than 50 years earlier.

Had I not had some understanding of Chinese history I wouldn't have had a clue what he was talking about. But, because I did, I was able over time to persuade him that perhaps a token technology transfer might equally soothe the hurt feelings of the Chinese people. He and his team members finally agreed, and we did the deal with their group.

The China Elephant doesn't forget. History plays a big part in the internal assumptions held by successful Chinese investors. And the impact of China's modern history should be one of the China Elephant's limbs that you likewise don't forget when evaluating investment opportunities.

Politics/Policy—The Head and the Brains: How the Chinese Communist Party Runs Business from the Shadows

The China Elephant's head contains several political drivers that shape and implement policies affecting business and investment. The influence of these drivers is immense. Under Mao's socialism, politics and the economy were one. With the reforms of Deng Xiaoping, socialism gave way to "socialism with Chinese characteristics" and an economic boom. In past 20 years, Deng's reforms have stalled and an increasingly entrenched state capitalism has emerged. Today, as the term *state capitalism* implies, the state controls much economic activity. But, is it really the state in control?

The challenge in evaluating an investment is figuring out which political driver is really in the driver's seat. In theory the Chinese government is made up of the state, the Chinese Communist Party, and the People's Liberation Army (more about the army later). Figure 11.1 illustrates this.

The diagram in Figure 11.1 is embodied in Hu Jintao, China's current leader. He is president (state), chairman of the Communist Party (party), and chairman of the Central Military Commission (army).

In investment, as in business, we usually focus our attention on the state. We pore over the state's latest Five Year Plan to get a sense of where opportunities might arise; we consider which foreign investments the state declares encouraged, permitted, restricted, or prohibited; we analyze new regulations for changes that might increase opportunities or risks. And all this is important.

But, the real driver and the one to watch is the all-pervasive Chinese Communist Party, the brains in the Elephant's head.

Within the Party, the Standing Committee of the Politburo, currently with nine members, is the ruling body of China. It makes all major decisions. The members are "elected" but in fact come to power through horse-trading between factions. The Standing Committee's process for coming to decisions is secret and impossible to penetrate. It rules the government, the people, and the economy from the shadows.

You can, however, discern its policies and intentions by watching how the Party members carry out their diverse posts—and, diverse as these posts are—by following the ebb and flow of factional politics within the Party.

The Central Organization Department and Appointments   All major appointments are made by the Party's personnel bureau, the Central Organization Department. According to Richard McGregor, "The best way to get sense of the dimension of the department's job is to conjure up an imaginary parallel body in Washington. A similar department in the United States would oversee the appointment of the:

- entire US cabinet,
- governors and their deputies,

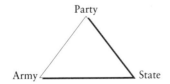

FIGURE 11.1   China's Troika

- mayors of major cities,
- heads of all federal regulatory agencies,
- chief executives of GE, ExxonMobil, Wal-Mart, and about 50 of the remaining largest US companies,
- justices on the Supreme Court,
- editors of the *New York Times*, the *Washington Post*, and the *Wall Street Journal*,
- bosses of the TV networks and cable stations,
- presidents of Yale and Harvard and other big universities, and
- heads of think-tanks like the Brookings Institution and the Heritage Foundation."[1]

The Party runs everything. So when you are evaluating investments, you must watch what the state says and does, but to understand the policies driving the state, watch the Party.

Factional Rivalry in the Party Monolith   You also have to follow factional politics within the Party. For all its attempts to appear otherwise, the Party is not a monolith of leaders with similar backgrounds, agendas, and outlooks. Instead, the leaders and high-ranking members are constituents of one or more of the Party's many factions. These factions compete for power and influence somewhat in the way political parties do in developed countries. Beyond struggling for power, they also provide checks and balances on each other. No one faction wins all the time or even has a clear victory. Decisions result from compromise and deal making.

For simplicity's sake (and this is very simple), let's say China has only two principal factions: the reform faction and the leftist faction.

The reform faction, headed by the current leader, Hu Jintao, has had the upper hand for 30 years. Since Deng Xiaoping effectively started it in 1978, the reform faction has focused on China's economic growth, stability, and harmony. The reform faction takes credit for China's spectacular economic growth and gets the blame for the problems growth has created, such as income/wealth inequality, the damaged environment, and the like.

The leftist faction seeks to cleave more closely to original Chinese communist doctrine and Mao Zedong principles. It would sacrifice economic growth for more equal distribution of wealth and a more egalitarian society. It advocates central economic planning and would concentrate even more greatly the means of production in government hands. And, it would focus the people's will on building the country as a whole populace rather than individually, all while submitting happily to Party rule.

For some time now, the leftist faction has been pulled even farther left by the New Left faction. This is very much like the gravitational pull that the Republican party in the United States has felt from the Tea Party movement.

By seeing what the New Left is for and against, you can get a sharper feel for the battle lines between the factions, as shown in Table 11.1.

All this is not to say that the reformers are the good guys, working toward open markets, free trade, and democracy. Quite the contrary—the reform faction created a state-capitalist economic system and has overseen increasingly repressive measures to quell dissent. But, compared to the leftist faction, the reformers are business friendly, although not necessarily foreign business and investment friendly.

Watching and understanding how the tide shifts between these factions should inform every China investment decision. And, deal making as well, as I learned a few years ago.

The Party Kills My Deal   I was negotiating a joint venture with a state-owned enterprise on behalf of a leading foreign insurance company. We had negotiated for a couple of months directly with the president and were days away from a final agreement. Documents were already being drafted. We said our goodbyes on a Friday. On the following Monday, when we arrived to finish negotiating a few details, we found that the president, with whom we had been negotiating, had been replaced.

The new president told us that the terms we had agreed on were entirely unacceptable. And, he placed before us a new term sheet. My comment on the term sheet: "Back to the future. In this case, the 1980s." The deal fell apart.

TABLE 11.1   Position of the New Left

Against	For
Reformers: Deng Xiaoping, Jiang Zemin, Hu Jintao	Socialism and Maoist thought
Capitalism	Strong rule by the CCP
Democracy	Economic central planning and control
Private enterprise	State ownership of business
Corruption	Egalitarianism
Wealth and income inequality	Wealth and income equality
Focus on urban instead of rural areas	Sharing Chinese recent wealth with all citizens, not just the elites
Lack of a social safety net for every citizen	Focus on rural areas
Too much foreign participation and investment in the Chinese economy	"Iron Rice Bowl"
Compromise in international relations	Limiting foreign participation and investment in the Chinese economy
	Nationalism

I had already made friends with the managers who remained. I asked them quietly what had happened. They told me that the secretary of the SOE's Party Committee had suddenly and unexpectedly become incensed at the "favorable" terms the president had given us. So incensed, in fact, that the secretary had persuaded the Party Committee to have the president fired.

I knew that all SOEs and now many private companies must have Committees. Quite often they are the ones really controlling the businesses, albeit again in the shadows. What surprised me is that former president, who was a member of the SOE's Party Committee as well as the Chinese Communist Party, had assured me that everyone on the committee, including the secretary, was following the negotiations and approved.

Was he out of the loop or just jollying us along? More likely he was a member of a reform faction and the party secretary a member of a leftist faction; the party secretary had bided his time, then used our nearly done deal to denounce the president and replace him with someone from his own faction. Such is Chinese factional politics.

Whether in the nitty-gritty of deal making or the evaluation of an investment, the Party is there, in the shadows. But, like an elaborate shell game, China encourages us to try to guess which shell the pea that is the state is under—while making us ignore that the real pea, the party, is not even on the table.

Economics/Finance/Business—The Legs: How China State Capitalism Controls the Economy

China calls its economic system Socialism with Chinese Characteristics. The rest of the world has begun to call it state capitalism. I go with the rest of the world. But, whatever the name, the state, through party policy, has, over the past 30 years, exerted increasing control of China's capital and means of production—the legs of the China Elephant.

Just as when looking at Chinese politics, we often focus more on the state rather than the Party, in economics we look at discrete bodies of information and miss how the underlying system of state capitalism shapes and even distorts the economy as a whole. And, just as with politics we should watch the Party to understand the state, with economics, finance, and business we should understand the nature of the China's state capitalism in evaluating investments.

During the 1980s, China's leaders did encourage entrepreneurship and development of the private sector, especially in rural areas. But, in the 1990s, with the advent of new leadership, these policies were reversed in favor of heavy investment in coastal cities, a bias toward massive state-connected (but not necessarily directly state-owned) enterprises and stronger, not weaker, state control of the economy and state-owned enterprises (SOEs) and state-controlled companies.

China State Capitalism's Long Reach   The true extent of this control is difficult to determine. Many companies classified as non-state are, in fact, still substantially owned or controlled by the Chinese government. For example, when SOEs go public in China, most are then reclassified as non-state companies. But, in fact, the state retains ownership and control of many of these, as well as many major non-public, non-state companies, through a convoluted network of cross-shareholdings. This means that when you are evaluating an investment in a private or non-state company, you have to look more deeply to understand just who is in charge.

Moreover, China's financial system is geared to support Chinese SOEs and state-controlled companies—they have priority in getting financing, with little left over for private companies. In a recent credit tightening, private companies were forced to turn to the curb markets for loans, with interest rates reaching as high as 120 percent a year. Many went out of business.

If you are a successful private company in a business the state wants to control, you could find the state as your competitor, as the *New York Times* reported in "Entrepreneur's Rival in China: The State." (December 7, 2011). Here, a manager at Cathy Industrial Biotech stole the company's secrets about an innovative process for "advanced nylon ingredients for use in lubricants, diabetes drugs and other 21st-century marvels," and started his own competing company. The twist—his new company, Hilead, was set up with the help of the state-run Chinese Academy of Sciences. And because the project fit national and local government policy goals, Hilead received a $300 million loan from the Central Government's China Development Bank. The loan came after the company won the approval of the party secretary of Shandong Province, one of the country's highest-ranking public officials.

According to Liu Xiucai, Cathay's founder and chief executive, "We created a great product and they [the state] stole it." And because of this, Cathay's plans to go public are on hold, and even the company's survival is in doubt.

So, just as you have to figure out whether the private company you are evaluating is truly private, and if it is, whether it can count on getting financing when it needs it, you must also determine whether top management has political connections sufficiently robust to protect it from the state.

"China Inc." versus the Messy Reality   China state capitalism has been described (but not using that appellation) as "China Inc." by noted China expert Robert Kuhn. He writes:

Because the Chinese government operates like "China Inc.," it oversees the activities of state-owned enterprises and even modulates private companies (which must always conform with policy) as well as maintains regulatory functions. All high-level officials, at central and local levels, and all senior executives of major state-owned enterprises are selected by the Party's Organization Department—and they are judged by their track record in achieving the objectives of the country's leaders. (For example, since leaders want a sustainable economy, governors are judged by how well they increase their province's ratio of GDP per unit of energy.) As such, to the degree that your company can advance the careers of senior officials or executives, your company can be favored.

("Designing a China Business Framework,"
on ChiefExecutive.net)

In fact, China state capitalism, like the Party itself, is not a monolith. It is messy, with conflicts, rivalries, and factional warfare between ministries, between the central government and local governments, between all governments and SOEs, just to mentions a few permutations. China's Premier Wen Jiabao summed up this up best:

China has achieved enormous progress and its development, winning acclaim around the world, yet I was one of the first ones to argue that our economic development still lacks balance, coordination, and sustainability.

Among the factors that pose obstacles to evaluating an investment, this messiness is the most difficult to penetrate. Yet, it is among the most important. No evaluation can be valid unless it situates and grounds an investment, as best it can, within this tangled and opaque system.

Society/Culture—The Heart: How Chinese Society/Culture Affects Analysis and Getting Deals Done

The heart of the China Elephant, like the human heart, has two sides: society and culture. These two are probably the most overlooked in evaluating investments. Yet, the heart might be the real force, as you will see, underlying any given investment.

As a society, the Chinese are a patient people—until they are provoked beyond endurance. Then, they get angry. And, when they get angry enough, dynasties and regimes fall. The Chinese Communist Party understands this well. The anger of the Chinese people brought it to power—and anger, they also understand, can topple it.

In Chinese society today, there are a lot of unhappy people. Farmers are angry that developers and corrupt officials are stealing their land. Farmers are also angry that China's economic boom made the urbanites rich while they remain poor. Urbanites are angry that many don't have decent housing or cannot afford to buy an apartment. Middle-class citizens are angry when polluting factories try to locate in their neighborhoods. Rural workers in the cities are angry they don't get social benefits and sometimes don't get paid. Both farmers and middle-class urbanites are angry as they watch the children of past and present Party officials, the princelings, gain wealth and position on nothing more than their connections. They are angry too that some officials profit from their positions through corruption in general and sometimes outright theft of public monies.

The list could go on. According to some estimates, these angry Chinese stage upward of 200,000 protests, demonstrations, and riots each year. The government response is sometimes to try to remedy the problem, but more often to quell the disturbances by force.

Anger Can Drive Policy and Create Investment Opportunities Focusing on investments, consider just two of these problems. First, farmers are angry because as just mentioned, developers and corrupt officials are stealing their land for residential, commercial, and industrial projects. Some reports say that as a result China now has 50 million landless farmers. China's leaders have pledged to end this practice. If they do, and if local government officials actually follow through (the big *if*), then real estate development and the profits from development will be affected. Companies that already own major properties and developers that have substantial land banks may see the value of their holdings and their enterprises increase as the supply of land decreases. Other developers may face higher land costs and possibly lower profits on their projects. Either case creates investment opportunities.

The second problem is the lack of affordable housing. To address this, the government instituted a program to build 36 million units of affordable housing between 2011 and 2015. The Party calls this a "solemn commitment" to the Chinese people. If this program is successful, then overall residential real estate prices should go down, with a corresponding effect on developers' profits. It will also affect China's demand for building materials, likely increasing their prices worldwide. And if, for example, each unit has a refrigerator, then Chinese white goods companies' profits will probably rise, as will demand for key materials such as copper, and worldwide prices for the metal will rise. But, the program is already running into problems. So, failure to meet the goal of 36 million units will have a corresponding and opposite effect. Either way, there will be an impact on investments in the relevant sectors.

Culture: The Overlooked Factor If societal concerns and how the Chinese government addresses them affect China and China-related investors directly, the impact of culture is more subtle but no less important.

Can you describe your country's culture with anything approaching an all-encompassing certainty? I cannot do that for the United States. And I cannot do that for China. And I don't believe many Chinese can, either. But, you can detect broad themes that do enter into the evaluation of investments. Here are two examples.

First, a hedge fund was considering an investment that depended on the pace of urbanization in China and asked me for an analysis. During our discussions, we examined urbanization from what seemed to be every angle. But, one factor didn't fit and kept coming up. China still has substantial excess rural population that has not yet moved to higher-paying jobs in factories in the cities; even so, urban wages are going up substantially. This shouldn't be happening—something called the Lewis Curve says this shouldn't be happening. Urban wages should not be going up until there are no more excess rural workers to move to the city to work. Simple supply and demand.

Then, as an analysts and I were discussing this, it dawned on us. This wasn't a matter of economics, of excess labor seeking more productive and higher paying employment—this was cultural. For a couple of thousand years, close-knit Chinese farming families have fed every member, productive or not, with whatever was available, feast or famine. These excess rural workers weren't going to the factories because they didn't want to, and they didn't have to. Where the economists saw excess labor, the analyst and I saw a long tradition of rural culture that explained the paradox. The economists had not figured in the cultural element in calculating excess rural labor, and so rising urban wages now made sense.

Second, after several months of tough negotiations I had reached an agreement for my client, a British insurer, to enter into a joint venture with a major Taiwanese industrial group to form a new life insurance company in Taiwan. I had drafted the joint venture agreement, and all concurred that the agreement captured the terms agreed to by both sides. But the Taiwan Group did not sign.

I dogged the Taiwan Group's negotiating team, asking what the problem was and whether there were still changes to be made. They could not or would not tell me why they were uncomfortable or what the problems were. Each day, they said they would sign; each day they didn't.

After a couple weeks of this, I was sitting in my office late one night. Taiwan's deadline for new life insurance company applications was coming up soon. There was one chance a year to apply, and we were going to miss it. Then I had a thought.

I knew that Chinese have traditionally been fond of slogans that we in the West consider banal or even corny. But the Chinese take them very seriously. With this in mind, I went through the joint venture agreement. At the start of each section, I laid out principles applicable to each. These principles included: "We will always work for our mutual good." "We will never knowingly take advantage of each other." "We are entering into this joint venture to make money." "We will work tirelessly to make our new company a success."

The next morning I presented the revised joint venture agreement to the leaders of the Taiwan Group. They signed it before the end of the day.

I have often told clients that, for Chinese, the real negotiations begin after the contract is signed. That was no exception for the new insurance joint venture. But later, when issues did arise between the parties, they were resolved more often by relying on the non-binding principles derived from Chinese culture—the heart—that guided their relationship than on the letter of the contract.

When you are evaluating an investment in China and some things just don't seem to make sense, take a step back, and see if you might have overlooked societal and cultural factors—China's heart. It's easy to do.

Military—The Tusks: How the Chinese Military Influences Economic and Business Issues

That the military could be a factor in evaluating an investment seems strange to those from countries where the military is firmly under civilian control. The People's Liberation Army, as the winner of a civil war in the not so distant past, still plays a role in shaping Chinese policy, although that role has diminished over time. For example, there is no longer anyone from the military on the Standing Committee of the Politburo.

That said, the Army remains a source of enormous political power. In his later years, after resigning all his other posts, Deng Xiaoping retained only the chairmanship of the Central Military Commission, the ultimate military position. After the current leader, Hu Jintao, became president and chairman of the Communist Party, he had to wait two years before becoming chairman—his predecessor, Jiang Zeming, wouldn't give up the position. And, in the upcoming 2012 leadership transition, there is much speculation about how long Hu Jintao will wait before reluctantly handing over the chairmanship to China's new leader. From this, you can see why the diagram of the Chinese government gave the army equal weight with the Party and the state.

In recent years, the army has become increasingly bellicose. And, because the army is a player in factional struggles, it has, as part of the usual haggling, won a measure of autonomy in developing strategies and taking actions, many of which China's neighbors find threatening. These strategies and actions can disrupt other more benign diplomatic and economic policies, and can unexpectedly affect China and China-related investments. To expect the unexpected, watch the China Elephant's tusks. Here's an example.

Not long ago a hedge fund, very active in Australia, asked me what would most likely disrupt China's purchase of Australian natural resources output and investment in resources companies. I told them they should focus on the tusks.

The Chinese military has developed a two-part Far Sea Strategy:

Part One: Control the East China Sea and the resource-rich South China Sea.

Part Two: Extend control to the Second Island Chain, driving the United States out of the Western Pacific.

This strategy is being implemented at the same time polls show that Aussies are increasingly wary of a potential China military threat against them and are worried that they are making a potential enemy stronger by selling China their natural resources. The Australian government is throwing in directly with the United States and also with Japan, Korea, and ASEAN to contain China's military.

If China continues to escalate military activity in the South China Sea, as its current strategy calls for, it will no doubt one day lead to a "hot" encounter. This will very likely turn Australian public opinion and government policy sharply against supplying China with Australian resources and against Chinese investment in Chinese Australian resources companies.

Like so much else in Chinese politics and policy, the army exerts influence mostly in the shadows. Often that influence can be discerned only from overt actions. But, by monitoring what key generals and admirals write and which Party leaders they are close to, you can nonetheless make reasonable predictions about what the army is planning and what impact that might have on your investment if carried out.

THE WHOLE ELEPHANT: HOW TO EVALUATE A CHINA INVESTMENT

Now that we have examined all the parts, here is a final example to illustrate how to see the whole China Elephant in evaluating an investment opportunity.

A hedge fund called and said that it was considering an investment in a US company that was acquiring another US company. The deal had to be approved by the United States, the European Union, and China. The US and EU had given their approval. The fund's question: What were the chances that China would block the deal?

Why this special concern? In January 2010, the United States announced a major arms sale to Taiwan. China protested as usual, but with a twist— this time it announced that it would punish not just the US government but also the US companies that sold the arms. One of the companies in the deal the hedge fund was evaluating is one of the companies that had sold arms to Taiwan. Would China kill the deal in retaliation?

This was my analysis.

The Tail—History

The Chinese civil war (1927–1949) was fought between the Communists and the Nationalists. When the Communists won in 1949, the Nationalists fled to the Chinese island province, Taiwan. China wants Taiwan back. But, the United States has been supporting Taiwan militarily since the beginning of the Korean War. This has been a consistent source of tension between the United States and China.

With past arms sales, China had always dialed up the rhetoric and temporarily cooled official relations. But, it had not in any way punished US companies' business in or with China.

The Head—Politics/Policy and the Tusks—the Army

No one in the state, the Party, or the army approves of the United States' selling arms to Taiwan. But, as with everything in Chinese politics and policy, you have to look at the factions.

The reform faction, with its focus on China's economic growth and stability, would protest the arms sales, but not go so far as disrupting China's foreign business relations. The hardliners of the leftist faction and the army would take a much tougher stance regarding Taiwan in every way, regardless of economic consequences. The question, then: Would the leftists and the army push so hard to punish US companies for selling arms to Taiwan that they would overcome the reformers' opposition? I didn't think so. The hardliners might go to the wall about regaining Taiwan, but they wouldn't for this issue. Too little gain, too much to give to the reformers in exchange.

Then I at looked at the entity that would make the actual decision to approve the deal or not, the Anti-Monopoly Bureau of the Ministry of

Commerce. I examined the actions, philosophy, factional ties, and attitudes of China's Minister of Commerce Chen Deming and, with more difficulty, of the Anti-Monopoly Bureau Director General Shang Ming. Both are reformers and, just as importantly, effective and professional in their work. I couldn't see either bowing easily to political pressures,

I also read comments from both foreign and Chinese law firms and others. I found general agreement that the bureau appears committed to attaining a reputation for international best practices and is on its way to doing so. Allowing political considerations to interfere with an impartial decision is not on the bureau's agenda.

But, what if I were wrong, and the bureau could be pressured? I calculated that cooler heads in the Chinese leadership would see that, even if the bureau were forced to withhold approval, it could not give punishment for the arms sales to Taiwan as its reason. Otherwise, it would lose all credibility as fair arbiter of antitrust cases on merits (something I felt the controlling reform faction would never permit). Since a punishment that cannot be clearly announced is no deterrent to future sales, killing the deal would ultimately serve no political purpose. And, thus, it would not be worth the political capital.

Finally, what about the initial threat to punish the arms sellers themselves? I interpreted it as either a compromise with the leftist faction and the army or the reaction of an overly incensed vice minister, probably a member of the hard line faction, speaking without authority.

The Heart—Society/Culture

More worrisome was the reaction of the Chinese people if the government didn't make good on its threat. The government often uses all its resources to whip up the population into a nationalistic fervor. And, US interference in China's attempts to reunify with its Taiwanese brethren is a hot button issue.

I reviewed other threats of various kinds and their outcomes with the populace. Some were indeed enforced, but many weren't. And, after checking in on China's more militant netizens, I found that those stillborn threats hadn't gained enough notice or traction to concern the government. So, not much to worry about if this threat just died quietly, too.

The Legs—Economy/Finance/Business

Lastly, for completeness, I looked into whether or not China had punished any of the companies that had sold arms to Taiwan in ways that could be done openly and with effect.

My research showed that not only was there no discernible impact, but the biggest offender had since made many billions of dollars in sales to China, all with government approval. And, in this case, because China had not signed the relevant WTO agreement, it could have stopped all these purchases—and announced that the reason was the arms sales, without repercussions to its reputation.

Taking all these into consideration, the whole China Elephant, I predicted that China would not kill the acquisition. And, I made my recommendation, with a very rare confidence of 95 percent, that the hedge fund should go ahead with its planned investment. It did, and not long afterwards, China approved the deal.

CONCLUSION

Tusks, hearts, heads, brains, tails, legs, whole elephants—all far from the normal vocabulary of investment. When we begin weaving in history, politics, society, culture, and even the military along with the usual economic, financial, and business consideration to arrive at an investment decision, it becomes counterintuitive, perhaps even a little nonsensical. And, if you are investing in a country where you already have a set of internal, integrated assumptions about the market, then it may not be necessary.

As soon as you consider investing in China, though, these are necessary. All these factors go into a successful Chinese investor's decision. If they aren't part of yours, and you just analyze the usual economic, financial, and business inputs, then you will be like the blind man grabbing the elephant's leg and believing you understand the whole beast.

So, whether you adopt the metaphor of the whole China Elephant and its constituent parts, or just the concepts it represents, you will in either case be better prepared to make better China investment decisions.

Or, to extend the metaphor, when you see the whole China Elephant, you will have an elephant rifle to blast it with.

NOTE

1. McGregor, Richard, *The Party: The Secret World of China's Communist Rulers* (HarperCollins e-books. Kindle Edition, June 2006).

CHAPTER 12

The Genesis of Markets: Colombia, Mongolia, and Haiti

Many largely unknown markets have potential. Three very different and starkly contrasting examples are discussed here. Colombia, an economy formerly known for its role in the drug trade, is today part of the next wave of South America investment candidates and already on its way to becoming part of emerging markets investment portfolios.

The Republic of Mongolia, until recently not known at all, had a spectacular rise in its stock market during 2010 and 2011 mainly driven by resource exploration companies. Abundant reserves of important commodities have put this country firmly on the map for growing investment, but stability in development is yet a step away. The genesis of the stock market in 1991, namely privatization of state-owned companies into the hands of the population, is an interesting approach to launching a stock market.

Haiti does not even have a stock market and suffered a tragic natural disaster that all but destroyed its economy. Multilateral aid and international support gave this country a new lease on life and with this new start, a small but remarkable player could emerge at the door step of the United States.

These three countries represent the 5- to 10-, 10- to 15-, and 20- to 30-year horizon for emerging market investors. They serve as examples of the genesis of future markets to watch.

COLOMBIA: FROM DRUGS TO INVESTMENT DESTINATION

Paul Stewart

This review of Colombia illustrates how a country notorious for its armed conflict has evolved into a favorable location for investors to seek lucrative business opportunities. Investors the world over, but most notably from

Canada, the United States, and Spain have already acquired assets in a country that is considered part of a new block of emerging markets: CIVETS (Colombia, Indonesia, Vietnam, Egypt, Turkey, and South Africa) predicted by Robert Ward, director of global forecasting for the Economist Intelligence Unit in 2009 to rise in economic prominence over the coming decades.

To the uninformed, Colombia conjures images of drug cartels, terrorist attacks, kidnapping, and guerrillas, perceptions that are all too often reinforced within the media. However, these undesirable elements are more symptoms of Colombia's past than indications of its future. In reality, peace settlements with FARC after decades of internal fighting have helped create relative stability that can be built on. And now, Colombia is on the cusp of achieving its full economic potential (see Figure 12.1A).

Colombia is already the fourth largest economy in Latin America after Brazil, Mexico, and Argentina, with strong inflows of foreign direct investment (FDI) that has increased over 500 percent in the past decade from US$2 billion in 2002 to US$13 billion in 2011, of which approximately 85 percent was invested in mining and energy. The increase in FDI has not been all positive; the country's currency, the peso, has appreciated by 12 percent against the dollar only in 2011, even as the central bank has purchased US$20 million within the currency market to slow its rise. Inflation remains one of the government's key economic concerns. The central bank has begun raising rates to 5.25 percent due to the decrease in global commodity prices and the economic weakness in China. Government also persuaded the central bank to hold rates steady through the rest of the 2012. Hence, inflation forecast for this year is around 2 to 4 percent.

With the second largest population in South America (after Brazil), with its rich endowment of natural resources such as oil, natural gas, titanium, copper, and coal and with more than 6.5 million hectares for agricultural development, global-investment industry interest is rising.

In 2004, during Álvaro Uribe's presidency, the government applied a more assertive military policy in the attempt to thwart the FARC and other militant groups. The offensive, supported in part by aid from the United States, improved several security indicators, including kidnappings, which decreased from 3,700 in 2000 to 172 in 2009. The overall reduction (Figure 12.1B) of violence has paved a path toward increased internal travel and tourism, which has helped improve the distribution of wealth to some of Colombia's poorest citizens. The middle class has increased and become wealthier, according to the World Bank, and Colombia's GDP per capita has increased 180 percent in the past six years to US$9,800.

The new investment policies of President Juan Manuel Santos, coupled with the country's ratings upgrade from Standard & Poor's, Moody's, and

(A) Economic Growth in Percent

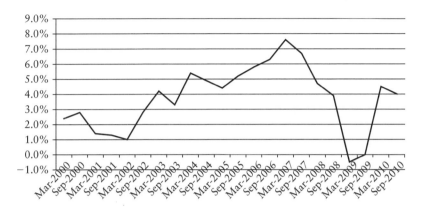

(B) Security Problem in Manufacturing—Index

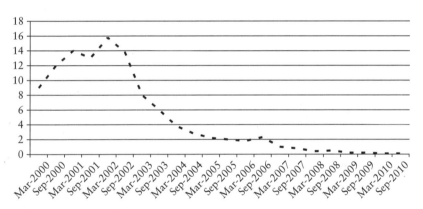

FIGURE 12.1 Colombia Economic Growth and Insecurity Problem
Source: DANE, National Accounts & ANDI, Monthly Industrial Survey.

Fitch, have brought additional demand for the country's bonds and lowered the cost of borrowing. However, in spite of a strong GDP growth of 5.9 percent in 2011, economists predict weaker growth in 2012 due to the sovereign debt crisis in the Euro Zone, high unemployment in the United States, sluggish growth in Japan, and weaker than usual growth in the BRICs.

Colombia is a net exporter of commodities and benefits from high global commodity prices. However, if prices remain persistently high, Colombia could experience a further increase in inflation. If this occurs, the

Central Bank will need to take corrective measures in order to stem inflation before it becomes entrenched.

Corruption presents a significant threat to Colombia's overall economy and its ability to attract foreign investors. Luckily, President Santos has adopted a direct approach to curtail corruption within the government by targeting infrastructure, health services, and the resource royalty management sector, areas of the economy that are deemed the most corrupt. Ultimately, these policies have helped improve Colombia's ranking in Transparency International's Index, which measures business transparency in over 180 countries. Colombia ranked eightieth in 2011, only seven places below Brazil (seventy-third), one of the lowest in the region.

Colombia has also benefited from being perceived by some as a good kid in a tough neighborhood. Left-leaning governments in Venezuela, Ecuador, and Bolivia provide Colombia the opportunity to market itself as a beacon of capitalism in a bastion of communism to capture higher foreign investment.

Economic Fundamentals[1]

Recently, strong consumer demand and improving labor market conditions have helped drive Colombia's economy. Retail sales are up 13 percent, and industrial output is up 4 percent year over year as of February 2011. Colombia is one of few countries in Latin America not plagued by hyperinflation in recent history and, besides El Salvador, was the only other country to avoid debt restructuring during the Latin American crisis of the 1980s.

Colombia's debt-to-GDP ratio (45.6 percent in March 2012) is higher than those of their regional neighbors, but short-term debt as a percentage of reserves is below 20 percent. The country has a current account deficit of US $5.9 billion, or roughly 2.5 percent of GDP, and had $22.5 billion in foreign debt. The government has recently approved a reform package to direct excess oil and mining revenue to a sovereign wealth fund, has reformed the distribution of royalties to regional governments, and has limited the level of debt the government can issue to strengthen economic fundamentals.

Colombia and Its Natural Resources

Colombia possess a wealth of natural resources including minerals, energy resources (hydroelectric, thermal, wind, and solar power), agricultural products, and fuels, offering investors a range of opportunities.

Coal Colombia has the highest coal reserves of Latin America, mainly concentrated along the northern coast in an open mine called El Cerrejon, that stores 7.4[2] billion metric tons of coke coal used as a reducing agent in iron smelters. This has brought many big-league investors interested in trading, extracting, and operating mines, such as Glencore and Xstrata, to the country.

Emeralds   Colombian emeralds are considered among the best in the world. Colombia produces 55 percent of world demand for these gems, known for their size and quality. In 2011 Colombia exported US$72 million in precious stones to its main export markets: Japan (50 percent) followed by the United States (25 percent) and Europe (12 percent).

Natural Gas   Colombia has about 114.4 billion cubic meters of natural gas reserves. With a pipeline network all regions of the country can be reached. The main pipeline, owned by Ecopetrol (Colombian oil company), extends over 584 kilometers and is supplemented by private pipelines over 1727 kilometers, mainly on the Atlantic Coast and in Santander.

Oil   It is estimated that the territory holds about 1.4 billion barrels of oil with a current extraction capacity of over 1 million barrels per day. There has also been an investment in the two main refining plants (Cartagena and Barrancabermeja) to expand their refining capacity and oil quality standards.

Electric Energy   There are 32 hydroelectric power stations producing 64 percent (2009) of internal electricity demand and 30 thermal generators covering 33 percent. The other 3 percent is mostly produced by aeolic/wind and solar energy. The construction of an electricity transmission line to Panama, connecting Colombia with Central America, has allowed power exports.

Agriculture   With the recent reduction of guerrilla groups, 6.5 million hectares have been made available for agricultural purposes. This sector currently generates 19.7 percent of employment, 19 percent of exports, and 9.2 percent of Colombia's GDP. Low land prices and the strategic location have attracted multinationals such as Cargill to start planting 10,000 ha of soy and corn. The government is also providing incentives to agricultural investors such as tax reductions and low loan rates.

Strategic Location

Colombia, strategically located between both the Atlantic and Pacific oceans, allows efficient transportation with competitive rates for international shipments[3] and the ability to access the North American markets from both the East and West coasts. As it stands, Colombia is only a three- to four- day sail, or a three-hour flight to two of the United States' largest markets, which provides a significant competitive advantage. This allows Colombian goods to reach major markets faster and at a lower cost.

To incentivize foreign investment, the government has created a free trade zone with a single 15 percent income tax rate. In addition, the government has provided tax exemptions for investments in tourism, aeolic and biomass energy, power generation, and medical and software products.

Export Markets   The past 10 years have been marked by the increase of over US $45.4 billion (or 222 percent) in exports, with a noticeable jump in 2008 when exports increased by 55.1 percent over the previous year (see Figure 12.2). According to the National Statistic Center (DANE), the positive trade balance in 2011 was 4.2 percent. Main imports were industrial materials with a 41.3 percent share, followed by construction materials with a 37 percent share.

In 2011, Colombia's largest export markets included the United States (38.2 percent),[4] the Netherlands (4.6 percent), and Chile (4.1 percent) (see Figure 12.3).

Thus, the Colombian economy has become more dependent on other economies. At the same time, the economy is influenced by international prices of commodities, as 57.5 percent of exports are based on oil and mining.

The recent free trade agreement (FTA) between the United States and Colombia, signed in October 2011, establishes tax-free access for most Colombian products exported to the United States, encouraging foreign investors to see Colombia as a springboard to the huge US consumer market. Similar trade agreements have also been concluded with South Korea, Canada, and Panama.

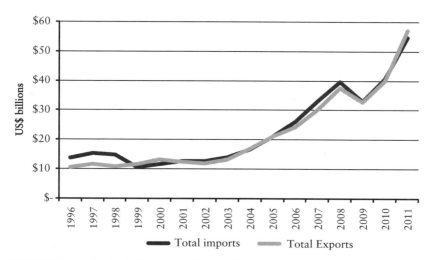

FIGURE 12.2   Colombia's Export and Import Trade, 1996–2011
Source: National Accounts & ANDI, author's analyses.

Colombian Stock Market

From its beginning on July 3, 2001, the Colombian Stock Exchange has contributed to the growth and development of the Colombian economy, facilitating the financing of industrial, commercial, and service companies that increasingly demand financial resources to further their production (see Figure 12.4).

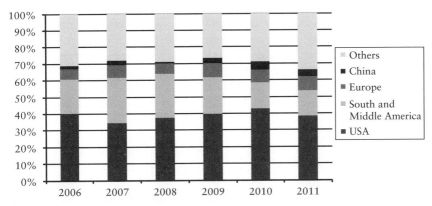

FIGURE 12.3   Colombia's Export Markets

Source: National Accounts & ANDI, author's analyses.

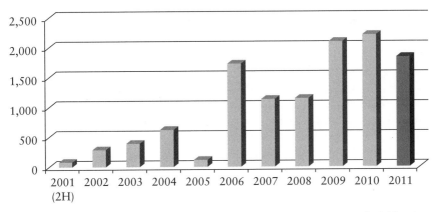

FIGURE 12.4   Colombia Stock Exchange (BVC) Turnover 2001 (Second Half) to 2011 (in US$ billions)

Source: BVC Report 2001–2011, author's analyses.

Transactions through the Colombia Stock Exchange (BVC) in fixed income securities and equities totaled COL$1,840.81 billion (Colombian peso currency equivalent to US$1 billion) in 2011. This was lower by 16.9 percent than in 2010, but an increase of over 2,254.7 percent since its beginning in 2001.

Currently only two Colombian companies trade on US exchanges, Ecopetrol (EC) and BanColombia (CIB). Ecopetrol, the state-owned oil company with a market cap of US$85.5 billion, yielded a 27.2 percent return last year and pays a dividend of 5.1 percent. BanColombia, one of the largest banks in Latin America, with a market cap of US$13.1 billion, returned 14.7 percent last year and pays a dividend of 2.2 percent. Two more Colombian companies were projected to be listed on the NYSE this year, EEB and Davivienda (the second largest national bank), but given market turmoil, it seems doubtful they will go ahead.

The BVC (Colombia Stock Exchange) is the stock market with the greatest turnover in the Latin American region. A significant portion of the BVC is composed of government bonds (98 percent), in part because it is the only stock market that has an organized of transaction system for government bonds. Considering only trading in shares, BVC would be in fourth place after Ibovespa (Brazil), Santiago Stock Exchange (Chile), and the Mexican Stock Exchange (Mexico).

In 2011, with an initiative from the Santiago Exchange (Chile), the Colombia Exchange and the Lima Exchange (Peru) created the MILA (*Mercado Integrado Latinoamericano*), which integrates the three stock markets. This unification of markets intends to become the largest in terms of number of issuers, the second largest in market capitalization, and third in terms of trading volume after Brazil and Mexico.

A good case of a success story would be the Canadian-based Pacific Rubiales (PRE), an oil company that took a chance on Colombia and bought an underexplored oil field formerly owned by Exxon in 2007.[5] Today it is the most productive oil pump with a production of 150,000 barrels a day and a revenue of US$3.4 billion in 2011.

This company is the second-largest company in Colombia, with over 4,000 direct employees. It has already expanded to countries like Peru and Guatemala. Although Pacific Rubiales is listed on the stock exchanges of Canada and Colombia, Pacific Rubiales seeks to increase its investor base through the Brazilian Stock Exchange to access capital in one of the world's most promising economies.

Government

Traditionally, Colombian politics have been bifurcated along liberal and conservative lines. Recently, alternative parties have entered the political landscape that provides more populist ideas of governance. Former Colombian president Alvaro Uribe Velez of the U party exemplifies these new elements. The U party supports the construction of a welfare state and recognizes the family as the foundation of society. It also recognizes and endorses globalization, with a strong emphasis on education, science and technology, and the opportunities of Colombia within the global market.

President Alvaro Uribe Velez's eight-year administration was highlighted by his Democratic Security Policy, which aimed to eradicate militant activity and drug trafficking. In spite of being highly criticized by political opponents, the policy did decrease murder rates. Uribe also helped Colombia play a greater role in regional trade through the establishment of trade agreements and strengthening the alliance with the United States.

Juan Manuel Santos took the presidency in 2010 and in his first year has shown diplomatic abilities by expanding the relations with neighboring countries. Santos has established an economic policy that focuses on five target sectors, housing, infrastructure, mining, agriculture, and innovation, to provide stable growth of the Colombian economy. In order to generate funding for these investments, the government created the Private Initiative project, that allows individuals or corporations, partnerships, joint ventures, or any other form of association to submit proposals for public infrastructural works to a state agency, and if approved, finance the projects through private means and obtain a concession to generate revenues through tolls or taxes.

As a result of these combined efforts, the global Doing Business ranking for Colombia was forty-second[6] out of 183 countries in 2012.

Taxation

Taxes on Colombian capital gains are zero if the investor is selling no more than 10 percent of holdings within each fiscal year, otherwise capital gain taxes are 14 percent. Dividends in Colombia are taxed at a flat 33 percent rate with a credit exemption for taxes paid. Repatriation of funds from Colombian equities sold is also subject to a .4 percent financial transactions tax on after-tax funds.

Main Deficiencies

Colombia's economic growth is highly dependent on global demand for its commodities, particularly from two of the economies that are experiencing significant economic slowdowns, the United States and the European Union. This risk is further increased as China, which is also experiencing an economic slowdown, becomes an increasingly important trade partner.

Colombia still suffers from an emerging market type of economy; there are still many problems to be solved. According to the World Bank, 37.2 percent of the population are said to live below the poverty level, 53 percent of the land is held by 1.08 percent of owners, and investment in education and infrastructure is wanting. While the overall security situation in Colombia has improved immeasurably over the last decade, problems are still prevalent, as evidenced by an escalation of FARC attacks on oil infrastructure including pipelines last year. While these incidents should not act as a major drag on economic growth, particularly as the security situation in major cities has been stabilized, investors need to be conscious that any escalation in the activities of armed groups is difficult to predict and can seriously affect the economy particularly the oil and tourism industries. This would have a negative effect on foreign direct investment.

Outlook

As the only country in South America with direct access to both the Pacific and Atlantic oceans, Colombia has the potential to facilitate trade along both coasts of the largest markets in the Western hemisphere (Canada, Mexico, and the United States). The recent signing of a free trade agreement (FTA) with the United States will help keep Colombia's manufacturing sector regionally competitive. Although challenges remain, such as weak infrastructure and lingering security concerns, Colombia has placed itself on a trajectory toward sustained economic prosperity for the foreseeable future.

Overall, Colombia, despite media stereotypes of being a violent and unstable country, presents a far more attractive investment option than Brazil or Argentina. Brazil presents a rising political and investment risk being driven by a leftist economic agenda and reactive economic policies of the Rousseff government. Also, Brazil is experiencing a significant economic slowdown that will impact on investment returns. In comparison, Argentina has typically run on an unpredictable boom-and-bust economic cycle with increased investment risk. It is expected that in 2012 Colombia GDP growth rate will be between 5 percent and 5.5 percent, an estimate supported by all current indicators. This would almost double Brazil's forecast rate of 3 percent, double the forecast 2.5 percent growth for the United States, and be higher than Argentina's forecast 4.6 percent.

MONGOLIA: OPPORTUNITIES IN THE NEW FRONTIER

Michael Preiss
Mongolia Asset Management

Most investors know Mongolia in the context of Genghis Khan, and the startling history of how one extraordinary man from a remote corner of the world created an empire that led the world into the modern age.

Today, Mongolia is opening up to foreign investors and keen to share its wealth with those who are willing to engage in long-term strategic investment opportunities. Mongolia is one of the fastest growing economies in the world. The IMF estimates that the local economy will grow above 14 percent on average through 2012 to 2016. Today, an increasing number of global investors are becoming convinced that Mongolia will be the success story in Asia in the coming decade. This is a very exciting time for the country with its unparalleled economic growth potential.

Illiquidity and a small market size are often considered a key risk in frontier market investing. However, it is also important to remind ourselves that very often the reasons why the investment opportunity exists in the first place is because it is largely overlooked and under-researched and considered boring or too illiquid by many.

The Mongolian economy is set to expand rapidly as the mineral and commodity sector gathers momentum, fueling a domestic consumption boom. Mongolia lines up an impressive pipeline of potential IPOs, including many state-owned enterprises, strategic mineral deposits, local industry leaders, and companies listed on foreign stock markets—a pipeline potentially worth US$45 billion in market capitalization. Government efforts to develop local capital markets are now taking place. The strategic partnership between MSE (Mongolia Stock Exchange) and LSE (London Stock Exchange) has successfully implemented a number of regulatory and system changes to bring the Mongolian capital market to international standards.

Mongolia is often considered a highly leveraged call option on the mining and China growth story. China, with over 1 billion people and consistently high GDP growth, is desperate for raw materials. The Tavan Tolgoi mine is considered by geologists to be the world's largest untapped coal deposit, and Oyu Tolgoi (which means Turquoise Hill in Mongolian) is the world's largest untapped gold and copper deposit.

The US$6 billion Oyu Tolgoi copper and gold project is on track to meet its initial production, targeted to commence in the third quarter of 2012. Installation of the two production lines in the concentrator and pre-commissioning work is progressing ahead of plan. The concentrator, which will have an initial capacity of 100,000 tons per day now is more than 80 percent complete. The first production line was scheduled to be completed during the third quarter, followed by completion of the second production line in the fourth quarter of 2012.

Mongolia is a landlocked country between Russia and the People's Republic of China. It is 550 kilometers from the capital, Ulan Bator (Ulaanbaatar), to Beijing, and 700 kilometers to the port of Tianjin. It has the longest land border, with 12 border crossings with People's Republic of China—4,600 kilometers; China's border with Russia extends 4,300 kilometers.

Mongolia has also a long land border with Russia of 3,500 kilometers; it is 235 kilometers from Ulan Bator to the center of the Siberian region, Irkutsk, and 3,000 km to Russia's industrial Ural region . It is 2,000 kilometers from Ulan Bator to Seoul and 3,000 kilometers to Tokyo.

Mongolia's strategic location is advantageous for resources exports to China compared, for example, with Kazakhstan and Australia.

With a massive land area of 1.5 million square kilometers, Mongolia is one of the top 20 largest countries of the world. It has 20 percent of Australia's land area, yet a tiny open economy of US$8 billion, which is not even 1 percent of Australia's. On the other hand, Mongolia has a stable, mature, and vibrant frontier democracy based on consensus building and a young, talented small population of 2.7 million with a lot of potential. Fifty-nine percent of the Mongolian population is below 30 years of age.

It is widely acknowledged that Mongolia is among the top 10 mineral - rich countries in the world. With only 17 percent of territory properly explored, it already has established in-ground value of top commodities in excess of US$3 trillion, compared to South Africa's US$2.5 trillion.

Inflation and Interest

According to the national statistics office of Mongolia, inflation was 10.8 percent nationwide in January 2012. According to the World Bank, inflation is forecast at 17 percent for 2012 (CPI). According to the IMF (November 2011), consumer prices (period average) are forecast to rise 18.7 percent in 2012.

According to the World Bank (October 2011), with budget expenditures increasing sharply in 2011 and 2012, overheating pressure will rise, feeding inflation that is already running at low double-digit levels. The 2012 budget envisages a 57 percent increase in wages and a 40 percent increase in transfers on the 2011 approved budget. There is therefore a substantial risk of a wage-price spiral, if higher inflation expectations become entrenched. Rising inflation, if not matched by preemptive tightening of interest rates, will push real interest rates close to zero or into negative territory, as happened in the run-up to the previous bust. High domestic inflation also causes the currency to appreciate in real terms, hurting the export sectors. Although the Bank of Mongolia has been quick to raise policy rates and reserve requirements, its efforts to control inflation will be more than offset if the extraordinarily large fiscal injections planned by the government materialize as planned.

According to the IMF (November 2011), the expansionary 2011 budget was a major source of the persistent inflationary pressures. The 2012 approved budget is still highly expansionary and continues to be a major source of inflationary pressure in 2012. Government spending, which was slated to grow by some 30 percent in the original budget, accounts for some two-thirds of the non-mineral economy and is thus a key determinant of aggregate demand. Any further increase in spending this year, therefore, is clearly not warranted. Additional spending this year would further overheat the economy, hurt the poor by driving up inflation, increase the vulnerability to a global commodity shock, and undermine credibility in fiscal policy and legal fiscal responsibility. Monetary policy, moreover, would not be able to offset a fiscal stimulus of this magnitude but would inevitably lead to a crowding out of private sector activity.

The consensus view is that although the 2012 budget is still highly expansionary, more realistic projections in the 2012 budget are a reflection of a political will to restrain inflation that is more widely perceived as a greater macro risk in case of prolonged fiscal expansion. 2012 is an election year and therefore there would be acceleration of politically motivated actions such as cash handouts. End result inflation in 2012 would be dependent on fiscal intentions and political commitments.

Stock Market

We believe that the Mongolian stock market and local currency assets in the fastest growing economy in the world are hidden jewels of frontier market investing.

The stock market in Mongolia was established in 1991 when the collapse of the Soviet Union compelled Mongolia to switch from a communist to a capitalist economy and democracy. Mongolia decided to privatize state assets through the creation of a stock market.

Since then the local capital market has developed and today is again at a major turning point as the country becomes the fastest-growing economy in the world.

MSE (Mongolia Stock Exchange) was the best-performing stock market in the world in 2010 with over 130 percent growth and despite a downward pull, Mongolia still managed to be the second-best–performing stock market in the world in 2011 with a 47 percent return.

We expect that the MSE will continue its multi-year bull market trend, as market liquidity improves and more and more Mongolian companies seek IPOs on the local market.

The MSE will likely see consistent success in coming years. The Mongolian stock market might not offer the best emerging market returns every year as it did in 2010, but investors worldwide have taken notice of the compelling long-term investment story (see Figure 12.5).

We expect market cap and daily equity average turnover to substantially increase in 2012, however gradually. The strategic partnership between the

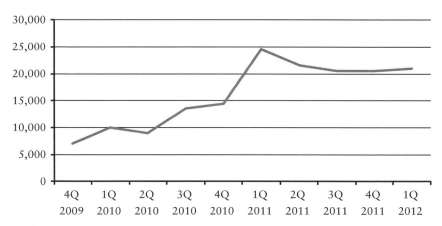

FIGURE 12.5 Mongolia Top 20, 2010 to 2012 First Quarter—Quarterly Index Levels
Source: Mongolia Stock Exchange.

MSE and the London Stock Exchange (LSE) to modernize the MSE and bring world-class standards by introducing a state-of-the-art trading system to the local market is revolutionizing the local capital market. The LSE has a three-year contract to actively manage the MSE.

The Mongolia Financial Regulatory Commission (FRC) is working on introducing new securities laws as well as an investment fund law.

We believe the downside risk in Mongolia equities is limited, as true profitability of Mongolian companies is still understated and the economy expands at a rapid pace. The balance sheet assets of many locally listed Mongolian companies are still undervalued or the book value of assets is much lower than their market value or replacement cost.

We expect an additional number of new share offerings and IPOs in 2012 as the Mongolian government is privatizing state-owned enterprises (SOEs) in mining, mineral processing, power generation and distribution, construction materials, telecom, and transportation.

Currency

The tögrög or tugrik (code: MNT) is the official currency of Mongolia. It is a resource and commodity currency similar to the Australian dollar but with much higher yield and real interest rate.

MNT was the second best performing currency in the world in 2010, appreciating 13 percent against the US dollar. According to the Bank of Mongolia, mining operations were in their initial stages, and demand for US dollars was low.

However, in 2011 the economy grew by 17 percent and the Mongolian currency depreciated by 11.4 percent against the US dollar. According to the Bank of Mongolia, mining operations were under heavy development and the demand for US dollars increased rapidly, both from the public and the government. Although the US currency inflow was the same, its outflow had increased causing the drop in the MNT rate.

In other words, the US$/MNT rate depends on the way Mongolia spends its income. According to the IMF, extraordinary growth in spending could lead to overheating the economy, high inflation, rapid growth in imports due to excessive domestic demand, and macroeconomic uncertainty, all of which are influencing the exchange rate. External considerations and domestic Mongolian factors tend to exert downward pressure on Mongolia's currency.

According to the World Bank, the trend for the year suggests that high domestic inflation is mirrored in the weakening of the currency. Rising global risk aversion and declining commodity prices are additional factors contributing to the depreciation, as has occurred in other mineral-rich emerging economies.

According to the Bank of Mongolia, the main indicators of the balance of payments of 2011 are:

- The current account deficit was MNT2.56 billion representing an increase of 2.9 times or US$1.68 billion. This was mainly due to a service trade deficit that rose 3.9 times to US$1.15 billion. The goods trade deficit rose 5.1 times to US$925 million.
- The current account deficit is financed by the inflow of capital and foreign exchange reserves reached US$2.3 billion in December of 2011, representing an increase of 8.7 percent or US$183 million.
- The surplus in the capital and financial account was US$2.3 billion, representing an increase of 1.3 times or US$556 million. This is driven by the 2.3 time increase in FDI to US$2.1 billion. Fifty-four percent of this FDI is loan funding, 37 percent is equity capital, and 9 percent is reinvestment of income.

After the massive increase in exports due to the production at Oyu Tolgoi comes to an end in 2014, it is expected that the MNT will appreciate against the US dollar and other major currencies. In the meantime, one of the highest interest rates in the world means that investors can compound capital at an attractive rate.

Exports and Imports

According to the National Statistics Office of Mongolia and the preliminary results for 2011, Mongolia traded with 127 countries and external trade turnover reached US$11.3 billion; exports amounted to US$4.8 billion and imports to US$6.5 billion. External trade increased overall by US$5.2 billion or 85 percent compared to 2010, with imports up by 104 percent and exports up by 64 percent.

Mongolia benefited from favorable commodity prices in 2011 for virtually all its export commodities such as coal, copper, iron ore, crude, (greasy) cashmere, zinc, and gold. At the same time, imports are rising due to mining, infrastructure, construction, and private consumption; terms of trade are getting more expensive.

Trade statistics (Tables 12.1 and 12.2) the rapidly growing importance of the primary sector as well as commensurate growth in consumer spending.

TABLE 12.1   Republic of Mongolia: Main Exports

Exports	Value 2011	Increase in Value over 2010	Increase in Volume over 2010
Coal	US$2.2 B	155.1%	26.2%
Copper	US$963 M	25%	0.7%
Iron ore	US$437 M	72%	61%
Crude	US$252 M	63%	22%
Zinc Ore	US$143 M	6.4%	0.8%
Raw (Greasy) Cashmere	US$132 M	26%	(9%)
Gold	US$113 M	37%	(4%)

Source: National Statistics, Mongolia Asset Management Analyses.

TABLE 12.2   Republic of Mongolia: Main Imports

Imports	Value 2011	Increase in Value over 2010	Increase in Volume over 2010
Diesel Fuel	US$706 M	75%	27%
Trucks	US$577 M	177%	100%
Gasoline	US$446 M	51%	13%
Passenger Cars	US$437 M	166%	113%
Bulldozers, etc.	US$273 M	268%	140%
Earth/Stone Machinery	US$148 M	167%	173%
Loading Machinery	US$102 M	125%	993%
Telecom	US$ 80 M	74%	65%
TV Appliances	US$57 M	157%	105%

Source: National Statistics, Mongolia Asset Management.

Banking

Banking is the life blood of any economy, especially for a fast-growing market like Mongolia. As the vast natural resource wealth filters through the general economy, it will create more government spending, more job opportunities, better infrastructure, and greater demand for loans and more sophisticated financial services.

There are 14 banks in Mongolia and the sector is growing rapidly. The key players are Khan Bank of Mongolia, Golomt Bank, Trade Development Bank of Mongolia, and Xac Banks. High economic growth and the multiplier effect of the natural resources boom in the country are creating a host of opportunities for banks in Mongolia.

According to the World Bank, lending is expanding at a healthy pace in order to deploy the strong influx of deposits. According to Bank of Mongolia (January 2012), total savings increased in 2011 by 41 percent to reach MNT3.89 trillion. Seventy-five percent of savings are MNT and 25 percent are in foreign currency.

According to the Bank of Mongolia, the weighted average interest of securities of the Central Bank increased by 3.3 percentage points to reach 14.25 percent. Weighted average interest for MNT loans declined 2.4 points to 15.5 percent and for foreign currency loans interest declined 0.5 points to 12.1 percent. Weighted average interest on MNT savings declined by 0.2 points to 10.5 percent and for foreign currency savings interest increased by 0.5 points to 4.5 percent.

According to the National Statistics Office of Mongolia (January 2012):

- Loans outstanding at the end 2011 amounted to MNT5641.1 billion, a growth of 72.8 percent or MNT2376.4 B.
- Principals in arrears at the end of 2011 stood at MNT73.7 billion, reflecting a decrease of MNT16.9 billion or 18.7 percent.
- At the end of 2011, non-performing loans in the banking system stood at MNT330.0 billion, a decrease of 44.4 billion MNT or 11.9 percent.

Mining

Mongolia is one of the richest countries in the world in terms of natural resources and is now making rapid progress with respect to exploiting these resources. The country is known around the world for its two major mining projects, OT (Oyu Tolgoi) and TT (Tavan Tolgoi).

OT appears to be on track and close to completing its funding. The latest developments include: Facilities required for the first ore production in mid-2012 remain on schedule and commercial production is expected to commence in the first half of 2013. The stringing of power cables was expected to commence in spring 2012. Bilateral agreements were expected in 2012 to ensure that imported power would be available at the site by the third quarter. Oyu Tolgoi LLC was finalizing a study on alternative power-generation arrangements to be implemented in the event that imported power would not be available by the third quarter of 2012.

Ivanhoe Mines, Rio Tinto, and a core lending group are working together to finalize an approximate US$4.0 billion project-finance facility for the Oyu Tolgoi Project, with the objective of signing the loan documentation in 2012.

The Tavan Tolgoi (TT) mine is to export 3 million metric tons (Mt) coal in 2012. 2012 prices to the buyer, Chalco, are adjusted according to an agreed index. The operating company (ETT) will build a two-lane paved highway beside the MMC highway, with construction to start in mid-2013. If there is a successful IPO for ETT, investments will maintain projects and growth in 2012 and 2013. A south railroad will be started at the same time as the east railroad to the Sainshand Industrial Hub.

The South Gobi region coal exports including value-added (washed) could reach a record in 2012 and we estimate volumes in a range of 25 to 30 Mt with a value of US$2.25–2.75 billion. Although there is a lot of progress with coal highways, industry consensus view is that infrastructure capacity is still a constraint to export growth. With softening prices the total value of coal exports is unlikely to increase as much as the new tonnage.

We expect record iron ore exports in the range of 8 Mt and a value of around US$500 million, softening commodity prices in 2012. We estimate the volume of copper exports should remain virtually the same as in 2012 with a value of around US$1 billion.

Democracy

Mongolia is a stable, mature, and vibrant frontier democracy based on consensus building: It is praised as model democracy by the United States, has more than 50 TV stations, is flourishing with robust media, and is a civil society.

The stable political system of Mongolia is its greatest advantage and encouragement for investors. Political risk premium overall is decreasing; however, 2012 is an election year. Overall, progress is there, but it is sometimes slow and riddled with challenges as the country learns to deal with its unprecedented natural resource wealth and economic boom. Patience and long-term commitment are required.

Governance

Mongolia has successfully managed a double transition—from an authoritarian state to a democracy, as well as from a centralized to a market economy. The political reform and democratization in Mongolia have been remarkably swift, smooth, and thorough. After almost 70 years of socialist rule in virtual isolation from the outside world (except for COMECON countries), Mongolia stands out as one of the front-runners in political and institutional reforms. An open and democratic society has been established and is being consolidated at all levels.

There have been positive developments in the level of governance in Mongolia. The overall drive toward democracy and a market economy is undoubtedly a national commitment and an irreversible process. Some results have been achieved in strengthening the institutions and mechanisms of government over the past few years and in putting into place mechanisms for redressing mismanagement and inefficiency.

HAITI: OUT OF TRAGEDY TO FUTURE FRONTIER MARKET?

Below the radar of most investors except multilaterals and those dealing with Least Developed Countries (LDC, a United Nations designation), the economy of Haiti in the Caribbean has many of the hallmarks of potential success looking extremely far out, possibly half a generation. This country truly represents the ultimate frontier.

There are three reasons to look at this country as an example of where a least developed economy could be in one to three decades:

- The country has a population of 10 million with a median age of 21[7] years which translates into abundant low-cost labor in the immediate proximity of the United States.
- An estimated 4 million diaspora comprised mainly of professionals and well-educated nationals generates remittances to the tune of 20 percent+[8] of GDP and represents a major source of potential inward investment and trained national talent.
- Between 2004 and 2006, the Haitian government made significant progress in the implementation of economic governance reforms.[9] These included actions to improve the legal framework and reforms to attract foreign investment.

The country was devastated by an earthquake in 2010 and has the opportunity to rebuild itself with very substantial debt relief and financial aid from multilaterals and the benefit of insight gained from observing the experience of comparable economies.

A democratic base is in place. The current president, Michel Martelly, has been quoted as saying that "everything is a priority in Haiti:[10] modernizing the economy, providing access to free education, strengthening the agricultural sector, and moving earthquake victims out of tents by jump-starting reconstruction.[11] as well as strengthening the rule of law and combating corruption." President Martelly announced, "starting May 14, Haiti will change. The state of law, like it or not, will become a reality. No person, no institution, will be above justice."

Haiti could emerge victorious from the disaster of the earthquake and start a modern and rapidly developing economy with a multitude of advantages over other Caribbean markets that already have demonstrated a capability to generate prosperity, stability, and economic success. This is the one after next opportunity for investors, nationals, and foreigners alike.

The Unfavorable Starting Position

Haiti is the second oldest republic in the Western Hemisphere, after the United States. It shares the island of Hispaniola with the Dominican Republic. Covering an area of 27,750 square kilometers, the 2011 population was estimated at 9.7 million.

10.4 percent of the population is employed by industry and 28 percent by the commerce, tourism, and transportation sectors. The largest segment of the population works in the agricultural sector and two-thirds of the population is dependent on subsistence farming. The World Bank categorizes Haiti as a low-income, chronic food deficit country, which means it is able to produce less than half of its food needs.[13] Haiti was categorized as a Least Developed Country (LDC) by the United Nations in 1971,[14] the "poorest and weakest segment" of the international community. Such designated countries enjoy tariff-free exports of certain products to most developed nations, including the United States and many European countries.

The 2010 earthquake, with its epicenter close to the capital, Port-au-Prince, caused damage in value greater than the country's total GDP for 2009. The government reported more than 300,000 homes destroyed or damaged. More than 1,300 educational establishments and over 50 hospitals and health centers became unusable, the main port became partly inoperable and many roads were left unstable, and government buildings were destroyed.[15]

Moreover, the international community has a less than favorable assessment of the current state of affairs. The 2012 Heritage Report states critically: "Overall progress in reforming the Haitian economy has been modest. The effectiveness of government spending has been severely undermined by political volatility that continues to sap the foundations of an already weak rule of law. Reforms to improve the business and investment climates have had little effect in light of Haiti's pervasive corruption and inefficient judicial framework. Limited efforts to liberalize trade have had little impact, and bureaucracy and red tape deter investment. Despite a UN

Stability Mission and a better-trained and equipped national police force, disorder is still easily sparked by paid gangs. Unemployment is very high, most economic activity is informal, and emigrants' remittances have yet to recover fully from the 2009 global economic downturn. Corruption, gang violence, drug trafficking, and organized crime are pervasive."[16]

Small improvements in reducing corruption and continued moderation of inflation offer signs of hope. It is hard to imagine a less favorable starting position. This is evidenced by the rise in the ranking of the Heritage Freedom Index. Haiti is ranked 142nd globally in terms of economic freedom with a score of just above 50 percent (still mostly not free) and about 20 percent below the world and regional averages. Still, this ranks Haiti ahead of Russia, one of the BRIC countries, and countries like Argentina, Venezuela, and the Ukraine in terms of economic freedom.

The Road to Economic Recovery

The estimated cost for long-term reconstruction in Haiti is US$11.5 billion. Immediately following the earthquake, the international community pledged US$9.9 billion over the next decade for relief, recovery, and development in addition to technical assistance and other non-financial resources.[17] The United States is Haiti's largest sovereign donor[18] and the Inter-American Development Bank (IADB) is its largest multilateral donor.[19]

After the earthquake, Haiti's government updated its comprehensive strategy, with a plan to raise medium-term growth and reduce poverty, with a focus on four main areas:

1. Territorial rebuilding, through the promotion of development centers outside Port-au-Prince; the rebuilding of affected areas; prioritizing growth-driving infrastructure; and managing land tenure.
2. Economic rebuilding, through the focus on modernizing and developing key sectors of the economy, such as agriculture, construction, manufacturing, and tourism.
3. Social rebuilding, through the emphasis of universal primary education, an adequate higher education system, a health system with essential coverage nationwide, and social protection for the most vulnerable.
4. Institutional rebuilding, to include core state functions modernizing the legal and regulatory framework, setting up institutions to manage reconstruction, and establishing a culture of transparency and accountability that deters corruption.[20]

The economic outlook is positive. For the first time in history, the state budget of Haiti exceeded HTG 100 billion (approx. US$2.5 billion), reaching a total of US$2.65 billion for the 2010–2011 fiscal year.[21]

Government revenue is heavily dependent on prevailing taxes that apply to most economic activities. Yet government revenues are low in comparison to expenditure needs and comparable economies.

The macroeconomic situation has also improved and prospects have been bolstered by debt forgiveness of countries (United States and Venezuela) and multilaterals (IADB, IMF, WB). Debt forgiveness, remittances, and global aid have allowed Haiti's central bank to build reserves and stabilize the currency. However, many believe recovery is being hampered by the delays in disbursement of pledged donations. Only one-fourth of the total US$5.5 billion pledged by the international community for 2010–2011 has been disbursed.

The Economy

Haiti is a market based economy with ample low-cost labor and a new pro-business government. Haiti's 2010 GDP was US$6.6 billion and its corresponding purchasing power parity (PPP) GDP was US$11.48 billion. Per capita GDP during the same period was approximately US$673 with PPP GDP at approximately US$1,164 per capita. Haiti's GDP growth in 2008 and 2009 had been 0.8 percent and 2.9 percent, respectively, after which it fell to -5 percent in FY 2010 due to the earthquake. However, the IMF expects GDP growth of 8.6 percent in 2011 and 8.8 percent in 2012.[22]

Inflation in Haiti is comparatively moderate and primarily attributable to a reduction in goods available, the increase in transportation costs due to global fuel prices, and significant inflows of external aid.[23] While inflation was forecast to rise to 8.5 percent in 2010, it was contained at 4.7 percent.[24] Nevertheless, the IMF expected inflation to peak at 9 percent in 2011, but then fall to 6.5 percent in 2012.

Trade is only emerging. The United States is Haiti's largest trading partner, accounting for 70 percent of Haiti's exports and 50 percent of its imports.

The banking sector in Haiti comprises eight registered banks, with 66 percent of all bank branches located in Port-au-Prince. Many Haitians do not have access to the formal banking system—micro finance does exist—because they are either too poor or do not live in or near Port-au-Prince. The average outstanding loan is US$12,700 and extension of credit is limited to a small number of firms and individuals. Banks currently lend to only 55,000 borrowers with a total loan portfolio of US$800 million. In 2011, interest rates on loans were approximately 9 percent for US$ and 14 percent for HTG lending while savings rates are around 1 percent.

Agriculture accounts for approximately 25 percent of Haiti's GDP and 50 percent of employment, comprising 72 percent of rural employment.[25]

Haiti produces a variety of crops including rice, sugar, cacao, coffee, sorghum, mangoes, hot peppers, pineapples, avocados, and sweet bananas.

Growth in the agricultural sector is limited by overuse of soil and poor irrigation techniques. The wide range of environments in terms of altitude, soil type, and climate allows for a wide variety of crops to be grown in Haiti.[26]

Coffee and cocoa are two of the dominant cash crops in Haiti. USAID estimates coffee production to be annually around 400,000 bags on 40,000 hectares of land.[27] Approximately 150,000 to 200,000 farm families depend on coffee.[28] Only 10 percent of the production is marketed through formal channels. Coffee used to be a major export item (up to US$70 million) however exports are now down to less than US$5 million.

The cocoa value chain is supported by approximately 20,000 microproducers. Total national production was estimated at 4,450 metric tons in 2008, with exports reaching approximately 3,800 metric tons (approximately US$10 million).

The government acknowledges the need to invest in modernizing farming equipment and techniques as well as intrastate support, such as better roads, improved irrigation, and storage units to prevent waste due to spoilage. Improving the efficiency of the sector could dramatically increase production and raise export volume. Exotic fruits and vegetables are promising sectors for Haiti, given their easy access to US consumers. Also, obtaining organic and free trade certification would be a way for Haitian products to gain access to foreign markets.[29]

The food processing industry in Haiti is underdeveloped. Currently, the most developed areas in the food processing industry are for traditional crops: sugar, cacao, and coffee. In addition to land-based crops, aquaculture has good prospects. Several international aid organizations have laid the foundation for a fish farming industry. Haiti also has access to open ocean for sea farming, with 1,100 miles of coastline and waters that extend 200 miles out to sea in an exclusive economic zone.

The manufacturing sector contributed only 7.6 percent to GDP in 2010.[30] The garment industry is the largest manufacturing sector, comprising 80 percent of Haitian exports to the United States and employing over 28,000 people.[31] Haiti was once a reliable supplier of assembled goods to the US market and employed as many as 100,000 workers during its peak production period,[32] which lasted from the 1960s through 1986.[33]

The biggest boost to the Haitian garment industry has come from the United States granting increased access to its market through the 2000 Caribbean Basin Trade Partnership Act (CBTPA) reforms, the 2006 US Congress HOPE Act, and the 2008 HOPE II Act. Under CBTPA, Haitian garment exports to the United States increased from $250 million in 2000 to

$450 million in 2006. The industry continues to grow at more than 20 percent annually, with 2010 garment and apparel exports valued at more than US$550 million.

Only 12 percent of Haiti has access to electricity and 80 percent of electricity demand comes from Port-au-Prince. Most of the energy is produced by light fuel oil at a cost of between US$0.22 and US$0.26 per kWh when crude oil is trading between US$60 and US$80 per barrel. Demand far outstrips supply, but electricity generation is projected to increase fivefold until 2028.[34]

Tourism has long been a priority but the 2010 earthquake caused widespread damage. The total contribution of tourism to employment is forecast to rise by 3.6 percent per annum from 182,000 jobs in 2011. The total contribution of tourism to GDP is equally projected to rise noticeably from 6.0 percent of GDP in 2011.[35] Plans include rehabilitating the Port-au-Prince airport and adding two international airports in Cap Haïtien and Les Cayes.

Although Haiti's telecommunications system is considered among the least developed in Latin America and the Caribbean, mobile density reached 40 per 100 persons in 2009, or 3.6 million cellular phones. Landline use is far more limited. Yet, as of 2009, there were an estimated one million Internet users in the country ranking Haiti 99th in Internet penetration in the world.[36]

Attraction to Investors

In a 2001 assessment of the investment climate in Haiti, the Organisation for Economic Co-operation and Development (OECD) identified political instability and physical security as the primary concerns for potential investors considering doing business in Haiti. The same report pointed out the advantages of investing in Haiti, which include its proximity to the United States and a large potential labor force.[37]

In 2007, the Haitian government affirmed Foreign Direct Investment (FDI) as a central pillar of its economic revitalization plan. Three key initiatives were enacted:

1. Creation of the Investment Facilitation Center to promote free zones, albeit with some restrictions.
2. Trade liberalization to reduce tariffs and duties.
3. Improvement to the legal framework for foreign investment.

All initiatives have created the right objectives for the first stage of a possible investment destination. Once implemented, they could form the base for significant progress. Stellar economic performances are not unheard of. This year Mauritius rose from 72nd to 8th in the world in terms of economic freedom (The Heritage Foundation).

Investment Facilitation Center and Free Zones

Haiti has several overlapping laws and decrees that govern, administer and regulate the establishment, operation, and governance of free zones and industrial parks. Both provide for duty- and VAT-free imports of equipment and raw materials, as well as similar exemptions from payroll and corporate income taxes for park/free zone operators and tenants.

Restrictions on foreign investment remain. Haitian law stipulates that any foreign investment with a potential impact on the country's economy is subject to presidential approval. Haiti also has more explicit restrictions in banking where foreign ownership is capped at 49 percent. The domestic air transportation sector is closed to foreign equity ownership. Seaports and airports are controlled by government monopolies. Other sensitive sectors include mining, energy and gas, electricity, and water. However, the private sector is making inroads in mining and energy production.

Foreign ownership of land is allowed, but restricted to one property for immediate operational needs. Foreign ownership of more than one property requires approval from the Ministry of Justice. Property rights of foreigners are limited to 1.29 hectares in urban areas and 6.45 hectares in rural areas.[38] Foreign companies may lease or buy land from private owners or from the state. Lease contracts can offer the lessee the right to sublease, mortgage, or subdivide the land.

All Haitian companies must have at least three shareholders and three board members; one member of each group is required to be a Haitian national. The minimum requirement for capital is the same for both domestic and foreign-owned companies.

Trade Liberalization

Haiti is a member of the Caribbean Community and Common Market (CARICOM) and applies common external tariffs. Liberalization measures include eliminating export duties, simplifying and lowering tariffs, and removing quantitative restrictions. According to the World Bank, Haiti's simple average most favored nation (MFN) tariff has remained at 2.8 percent, which is lower than the average low-income country. Imported goods bear a heavier effective tax burden of 6.9 percent. A 2 percent tax on import duties is also imposed, along with a turnover tax of 10 percent and excise duty on both imports and domestic products.[39]

Haiti does not have free trade agreements, but rather framework agreements drawn up according to the most-favored-nation principle with multiple countries and through the CARICOM agreement.[40] Haiti is a beneficiary of the WTO General System of Preferences; the Caribbean Basin Initiative (CBI) with duty-free access to the US market for many products;

the Canadian Programs for Commonwealth Caribbean Trade; and the Investment and Industrial Cooperation (CARIBCAN) with preferential treatment for exports to Canada.

Legislative Framework

Haiti adopted the French civil law system. French doctrine and jurisprudence guide interpretation of the law.[41] Haiti is a contracting state to the 1966 Convention on the Settlement of Investment Disputes Between States and Nationals of Other States (ICSID or the Washington Convention) and the 1958 UN Convention on the Recognition and Enforcement of Foreign Arbitration Awards.[42] Haiti abides by regional arbitration mechanisms under its agreement with CARICOM.[43]

All commercial matters are subject to arbitration, except for disputes involving the state, government entities, minors, and incompetent adults. The Chambre de Conciliation et d'Arbitrage (CCAH) it is not yet fully operational but on its way. Arbitration agreements must be concluded in writing and proceedings must be conducted in French.

Haiti has a long history of protecting foreign investment. The 1987 constitution reinforced protections on foreign investment. In 2002, the Haitian parliament passed an investment code that explicitly recognizes the rights of foreign investors, such as in Article 11 of the Investment Code: "No other authorization, license or permit, which is not required of Haitian investors, is applicable to foreign investors." Foreign investors pay taxes, duties, and levies according to the schedules and regulations that are applicable to Haitian investors. The right to real estate is guaranteed to foreign investors for the needs of their enterprise. Foreign investors enjoy free transfer of interest, dividends, profits, and other revenues stemming from their investments.

The judicial system as a whole is still weak and needs substantial revamping and strengthening. The precariousness of land titles, in the absence of a clear official registry, can also be a major constraint.

Outlook

The key to success for Haiti is proper governance, adequate infrastructure, and institutions to give the ready and young work force a mandate to develop. In the past, Haiti was one of the major exporters to the United States and the proximity to the largest consumer market in the world represents a major opportunity to turn around the fortunes of the country. Haiti only serves as an example of an economy largely ignored but with many of the attributes to become a successful investment destination. We should not ignore economies in the long term just because they do not have the right characteristics at this point in time; they may well be part of a winning proposition in the years or decades to come.

CONCLUSION

Despite its tumultuous past, Colombia is strategically located and poised for strong economic growth in the coming decade and could emerge as a leading economy in South America. Colombia's government has begun to make inroads toward stemming violence, which has helped increase domestic production, consumption, and foreign investment, while decreasing unemployment. In addition, Colombia is now better equipped to capitalize on its natural resource deposits, which include oil and natural gas that will fuel domestic growth.

The Mongolia Stock Exchange, small and narrow as it stands today, has outperformed most other markets driven by attractive resource stocks. Farsighted investors realize that in a world with too much debt and structurally weak Western economies, investment in resource rich economies is one of the best macro trades.

Consider Haiti as a market without a stock exchange and without any decent capital market. This would be of no interest to investors except multilaterals and private equity investors. Now consider Haiti as a mid-sized multinational corporation that will receive an equity capital injection one and half times the size of its business. That would be an investment proposition.

NOTES

1. "Seeking Alpha," seekingalpha.com (July 22, 2011).
2. "El Cerrejon," www.cerrejon.com.
3. "Zona franca Bogota," www.zonafrancabogota.com/en/.
4. Proexport, www.proexport.com.
5. "Pacific Rubiales," www.pacificrubiales.com/corporate/company-history.html.
6. "Doing Business," www.doingbusiness.org/.
7. CIA, The World Factbook: Haiti.
8. Ibid.
9. World Bank, "Haiti: Recent Progress in Economic Governance Reforms," siteresources.worldbank.org/INTHAITI/ . . . /Governance_reforms_Haiti.pdf.
10. Georgianne Nienaber, "Haiti's Michel Martelly: The Election, Fraud, and the Future," *La Progressive* (December 8, 2010).
11. Moni Basu, "Haiti's New Leader Makes Rounds in Washington, Vows Transparency," CNN World (April 21, 2011).

12. News 24, "Haiti's Martelly Vows 'Rule of Law,'" (April 6, 2011).
13. Food and Agriculture Organization (FAO) of the United Nations, *Low-Income Food-Deficit Countries (LIFDC)—List for 2011.*
14. United Nations, Handbook on the Least Developed Country Category: Inclusion, Graduation and Special Support Measures (November 2008).
15. Government of Haiti. Haiti Earthquake PDNA.
16. 2012 Index of Economic Freedom, The Heritage Foundation and the *Wall Street Journal* (2012).
17. United Nations, News & Media: UN/HAITI DONORS 3.
18. US Department of State, Background Note: Haiti.
19. Inter-American Development Bank, History of the IDB in Haiti.
20. Government of Haiti, Action Plan for the National Recovery and Development of Haiti (March 2010).
21. Haiti Libre, Haiti—Economy: "The Budget of Haiti 2010–2011, Passes 100 Billion Gourdes" (December 14, 2010).
22. International Monetary Fund, World Economic Outlook Database (April 2011).
23. Economist Intelligence Unit, Haiti: Country Report(February 2011).
24. World Bank, "One Year Later: World Bank Group Support for Haiti's Recovery" (January 2011).
25. Government of Haiti. Haiti Earthquake PDNA: Assessment of damage, losses, general and sectoral needs (March 2010).
26. Government of Haiti, Action Plan for the National Recovery and Development of Haiti (March 2010).
27. USAID, "The Haitian Coffee Market Chain."
28. Fernando Rodriguez et al., Assessment of Haitian Coffee Value Chain, Catholic Relief Services.
29. World Economic Forum, Private Sector Development in Haiti: Opportunities for Investment, Job Creation and Growth, 2011.
30. J. F. Hornbeck, "The Haitian Economy and the Hope Act," Congressional Research Service (June 24, 2010).
31. International Trade Administration, "Haiti Uses a Bit of MAGIC to Energize Their Textile Industry."
32. Embassy of the United States in Port-au-Prince, Fact Sheet: North Industrial Park (January 11, 2011).
33. J. F. Hornbeck, "The Haitian Economy and the Hope Act," Congressional Research Service (June 24, 2010).
34. Nexant Caribbean Regional Electricity Generation, Interconnection, and Fuels Supply Strategy Final Report (March 2010); submitted to the World Bank.
35. World Travel and Tourism Council, "Haiti: The Economic Impact of Travel and Tourism (2011).
36. CIA, *The World Factbook.*
37. Martha N. Kelley, "Assessing the Investment Climate in Haiti: Policy Challenges," Organisation for Economic Co-operation and Development (2001).
38. US Department of State. Background Note: Haiti, Bureau of Western Hemisphere Affairs (August 10, 2011).

39. World Bank, "Haiti: Trade Brief" (2008).
40. Caribbean Export Development Agency, "Doing Business With Haiti" (May 2007).
41. Marisol Florén-Romero, "Researching Haitian Law," New York University GlobaLex (May/June 2008).
42. United Nations Commission on International Trade Law, "About UNCITRAL."
43. Martha N. Kelley, "Assessing the Investment Climate in Haiti: Policy Challenges," Organisation for Economic Co-operation and Development (2001).

CHAPTER 13

Nascent Stock Markets: Myanmar, Laos, and Cambodia

Scott Lewis, Ken Stevens, and Gordian Gaeta
Leopard Capital

Three neighboring economies in Southeast Asia have recently started or are upgrading their stock markets. While they each have only one or two stocks listed, they have the potential to expand and become attractive investment destination candidates down the road.

For private equity investors they are rising in terms of interest and offer the promise of the few last and large frontier markets heretofore not considered.

MYANMAR: CHANGE TOWARD LONG-TERM ATTRACTION?

In recent times, few emerging countries have attracted more media interest than Myanmar (Burma). After some troubled history throughout the second half of the twentieth century and a general isolation from the world, the government embarked on a set of significant political reforms that rekindled foreign interest and support. The continued path of reform is leading to a widely expected relaxation of sanctions imposed by the United States and the EU. The country has a population of some 58 million, abundant natural resources, a compound GDP growth rate of around 10 percent over the period 2001 to 2011(E),[1] and is surrounded by generally booming neighbors and fellow ASEAN members. Within ASEAN, Myanmar is the fastest-growing, second-largest, and least-developed major economy by GDP per capita (see Table 13.1). However, prior to the military coup in 1962, it was the richest country in Asia, with

TABLE 13.1 Myanmar within ASEAN

By Land Area	By Population	By GDP	By GDP per Capita 2011 (E)
Indonesia	Indonesia	Indonesia	Singapore (US$50,713)
Myanmar	Philippines	Thailand	Brunei (US$36,532)
Thailand	Vietnam	Singapore	Malaysia (US$8,617)
Vietnam	Thailand	Malaysia	Thailand (US$5,281)
Malaysia	**Myanmar**	Philippines	Indonesia (US$3,469)
Philippines	Malaysia	Vietnam	Philippines (US$2,255)
Laos	Cambodia	**Myanmar**	Vietnam (US$1,362)
Cambodia	Laos	Brunei	Laos (US$1,204)
Brunei	Singapore	Cambodia	Cambodia (US$912)
Singapore	Brunei	Laos	**Myanmar (US$804)**

Source: UBS research, IMF estimates for 2011, author's analyses.

a strong legal system, leading training and educational systems, and a high proficiency in English.[2]

Given its size, resource endowment, and history, Myanmar is the last large frontier market of Asia that could become of interest to global capital flows.

The Economy

The economy is dominated by the primary sectors: agriculture and resource extraction, which also account for the lion's share of exports.[3] Manufacturing has increased, primarily in state-owned enterprises, but remains of secondary importance, as do services.

Externally estimated composition of GDP would indicate that about 51 percent of GDP is agriculture, about 37 percent services, and about 9 percent industry.[4] The labor force is predominantly employed in agriculture (~64 percent) which may explain the high labor participation rate: 83 to 86 percent male and 63 to 69 percent female.[5] Primary school enrollment is 100 percent (secondary school enrollment is 24 percent) and consequently the adult literacy rate is 81 to 85 percent.

External trade in 2010/2011 (see Figure 13.1), the combined value of exports and imports, amounted to around 32 to 35 percent of GDP, somewhat ahead of other least developed economies (LDCs). Average trade to GDP ratio for LDCs in 2009 amounted to 26 percent; for the world it amounted to 27 percent.[6]

International sanctions are a main constraint for Myanmar as is the low development of its industries. Due to sanctions from the United States and the European Union, the major trading partners for exports are Thailand, China (including Hong Kong), and India(see Figure 13.2).

Gas, teak, plywood, and hardwood as well as aquatic products are the major export items; garments are the major manufactured export (see Figure 13.3). Production of rubies and sapphires amounted to 6.5 million and 4.0 million carats respectively over the same period. Jade extraction

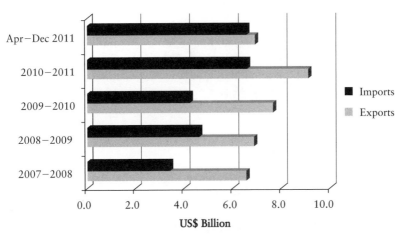

FIGURE 13.1 Myanmar External Trade, April 2007 to December 2011
Source: Central Statistical Office, Myanmar, December 2011, author's analyses.

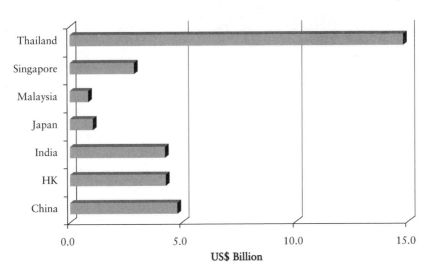

FIGURE 13.2 Myanmar Major Export Destinations, April 2007 to December 2011
Source: Central Statistical Office, Myanmar, December 2011, author's analyses.

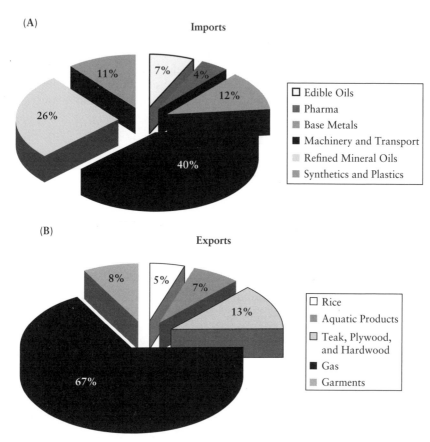

(A) Imports

☐ Edible Oils
■ Pharma
■ Base Metals
■ Machinery and Transport
▨ Refined Mineral Oils
■ Synthetics and Plastics

(B) Exports

☐ Rice
▨ Aquatic Products
☐ Teak, Plywood, and Hardwood
■ Gas
▨ Garments

FIGURE 13.3 Myanmar Major Imports and Exports, April 2007 to December 2011
Source: Central Statistical Office, Myanmar, December 2011, author's analyses.

resulted in 157.5 million metric tons between 2007 and 2011. These and other precious stones are presumably exported but not disclosed separately. They are included in the category "others" that accounts for over US$12 billion of exports for the period.

Agricultural produce is equally growing in export importance. Pulses (legumes used for food and/or animal feed) and rice are the major export items that are rising in importance.

Not surprisingly, machinery and transport equipment and refined mineral oils are the major imports. They go to support the primary industries.

In absolute value, external trade is not significant. However, the potential needs to be considered. Despite the limitations of the economy due to its political system and international sanctions, Myanmar has already carved out an appreciable position in global terms. While still a least developed economy and in the bottom 10 percent of economies by GDP per capita, it excels in several areas of economic activity (see Table 13.2).

Teak cultivation and production, although not critical in a global context, is a case in point that highlights the economic potential based on the history of the country. Myanmar established plantations to produce teak in 1856 and those early foresters had the foresight to make it possible for future generations to reap the financial benefits of the plantations on a sustainable basis.[7] Today, the country is the world's most important teak producer and trader.

Such pockets of strength and the abundant natural resources attracted foreign direct investment despite the restrictions placed on the country. Most of the investment went into power generation and oil & gas exploration, followed by mining. Relatively small investments (still above US$100M over five years)—are made in agriculture and smaller in industries (see Figure 13.4).

The country of origin of foreign direct investment over the past five years is not dissimilar to the trade pattern. According to national statistics, China was the largest foreign investor with some US$13.5 billion, followed by Hong Kong with US$5.8 billion, Thailand with US$3.0 billion, and Korea with US$2.7 billion.

TABLE 13.2 Global Share and Rank of Key Myanmar Products and Commodities

Product/Commodity	Share of Global Value	Global Position
Population	0.8%	Top 25
GDP nom	0.1%	70–75
GDP PPP	0.1%	73
GDP/PPP/ per capita	n/a	163
Teak Wood	60–80%	Top
Rubies	30%+ (E)	Top 2
Sapphires	10%+ (E)	Top 6
Fuel Wood	2.1%	Top 10
Aquatic Products (captured)	1.3%	Top 15
Garments	0.2–0.5%	Top 30
Natural Gas Production	0.4%	Top 35
Natural Gas Reserves	0.2%	Top 40

Source: Central Statistical Office, Myanmar, December 2011, FAO, WTO, UN statistics, UNIDO, World Bank, BP, industry news, Haik Zarian, author's analyses.

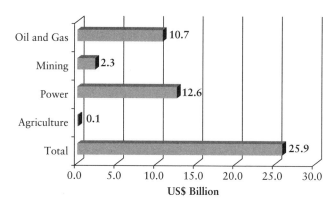

FIGURE 13.4   Foreign Direct Investment in Myanmar, April 2007 to December 2011
Source: Central Statistical Office, Myanmar, December 2011, author's analyses.

Stock Market

A stock market small in nature was established in Myanmar before the great depression of 1930s in the form of Yangon Stock Exchange, but trading was limited. In fact, there were only seven members, all of which were European firms. Trading took place within an informal OTC framework. A leading European firm issued quotations of prices, which were published by their newspaper. A majority of the stockholders were Indians. There were no Myanmar companies listed in that fledgling market.

In the late 1950s, with a view to encouraging private sector development, the government formed nine joint venture corporations with the private sector. Shares of those joint venture corporations were traded as preferred stock in an unofficial OTC market. This market was closed when nationalization of economic entities took place as the centrally planned system was adopted in Myanmar, in 1962.[8]

A small stock market was reopened in 1996 (a Daiwa Securities JV) and in 2006, a government committee drafted a road map for the development of capital markets in Myanmar with a view to an ASEAN interlinked stock market. In 2008, the government set up a Capital Market Development Committee. Most of the work included in the first phase has already been implemented successfully, with the second phase planned for 2010 to 2012 and phase III from 2012 to 2015.

At present, two stocks, Myanmar Citizens Bank and Forest Products JV Corp., both majority owned by government, are thinly traded over the counter, as are government treasury bonds. The stocks provide attractive dividend yields of about 25 percent and the bonds do equally well. There is a shortage of supply and no liquidity.

The Tokyo Stock Exchange with Daiwa Securities recently announced a partnership with the Myanmar Securities Exchange Centre Co. and the Central Bank. The aim is to create a full-fledged stock exchange by 2015 using the technology and trading platform of the Tokyo Stock Exchange.[9] Competition comes from the Korean Exchange, equally keen to open a new exchange/rekindle the exchange in Myanmar. The Korean Exchange already operates the Lao and Cambodia exchanges and the potential of these economies for an attractive stock market is considerable.

Investor and Capital Market Legislation

The general characteristics of the legal system are dominated by the British common law system established during the period 1886 to 1948 and these laws continue to be applied, such as the Contracts Act of 1872 as well as related precedent.[10]

The current Foreign Investment Law of 1988—the revised Foreign Investment Law is under debate by the National Assembly—allows foreign investment in many sectors and provides a tax holiday, export concessions, and depreciation allowances/preferential accounting rules as well customs and tax relief for certain investment goods and periods. The Myanmar Investment Commission (MIC) and the Directorate of Investment and Company Administration are mandated with implementation of the law. The revised law will extend the tax holiday from three to five years and allow foreigners leases on land for 30 years plus 30-year extensions. However, foreign investors will be required to progressively employ more Myanmar citizens.

The government guarantees investors against nationalization and expropriation. Foreign currency from profits, capital gains, and salaries can be transferred.

In addition, the country has enacted the Special Economic Zone Law and two SEZs are approved. SEZs offer additional benefits to foreign investors. The Dawei Special Economic Zone is close to Thailand and plans a deep sea port, power plants, and an industrial estate. The project value is equivalent to the country's GDP today.[11] The exchange rate regime is being liberalized with a floating exchange rate adopted in April 2012. Consideration is given to allow foreign bank joint ventures and branches. A securities and exchange commission law is being drafted as well as a capital markets law.

Myanmar has its Arbitration Implementation Act of 1937, but lacks implementation thereof. Myanmar is considering joining the New York Convention on the Recognition and Enforcement of Arbitral Awards in the near term. Trademark registration is possible.

Currently economic sanctions against the country are severe. To date, the United States prohibits investment or facilitation, export of financial services, and imports related to Myanmar. Any dealings with Specially Designated Persons (SDNs) deemed to be involved in human rights abuses is prohibited. The European Union restricts investment, trade, and services with respect to defense and military, extractive industries, forestry, and steel and iron.

However, the EU travel and visa ban has been lifted. Generally, the ease or lifting of most restrictions is expected if Myanmar continues to liberalize its political regime.

The history of the country and its people augurs well for rapid development and progress. Provided political change continues, economic attractiveness should follow. Most building blocks for a frontier economy are in place and the English legal system is a very good starting point.

With a labor force of more than 40 million people, mostly literate and conversant in English, access to natural resources and a very low-cost base, manufacturing industries would benefit greatly. If the legal system strengthens and sanctions are lifted, foreign investment is likely to follow. All industrial sectors should benefit and develop accordingly. Even just getting back to the heyday of the garment and textile industries would be an accomplishment. Health care and education, tourism, retailing, and telecoms are some of the most promising service sectors. Construction of infrastructure but equally of housing, low cost and urban, will be in high demand.

Membership in ASEAN and the growing importance of regional trade (25 percent of all trade by ASEAN members and 53 percent of all exports by Asian economies are intraregional according to a WTO 2011 report), could allow Myanmar to become a low-cost producer for neighboring and booming economies and attract significant investment. At the same time, the large population has the potential to gradually migrate toward more consumption of basic goods and services and develop into a noticeable low-to-middle market.

LAO PEOPLE'S DEMOCRATIC REPUBLIC: EMERGING FROM ISOLATION

Long considered an unspoiled, charming, vast but sleepy country about the size of the United Kingdom in area, Laos, with some 6.5 million inhabitants, has emerged from nearly three decades of self-imposed isolation to become one of the fastest-growing economies in Asia and a recent destination for foreign investment. In 1986 the government shifted away from a Soviet-style command economy and began to introduce some market reforms that developed private sector activity.

Laos has a one-party political system with active central planning by the government. The head of state is the president and head of government the prime minister. Government policies are determined by the party through the powerful 11-member Politburo and the 50-member Central Committee.

The National Assembly, which added seats at every election, approves all new laws, although the executive branch retains the authority to issue binding decrees.

Since the decentralization, the forces of globalization (in 2004 Laos gained Normal Trade Relations status with the United States) and regionalization (ASEAN membership) have further driven Laos toward a market-oriented economy. The country's GDP (PPP) was US$1.8 billion in 1984 and US$7.3 billion in 2010. The economy has expanded at a rate of over 7 percent per annum since 2004, driven by foreign investment in hydropower, mining, agriculture, and tourism. GDP is expected to increase by 7.6 percent per annum on average from 2011 to 2015. Tourism is the fastest-growing industry in the economy. The number of tourist arrivals tripled in 10 years to 1.2 million tourists in 2010.

Several factors are expected to underpin its growth over the next decade, including: strong demand for its vast resources, particularly by its industrializing neighbors; accelerating integration of the ASEAN group of nations and with China; favorable demographics offered by its young population; and the return of successful Laos expatriates to their homeland to provide sorely needed capital and entrepreneurial expertise.

Recent Trends in the Lao Economy

Laos is a relatively poor, landlocked country with an inadequate infrastructure and a largely unskilled workforce. The country's GDP (PPP) in 2010 was approximately US$7.3 billion, with per capita income (PPP) estimated at US$1,176. Agriculture dominates the economy, employing some 75 percent of the population and producing approximately 31 percent of GDP, while the industrial sector and the service sector account for approximately 25 percent and 39 percent, respectively (see Table 13.3).

During the global economic slowdown of 2008 and 2009, the Lao economy held up very well compared to its neighbors as GDP expanded at a brisk rate of 7.8 percent (2008) and 7.1 percent (2009), making Laos the second fastest-growing economy in Asia after China. The main reasons for this resiliency were likely the country's limited integration with global monetary and trading networks. Also, resource-rich Laos was a major beneficiary of rising commodity prices during the period.

TABLE 13.3   Lao PDR Economic Snapshot

Industrial Production Growth (2010)	19%	GDP Growth (2010)	9.4%
Exports (2010)	US$2.3B	Partners (2010)	Thailand 31% China 23% Vietnam 13%
Imports (2010)	US$2.9B	Partners (2010)	Thailand 66% China 15% Vietnam 7%
Public Debt (2008)	49%		

Source: National Statistics of Lao PDR, author's analyses.

More than 80 percent of the country's trade is with the neighboring countries of Thailand, Vietnam, and China. Only a small portion of Laos' exports are manufactured products or finished goods. Instead, most items sold abroad are basic products, raw materials and semi-processed goods. The largest export categories are minerals (30 percent of total), base metals and related products (27 percent), textiles (including garments 14 percent), and jewelry and gemstones (6 percent). As a less developed country, Laos enjoys preferential trade tariffs and other trade benefits from the European Union and other OECD nations under the "everything but arms" program.

Laos has followed a market-oriented reform program since the launch of the New Economic Mechanism policy in 1986, although partial reforms were introduced as early as the late 1970s. Many current economic problems stem from the legacies of central planning and the difficulties associated with the shift from central planning to market forces. The government's ability to enact reforms is hindered by a lack of consensus within the ruling party over the suitable pace of reform. Although top party leaders are regarded as from its reformist wing, their approach to reform has been gradual in the face of ideological and political resistance.

Foreign Investment Surge Since 2004

The Lao PDR government depends heavily on foreign investments to supplement foreign aid and lift the country from its underdeveloped status. The creation of additional jobs is a major objective, as Laos has a very young population (60 percent of its people are under the age of 25) and the workforce is expected to expand rapidly. As part of that plan, the Lao government seeks to promote greater foreign investment in agriculture, electricity generation, alternative energy, hotels and tourism, and logistics and services. It is also promoting expanded investment in infrastructure as part of its plan to transform the country from "land-locked to land-linked" as a trade crossroads in mainland Southeast Asia.

Foreign investment will continue to play a major role in Laos' development. However, foreign investors are restricted from engaging in certain commercial activities without the permission of the Lao government, such as forest exploitation, accounting, tourism, heavy vehicle or machinery operation, and rice cultivation.

Foreign direct investment has surged in recent years, coming mainly from neighboring Thailand, China, and Vietnam (nearly 80 percent of FDI approvals in recent years). Investments from Thailand and Vietnam increased notably after 2004 when the second revision to the investment law made major changes to investment policy and provided improved incentives.

Chinese investment into Laos tends to focus on companies that can provide natural resources (minerals, agricultural goods, etc.). Often these are government linked projects that have received long-term concessions from the Lao government. Many of the largest Chinese investors tend to come from provinces located close to Laos, such as Yunnan province.

Thai and Vietnamese businesses take a different approach, as they are mainly prominent business groups that seek to extend their presence into neighboring Laos. Thai investors have successfully extended well-known Thai brands into Laos (such as banks, building materials, and retail businesses) and have also focused heavily on the hydropower industry, which exports much of its output to Thailand. The Vietnamese are also very active in the financial sector and construction services.

One criticism leveled against foreign investment is that many of the companies seek only to acquire raw materials and basic goods from Laos and then process them elsewhere. The Lao government has moved in recent years to require greater value addition in Laos and thus stimulate investment in processing facilities. This is most evident in the wood-processing industry where the sale of unprocessed logs and timber has been halted. Similar plans are being considered for the agricultural sector, as Laos currently has some basic processing capacity for farm goods.

Another important source of foreign investment comes from individuals of Lao descent, the overseas Lao who have focused on developing small to medium enterprises (SMEs). Many of these individuals are successful businessmen who emigrated to North America, Australia, or Europe in the 1970s. As they usually hold passports from their adopted countries and do not have Lao passports, their investment is classified as if they were foreigners. They are an important source of capital and entrepreneurial expertise to the SME sector.

Strong Demand for the Resources of Laos

Laos is blessed with an abundance of natural resources, including vast minerals, large forested areas, and, with its extensive water resources, the opportunity to develop large hydropower and agriculture industries. Relatively little exploitation occurred during the country's self-imposed isolation from the mid-1970s until recently.

Given the hefty rise in most commodity prices over the past decade, Laos is now well positioned to develop and exploit these resources. The government has expressed its interest in pursuing a strategy of sustainable development and is keenly aware of the damage caused to the economy and society of its neighbors as they aggressively developed their resources in the past few decades.

Power   Under an ambitious plan to become the "Battery of Asia," Laos is expanding its power-generating capacity so as to export electricity to its rapidly industrializing neighbors. The Mekong River and its tributaries, the Nam Ou and Se Kong rivers, flow through the country for over 2,000 kilometers and provide ample water supplies that provide Laos the potential to produce up to 20,000 megawatts (MW) of hydropower capacity. Plans are in place to expand installed capacity from nearly 2,000 MW at present to 5,000 MW by 2020. Earnings from these projects, if used wisely, can be used to solve a number of important social and economic issues, such as improving the country's domestic infrastructure and upgrading its academic systems.

Laos has been successful in attracting foreign investors from both Asia and the OECD into its hydropower program. Within Asia, the only countries which have a similar or greater benefit from hydropower development are the Himalayan countries of Nepal (estimated potential of 30,000 MW) and Bhutan (estimated potential of 20,000 MW).

Mining   Laos has large quantities of gold, copper, aluminum, and potash and is also believed to hold important deposits of lead-zinc, tin, iron, gypsum, and coal. Mining operations in recent years have accounted for nearly 10 percent of GDP and can expand substantially since the government has only granted exploration licenses for 21 percent of the total land area believed to hold mineral deposits. Mining operations have begun on less than 10 percent of that area. At present there are about 150 mining projects at various stages of planning, but many licenses appear to be held by companies that lack the financial resources or expertise to develop the projects.

Two major mining companies, Min Metals Lao and Phu Bia Mining, are increasing their extraction of copper and gold and now produce more than double their output in 2008. An estimated 2 to 2.5 billion tons of bauxite await extraction in the southern provinces of Champassak, Sekong, and Attapeu. Potash, an essential element in the production of fertilizer, is becoming increasingly valuable as world prices of fertilizer continue to rise. Several Chinese and Indian businesses are competing for the right to mine potential potash deposits south of Vientiane that could yield almost 50 billion tons.

The government remains concerned that mining resources should be developed in a sustainable manner. In July 2010, it announced it would suspend new mining projects until further notice and would improve its monitoring of mining concessions.

Integration within ASEAN and with China

Laos shares a border with four other ASEAN nations and development of the country's transportation infrastructure is a key strategy to integrate resource rich Laos with potential markets in the region and is also designed to reduce its typically expensive transport costs. Much of the improvement to roads and the rail system are being funded by international donors and grants by foreign governments. Presently three major highway networks are under construction that will pass through Laos and will convert Laos from a land-locked nation to a land-linked nation.

Laos currently does not have a functional railway network, but a Chinese railway project has been proposed which would link Laos to southwestern China. The 400-km line will link the Lao cities of Luang Namtha, Luang Prabang, and Vang Vieng with Vientiane and China's Yunnan province. The railway is a joint investment between Chinese companies, which have a 70 percent stake in the project, and the Lao government, which holds the remaining equity.

Recently, the Thai government has proposed a plan to complement the Chinese project and extend the line from Vientiane into Thailand and on to Malaysia by establishing a high-speed train that would integrate with its existing rail system in Thailand. This immense project could provide a significant boost to Laos' GDP, develop numerous rural areas in Laos, and dramatically reduce transport costs and transit times for Lao exports.

Favorable Demographics: Laos Is Young and Hungry

Laos is an extremely young country with a median age of only 19 years. It is not uncommon to find families with five or more children. These young consumers will bolster consumption as they require housing, major goods, and services. Laos is not likely to develop a large manufacturing sector and most consumer goods will be imported, offering significant opportunity for substitution production facilities.

Laos is well suited to provide labor to its neighbors and ASEAN. There are plans to establish Thai and Vietnamese industrial estates close to the borders of Laos to tap Lao labor and produce goods for sale in their countries and Laos. For Thailand this is especially attractive as the two countries share a comparable culture and a similar language. Eighty percent of the Lao population is said to live near the Thai border and can meld easily with the people of Thailand's northeastern region of Isaan, most of whom are ethnically Lao, as the area was once part of the Lao kingdom.

Overseas Lao: Providing Needed Capital and Entrepreneurial Expertise

An estimated 500,000 to 600,000 overseas Lao live largely in North America, Europe, and Australia. These expatriates are returning to Laos in increasing numbers and many have returned indefinitely to establish businesses and settle in Laos. Many of these individuals emigrated in the late 1970s as the communist regime (Pathet Lao) seized power.

The Pathet Lao allowed their residents to depart the country, but at a cost of losing their passports and citizenship. The only outward discrimination against returnees is that they cannot own land as they do not hold Lao citizenship, and hence are treated as foreigners in this regard. As many returnees want to buy homes, an initiative is considered by the government to establish a process for them to buy land. In the future we expect to see modern housing in Vientiane and other cities, full of expat owners and their families.

Many of the new startups and SME investments are pioneered by the overseas Lao, who thus fill a vital role of creating jobs and providing entrepreneurial innovation. Having had a taste of Western-style consumerism and having recently enjoyed Western-level salaries, these expats will play an increasingly important role in bolstering consumer spending in Laos and modernizing its retail and service sectors.

Laos Securities Exchange (LSX)

In September 2007, the Bank of Lao PDR (BOL) and the Korean Exchange (KRX, 49 percent shareholding) signed a memorandum of understanding (MOU). The Securities and Exchange Commission Office (SECO) was formed and in January 2011, the Lao Securities Exchange (LSX) was officially opened with two initial public offerings (IPOs): Eléctricité de Lao Generating Co (EDL), a state-owned power company and Banque Pour Le Commerce

Extérieur Lao (BCEL), a state-owned bank. Their IPOs raised a combined US $140 million. Share offerings have attracted significant international and domestic investor interest, with heavy oversubscription of foreign investors from over 20 countries. Total funds raised by these two Laotian companies are almost three times larger than all IPOs (US$50 million in total) at the Mongolian Stock Exchange (MSE) for the past six years.

To be listed, companies have to be profitable for at least one year, demonstrate transparency and sound management, and have a sound business plan. A share offering must not exceed 10 times the company's registered capital. The procedures for an IPO are generally similar to those in other countries. Once SEC approval has been obtained, a prospectus for potential investors must be prepared and publicly advertised within 60 days. Securities may then be sold by SEC licensed brokers within 90 days (or 120 days). There are currently two licensed brokers.

Currently, securities may be bought, sold, and transferred at the LSX only in Lao kip; however, the SEC appears to be considering other currencies. Foreign investors are entitled to purchase securities. However, some restrictions apply: Individual investors may not hold more than 10 percent of total shares of a single company, and a group of investors together may not hold more than 49 percent of total shares of a single company. The SEC has stated that as long as there are no industry restrictions (e.g., media industry), listed companies may allow any percentage of foreign ownership.

Current Publicly Traded Securities: Eléctricité du Laos Generating Co. (EDL)

EDL Generating Company (EDL Genco) is currently the largest listed company on the LSX and operates seven hydropower dams totaling 387 MW; they acquired an additional 210 MW in 2011 and expect to grow to 1,096 MW by 2016.

The government of Laos established the company to raise funds to invest in acquiring the power plants and assist in the development of the Laos power sector as well as become the first publicly traded stock on the Laos Stock Exchange.

The company sells electricity to EDL (the government holding co) under a series of power purchase agreements with terms of 30 years and an option to extend 10 years. Company sales are denominated in Lao kip and not US dollars The company does not own or operate transmission lines or distribution assets, these services are conducted by EDL Genco.

EDL-Genco offered 25 percent of its shares for purchase, with 10 percent of its IPO going to foreign investors and 15 percent to domestic investors. The government holding company EDL will maintain a 75 percent holding. Thailand's Ratchaburi Electricity Generating Holding PCL is the largest single minority shareholder through a US$43.3 million holding in the company.

The stock performed strongly at the outset during which several international investors rebalanced their portfolios. Over the course of the year 2011, the stock moved sideways slightly below issuing price (excluding dividends paid) and is now moving in a 5 to 10 percent range above the IPO price (see Figure 13.5). With a 10 percent dividend yield (see Table 13.4) and a long-term stable outlook for electricity generation and export sales, this investment—despite being listed on an unclassified market – has all the hallmarks of an early investment into an emerging economy.

The second listed share is the largest commercial bank of the country, Banque Pour Le Commerce Extérieur Lao Public (BCEL).

BCEL was established at the end of 1975 as a specialized branch of the former state bank (Central Bank). In November 1989, BCEL was transformed into a full commercial bank. BCEL's activities continue to grow with 18 branches, 20 service units, and 10 foreign exchange service offices. BCEL has over 100 correspondent banks worldwide.

BCEL offered 20 percent of total shares to the public, of which 75 percent were allotted to Lao citizens and 25 percent to BCEL's staff. Foreign investors were not eligible to participate in the IPO but can purchase shares in the market.

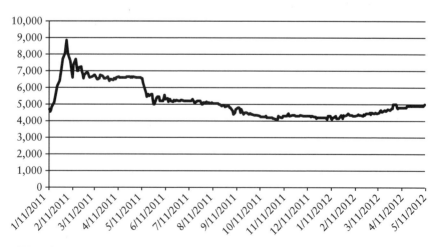

FIGURE 13.5 EDL Share Prices Since the IPO
Source: LSX, author's analyses.

The stock performed similarly to the EDL stock and trades now above the offering price (see Figure 13.6). Given that foreigners were excluded from the IPO, this stock may demonstrate the pent-up demand in the country for financial assets

As with EDL, financials (Table 13.5) and consequential valuation seem reasonable given dividend yield, return on equity, and price earnings ratio.

TABLE 13.4 EDL Financials and Valuation Report

FY ended 31 Dec	2009*	2010*	2011	2012(E)†	2013(E)†
Revenues (US$M)	82	95	111	208	269
Net Profit (US$M)	34	31	71	105	118
EPS (US$)	0.05	0.05	0.08	0.11	0.1
EPS Growth in %	−1	−8	70	30	−9
Dividend (US$)			0.06	0.06	0.08
Book Value (US$)	0.5	0.51	0.57	0.68	0.70
PER (x)	11.36	12.35	7.26	5.24	6.14
PBV (x)	1.18	1.17	1.04	1.05	0.08
EV/EBITDA (x)	Na	Na	6.07	7.61	5.83
Dividend Yield (%)				10.60	10.60	13.02
ROE (%)	10.7	9.5	17.2	15.8	12.7
Gearing (%)	63	50	27	92	69

*Pro forma as if the company had existed and was operating.
†Per-share data and EV for 2012 is based on share capital of 1,226.22 million shares.

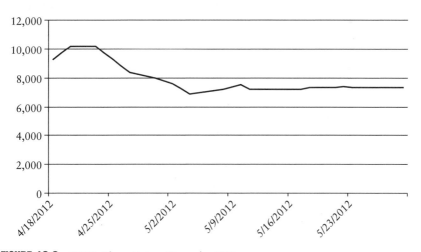

FIGURE 13.6 BCEL Share Prices Since the IPO
Source: LSX, author's analyses.

TABLE 13.5   BCEL Financials and Valuation Report

FY ended 31 Dec	2009	2010	2011	2012(E)	2013(E)
PPOP (US$M)	16.7	22.7	36.6	48.3	65.6
Provision (US$M)	−0.8	−2.4	−5.1	−6.8	−9.2
Net Profit (US$M)	10.5	13.6	24.3	29.0	39.5
EPS (US$)	0.08	0.10	0.18	0.21	0.29
EPS Growth in %	na	22	89	23	30
Book Value (US$)	0.36	0.71	0.91	1.06	1.32
Dividend (US$)	na	na	0.09	0.06	0.09
PER (x)	12.2	10.0	5.3	4.4	3.2
PBV (x)	2.61	1.39	1.03	0.89	0.71
Dividend Yield (%)	na	na	10.2	7.3	10.0
ROE (%)	21.4	13.9	19.5	20.1	21.9

IPO Pipeline

Laos sports a number of potential future IPOs and several companies have expressed their interest to list. The Lao-Indochina Group Public Company is planning to be listed on Lao Securities as the first private company. Growing cassava and tapioca is the main focus of its business.

Enterprise of Telecommunications Lao is a state-owned company. The government intends to sell 30 percent of its shares. Five percent will be offered to ETL staff, 15 percent to Lao nationals, and 10 percent to foreign investors. ETL has about 960,000 mobile phone subscribers and is confident it can attract more customers despite strong competition in the domestic telecom market.

Lao World Group, privately owned, is a diversified group that invests in agriculture, engineering, construction, hotels, and tourism sectors. Lao World Group is known to be a prominent group of companies working with the government in various development projects.

Lao Airlines is wholly owned by the Lao government. It is the national airline of Laos, operating domestic services to 10 destinations and international services to Cambodia, China, Thailand, Vietnam, and Singapore.

Lao Brewery Company is a 50-50 joint venture between a state firm and the Danish brewer Carlsberg and is also looking at an IPO. The company's beer production capacity will reach 310 million liters in 2012 and holds a 98 percent market share.

KINGDOM OF CAMBODIA: A NEW MARKET

The kingdom of Cambodia with 15.5 million people is considered a new economy. The country faced civil conflict for over 30 years from the mid-

1960s to the late 1990s. Political stability improved over the course of the early 2000s and the economy began to gather momentum with average GDP growth per annum of 9.5 percent between 2000 and 2008.

Cambodia's system of government officially is a multiparty liberal democracy under a constitutional monarchy. The current system was established and adopted in September 1993. Under the framework established by the constitution, HM the King serves as the head of state for life but does not govern. HM serves as symbol of the unity and continuity of the nation.

The head of government, elected since 1998, is the prime minister. The National Assembly constitutes the first of the two legislative branches of the system of government. Its 122 members are elected by popular vote to serve five-year terms in parliament. The second legislative branch of the government is the Senate. The Senate currently has 61 members, whose appointments are officially made by HM the King.

Recent Trends in the Economy

The growth of the Cambodian economy has averaged 7 percent on an annual basis since the government began its measured shift toward free market economic policies in late 1980s. Today the Cambodian economy is driven by four sectors: agriculture, tourism, property/construction, and light industry (primarily garment and footwear manufacturing). GDP per capita (PPP) reached US$2,100 in 2010 (see Table 13.6).

Since 1995, the agricultural sector's contribution to GDP has fallen from 45 percent to 31 percent as industry and services have grown faster, although agriculture has seen a resurgence of investment. Rice is by far the largest crop, with rubber and cassava second but growing rapidly in recent years. Sixty percent of the workforce is employed in the agriculture sector.

The garment industry is considered the biggest industrial employer in Cambodia, employing more than 350,000 workers—about 5 percent of the workforce in 300 factories contributing more than 70 percent of Cambodia's exports. The industry began to grow after the country passed a new labor law encouraging labor unions and allowed the International Labor Organization (ILO) to inspect factories and publish its findings. In turn, the United States signed the least developed countries (LDC) agreement, agreeing to cut tariffs on Cambodian garment exports and buying 70 percent of all of the country's textiles in the 1990s.

Tourism is Cambodia's fastest-growing service industry, representing 18.4 percent of GDP and 14 percent of employment in 2010. In 2011, 2.8 million people visited Cambodia and tourism is expecting growth at 15 percent in the coming years.

TABLE 13.6 Kingdom of Cambodia Economic Snapshot

Industrial Production Growth (2010)	6%	GDP Growth (2010)	6%
Exports (2010)	US$5.5B	Partners (2010)	US 47% Canada 8% UK 7%
Imports (2010)	US$7.4B	Partners (2010)	Thailand 27% Singapore 25% China 15%

Source: National Statistics of Cambodia.

The construction industry was affected by the global financial crisis but got back on track in 2010 and 2011, with investment reaching US$840 million over 2,149 projects and government-approved investment in 2011 worth US$1.7 billion.

In 2005, exploitable oil deposits were found beneath Cambodia's territorial waters, representing a potential new revenue stream for the government if extraction proves commercially viable. Mining for bauxite, gold, iron, and gems also is attracting investor interest, particularly in the northern parts of the country.

The major economic challenge for Cambodia over the next decade will be to create employment opportunities. More than 50 percent of the population is less than 25 years old.

The IMF assessment of Cambodia's fiscal policy has been broadly positive. Fiscal restraint has led to consistent reductions in the budget deficit over the past few years. However, revenues as a percentage of GDP remain low. Tax collection and legislation have been of particular concern. The authorities are now placing a stronger policy emphasis on the enforcement and reform of taxation law.

Cambodia Securities Exchange (CSX)

In 2006, the Ministry of Economy and Finance of the Kingdom of Cambodia and Korea Exchange (KRX) signed a memorandum of understanding on the development of the securities market in Cambodia and in 2009 established a stock market, the Cambodia Securities Exchange Co, Ltd, a public enterprise with a 45 percent shareholding by KRX under the supervision of the SECC, the Securities Exchange Commission of Cambodia.

With advice from KRX and input from the private sector, the SECC established the listing requirements. Companies need to have a three-year history of complete financial and tax records, a current capital of at least US

$1.2 million, and an annual net profit of over US$ 125,000, plus an accumulation of US$250,000 of net profit in the previous three years. The company's board shall be composed of at least 5 and not more than 15 members with at least one-fifth independent directors. Where the company employs non-Cambodians as independent directors, such directors shall have worked six months in Cambodia.

For companies with capital below US$5 million, the issue size shall be at least 20 percent of the share capital, otherwise it shall be at least 15 percent of the share capital. Twenty percent of the total public offering is reserved for Cambodian citizens and 80 percent is open to the global market.

There are four registered brokers and seven licensed securities underwriters in addition to two securities dealers and three investment advisors.

First IPO: Phnom Penh Water Supplies (PPWSA)

PPWSA was founded in 1895 and currently produces and supplies potable water to consumers in Phnom Penh and the surrounding areas by treating raw water from the rivers surrounding Phnom Penh. Water supply accounts for approximately 90 percent of revenues. Other services include new water connections and water supply consulting services.

The company currently (2011) operates three production facilities with a total capacity of 330,000 cubic meters/day and is constructing a fourth facility that will add 260,000 cubic meters/day by 2015 (130,000 cubic meters/day in 2013 and another 130,000cubic meters/day in 2015). PPWSA's distribution network is currently approximately 2,000 kilometers covering 90 percent of Phnom Penh. The efficiency of the network is good, with only 5 to 6 percent water loss, down from 20 percent + 10 years ago.

The tariff structure for water is progressive. Tariffs were last revised in 2001 and there is no further review scheduled. The average tariff is US$0.25 per cubic meter versus US$0.30 per cubic meter in Thailand and US$0.45 to $0.50 per cubic meter in the Philippines. PPWSA has achieved a 99 percent collection rate on billing in recent years.

The company is considered well managed from an operational standpoint. It has a seven member board of directors, all of whom are Cambodian and five of whom are government officials. The company's financial statements are audited by PWC.

The company has steadily grown its customer base (7 to 8 percent per annum) but revenues have grown faster (8 to 10 percent per annum) due to a more favorable customer mix. Operating expenses have been 45 to 50 percent of revenues. Electricity and staffing are the major operating expense items. The company has generated a healthy ROE.

Revenues are expected to grow 10 and 12 percent in 2012 and 2013 respectively due to new customers and industrial/commercial customers paying a higher tariff (see Table 13.7). Phnom Penh is expanding rapidly, with the population forecast to increase from 1.4 million in 2009 to 2.2 million by 2020. Dividend policy has not been defined but historically the company has paid out 9 to 10 percent of profits.

The company has fairly low leverage. Most debt is low-cost debt from government and development organizations such as JICA, AFD, and the World Bank. Leverage will increase modestly to fund new plants.

PPWSA offered 13.5 percent of its shares to the public through a book building process at a price range of 4,000 riel (national currency of Cambodia and equivalent to US$1) to 6,300 riel (US$1.57) for gross proceeds of US$13 to US$20 million. The CSX intention is to have stocks trade only in riel. Following the offering, the government will continue to own 85 percent of the outstanding shares subject to a one-year lock-up. 1.5 percent of the company's shares will be reserved for with a three-year lock-up period. The book-building process generated huge demand and was oversubscribed 17 times with more than 800 foreign and domestic investors putting in offers. A small number of shares were subsequently offered at the book building price by way of subscription.

In terms of valuation, PPWSA is at the high end of comparators across the region (see Table 13.8).

PPSWA pricing appeared to be pretty aggressive. However, underlying growth potential, performance, and excess liquidity may have been a key factor in the book building price finding.

TABLE 13.7 PPWSA Financial Snapshot

In US$ M	2007(A)	2008(A)	2009(A)	2010(A)	2011(F)	2012(F)	2013(F)
Total Assets	149.1	161.1	169.8	184.1	208.8	227.8	227.7
Total Debt	24.1	27.8	39.8	34.1	47.2	32.2	23.2
Total Revenues	21.0	22.9	23.8	26.2	28.4	31.3	35.0
EBITDA	12.7	12.1	13.1	13.3	15.6	15.9	18.9
EBIT	8.0	7.3	8.3	8.3	10.5	10.4	12.9
Net Profit	5.5	6.0	6.6	7.5	8.6	8.0	9.9
ROE		40.9%	32.0%	27.4%	24.0%	17.9%	19.0%
EPS					0.10	0.09	0.11
Debt/Capital	18%	20%	20%	21%	26%	18%	13%

Source: PPWSA, prospectus, Tongyang Securities (Cambodia) Ltd. March 2012, Leopard Capital.

TABLE 13.8 PPWSA Comparators

	P/E 2011	EV/EBITDA 2011	ROE 2011
Thai Tap Water Supply	10.8	7.3	22.5%
Eastern Water resources (Thai)	11.8	8.2	13.5%
Manila Water Company	10.7	6.8	19.1%
Hyflux Ltd (SIN)	22.3	8.7	16.5%
Beijing Enterprises Water Group	20.1	15.3	13.6%
China Water Affairs	8.4		14.7%
United Utilities Group (UK)	9.2	10.6	18.2%
Pennon Group (UK)	15.4	11.4	20.8%
Severn Trent (UK)	13.6	9.7	24.5%
American Water Works	19.3	n/a	7.5%
American States Water	15.9	n/a	11.2%
Aqua America	21.2	n/a	11.4%
California Water Service Group	17.8	n/a	8.4%
PPWSA	**< 15.9 <**	**< 12.5 <**	**< 24.0% <**

Source: Leopard Capital.

Despite the high valuation and the upper end IPO price of Riels6,300 (US$1.57), the stock gained some 60 percent from its IPO value during the first few days of trading and was trading at Riels10,200 (US$2.54) on April 20, 2012. This demonstrates both latent demand and opportunities in unknown markets. Given the great success of the first issue, several other state owned or related companies are now looking to follow soon.

IPO Pipeline

As in other developing stock markets, additional early listing candidates are generally large utilities, telecom companies, and financial institutions. Cambodia is no different but there are reportedly a number of garment manufacturing companies, hotel companies, and others contemplating a listing (see Table 13.9).

CONCLUSION

The three main Mekong river economies represent individually and collectively one of the last true frontiers of rapid development. While today not classified as frontier economies by international standards, their endowment

TABLE 13.9   Cambodia IPO Pipeline

Telecom Cambodia	Communications	Founded in 2006, state-owned corporation considered the principal telecom company of the country
Sihanoukville Autonomous Port	Commerce	Founded in 1960, PAS is a government agency that operates the country's sole deep water port
ACLEDA Bank	Bank Services	Founded in 1993 as an NGO providing microfinance loans, now a full service commercial bank with 234 offices nationwide

with human and natural resources and their strategic location embedded in historically strong legal systems augurs well for the future. As trading partners within ASEAN and as rapidly growing labor and consumer markets, Mekong river economies are prime candidates to watch as investment destination. Tiny and new stock markets are a first step in joining the ranks of investable markets.

Membership in ASEAN and its people endowment will allow Myanmar to rapidly shed the least-developed economy status and become a fast-growing support economy to ASEAN and wider Asia. This looks like a frontier market in the making and its future depends only on the political will to making it happen and convincing the international community that efforts are sincere and sustained.

In the same vein, Laos offers upcoming opportunity with advantages to foreign investors over some of its neighbors (China, Thailand, and Vietnam). Foreign firms may wholly own and operate a business in any promoted sector, which includes a broad range of industries, many of which are protected in other countries. The countries nascent stock market could develop over the coming years to list attractive investments.

It's hard to find a country that has recovered faster from more than 30 years of turmoil, ending only in the mid/late 1990, than Cambodia. The opening of the Cambodian Securities Exchange is an important milestone for Cambodia on its path to becoming an accepted frontier economy. With a number of larger companies, the country may well develop an attractive, although smaller, stock market.

NOTES

1. UBS, Investment Research, April 2012 quoting IMF.
2. UBS, ibid.

3. Central Statistical Office, Ministry of National Planning and Economic Development, *Monthly Economic Indicators*, December 2011, www.csostat.gov.mm.
4. www.populstat.info.com.
5. UN data, various.
6. World Trade Report 2011, WTO.
7. www.teakindustry.com.
8. Central Bank of Myanmar, www.cbm.gov.mm.
9. Reuters, Agence France Press, Gulf News (May 14, 2012).
10. Hogan Lovells, "Change and Opportunity in Myanmar" (April 2012).
11. UBS, ibid.

CHAPTER 14

Credit and Real Estate Markets in Emerging Economies

This chapter looks at two economic aspects of developing economies that are often overlooked but often of critical importance to investors: credit and property markets.

Credit markets are central to the well-being of the financial system and are a lead indicator for the outlook of investors. Once the banking system is burdened with bad debts, investor opportunities rapidly decline. We review the credit markets of Eastern and Central Europe as an example of a burdened investor opportunity.

Property markets are often used as a gauge of the strength of an economy and hence investor attractiveness. In developing economies this indicator is distorted by restrictive laws and practices. A review of the laws and development aspects of property markets in Southeast Asia provides a supporting guide to the attractiveness of these economies.

CREDIT MARKETS OF EMERGING CENTRAL AND EASTERN EUROPE

Dr. Emanuel Maravic

At the time of writing about the effects of on-performing loans (NPLs) on the financial systems of Central and Southeastern Europe (CE and SEE), a EUR100 billion-plus write-down of sovereign debt to Greece occurred and crisis had gyrated into the fifth year of its existence. Anything that is described or stated is to be seen in the light of a very fast-changing economic, financial, and regulatory environment with, so far, unprecedented repercussions on the economies.

The Recent History of CE and SEE Emerging Markets

Shortly after the fall of the Iron Curtain in 1991, several banks operating in the developed, yet overbanked, markets of what was then the European Union of 13 member states made the decision to expand into the countries of the collapsed COMECON (Council for Mutual Economic Assistance)[1] area, partly by acquiring existing banks or branch networks, partly by creating new greenfield operations.

At the time, this strategic move of paramount importance was strongly applauded by the governments of host as well as home countries of the expanding organizations. It provided welcome support by the so-called house banks of the Western foreign direct investment (FDI) investors to their existing client base in their new expanded home markets while it helped the countries of the region in their transition from command economies to market-determined economies.

By the same token, it jump-started effective short- as well as long-term money supply by commercially well-versed and effective organizations and was a first step in the development of local currencies at a time when all countries of Central and Eastern Europe still had their own legal tender. Cheap money supply by the central banks on both sides of the Atlantic and over an extended period of more than a decade coupled with a period of growth, the prospects of adopting the euro as a common currency, financial stability, and a generally benevolent lending climate to creditors, specifically in the years 2003 to 2008, led to a gradual relaxation of credit standards in the region and elsewhere and ultimately to the phenomenon of a boom-bust cycle in Central and Eastern Europe.

A Bird's-Eye Glance at the Credit Situation in the Region

Spread out over households and small and medium-sized enterprises (SMEs with a workforce of less than 250 and an annual turnover not exceeding euro 50 million and/or an annual balance sheet total not exceeding euro 43 million) and with a differing pattern of exposure per country, jumping from a mere 3.5 percent shortly before the emergence of the crisis volumes of non-performing loans (NPLs) reached a regional average of 11 percent in early 2012. NPL data are difficult to compare and interpret due to a lack of internationally accepted standards and little, if any, harmonization in this respect and the inability of national supervisors to enforce NPL reporting and its harmonization. A generally accepted principle, however, seems to be the rule that a claim having fallen overdue 90 days or more is to be qualified as non-performing (90 days delinquency rule). Practices dealing with collateral however are heterogeneous across the region.

The Working Group Report on NPls of the European Banking Coordination Initiative of March 2012 stated: "The boom-bust cycle in CESEE countries has left a legacy of non-performing loans (Npls) in the region. In some countries Npls reach levels comparable to those seen in the wake of earlier financial crises. Although the problem is serious, there are important differences in its gravity across countries and sectors and it is not found to be on a scale where it would imperil financial stability or where it would be symptomatic of a generalized debt overhang in the countries of the region. Rather, the danger lies in lingering Npls becoming a drag on economic growth as they weigh on credit growth, which remains subdued in most of the region. More generally, unresolved Npls tend to mute activity of overextended borrowers and hinder the reallocation of their assets to more productive uses. The clouded economic outlook for CESEE countries suggests that 'growing out of the NPL problem' is probably not a realistic option for the region. Instead, a more proactive and cooperative approach to NPL resolution is needed. This holds the promise of improved growth performance, with positive knock-on effects on banks' asset quality and credit demand."

With predominantly leverage-financed economies of CE and SEE beset with households and corporations not having had sufficient time for the development of savings and equity positions, plus little domestic investment from their own savings, the region's economy fell into a deep recession, creating asset quality problems on the banks' books and preventing loans to households as well as to companies.

The Vienna Initiative as Response to CE and SEE Emerging Markets

Commercial banks, international financial institutions, the European Investment Bank (EIB), Luxemburg, the European Bank for Reconstruction and Development (EBRD), London, and the World Bank Group, jointly with home country and host country regulators, created in January 2009 under the auspices of the European Commission and the International Monetary Fund the European Banking Co-ordination Initiative/EBCI, dubbed the Vienna Initiative.

This informal and highly flexible platform of organizations and institutions proved a most useful liaison and discussion platform to coordinate the efforts in resolving the NPL situation in CE and SEE, but also for dealing effectively with several other issues of importance for the financial systems and the credit markets of the countries of CE and SEE.

Topics of relevance for EBCI are local currency and capital markets, the problematic exposures stemming from large volumes of unhedged FX borrowing to SMEs or households in some countries in the region, and the absorption of EU Structural and Cohesion Funds et al. Several of the topics are dealt with in working groups, then the results are presented in the full forum.

During the first phase of the crisis in the region, the participating IFIs put together the so-called Joint Action Plan (JAP) for providing jointly over 30 billion euro through the intermediation of commercial banks. While it is certainly the role of the European Central Bank (for those countries who have already joined the euro arena) and the central banks of the non-euro countries, respectively, to provide the national banking systems with sufficient liquidity, EBCI's two-year support action under the JAP resulted in a tangible contribution to the stabilization of banks for the benefit of the real economy.

Although liquidity needs of the banking systems are now as severe as they were in 2008, as can be seen from the huge money tenders of EUR500 billion + by the ECB, the challenges to EBCI in 2012 and the years ahead are different from those in 2008 and 2009. Markets and supervisors now require a much stronger capitalization when home country (parent) banks are under capitalization stress themselves. On a broad basis a deleveraging of banks in the region is going on while countries are seeking ways to jumpstart their economies. There is a clear difficulty of maintaining credit lines by parent companies to their subsidiaries when mothers in fact want to tap the liquidity of their subsidiaries in the face of a limited savings rate in the host countries. The consequence is that banks are retrenching their branch networks or even putting subsidiaries increasingly up for sale to competitors.

How Did CE and SEE Countries Fare on an Individual Basis?

While some economies, such as Poland or the Czech Republic, battled through the situation since 2008 and 2009 better than others, the crisis legacy in other economies will need a considerable cleaning up of the banks' balance sheets (see Figure 14.1). The Western Balkan economies recently showed scattered signs of recovery with considerable delays while others, such as Hungary or Serbia, are at the time of this writing still severely suffering from their home-grown or imported problems of, for example, their SMEs' and households' unhedged exposure from excessive borrowing in foreign currencies such as the Swiss franc or the euro.

The so far unresolved problem of large amounts of NPLs in Central and Eastern European countries (see Figure 14.2) may in the short term prevent banks from expanding their lending activities in the region, causing the much-feared credit crunch.

Such lingering weakness in the loan portfolios coupled with partly insufficient provisioning against losses (see Figure 14.3) will become a drag on future economic growth.

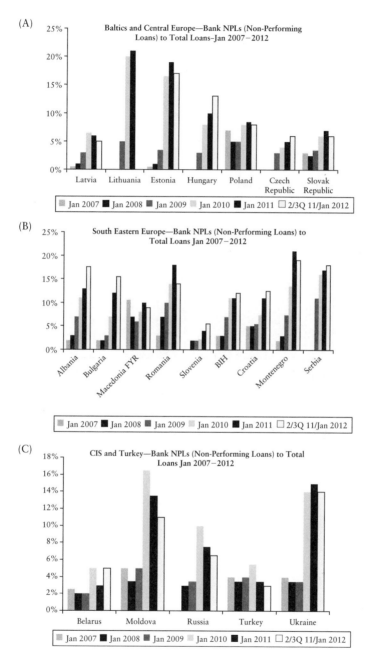

FIGURE 14.1 CE and SEE Bank NPLs to Total Loans, January 2007 to January 2012 (in percent)

Source: EIB, author's analyses.

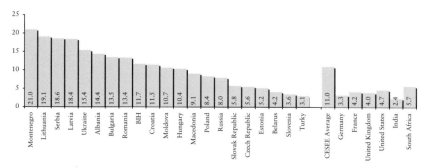

FIGURE 14.2 CE and SEE Bank NPL Ratio
Source: EIB, author's analyses.

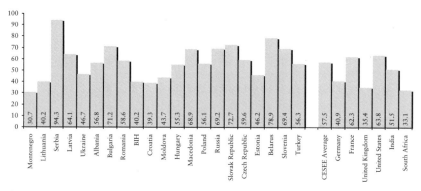

FIGURE 14.3 CE and SEE Provisioning Ratio
Source: EIB, author's analyses.

What Is the Effect on the Banking Systems of the Region?

Banks' positions in this new situation are to be seen in light of the fact that their host countries are experiencing the first such crisis of this magnitude after an era of continuous and benevolent growth following the introduction of the market economy in the early 1990s. Lending to consumers and SMEs on a very broad scale by commercially oriented banks had not happened before, and consumers as well as small-scale entrepreneurs were not fully cognizant of the rules of the capitalists' game. Legal and accounting systems were not developed by CE and SEE (Figure 14.4), countries' legislators at a speed commensurate with the need for liquidity by the respective national economies and the expansion of credit. In some countries the land registers

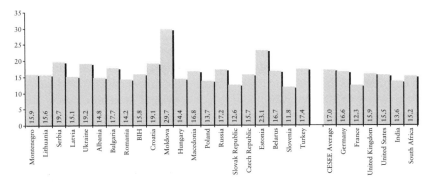

FIGURE 14.4 CE and SEE Capital Adequacy Ratio
Source: EIB, author's analyses.

as a core instrument of banks' collateralization mechanisms for mortgage loans are still not operating according to high Western standards.

Still, the situation is manageable: On the basis of comparably high capital adequacy ratios (CARs) of banks active in CE and SEE (Figure 14.4), recent data collected by the IMF suggest by and large a general stability of the banking systems of CE and SEE. Prudent provisioning up to levels of 60 percent is generally deemed a sufficient buffer, still providing for a CAR of close to 17 percent on average across the region.

However, in a county-to-country comparison, the capitalization of banks and the level of NPL provisioning differ considerably. With some exceptions, namely in the economies of Lithuania and Montenegro, write-offs of NPLs would not result in significant capital deficiencies on banks' balance sheets and capital adequacy would remain above regulatory minimum requirements. At the level of individual banks, write-offs in Latvia, Hungary, and Bulgaria could cause the banks' capital to fall below minimum regulatory requirements, hence triggering the need for capital injections to stabilize them at a level of 8 percent. Banks in the Ukraine could require substantially higher amounts in terms of recapitalizations. Most regulators of CE and SEE countries stipulate a minimum CAR of 8 percent of risk-weighted assets; 10 percent is applied in Estonia, Russia, and the Ukraine; and 12 percent in Bosnia-Herzegovina, Bulgaria, Croatia, and Serbia.

Stress testing of recent months has revealed that all larger Western banking groups active in the region (for example, Raiffeisen, Unicredit, Erste Bank, et al.) are at group level well enough capitalized to maintain a CAR above 10 percent, even when effecting write-offs bringing down their capitalization levels by 0,75 to 2,25 percentage points.

The Banks' Reaction to the Situation in the CE and SEE Credit Markets

Clearly, less than two decades for the transition to a full open market economy did not suffice to fully develop all necessary legal, accounting, and other systems—and in particular the culture of market participants—to deal effectively with the situation of a severe economic downturn with all its consequences.

As one example, at the beginning of the crisis experienced bankruptcy practitioners and reliable judges, well-versed in receivership law, were not available in sufficient numbers to cope with the situation. Professional experience with NPLs had to be transferred from the bank's home countries. Meanwhile, local banks gained substantial expertise, upgraded their internal systems, improved portfolio monitoring systems, and standardized solutions dealing with distressed loans to households as well as SMEs.

The banks, faced with swiftly growing NPL portfolios, reacted by adjusting their internal organizations and procedures. It became important to separate business origination from the hitherto hardly existing work-out and recovery functions. Only a handful of banks went to the point of creating legally independent "bad banks," as such a move would have resulted immediately in questions of the transfer price of the assets concerned. There is a clear trade-off between the principle of "know your client and his history of borrowing" followed in the good years by successful relationship managers and the possibilities of work-out manager to operate more independently and with a more appropriate toolbox for the benefit of the resolution of NPLs.

Some banks created multiple work-out units across their branch networks, while others reinforced the central credit units in their headquarters to handle the increased number of NPLs. Large corporate cases are generally handled on a joint basis. By the sheer nature and size of the situation it was at times difficult to recruit sufficient talent internally, resulting in an externalization of some functions as well as persistent competition for experienced work-out managers. A sufficiently high number of skilled work-out personnel to deal hands-on with the problem appears to be more important in order not to lose momentum in the recovery process. Experience has shown that typically one third of the value of an asset will have perished once payments have fallen overdue for more than 90 days.

Do Banks in the Region Have a Uniform Policy to Deal with the Situation?

Since the economic recovery in several markets is at best scattered, banks are not eager to generate further unnecessary losses on their books by a hasty liquidation of collateral. Surveys have revealed that the current economic situation in several of the credit markets of the region does not support an aggressive work-out policy by creditors. This induces many banks to seek an amicable solution with their clients; however, strategies differ to reach the goal to smooth the losses. After all, none that are qualified as systemic banks have so far left the region and commercial institutions have in the past repeatedly stated that they are there to stay. In the current economic phase and when secondary markets for selling collateral collapsed, creditor banks often emphasize the importance of working closely alongside their debtors to resolve the situation. Although banks had limited experience with corporate "going concern" situations on a distressed basis when the crisis hit in 2008–2009, they now generally try to avoid breaking up companies.

Why Can the Situation Not Be Resolved Faster?

There are numerous obstacles to a faster resolution of NPLs in the region. A particularly critical role is the lack in many countries of a robust legal framework for the enforcement of creditor claims, relying on a strong institutional infrastructure and in particular an independent and competent judiciary that is in the position to apply the national law in a consistent manner. Speeding up of foreclosure proceedings and allowing enforcement without extensive court involvement would be helpful in this respect. Fast-track court approval procedures for restructuring agreements that are reached by parties in a consensual manner and before the initiation of an insolvency proceeding would help to take a substantial burden off the judges, achieving tangible and positive results for creditors and debtors alike.

The tax treatment of loan losses varies greatly from country to country as much as the definition of what in fact creates a loss. When and how it is to be recognized varies widely across the region. An effective use of loss carry-forwards is not uniformly permitted by the national laws in CE or SEE countries and harmonization of the applied tax rules would clearly make life easier for international creditor banks operating in several different markets of the region.

The trading of distressed debt as one way of cleaning up banks' balance sheets is so far only utilized to a limited extent in the ongoing situation. This can be explained by some of the phenomena specific to the markets of the region that have been explained. Yet, experience in the Asian and the South American crises have shown that there is a benefit in also applying these instruments in the years to come in order to help stabilize the credit markets of the region and help the banks to recommence their lending to the economies soon.

From an equity investor's angle or as a long-term lender, committed to the region, each economy in Central and Eastern Europe is to be assessed on the basis of its own merits and strengths. Obviously, there is no uniform one-size-fits-all solution for the region, which, to a large extent, already forms part of the European Union, having to apply its rules under the Acquis Communautaire while countries of the Western Balkans are at the doorstep of joining the Union. Under the new European policy of austerity, countries will be applying more and more harmonized fiscal and economic policies. Regulators will at the same time push for a further alignment of rules and regulations to NPLs, an enhanced coordination between the banks exposed to the region, better coordination with the IMF and IFIs, regulators, and central banks of home and host countries and all the other stakeholders. On an individual bank's level, all this will go along with a gradual further provisioning for exposures that have so far not been fully valued on the grounds of mark-to-market principles. A full restructuring of the bank's balance sheets will have to be synchronized with the already ongoing deleveraging exercise of the financial industry, while national economies must not be starved of the necessary lifeline of liquidity—all in all a tightrope to recovery, but doable.

REAL ESTATE MARKET IN THE MEKONG REGION

Martin Desautels and Guillaume Massin
DFDL

The Mekong region is one of the most up-and-coming dynamic markets with notably diverse and innovative opportunities in the real estate sector, as real estate investors' and developers' confidence in the region steadily increases, with a focus on long-term prospects. The potential for developing countries such as Cambodia, Laos, and Myanmar is promising, while more advanced countries such as Thailand and Vietnam are expected to continue enjoying exponential growth.

In this section, we aim to provide you with an overview of the real estate markets in the Mekong region, discussing each country's (1) legal environment and key constraints, (2) market trends, and (3) other opportunities based on our experience in these countries.

Thailand

Thailand is still the most secure and developed of Southeast Asia's property markets, but regional competitors could potentially offer more liberal and less restrictive opportunities in the years to come.

Legal Environment and Key Constraints   Under Thai law, foreign individuals or legal entities or Thai companies with foreign shareholders holding more than 49 percent of the registered and issued share capital cannot own land. However, there are a few exceptions.

Commercial and industrial property investments by foreign investors through Thai companies, even in cases where the shareholdings owned by foreigners exceed 49 percent of the registered share capital, can be made under certain conditions and in certain areas in Thailand where investment privileges can be obtained from the Thai Board of Investment, or from the Industrial Estates Authority of Thailand for properties within qualified industrial estates.

Foreigners may also invest in immovable properties by acquiring units in property funds registered with the Securities and Exchange Commission. There are several types of these funds, but currently only a so-called Type I Fund can be established.

Investments in listed Thai Real Estate Investment Funds (REIT) will also soon be possible. Implementing regulations are being drafted. REITs offer more flexibility than property funds in terms of real estate investments.

Foreigners can, however, own buildings and houses and may have long-terms leases registered in their own names. Foreigners may also own, in their own names, up to 49 percent of a total condominium unit space (less the common property areas).

Market Trends   Thailand has a significant amount of investment by foreigners in immovable property, especially by individuals who invest in condominiums in Bangkok, and by those who invest in second and/or retirement homes and condominiums in resort destinations such as Phuket, Pattaya, Koh Samui, and Hua Hin.

The Ministry of Interior has recently increased its scrutiny of land transactions involving Thai companies with foreign promoters, shareholders, and/or directors. Land Department officials now check the Thai shareholders' source of funds and background, and will often require the presence of these Thai shareholders. Hence, it has become very difficult to acquire land using Thai companies that are partially owned or managed by foreigners.

As a result of this official scrutiny, leasehold constructions have become popular, and the bulk of property developments aimed at foreign investors offer long-term land leases in combination with the sale or construction of a house. A feature that is often included now is indirect ownership (via an offshore company) of the Thai land-owning company by all the lessees, who are thus able to control the board of directors of that company. This ensures unlimited lease renewals.

Opportunities   Despite the current global economic turmoil and the polarizing domestic political issues that have afflicted the country over the past few years, Thailand still remains the preeminent Asian investment destination for many foreigners looking for second or retirement homes and condominiums. We do not believe that any relaxation of the currently applicable land ownership restrictions or lease terms will happen in the near future. Nevertheless, under the current legal framework, investment by foreigners in immoveable property can be structured safely and securely, and for the long term.

Vietnam

The property sector in Vietnam is growing rapidly, offers a range of opportunities, and with the potential relaxation of laws and regulations, could offer lucrative opportunities in the near future.

Legal Environment and Key Constraints   The real estate market in Vietnam is still in its early stages of development, but offers numerous opportunities for foreign investors. Since the country's accession to the World Trade Organization, the Vietnamese government has made significant changes to the property investment laws. Nevertheless, there are legal constraints that may cause foreign investors to hesitate to enter the local market.

The most recognizable constraint is that foreigners are not permitted to own land. Indeed, there is, technically, no private ownership of land in Vietnam. The state either allocates or leases land through the grant of long-term land-use rights (LURs), which are subject to specific use and time limitations.

Foreign organizations and individuals are not entitled to land allocations. They may only acquire LURs through a land lease with the state, under which they can pay for land rental on an annual or lump-sum basis. Foreigners wishing to obtain LURs for the purposes of real estate investment can do so by entering into a joint venture or business cooperation contract with a local Vietnamese partner or by leasing land from the state.

Market Trends   There is a huge shortage of low-cost housing in Vietnam; therefore, to help ease this problem and to ensure a more adequate supply of houses designed for lower-income people, the government has directed the Ministry of Construction (MOC) to take all necessary measures. This has resulted in the MOC cooperating with and supporting investors to mobilize capital in an effort to increase the number of low-cost housing projects and to speed up their implementation.

Another shortage is in student housing, with similar initiatives being taken by the relevant authorities. With the low-cost base for investing in affordable housing and student accommodation, we are seeing a number of investors returning to this market sector, especially in private investments, with a shift in their investment strategy.

In addition, coastal areas such as Da Nang, Nha Trang, Vung Tau, and Phu Quoc Island are witnessing significant new interest, driving property prices and sales to a record high.

Finally, another shift is the focus on investment in, and development of, industrial zones and new urban areas just outside the main cities.

Opportunities   In Vietnam, as in any nation witnessing rapid development, there are features in the legal and financial setup that remain a hindrance to growth. But, even though the Vietnamese economy is expanding at a rapid rate, entry costs for investors are still low. With cheap labor costs and a young, literate, and energetic workforce, plus an increasing number of tourist attractions, investment generally, and real estate specifically, can be viewed as a very attractive and lucrative prospect in Vietnam.

Cambodia

Cambodia is a friendly environment for property investment, which offers the potential of becoming more liberal as the country develops further.

Legal Environment and Key Constraints   In 2001, a new land law was enacted in Cambodia. This law has considerably improved the legal infrastructure for land-related investments and has clarified the various types of rights relating to land. This legal framework was supplemented by the implementation of a new civil code, which came into force in December 2011.

Under Cambodian law, a foreign national or entity cannot hold a 100 percent stake in immovable property within the kingdom. Foreign investment in immovable property can, however, be in the form of a permanent lease, a concession from the state, or a minority interest in a Cambodian-owned company that owns the land, coupled with secured lending against the land.

Market Trends   With respect to commercial and residential developments, a major advancement was achieved with the promulgation of the 2010 Foreign Ownership Law, according to which foreigners are allowed to own up to 70 percent of private units in co-owned buildings or condominiums, excluding ground and underground floors. This new land ownership structure is intended to help promote residential and mixed-use projects and to attract new investors, as well as customers from Cambodia's expanding middle class, notably through the development of satellite cities, which have been initiated in the Phnom Penh area since 2007.

Another interesting focus is the retail property sector, which is a relatively new phenomenon in Cambodia and especially in Phnom Penh. This is an area that is primed for growth over the next decade and is essentially wide open for lucrative retail investment corporations to step in.

Additionally, the agriculture sector is now positioned as one of the up-and-coming areas for investment, and is slated to become one of Cambodia's key economic sectors, particularly in a production and export capacity.

Economic land concessions granted by the government on state private lands have brought a large flow of foreign investment into Cambodia, notably through the development of rice, rubber, palm oil, and jatropha plantations, toward which investors are looking long term with regard to capital growth and positioning themselves in a developing nation that is rapidly growing and provides numerous new economic opportunities.

Opportunities Undoubtedly, Cambodia has repositioned itself in the Mekong region as an emerging "dragon," especially in regard to property-based foreign investment. For the past decade, there has been a steady influx of companies looking to take advantage of the opportunities on offer with regard to Cambodia's attractive tax incentives, low-cost labor, available land for industrial and agro-business development, and open attitude toward foreign investment.

Lao People's Democratic Republic

The property sector in Laos is still in its early stages, but large-scale business investors should be able to secure acceptable conditions under the current regulations.

Legal Environment and Key Constraints Under Lao PDR law, land is owned by the "national community," and as such, individuals or entities, Lao or foreign, cannot own land; instead, Lao individuals and entities may be granted land-use rights or usufructs. Foreign individuals and foreign-invested companies, including joint ventures, are restricted to leasing land or receiving land concessions from the state.

Leases from Lao citizens to foreign investors are limited to 30 years duration. Leases and concessions from the state are limited in accordance with the specific laws for each sector. Foreign investors are entitled to own structures located on leased land. However, title to such structures will automatically transfer to the lessor of the land on which the assets are situated, upon the expiration of the lease term, without compensation, unless the details of the lease provide otherwise.

Under the new Investment Promotion Law, foreigners and foreign-invested entities that invest at least US$500,000 in equity in the Lao PDR are to be allowed to hold land-use rights for residential, office, or unspecified business purposes. However, these provisions allowing foreigners and foreign-invested entities to hold land-use rights are still regarded as controversial in some official quarters and have not yet been implemented.

Market Trends There is increasing interest in land-related investments in the Lao PDR, such as in agro-businesses and the hotel/resort/tourism sector. Foreign investors generally seek long-term leases or land concessions for such projects, and in order to achieve this, the establishment of a Lao PDR subsidiary is nearly always required.

Agro-business projects include plantations for industrial trees (eucalyptus or acacia), rubber trees, cassava, maize, and bananas. Hotel/resort and tourism-related developments have so far generally been centered in the main cities of Luang Prabang and Vientiane, with a few casino hotels located elsewhere in the country near international borders. In addition, a large international big box retailer has recently been licensed in the Lao PDR, whose store will provide the anchor for a large shopping mall in Vientiane. If this commercial project is successful, further shopping mall developments can be expected in the coming years.

Opportunities The real estate market in the Lao PDR is rapidly developing; however, the laws and regulations in this sector are complicated. Investors will certainly require attorneys with the technical expertise and practical approach to both creatively structure the transaction and deal with the relevant government authorities. Many such investments will involve a secured project loan, a long-term lease, and a turn-key construction contract.

Myanmar

Myanmar's property sector is undeveloped and restricted, and potential investors will certainly need legal advice in order to secure acceptable conditions according to the current laws. Significant legislation that will reform many current restrictions is currently under consideration.

Legal Environment and Key Constraints Under the current laws, foreign individuals or companies are not permitted to own land in Myanmar. In addition, foreigners may not take any security interest, other than the creation of a charge, in or over land. A foreign individual or entity may lease real property from a private landlord for a period of not more than one year at a time.

Market Trends Foreign developers or investors can obtain land rights by way of leasing government-owned land on a BOT or joint-venture basis, since, under the present policy, foreign investors must lease government-owned land to establish their business, other than land for the use of office space.

A foreign investor may enter into a 30-year lease, and if the amount of the investment is substantial and the economic activity is deemed beneficial to the state, and the Myanmar Investment Commission recommends that the foreign investor needs more than the specified duration for a lease of 30 years, the foreign investor may obtain leasehold right for more than that 30-year period.

The new Central Committee for the Management of Cultivable Land, Fallow Land, and Waste Land was formed in July 2011, whereby foreign investors or those foreign investors wishing to do business in the form of joint ventures with government enterprises, or with local entrepreneurs, may submit an application to the Central Committee for the use of cultivable land, fallow land, and waste land, for the purposes of agricultural production, livestock breeding, mining exploration, or other permitted enterprises. Application procedures for these activities will be established at a later date not yet specified by the relevant authorities.

Concession rights to land, however, cannot be granted by the Central Committee alone, since they must be granted in accordance with specific laws such as the 1989 State-Owned Economic Enterprises Law, the 1994 Mines Law, and the 1984 Electricity Law.

Opportunities The Myanmar Special Economic Zone Law and the Dawei Special Economic Zone Law of 2011 give foreign developers and investors a minimum leasehold right for 30 years, which is renewable for two additional terms. A maximum renewable term for large-scale investment is 45 years, with 30 years for medium-scale investment, and 10 years for small-scale investment. However, the regional special economic zones provided for under both of these laws are yet to be made operational.

CONCLUSION

The largely weak credit markets in Central and Southeastern Europe raise a warning signal for investors because funding for growth is hardly available and restrictive economic policies are to be expected. The health of the monetary sector cannot be taken lightly and expansive credit in the past has led more often than not to asset inflation followed by a bursting of the bubble. It is therefore important to look at the finance sector even if investment in this sector is not the target. Credit markets are one important snapshot for investors in a region.

The increasingly liberalizing real estate markets in Mekong-Asia, comprising countries of different economic development stages and challenges, is another type of snapshot for investors in a region. The rapidly developing legal environment demonstrates that the high-growth region of Asia increasingly translates its economic success into offering investment opportunities both on the individual and corporate levels.

Any one perspective is insufficient but both approaches have validity and can be a valid assessment for investors interested in specific opportunities.

NOTE

1. The Council for Mutual Economic Assistance (1949–1991) was an economic organization under the leadership of the Soviet Union comprising the countries of the Eastern Bloc along with a number of communist states elsewhere in the world. The COMECON was the Eastern Bloc's reply to the formation of the Organisation for European Economic Co-operation in Western Europe that emerged in 1948 from the Marshall Plan.

CHAPTER 15

Critical Business Issues in Developing Markets

M any investors and executives tend to see businesses in their local and regional environment. A much-overlooked subject is the responsibility with respect to good governance and avoidance of corruption. The international community, however, is increasingly rallying support for a global system of combating inappropriate behavior no matter where it occurs.

Institutional investors will need to devote more resources to this issue or risk facing unpleasant questions and possibly consequences.

One of the critical ingredients in considering, making, or having an investment in developing economies is access to information and some degree of reliability of such information. Aggregate information we use to make decisions is often nothing but the accumulation of poor lower-level information. This is particularly relevant when analyzing company reports, research, and other external information. Looking at the sources of mistakes and flawed information flows is a necessary corollary for any developing market investor.

THE IMPORTANCE OF BEING EARNEST: THE UK BRIBERY ACT GLOBALLY

Robert-Jan Temmink
Quadrant Chambers

Standing in the dock of an English Crown Court facing trial for an imprisonable offense is an unpleasant place to be any time. Imagine that the accused is the CEO of a major US company who is there not because of any act he did while sitting in his office somewhere in the United States, but because of the act of one of his junior employees whose name he has never heard, or an employee of a subsidiary or maybe that of a supplier, or as a result of an act done in a far-flung country that the CEO could not even have found on a map. Such a scenario is entirely possible as a result of the UK Bribery Act 2010, which came into force in mid-2011. There has already been one successful prosecution in the United Kingdom of a corrupt court clerk; most commentators are expecting a headline-grabbing multinational trial in the near future, a showcase of the global reach of this important legislation.

This chapter highlights a few of the legal issues facing directors, individuals, and businesses considering investing in emerging markets in the context of this far-reaching piece of English legislation, legislation which now challenges the US Foreign Corrupt Practices Act for the extent of its long-arm nature. Murky business practices and even practices that the United States considers to be clean (facilitation or "grease" payments) now potentially render international individuals and global businesses subject to prosecution within the United Kingdom.

Prior to the new act coming into force, the United Kingdom law that criminalizes acts of bribery and corruption was to be found scattered across the common law and no less than 12 different statutes dating from as long ago as 1551. All of that has been swept away by the new Act.

Drivers behind the New Act and the International Perspective

The United Kingdom came under increasing pressure to reform the existing legislation. The key driver behind the Act was the Organisation for Economic Co-operation and Development (OECD) Anti-Bribery Convention and its revised recommendation produced in 1997, the purpose of which, according to the secretary general of the OECD, is to tame "the dark side of globalization." In 2009, the OECD produced a Recommendation on Further Combating Foreign Bribery, which called on parties to review the position on small facilitation payments, increase the effectiveness of corporate liability, protect whistleblowers, and encourage the private sector to adopt stringent anti-bribery compliance programs. The Annex to the Recommendation gave good practice guidance on compliance.

The six principles produced by Transparency International, the world's leading non-governmental anti-corruption organization, underpin both the Anti-Bribery Convention and the UK Act. The principles are risk assessment, top-level commitment (a business culture in which bribery is unacceptable), due diligence concerning business partners, clear policies and procedures, effective implementation, monitoring and review of controls, and external verification of their effectiveness. Other international instruments include the United Nations Convention against Corruption (2003), European Union measures such as the Convention on the Fight against Corruption involving Officials of the Member States of the EU (1997), and a Framework Decision on Corruption in the Private Sector (2003). The latter requires the criminalization of both active and passive corruption (giving and receiving a bribe), and stipulates that legal persons may be held accountable. The Council of Europe Criminal Law Convention on Corruption (1998) and additional Protocol (2005) covers bribery of domestic and foreign officials as well as private sector corruption, trading in influence, money laundering, and accounting offenses connected with corruption offenses. The Convention includes provisions on corporate liability, accounting offenses, and mutual legal assistance. The Protocol covers bribery of domestic and foreign arbitrators and jurors.

Structure of the Act

The act abolishes the common law offenses and sweeps away the nineteenth- and twentieth-century Prevention of Corruption Acts. The purpose of the act is to codify the common law principles and enshrine the principles just set out in one unifying piece of legislation.

Using a novel form of drafting (the introduction of *cases*, samples of statutorily restricted behavior), the new offenses created by the Act reach directors, managers, and secretaries of companies as well as the corporate bodies and partnerships themselves. They have very broad jurisdictional reach that can affect any business, or part of a business, in the United Kingdom, even if the underlying behavior does not have any substantive connection with the United Kingdom.

The Key Provisions Broadly, the act creates four categories of offense:

1. Bribing a person (section 1).
2. Being bribed (section 2).
3. Bribing foreign public officials (section 6).
4. Failure by a commercial organization or partnership to prevent bribery (section 7).

The latter offense is a strict liability offense for companies and extends to "associated persons," which includes employees, agents, or subsidiaries, subject to the defense that the company had in place adequate procedures to prevent the bribery.

The secretary of state in the United Kingdom is required by the Act to publish guidance,[1] the legal status of which is a little uncertain and yet to be tested in court, that sets out procedures that relevant commercial organizations can put in place to prevent people associated with them from bribing. The introduction to the guidance by the justice secretary is salutary:

> *Ultimately, the Bribery Act matters for Britain because our existing legislation is out of date. In updating our rules, I say to our international partners that the UK wants to play a leading role in stamping out corruption and supporting trade-led international development. But, I would argue too that the Act is directly beneficial for business. That's because it creates clarity and a level playing field, helping to align trading nations around decent standards. It also establishes a statutory defense: organizations which have adequate procedures in place to prevent bribery are in a stronger position if isolated incidents have occurred in spite of their efforts.*
>
> *Some have asked whether business can afford this legislation – especially at a time of economic recovery. But the choice is a false one. We don't have to decide between tackling corruption and supporting growth. Addressing bribery is good for business because it creates the conditions for free markets to flourish.*

The rhetoric acknowledges the economic burden on companies engaged in international trade of complying with the legislation and the risks of not taking this legislation seriously. In England and Wales, no prosecutions under the Act may be instituted without the consent of the Director of Public Prosecutions (DPP), the Director of the Serious Fraud Office (SFO), or the Director of Her Majesty's Revenue and Customs Prosecutions. The Director of the SFO and the DPP have also issued guidance and given lectures concerning the principles they intend to apply to any circumstances that may give rise to a decision to prosecute. The extent and legal effect of such guidance has yet to be tested in the courts.

Penalties range from fines to imprisonment for up to 10 years, or both, and can extend not only to corporate bodies but also to the senior officers of the corporate bodies if the offense were committed with their consent or connivance.

The Different Offenses The section 1 offense prohibits a person (which definition also includes a body corporate) from offering, promising, or giving a financial or other advantage:

- In order to induce a person improperly to perform a relevant function or duty.
- In order to reward a person for such improper activity.

- Where the person knows or believes that the acceptance of the advantage would itself constitute an improper performance of a function or duty. It does not matter whether the advantage is offered, promised, or given by a person directly, or through a third party.

The section 2 offense prohibits a person from requesting, agreeing to receive, or accepting a financial or other advantage (a bribe) intending that a relevant function should then be performed improperly, either by that person or by another person at the request of, or with the assent or acquiescence of, the first person. Again, it does not matter whether the bribe is requested, received (or agreed to be received), or accepted directly or through a third party; nor does it matter whether the bribe is or will be for the first person's benefit, or for the benefit of another person. Furthermore, it does not matter whether the person requesting or accepting the bribe knows or believes that the performance of the relevant function is improper.

A "function or activity" is "relevant" for the purposes of the Act if it fulfills a number of criteria. First, it has to be:

- Any function of a public nature.
- Any activity connected with a business.
- Any activity performed in the course of a person's employment.
- Any activity performed by or on behalf of a body of people (whether corporate or not corporate).

The relevant function or activity has also to be performed by a person who is expected to perform it:

- In good faith.
- Impartially.
- From a position of trust by virtue of performing the function.

Section 6 provides that it is an offense for a person (which definition also includes a body corporate) to offer, promise, or give any financial or other advantage to a foreign public official, either directly or through any third party, where the person's intention is to influence the official in his capacity as a foreign public official and the person intends to obtain or retain either business or an advantage in the conduct of the business. "Foreign public official" is defined in section 6(5) of the Act as an individual who holds a legislative, administrative, or judicial position of any kind, whether appointed or elected, in a country or territory outside the UK; or who exercises a public function for or on behalf of a country or territory outside the United Kingdom or for any public agency or public enterprise in such a country or territory, or who is an official or agent of a public international organization.

Section 7 creates a strict liability offense on commercial organizations where a person associated with the commercial organization bribes another person (where the associated person commits an offense under sections 1 or 6) intending to obtain or retain either business or an advantage in the conduct of business save where the commercial organization can prove that it had in place adequate procedures designed to prevent bribery. "Associated person" is defined in section 8 of the Act as a person who performs services for or on behalf of a commercial organization. The capacity in which that person performs services for the organization does not matter and the person can therefore be an employee, agent, or subsidiary of the organization. All the relevant circumstances can be taken into account by a court when determining whether an individual is or is not an associated person of a commercial organization and it is assumed that an employee is an associated person. It is this wide definition, coupled with the territorial extent of the Act, that poses the most risk for companies investing in emerging markets, particularly when investing in markets where the standards of business and ethics may not be those expected in the United Kingdom.

Territorial Scope   Uncontroversial, section 12 of the Act provides that the offense under sections 1, 2, and 6 are committed if any act or omission that forms part of those offense takes place in the United Kingdom. More controversial, the Act also criminalizes acts or omissions abroad by individuals with a close connection with the United Kingdom if those acts or omissions would form part of the offense if they had been done or made in the United Kingdom. "Close connection with the United Kingdom" is defined in section 12(4) of the Act and includes a United Kingdom citizen, an individual ordinarily resident in the United Kingdom, and a body incorporated under the law of any part of the United Kingdom.

An associated person can also be a joint venture—when deciding whether to invest in an emerging market companies that have any connection with the United Kingdom will now need to be assiduous in ensuring that they have done their due diligence on any joint venturer or agent abroad to satisfy themselves that they have in place adequate procedures to prevent bribery. This concept of adequate procedures is examined in further detail later. The concept can lead to problems if, for example, that joint venturer is a US corporation. Under the equivalent US legislation, the Foreign Corrupt Practices Act, it is not an offense to make what are called facilitation or grease payments, that is, payments to a foreign government employee to provide what you are entitled to have, for example giving a border guard

$20 to stamp a passport immediately, instead of waiting a few hours or days. But under the English legislation, that is capable of being an offense, and you have to hope that the prosecuting authorities would consider that it was not in the public interest to prosecute.

An investor might think this a rather unsatisfactory state of affairs. It is, perhaps, analogous to the famous judicial comment in the Vestey tax case about it being better to be taxed by statute rather than untaxed by Inland Revenue concession: It would be better to know that making such a trivial payment was within the law rather than be put at risk of a prison sentence if a prosecuting authority decided, for whatever reason, to make an example and prosecute.

The person paying the bribe does not have to be prosecuted before the organization is prosecuted. Thus a UK company may incur liability for the acts of foreign nationals working abroad, even if their acts have no connection with the United Kingdom.

There is a restricted defense. The organization must prove (on balance of probabilities) that it had in place "adequate procedures" designed to prevent associated persons from undertaking such conduct.

As stated above, the Act applies to any entity that carries on a business, or even part of a business, in the United Kingdom whether the acts or omissions, the constituent elements of the relevant offenses took place in the United Kingdom or elsewhere. The secretary of state's guidance now indicates that mere listing on the London Stock Exchange is unlikely to constitute a sufficient connection with the United Kingdom, but investors can be sure that any trade in, from, or to the United Kingdom will be enough to be caught by the reach of this Act. This far-reaching territorial scope places the United Kingdom's anti-bribery legislation on a par with the US Foreign Corrupt Practices Act and with the obligations under the OECD Convention, to which the United Kingdom is a signatory—but it goes further.

The Risk Factors and Adequate Procedures The legislation includes a number of risk management and mitigation approaches aimed at giving effect to the legislation.

Risk Assessment Risk Assessment involves regular and comprehensive assessments of the nature and extent of the risks relating to bribery to which the organization is exposed. The organization should consider whether using external professionals may be appropriate in this regard. Transparency International offers a useful Self-Evaluation Tool on its website,[2] which is intended to assist companies to evaluate their current anti-bribery provisions.

Key bribery risks include:

- Country risk (e.g., corruption league tables and absence of anti-bribery legislation and implementation). In October 2010 Transparency International published its latest Corruption Index,[3] with Denmark being cited as the least corrupt nation, and Somalia as the most. The United Kingdom was placed 20th.
- Transaction risk (e.g., charitable or political contributions, as allegedly requested by FIFA committee members in a recent *Sunday Times* investigation). Short-term, high-value, one-off transactions are likely to pose more of a risk than a prolonged and sustained series of transactions with a trusted partner.
- Partnership risks (e.g., business partners who are present, or trade in higher-risk jurisdictions).

In a speech before the Act came into force, a representative of the Serious Fraud Office stated:

We also recognize that some companies have in the past chosen not to ask too many questions about how those doors are being opened by those intermediaries. Often either not conducting sufficient due diligence or ignoring clear and cogent warning signs. Under the Bribery Act, that simply won't do.

Top-Level Commitment Top-level commitment requires the establishment within the organization of a culture in which there is zero tolerance of bribery. Steps are taken to ensure that the organization's policy to operate without bribery is clearly communicated both within and outside the organization.

Due Diligence Due diligence should cover all the parties to a business relationship, including the organization's supply chain, agents and intermediaries, joint venturers and the like, for example so-called politically exposed persons where the proposed business relationship involves, or is linked to, a prominent public office holder. It should also extend to all the markets in which the organization does business.

Clear, Practical, and Accessible Policies and Procedures Clear, practical, and accessible policies and procedures should include comprehensive and clear policy documentation, for example a clear prohibition on all forms of bribery, and guidance on making political or charitable contributions, and appropriate levels of bona fide hospitality or promotional expenses.

Bribery prevention procedures should be put in place; for example, modification of sales incentives to give credit for orders refused where bribery is suspected, or whistle-blowing procedures to be implemented.

Procedures might be implemented to deal with any incidents of bribery promptly, consistently, and appropriately. Transparency International states in its Guidance[4] that:

> *To be effective, the Program should rely on employees and others to raise concerns and violations as early as possible. To this end, the enterprise should provide secure and accessible channels through which employees and others should feel able to raise concerns and report violations ("whistle-blowing") in confidence and without risk of reprisal.*

Effective Implementation Effective implementation would involve an implementation strategy including, for example, who is responsible for implementation, how training is done, internal reporting of progress to top management, defined penalties for breaches of agreed policies and procedures. Bribery prevention training should be considered. External communication should be considered and a company might seek to publicize its anti-bribery credentials by posting information on its website.

Monitoring and Review The OECD Guidance recommends "periodic reviews of the ethics and compliance programs or measures, designed to evaluate and improve their effectiveness . . . taking into account relevant developments in the field, and evolving international industry standards."[5] This could include financial and auditing controls. The Ministry of Justice suggests that large organizations might consider periodically reporting the result of reviews to the audit committee or the board, who in turn might wish to make an independent assessment of the adequacy of anti-bribery policies, and disclose their findings and recommendations in the company's annual report to shareholders. This is potentially good news for lawyers and anti-bribery consultants, but it significantly increases the cost burden on organizations. However, that cost burden has to be seen in the context of a potential investigation and prosecution. The consequences in the United States of an SEC investigation are well-documented: Companies tend to disclose fully and frankly and to fall on their swords, all in an effort to avoid the publicity and public shaming of SEC enforcement action. It remains to be seen whether such a culture will develop in UK companies investing in high-risk markets or sectors.

The guidance does not supersede preexisting guidance such as the FSA's rules and principles for regulated financial sector firms, which remain in force.

The DPP and the SFO are preparing joint guidance, and the Ministry of Justice has published its *Quick Start Guide* and wider guidance on the Act. However, the publications have an untested weight at law and, in any event, "guidance" can be no more than that: The real test will come when courts—judges and juries—hear factual scenarios and apply the law to real-life situations.

A Comparison of the US Foreign Corrupt Practices Act and the UK Bribery Act 2010

A comparison of the UK Bribery Act with the US Foreign Corrupt Practices Act (FCPA) supports the notion of the far-reaching nature and potentially wide application of the English legislation.

The US FCPA   The US Foreign Corrupt Practices Act has long been in the vanguard in relation to the compliance and ethical conduct of international businesses. Following investigations by the Securities and Exchange Commission (SEC) in the mid-1970s, over 400 companies in the United States voluntarily admitted making questionable or illegal payments in excess of $300 million in corporate funds to foreign government officials, politicians, and political parties.

After the enactment of the FCPA in 1977, amendments followed in 1988 and 1998. The 1998 amendments were introduced to implement the 1997 Convention on Combating Bribery of Foreign Public Officials in International Business Transactions, which was negotiated under the auspices of the Organization for Economic Cooperation and Development (OECD); the expectation was that the other 32 signatories to the convention at the time would follow suit with similar legislation (see President Clinton's presidential signing statement dated November 10, 1998).* The "prohibited foreign trade practices" anti-bribery provisions essentially make it unlawful to bribe (meaning to make a corrupt offer, payment, promise to pay, or authorization of payment of any money or anything of value: e.g. 15 U.S.C. §§ 78dd-1(a)) a foreign government official or foreign political party or party official (referred to in this article as a "foreign official"), whether directly or indirectly through other persons, in order to obtain or retain business. Depending on the type of conduct, the place where such conduct takes place, and the nationality or place of residence of the person concerned, the FCPA potentially applies to individuals, partnerships, and other forms of business association or organizations including trusts, companies, officers, directors, employees, or agents of a company and stockholders acting on behalf of a company.

---

*Available online at http://www.presidency.ucsb.edu/ws/index.php?pid=55254

The targets of the legislation may also be penalized if they order, authorize, or assist someone else to violate the anti-bribery provisions or if they conspire to violate those provisions.

Jurisdiction is not limited to conduct taking place in the United States in all cases. The provisions cover:

- Conduct outside the United States in furtherance of a bribe of a foreign official, as long as it is the conduct of US issuers of securities ("issuers") or "domestic concerns" or of any US person who is an officer, director, employee, or agent thereof (the so-called alternative jurisdiction to the principal jurisdiction that holds such entities or persons liable for such conduct undertaken within the United States).
- Conduct within the United States in furtherance of a bribe by any person or entity who is not an US issuer, domestic concern, or national, certainly if the person or entity is physically present in the US when undertaking the relevant act but possibly even if not. The US Department of Justice argues that a person is liable under this provision provided that he causes, directly or through agents, an act in furtherance of the corrupt payment to take place within the territory of the United States. US parent corporations may also be held liable for the conduct within the United States of foreign subsidiaries where the parent corporation authorized, directed, or controlled the activity in question, or can otherwise be seen as the agent of the foreign subsidiary in relation to the conduct in question. This also applies to domestic concerns, which were employed by or acting on behalf of such foreign-incorporated subsidiaries.

The definitions of domestic concerns and US person are wide ranging. The former is defined as an individual who is a citizen, national, or resident of the United States or any corporation, partnership, association, joint-stock company, business trust, unincorporated organization, or sole proprietorship that has its principal place of business in the United States, or that is organized under the laws of a state of the United States or a territory, possession, or commonwealth of the United States. A US person is defined as, for example, a US national or a corporation, partnership, association, joint-stock company, business trust, unincorporated organization, or sole proprietorship organized under the laws of the United States or any state, territory, possession, or commonwealth of the United States, or any political subdivision thereof.

Not all payments to foreign officials give rise to liability under the FCPA (for example, see the discussion in "Defenses").

UK Bribery Act 2010 The scope of the UK Bribery Act 2010 is in some respects wider than that of the FCPA and it may come to be regarded as amounting to tougher anticorruption legislation, providing as it does for wider territorial effect, liability by omission, fewer defenses, and stiffer penalties. The details of the offenses created by the Act are set out elsewhere in this chapter. Now we deal, in summary, with some of the principal differences between the two pieces of legislation.

The FCPA applies to bribery of non-US government officials, political parties, and party officials. The Act is potentially engaged by bribery not only of non-UK public officials, but also of UK officials and private sector individuals, an important factor that will need to be borne in mind by US entities operating in the United Kingdom.

Under the FCPA, companies operating in the United States that do not issue securities in the United States or make securities filings with the SEC and are not domestic concerns can only be liable if the conduct relating to the bribery occurred in the United States.

The Bribery Act provides extraterritorial jurisdiction to prosecute offenses where the corrupt conduct occurred in the United Kingdom and where the conduct occurred outside the United Kingdom. In relation to the section 6 offense of bribery of foreign public officials, for example, this applies to conduct occurring wholly outside the United Kingdom where the conduct would have been an offense if carried out in the United Kingdom, provided the defendant has a close connection with the United Kingdom (essentially if the defendant is a UK national or UK overseas territories national, a UK resident, or a UK corporate body).

Under section 7, the Act has created a strict liability corporate offense of failure by a commercial organization to prevent bribery by a person associated with the organization, that is to say any person performing services for or on behalf of the organization. This offense applies to corporate bodies or partnerships incorporated in the United Kingdom or formed under the law of the United Kingdom, who are carrying on business in the United Kingdom or elsewhere; or any other corporate body or partnership carrying on business or part of a business in the United Kingdom.[6] Provided at least one of these requirements is met, the commercial organization will be liable even if all the relevant conduct takes place outside the United Kingdom and has no connection with the United Kingdom.

Consequently, for a non-UK body that carries on only a part of its business in the United Kingdom, circumstances in which every aspect of the conduct relating to the bribe occurs outside the United Kingdom and where the commercial entity has done nothing more than fail to prevent the making of a bribe may still result in prosecution.

There is no similar offense under the FCPA to the Bribery Act offense of failing to prevent bribery, although it may be possible for a person to be liable where they have knowledge that a corrupt payment has been made on their behalf.

Defenses The United Kingdom legislation provides a defense to the section 7 offense when it can be shown that the organization had in place adequate procedures designed to prevent the bribery.[7] Generally, adequate procedures will not provide a defense under the US legislation. However, it is one of many factors considered when deciding whether to bring a charge. It is included within the US sentencing guidelines as a mitigating feature.

There are three exceptions, or "affirmative defenses," provided for under the FCPA, only one of which is reflected in the Act. They are:

1. The payment was a reasonable and bona fide expenditure directly related to the promotion, demonstration, or explanation of products or services or the execution or performance of a contract with a foreign government or its agency; or
2. The payment was made in order to facilitate or expedite routine governmental action; or
3. The payment was authorized by local written law.

Under the Act there is no defense for bona fide expenditure or facilitation expenditure. However, it would be a defense under the Act to the offense of bribing a foreign official if the foreign official were permitted by the written law applicable to him to be influenced by the offer, promise, or gift.[8]

Penalties and Enforcement The maximum penalties under the Act are more severe than the FCPA penalties—five years' imprisonment under the latter and ten years under the former.

The United States has adopted a scheme of self-reporting, which it encourages, alongside internal investigations, in return for negotiation in plea agreements and reduced sanctions. There may be lesser penalties where the management of a company is changed before the misconduct came to light and in some cases no sanctions at all.[9] This practice has been adopted by the Serious Fraud Office in the United Kingdom in other contexts.[10]

Prosecutions in the United States have affected companies and individuals in the United Kingdom. The US government is currently seeking the extradition of Jeffrey Tesler and Wojciech Chodan, both United Kingdom citizens who were indicted for their involvement in the Bonny Island, Nigeria bribery scheme. There have also been prosecutions in the United States of United Kingdom companies and of companies with a UK connection, including Mabey & Johnson in 2009, Aibel Group Ltd in 2008, and York International Corporation in 2007.

The FCPA was the long-time flag bearer for anti-corruption legislation, although it now appears that, through the Act, the United Kingdom is seeking a comparable international policing and enforcement role. It remains to be seen what the result of this new intervention will be. However, given the extraterritorial extent of the Act in certain circumstances and in particular its potential application to conduct wholly unconnected with the United Kingdom, foreign corporations carrying on even a small part of their business in the United Kingdom will need to review carefully their worldwide practices and procedures so as to attempt to ensure that, should a bribe be paid by someone performing services on their behalf anywhere in the world, they can rely on the adequate procedure defense.

INFORMATION TECHNOLOGY IN DEVELOPING MARKETS

Charles Brewer
NaMax DI Limited

The purpose of all business activity is profitable investment. This can only be reliably achieved through the implementation of sound plans and strategies which themselves can only be brought about through the conversion of analysis into practical action.

In all cases, this involves the analysis of data, and in today's circumstances will involve the examination of data using information technology (IT), in particular software allied with ever-increasingly powerful hardware.

In this section, we explore the two critical components: the data and the tools available for its analysis. We also examine some of the critical differences that may occur in the circumstances of the analysis in developed and developing markets and seek to highlight some of the dangers of using methods appropriate for the former in the latter, in particular as regards the validation of "rolled up" data, and finally briefly review some suggestions for the use of information technology in the analysis of investment decisions in developing markets.

The section does not address, except in passing, the actual methods of analysis applied or their particular relevance to one case or another. Rather, it seeks to elucidate the data environment in which analysis takes place and how the different circumstances should condition the analysis. Above all, it does not address directly the skills and critical faculties of those carrying out the analysis, and on whom, ultimately, all responsibility must fall; a poor analyst may derive bad plans from perfect data, whereas a good one will be distinguished by extracting good decisions from flawed data.

This section seeks to elucidate the environment in which good and poor analysts actually work and their dependence on IT.

The Characteristics of Analytical Data

The objective of investment analysis is the evaluation of the probabilities of acceptable returns in the given circumstances of risk. The standard models for this invoke assessing the likelihood of a given outcome given both latitudinal (contemporaneous/similar company or market) and longitudinal (asynchronous/dissimilar company or market) comparison and ranking investment options prior to formulation and execution of plans. The term *company* should be taken as an abbreviation for company/market/country.

Data for investment decisions has a number of broad characteristics. We may roughly group these into two categories that we shall term quantitative and environmental. These should not be considered firm distinctions, for some of our quantitative measure may be little more than rankings or estimates, and some of our environmental factors may be susceptible to precise formulation, but in the broad sense, the qualitative factors relate to the actual constitutive qualities of the data, while the environmental factors primarily affect the manner in which the data should be regarded and treated. Each of the factors has constraints and may be seriously compromised if other factors are only weakly present.

Qualitative Factors

Qualitative factors that relate to the constitutive qualities of the data comprise:

- *Latitudinal:* This is the degree to which data covers and represents the totality of a company's activities. Normally this is a snapshot of information.
- *Longitudinal:* This is a measure of the depth of data, normally in two separate dimensions: first in terms of time (data from an extended period is desirable) and secondly in terms of levels of detail, in general the more the better. It should be noted that the periods involved are not necessarily the obvious quarterly/annual measures, but in the case of (say) a fast-food operation, it may be important to have data relating to (for example) different times of day (breakfast, lunch, dinner), different calendar periods (school holidays, national or religious holidays).
- *Consistent:* If the same term is used to describe materially different aggregations of data, then comparisons may be severely compromised;

it is critical that measures are consistent over time, or at least that it is possible to progress through them with an auditable/provable/operational thread of consistency.

■ *Comparable:* The standard statistical qualifications of nominal, ordinal, interval, and ratio scales give a good basis for the increasing quality of comparability.

These are the factors that are normally considered as part of an analysis. In a developed economy, and for larger enterprises, these will normally be available in good measure. The regulatory returns, annual reports, and corporate analysts' statements will generally give all the information necessary to conduct a sound standard analysis of the data and a ranking of likely risks and returns given whatever circumstances the analyst chooses to make use of in forecasting scenarios.

Environmental Factors

These are the lenses through which the more concrete qualitative factors are seen, and frequently are little more than an adjectival gloss on a standard analysis. However, these factors can have and should be considered to have a profound influence on how data should be interpreted.

■ *Accuracy:* In a report, a "7" measured with absolute accuracy (e.g., position in the English Premiership at 1700 on January 1, 2012), is no different from one mistyped by a tired intern at 4:00 in the morning before a meeting. Accuracy of data input depends critically on the input medium (T. Shelby-James, 2007) but error rates of around 0.675 percent are typically found for data input on handheld devices, declining to around 0.1 percent for double-keyed entries from paper sources. It is far from uncommon for organizations to know that their data is inaccurate, but the organization has neither the time nor resources to correct the matter.

■ *Reliability:* Here also, the final version of an analysis may fail to distinguish between a journalist's overheard rumor and the signed-off audit from a Big Four accounting firm (which is not to say that the latter is perfect, as the demise of Arthur Andersen demonstrated). A particular problem here is where there are disconnected systems and manual intervention is possible.

■ *Relevance:* In his seminal paper Altman (1968) relates that, at least from his perspective in 1968, "Academicians seem to be moving towards the elimination of ratio analysis as an analytical technique in assessing the performance of the business enterprise." In the past two decades, valuations based on "clicks," "eyeballs," brand awareness, and share of wallet/mind/voice have all been considered factors of greater or lesser weight in assessing companies. It is clear that fashion and opinion may have a significant effect on the valuation of enterprises. The degree to which these are objectively significant (and indeed, what counts as objective) is something that changes over time.

Environmental factors can have a profound effect on any assessment based on the quantitative factors, even though we would normally place significantly more weight on the former in actually finalizing assessments of investment opportunities.

Volumes

As any end-of-year review of the IT technical press will show, the volume of data held on computer networks is growing exponentially. A recent paper (Makarenko, 2011) suggests that as of 2012 there is approximately 3 zettabytes (3×2^{70} bytes) of data stored globally, and that this will continue to grow in a non-linear manner for some time. To put this into perspective, in 2009, the entire Internet was estimated to contain 500 exabytes (500 billion GB) of data, which is half a zettabyte.

Of course, vast amounts of this data are images on Facebook, the result of particle collisions at CERN or copies of copies of copies of documents in Word, but it is certainly true that the longitudinal and latitudinal data held on financial and economic databases in immense and grows continuously.

It is now possible to obtain extensive, multiyear data on 6,548 companies listed on the three major New York exchanges and 9,021 listed in London. There are 2,823,554 companies and LLPs registered at Companies House London. For a single, randomly chosen company, in a single page, the *Morningstar Report* gives 503 items of summarized data (excluding attribute names and column headings) plus four pages of commentary. If we take into account the volumes of data in Bloomberg, Thomson Reuters, Zawya (Middle East), Quick (Japan), and others, the volume of data is enormous and certainly well beyond the capabilities of any individual to handle manually.

Analysis Tools

We next consider the main types of tool used for analysis. These fall into three main categories:

1. Spreadsheets (essentially, Excel and add-ons): general purpose calculation software where small-to-medium-sized data sets can be manipulated and calculations applied to data.

2. Standard analytical software: software developed to carry out standard analytical interrogation of datasets from small to very large; often this is part of larger software packages.
3. Data mining and visualization software: software that allows data to be manipulated and interrogated and presented in a variety of forms.

Excel is the dominant analytical software used.[11] Close to all users use Excel in one form or another. Access and ACL are also frequently used by some 35 to 45 percent of users respectively. All other software is used by less than 20 percent of users.

Spreadsheets   The most common method of analysis of data by far is the by means of spreadsheets, which for all practical purposes means Microsoft Excel and various add-ins which may be used to carry out more specialized functions than are normally available in the standard package. Accuracy in spreadsheets has been studied over a reasonably lengthy period, and studies over the years appear to confirm the profound risks that are common. Table 15.1 shows the findings of a meta-analysis carried out by Panko (1998, revised 2008), one of the leading researchers in the field, which shows that nearly all spreadsheets in business have material errors. Kruck (2001) and others have demonstrated that even under so-called ideal conditions (team development, spreadsheet review) errors are very common. Worryingly, some software vendors appear to make a virtue of their ability to incorporate spreadsheets into other models. For example, the insurance rating package DecisionMaker Rating "facilitates the rating development cycle by allowing automated rating and underwriting services to be built from existing Excel™ spreadsheet models."[*] This may not be considered an unqualified virtue or benefit.

Standard Analytical Software   A wide range of tools exists, ranging from the relatively generic (Crystal Reports, Microsoft Access) to the more sophisticated (Oracle Financials, IBM COGNOS) to the specialized (ACL, SAS, SPSS). These are typically used to extract data from operational sources, such as accounting and production systems, and to carry out standard functions on the data.

The two main drawbacks for software of this nature for use in data analysis are the time and effort required for collection and preparation of data and the general inability to deal with defective data.

Extraction and preparation of data for these systems is often a major effort, and often the analytical tools themselves will have expectations as to the

---

[*]See http://decisionresearch.com/Products/rating.html#

TABLE 15.1 Spreadsheet Errors

Study	Number of Spreadsheets Audited	Average Size (Cells)	% of Spreadsheets with Errors	Cell Error Rate	Comment
Coopers & Lybrand (1997)	23	More than 150 rows	91%		Off by at least 5%
KPMG (1998)	22		91%		Only significant errors
Lukasic (1998)	2	2,270 & 7,027	100%	2.2% 2.5%	In Model 2, the investment's value was overstated by 16%. Quite serious.
Butler (2000)	7		86%	0.4%	Only errors large enough to require additional tax payments
Clermont, Hanin, and Mittermeier (2002)	3		100%	1.3%, 6.7%, 0.1%	Computed on the basis of non-empty cells
Lawrence and Lee (2004)	30	2,182 unique formulas	100%	6.9%	30 most financially significant SSs audited by Mercer Finance & Risk Consulting in previous year.
Powell, Lawson, and Baker (2007)	25		64%		11 of 25 spreadsheets contained errors with non-zero impacts. Among the 10 spreadsheets with non-zero impacts for which error size was reported, all 10 had an error that exceeded $100,000, 6 had errors exceeding $10 million, and 1 had an error exceeding $100 million.
Powell, Baker, and Lawson (2007)	50		86%	0.9%	Percent of formula cells containing errors that give an incorrect result. Including poor practices, 1.8% of all formulas had issues. Including poor practices, 94% of the spreadsheets had issues.
Total since 1995	113		88%		

Source: Adapted from (Panko, 1998, revised 2008).

content and format of data to be processed. In most cases, data sources need to be analyzed and converted into data cubes before any real analysis can be done.

This has two major drawbacks for data in developing markets: First, data deficiencies (missing or erroneous data) will not be highlighted but will be subsumed in the mass of information and tend to lose those features that might alert an expert analyst. Second, the analytical elements of the systems will tend to have certain expectations as to relevance and comparability of data that may not be fulfilled (or may only be fulfilled by indirect analysis of the data).

Data Mining and Visualization Software   This is software that has few or no preconceptions about the data to be analyzed. Wickham (Wickam, 2009) describes a grammar of graphics such that "a statistical graphic is a mapping from data to aesthetic attributes (color, shape, size) of geometrical objects (points, lines, bars)." the important aspect being the relative success of the aesthetic element to depict, represent, or highlight some aspect of the data which would otherwise be obscured or lost.

Data mining is the process of iterative search and analysis where both the search and the result will tend to be informative. The mere act of investigation, even if it does not lead to interesting answers, will tend to make the investigator more informed and hence more generally under-standing of situations.

Data mining is often carried out with highly technical software such as SAS or SPSS, both of which require significant effort both to use and to interpret, and are sometimes limited in terms of the forms of output available. More modern tools, such as Tableau, Qlikview, and Mosaic, place more emphasis on the interaction between mining and visualization and the ability to modify or add new attributes and values to give "what if" and other data modifications.

The weaknesses of these types of software to some degree match those of the other categories: They may require significant data preparation, or have difficulty handling large volumes, but overall are well-suited to the analysis of non-standard data forms.

Data for Analysis

It is often said by business managers or frustrated analysts that there is not enough information available, but this is almost the exact opposite of the truth; we have moved from a world where data was indeed sparse to one where it is superabundant. What has failed to keep pace is the ability to manage, access, process, and present the data in a comprehensible and relevant manner.

However, in developing markets, it will often be the case that the data available fails to conform to one or more of the desirable characteristics and that we must apply compensating factors in order to be able to carry out our investigation. Table 15.2 shows some tactical approaches for this.

Each of these involves a measure of modification of the original data in order for it to be properly susceptible to analysis and comparison. Furthermore, it is important to take note of the degree to which data has been modified and substituted. The importance of the expertise of the analyst is heightened rather than diminished by rendering the data more capable of comparison.

To allow for the differences between the regular data of developed markets and the less formally based data of developing markets a variety of tasks will therefore need to be undertaken. These will include:

- *Ad hoc creation of new dimensions*: There may be categories of data that are poorly represented by standard attributes; for example, there may be important family linkages between enterprises that make a difference to its access to markets. Standard analysis tools will often have difficulty with this.

TABLE 15.2   Comparison of Data Usage Issues: Developed and Developing Economies

Developed Market	Developing Market	Correcting Action
Latitudinal data: Covers all activities in detail	Covers some activities	Identify missing data Use proxies from similar entities
Longitudinal data: 5+ years	Limited or no time series	Extrapolate from similar markets/companies
Consistently used terms between companies and over time	Non-standard terminology or categorization	Go back to source data and recompile using preferred attributes
Comparable data, e.g., standard calendar	Non-comparable data: e.g., non-standard calendar (e.g., effect of Ramadan on year-on-year results/unusual holiday or political events)	Create new attributes categorizing information appropriately
Integrated/ consolidated books	Separate books for different entities/activities	Apply ETL and data dictionary to standardize. Apply bottom to top reconciliation
Audited data	Erroneous data	Apply reasonability rules
Complete data	Missing data Deceptive data	Proxies or extrapolation Apply delusive data rules

- *Time manipulation:* A great weakness of many tools that require the creation of data cubes prior to analysis is that all formulations relating to time (year/quarter/month/day/hour, etc.) must be defined in advance. If it is later discovered that some other temporal measure is required, this may be extremely inconvenient to add.
- *Modification of given data:* It may be found that selected data required systematic modification (e.g., because two values have been combined in one data set but not in another); it should be possible to create new data from existing (or added) data.
- *Processing of missing/invalid data:* It is important to be able to recognize where a set of data is absent or clearly defective. In spreadsheets this can be particularly difficult because it is only possible to see a very small part of the data at any one time.
- *Roll-up of data from detail in new configuration:* We saw earlier that sometimes it is necessary to revert to basic data and recalculate values. This will involve the creation of new summaries that did not exist in the original data.

A particular issue may arise where there are multiple loosely integrated systems in which information is subject to potential or actual intervention. In many environments, there is a tendency to avoid presenting difficult news, and managers at various levels may intervene in data which is being passed upward. An account where payment is overdue may be "smoothed" to show overdue payments as less problematic than they are; for example, an invoice 130 days overdue may be included as a probable future revenue, when in fact it should probably be regarded as a loss for practical purposes.

The situation is portrayed in Figure 15.1.

A potential investor would do well to see whether it is possible to make use of very low-level data and examine a consolidated version of this rather than take the over-sanitized versions that may be presented through the normal management reporting route. Such an approach is often difficult, but some modern investigative tools exist that allow this.

CONCLUSION

Data is the key to sound analysis in all markets and all situations, and this is no less true in markets where the data is less available or presented in non-standard ways. The role of information technology in assisting the quality review of data and presenting it in an enlightening way is the first, and in some ways, the most critical step in allowing the investment analyst to assess whether an investment should or should not be made.

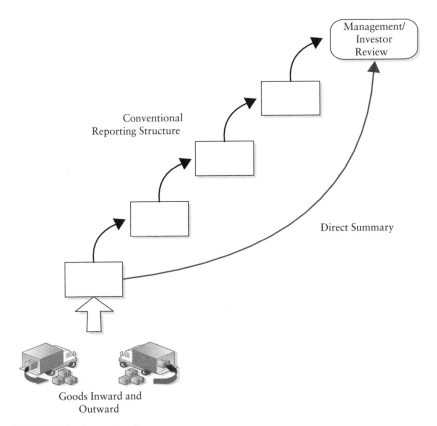

FIGURE 15.1 Reporting Structures

Developing market data in particular requires the analyst to be able to take a broad view of the available data, to be able to modify given data, and to be able automatically to apply rules to make the data susceptible to intelligent, accurate, and insightful analysis.

NOTES

1. Available at www.justice.gov.uk/downloads/legislation/bribery-act-2010-guid-ance.pdf.
2. www.transparency.org.
3. Ibid.
4. "Business Principles for Countering Bribery," www.transparency.org.

5. "Good Practice Guidance on Internal Controls, Ethics, and Compliance," February 18, 2010, OECD. www.oecd.org.
6. Act s7(5).
7. Act s7(2).
8. Act s6(3)(b).
9. See publications by law firm Bristows and others.
10. UK actions against Mabey & Johnson and ActE Systems.
11. IIA, The Institute of Internal Auditors, 2006, www.acl.com/pdfs/iia_survey_summary.pdf.

CHAPTER 16

Operating in Emerging Markets

In emerging markets, businesses often underestimate realities. Any successful undertaking needs to master the market, but marketing in developing economies does not always respond to traditional wisdom. Understanding the issues goes a long way in evaluating or driving a company toward better customer penetration and successful product launches.

Even the most successful businesses are occasionally faced with unpleasant surprises and must find ways of securing their future despite the adverse conditions. A very early entrepreneurial experience in Southeast Asia is illuminating and entertaining.

Finally, we must not forget that cultural differences can create both a divide and a bridge. Acting in the right way often helps as investor, or as partner in a business venture.

THE SUBSTANCE OF MARKETING IN DEVELOPING MARKETS

Eric Rosenkranz

On November 9, 1989, the Berlin Wall fell. After decades of isolation millions of consumers in markets such as Poland, Czechoslovakia (soon to be the Czech and Slovak Republics), Hungary, East Germany, and Russia were suddenly thrust onto the world stage, ripe for development by the global multinationals.

I was there to sell soap. Working with Procter & Gamble, arguably the smartest and most successful FMCG (fast-moving consumer goods) company, we developed a formula for a superior liquid detergent and went to sell it in Poland. Given P&G's propensity for research, we tested the product, the pricing, the advertising, the jingle, the slogan, the packaging. Every element of the marketing plan was found, quantitatively, to be superior to anything on the market.

With great fanfare, we launched the product into the Polish market. Initial sell-in was very strong. When we had reached optimum levels of distribution, we started the advertising. Sales dropped.

We studied every element of the marketing plan and found it to be class A. So we doubled the advertising spending levels. Sales dropped more.

We retested the advertising, the jingle, the slogan, all of which consumers told us they loved. So we doubled the ad spend again. And sales dropped even more.

We had discovered a perfect inverse correlation between advertising spending and sales. Why was this happening?

Successful marketing in frontier, developing, and even emerging markets (FDE) continues to be a challenge. For the investor, finding a suitable investment, doing due diligence, determining the appropriate valuation, and putting into place seasoned management are all necessary, but not sufficient, steps to create positive payback. Selling your investment company's offering into the market, be it a product or a service, be your end purchaser a consumer or a business, is key to strong returns.

The best investment will fail if the product does not sell. Luckily, there are patterns we can detect and use to our advantage.

For example, there is what I call the "Pendulum Theory of Emerging Market Product Development."

If we look at what happened when the Berlin Wall fell, when China and Vietnam opened, when Thailand and other markets in Southeast Asia finally became wealthy enough to develop consumerist societies, we see a familiar pattern emerge.

- When a market first opens, consumers flock to international products. Long deprived of high-quality products, consumers stop purchasing everything they grew up with for the new, unfamiliar, and, frankly, superior products from the multinational corporation. A closed market, deprived of competition from outside, usually does not create strong products, and these local products are often swamped by the superiority from outside the country's borders. Consumers pay higher prices for vastly improved performance.

- At some point, usually one to three years after the market opens, there is a countering of this initial reaction. Consumers start to doubt the higher prices they are paying, doubt whether the superior performance is real or imagined, and begin to retreat back to the products of their childhood. "If it was good enough for my parents, it is good enough for me" is often heard. Nationalism begins to creep in. "I love my country and products made here are as good as those from anywhere in the world."

■ As consumers become more savvy, they begin to examine each product (or service) on its own merits, and a steady state emerges. Some multinational products continue to be purchased for their superior performance, some local products are purchased for their price and value proposition. This is the pendulum.

First a swing one way, then a swing back, then the pendulum settles somewhere in the middle.

This phenomenon can be seen in many markets. China, when it first gradually started to open in the late 1990s/early 2000s, violently exhibited this. From one day to the next, in white and brown goods, consumers immediately dropped every locally made TV, VCR, refrigerator, microwave, and stereo, and would only buy foreign. This lasted the shortest period, about one year, before there seemed to be an instant return to domestic products. The steady-state period followed shortly thereafter.

The developing market investor needs to understand this. By definition, he is investing in a local company whose fortunes he hopes will grow as the market matures. But this maturation and opening up to the West will entice the multinational, who will attempt to dominate the market by bringing successful products into the local space.

Thus, the developing markets' emergence into the world is a threat as well as an opportunity.

It is the rare local company that can beat the multinational over the long term. Look at the countries of the former Eastern Europe Soviet Bloc, and see how many local companies have survived.

The strategy of the local company must be to grow stronger, not to compete with the multinational, but to be able to sell out to them. This becomes the investor's exit strategy.

While the multinational has superior products, technology, systems, and strong cash positions, the local company has its own advantages, things the MNC lacks:

■ Local knowledge
■ Distribution and sales
■ Factories
■ Government relations
■ Good local people

These five elements are basic and need not be explained in further detail. But it is important to recognize that each element is a double-edged sword.

The local company, by definition, has local knowledge. But often it has not been updated in many years, and quite often reflects a view of the market that is hopelessly out of date, especially in a country that is rapidly growing. The MNC, not having this local knowledge, needs to do exhaustive consumer research, very often uncovering insights that the local company has passed over. (However, later in this section you will read a case history of a local company that defied this.)

Distribution and sales methods can often be updated, as can the factories. Government relations are often strong, but people change, and regimes fall. Manufacturers who for years grew rich on the relationships with, for example, the cronies in Myanmar, struggle when a new class of leadership comes into power.

Lastly, good local people desert their company in a nanosecond when offered the chance to work and be trained by a multinational.

For the investor putting money into a local company, hoping for an exit strategy to an MNC, the strategy becomes clear. Additional monies need to be spent on consumer understanding, upgrading factories and sales operations, retaining people (through incentive programs, quite often by offering stock options, which an MNC rarely can do), and especially by continuing to focus on strong government relations.

The theme of understanding the consumers brings us back to the opening of this piece, on marketing to the consumer of the frontier, developing, or emerging market.

Consumers in developing countries are the same, and want the same things, as consumers in developed markets. They want products and services that will improve their lives, while offering value for money paid. Consumers in FDEs are often earlier on a value chain than elsewhere in the world.

Consumers in frontier markets need basic services: infrastructure, clean water, electricity, hospitals. As the market moves to a developing status, there is an increased demand for basic FMCG products, motorcycles, simple washing machines, TVs, and other consumer durables. And as a market emerges, we see demand for automobiles, better housing, and eventually banking services (i.e., credit cards).

An obvious caveat is that no market fits neatly into any one category. In Thailand today we can see four stages of development occurring simultaneously: from Bangkok, which has first world developed market status, all the way to Northern Isaan near the Laos border, which is still in the frontier market stage. In fact, one can start in Bangkok and drive to Isaan, viewing all four stages during the day's journey.

The sophisticated marketer must take this into account, and very often produces and sells two (or even three) products in the same segment, differentiated on product quality as well as price. Kingdom Breweries, a microbrewery in Cambodia, sells an expensive, high-quality beer to high-income Cambodians and expats/tourists, while selling a lower-priced product designed to appeal to a less affluent target market in the countryside.

Earlier it was noted that many times the local marketer fails to understand his own market, while the outsider, using the latest research techniques, often has clearer consumer insights. This is not always the case.

Let us consider one example of a highly successful company in a developing market, a company that returned 100 times their original investment to its early stage investors.

Focus Media China was conceived of by Jason Jiang, a young (early thirties) PRC national, in the early years of the 2000 decade. Coming from an advertising background, he noticed that it was very difficult to reach the Chinese businessman with television advertising. This target group usually worked late at night, and if they were not working, they were invariably out drinking with associates or customers. On the rare occasions when the businessman was at home in the evening, the housewife controlled the remote on the one TV in the apartment, and watched the programs she wanted to see. Even if the businessman could grab the control, there was little he wanted to watch, programming in those years being mass-market oriented, with no news, sports, or business channels focused on his interests.

For obvious reasons, this target audience was highly sought after by certain groups of advertisers, including real estate, banking, automotive, cell phones, and cell phone carriers. How to reach this unreachable target and grab those lucrative advertising dollars? (Chinese currency, in this case.)

The simplest ideas are usually the best, and Jiang noticed what many others saw but failed to understand. He realized that the businessman was most often in his office, and to get there he had to take the elevator in his building.

For two reasons, elevators in Chinese office towers take longer to arrive than in the West. First, there are more people per floor in China than elsewhere, due to a higher density of people per building. Second, Chinese buildings are designed with less elevators. These two factors combine so that, while in the West an elevator usually arrives within seven seconds after the call button is pushed, in China it takes an average of 2.2 minutes.

Jiang put all this together and arrived at a simple answer—install TV screens in the elevator lobbies of office buildings and run advertising content.

A little over $1 million was raised in a series A round, through a total of 10 investors; Series B raised about $6.5 million and Series C, a year before an IPO, raised $20 million. As vice-chairman of Focus Media, I helped to list the company on NASDAQ. Listing valued Focus Media at slightly below $700 million; about 18 months later the company was valued at $7.5 billion.

This tremendously successful investment and subsequent listing provides a number of lessons:

- Developing market successes are often concepts that would not work elsewhere, as FDE markets are on a different life cycle. The Focus Media concept has been tried and failed in many western markets. In Asia today, there are Focus Medias in most countries, with varying degrees of success. The concept seems to work well in Vietnam, and Focus Media HK and Singapore (both owned by serial entrepreneur P.J. Wong and independent of Focus China) successfully listed on the Hong Kong Stock Exchange in 2011.
- Understanding the customer is key to any success. In the case of Focus Media, Jiang had to understand two customers: the advertiser as well as the businessman.
- Usually, it takes a local person to uncover the success factors of a new idea. Foreigners very often cannot deeply penetrate the local culture enough to gather the right insights. (This is potentially contradictory to the earlier statement that MNCs use the latest research to understand the local mindset. One needs to differentiate between the gathering of facts and the interpretation of those facts into consumer insights.)
- Outside investors bring operating experience, knowledge of money markets, and best practices that local management does not have. Jason Jiang had incredible foresight to hire the outside experience he knew that he and his team lacked.

Putting this all together, what should potential investors do pre-investment as part of their non-financial due diligence on a target company?

- **Determine depth of consumer understanding.**
  How well does the Target Company (TC) truly understand its consumer (or potential consumer)? Is the TC producing and selling products to meet consumer needs, and does the TC understand that as the market develops those needs will also develop?
- **Look at down-the-road product development.**
  Does the TC have in its product development pipeline new products that address the previously mentioned emerging consumer, and will its new products be able to hold off, at least for a while, the onslaught of products from outside?
- **Price ranges.**
  Are products/services being developed that will address the needs of different income earning classes, since in FDEs consumers will get wealthy at different rates of progress?

- **Sales/distribution.**

  Are sales and distribution methods up to date? How much money will be needed to upgrade them (and the factory)?
- **Brand building.**

  Is enough money set aside for advertising? Does the TC have a strong brand in the hearts and minds of its consumers?
- **People.**

  Does the TC have a marketing/sales director? How strong is she or he? How well does she or he understand the consumer and marketing process? What about top management? Are they only bottom line focused, or do they also have a strong insight into their customer base?

So why did sales plummet for the liquid detergent in Poland when advertising increased?

Under the Communist regime, products were produced by decisions of the Soviet, not necessarily according to consumer demand. There were often shortages of basic consumer durables as well as nondurables. An average product sold simply because it was the only one available, a good product sold out quickly. It was the inferior products that stayed on the shelves.

When a product did not sell, the only way to move it was to advertise. Polish consumers learned through bitter experience that only inferior products were advertised.

The more we advertised, the more we shouted to the consumer "Our product is bad! No one wants it!" So no one did.

The pendulum swung, however, as the few daring souls trying our product recognized its superiority, told their friends, and eventually our product became the number-one–selling detergent.

CORRUPTION UTILE

Bernard Forey

When working for a French company studying the construction of a hydro-electric dam, the group wanted to start an unrelated activity, a logging operation for the very important Japanese market.

In 1966, after three months of training in a logging operation in West Africa, we spent about one year for the delimitation of a logging concession of 360.000 hectares.

After obtaining a 20-year renewable license from the appropriate ministry of agriculture, we ordered all the necessary equipment including

50 Caterpillars, loaders, scrapers, cranes, and so on to start a large-scale operation. A fleet of barges and tugboats was required as the concession was 600 kilometers upstream of a river. We sourced generators, workshop equipment, and even a small aircraft for which we had to build a 1,200 meters airstrip. The estimated total investment was about US $10 million.

First we built a camp for about 1,000 people, workers and families. Three months after the delivery of the equipment we started the logging operation to export logs to Japan. The Japanese market was booming due to building construction.

Few years later, the French group expressed their intent to sell the timber business, as they failed to obtain the hydroelectric dam contract. To me, the decision was not logical, as the logging was starting to make a profit. Why abandon such a promising project?

So, I asked the CEO of the French company under what conditions he was prepared to sell the logging company. He replied that they were willing to sell for US$5 million. When I told the CEO that I was interested in buying the company, he was surprised, yet he agreed to give me six months to raise funding and complete a transaction.

Being French, I went to see the French banks first, and some foreign banks in Singapore, trying to get them interested in the company and prepared to give a loan of US$5 million against full mortgage of the company. All the banks had the same reaction and asked for collateral outside of the logging business. The bankers did not understand the potential of the business and the size of the Japanese market.

After my negative experience in Singapore, I decided to approach a local bank involved in timber. They were receptive to the proposal and surprised that a foreigner would understand and invest in such a local business.

The bank decided to send two appraisers to inspect the company, the equipment, and the audited accounts, even if accounts are unreliable. After two weeks the bank appraisers came back with a positive report and, confidentially, the bank executive told me that he would require US$500,000 as a transaction fee for the work to get the transaction approved.

The loan was increased to US$5.5 million and one month later the French company received the $5 million asking price. We took over the operation, kept all the manpower, and developed production to respond to the increasing demand from Japan. We built a sawmill and one of the first plywood factories in the country.

From a village of 1,000 people, within five years the place became a small city of more than 5,000 people, with schools, clinics, shops, warehouses, and workshops in the middle of the jungle, with the only possible access by the river or by small aircraft.

Besides timber, we started a tuna-fishing operation and a canning factory, and soon the factory was canning for John West, Saupiquet, Migros, and others, employing about 1,500 people on fishing vessels and at the factory.

Several years later, I was contacted by one lawyer working for one of the country's leading families, who tried to convince me to take them as partners in my business. I explained that we already had a local partner, a local company financed by us for the benefit of local staff. They told me that our local partners do not have political connections or the right clout to make things happen. Finally they offered to take 50 percent of the business for 1 US dollar, which would provide the support of the family at the highest level, meaning many new opportunities and financing of new projects under special conditions.

We refused the proposal and three months later we had no more export licenses, no more credit, and a refusal to extend the renewable timber license. We then hired a lawyer to sue the administration and were contacted by the family lawyer, offering, after aggressive meetings, some 20 percent of the real business value.

In retrospect, we were wrong to refuse the offer of indirect participation with the family. Our decision stopped all our planned developments in country, including an important plantation.

A Chinese businessman, in the same circumstances, might have accepted the offer of 50 percent for US$1, knowing that unlimited credit facilities would give him the opportunity to develop bigger business and also find a satisfactory compromise in other respects. After working with Chinese for so many years, I was, in many ways, under the influence of the Chinese way of building a business. My refusal to the family proposal was the result of my Western education, not prepared to accept a deal that was offensive.

Ultimately, success was made possible because of the commercial mindset of the director of credit of the bank. For us, it was positive facilitation. At the same time, the success was its own downfall when similar principles were applied to get us out of the business. There are always two sides to success in developing economies and today this may be different altogether, but in many emerging economies the principles may still hold.

BUSINESS STYLES AND REQUIREMENTS

Walter Vieira

At first sight, it might seem that a section on business styles and requirements is greatly misplaced in a book focussed on investing. On reflection, interpersonal culture and investing are two sides of the same coin. One is dependent on the other, although we do not generally give much thought to this aspect.

The Economist of February 14, 2009 contained an article by Adam Galinsky of the Kellogg Business School that stated the obvious, but is worth repeating: "During this crisis, when there is so much uncertainty about who will end up having power, the best strategy is to be civil to everyone." Significantly, the newspaper headline of January 11, 2012 screams, "China and India contribute towards 50% of the current growth in GDP worldwide." A long way from when United States, Europe, and Japan dominated the world economic scenario!

The Role of Business Styles

The first time I realized the role of what is called business etiquette was in a business discussion when a client, the CEO of a very large textile mill in India, went to see the chairman of the Industrial Development Bank in India, to seek a loan for a large expansion project. The company's vice president, Finance, and I, as management consultant, accompanied the CEO, both as rather passive attendees, since much of the conversation was between the CEO and the chairman of the bank. After some time, the finance VP got either tired or bored, or perhaps both, and involuntarily began rocking his chair, only slightly but still noticeably. A while later, the chairman turned sternly to him and said, "You seem to be uninterested in what is going on. I think we'd better end this meeting now" and he got up from his chair to say good-bye. In parting, he said to the CEO, "Why don't you send a complete written proposal and I will see what we can do."

The proposal was sent soon after to the bank, which rejected it. The CEO later confided to me that it was perhaps the annoyance caused by his VP that resulted in the rejection. If it were a deficiency in the report or proposal, the bank would have asked for clarifications, but they did not. This was in spite of the mill being one of the leaders in the industry.

A clash of business styles by a senior manager had caused the company to pay a very heavy price—totally disproportionate to the potential offense! If this can happen in interactions between leaders in the same country, how much more challenging can situations be between businesspeople and executives from different cultures?

A Question of Attitudes—East and West

There is the situation of Dr. Ben, an eminent investment consultant from India. We met in the lobby of a hotel in Dubai and I asked him what he was doing there. "Wasting my time," was the terse reply. I could see that he was angry about something. "Why?" I asked.

He told me that he had been invited by a wealthy sheik for discussions to start an investment firm in the United Arab Emirates. He had arrived two days prior and he had met the Sheik just twice, once on the first day when he came to check that Ben was comfortable and to make arrangements for his sightseeing in Dubai (which Ben was not keen on) and again the next evening to have dinner with him. Both times there was no discussion about the business he had come for. Even when Ben broached the subject, the Sheik avoided this with "We will talk about this later." The hospitality was excellent, there were no complaints. There was a car with a chauffeur at his disposal and the hotel was five stars. But no work got done! Ben had planned a visit of only two days! I learned later that it took five days before a deal was concluded.

Ben had forgotten that in the Middle East, you need to be a friend first, before you do business. In the West, you first do business, and then, perhaps, you may become a friend. Dr. Ben went through the motions, albeit reluctantly, and he was rewarded. He now has a partnership in a successful investment company in the United Arab Emirates.

A Question of Time

The management of time is such a cultural issue that tempers are lost, and relationships shattered, because one does not put time into the cultural context.

There is the German and the Scandinavian view of time, which demands that you be there a few minutes before the appointed time. The American, the English, the Japanese, and Singaporean will be there on time. The Italian will be punctual for the business meeting, but allow certain flexibility for the social meeting. The Iberian and the distant relative, the South American, will perhaps allow a delay of a quarter to half an hour. So will the Indian and the Malaysian. That is why Malaysian time is called rubber time—it is stretchable!

When you travel abroad, you can hold to your own view of time, but not if you want to succeed in business worldwide. You have to view punctuality in a cultural context.

A Problem of Attention

When the Arab tycoon was invited to Canada by his prospective business partner to sign the agreement, the Canadian hosted a large dinner party for 50 important guests. He made sure not to serve pork and to offer his host only nonalcoholic beverages. The guest of honor did not accept any food or drink immediately. He said he would have some later. The host assumed that he would then help himself, and went to look after his other guests. An hour later, the guest of honor could not be found. He had quietly slipped out and gone back to his hotel, in annoyance that his host had not given him sufficient importance.

It was necessary to offer him a drink at least three times before he would accept. It is not good custom to say yes immediately on being asked. And the host, instead of spending all the time with him, was circulating among his other guests without giving him personal attention. The host felt he had to be fair to his other guests too. The guest of honor did not see it this way. The agreement was never signed. There was a mismatch in cultural values.

Differences in Verbal Communication

Verbal communication is managed differently by people of different nations. When you sit across the table from an executive in the United Kingdom, and he receives a phone call, you cannot hear the conversation. It is clear and audible to the person at the other end of the telephone, but inaudible to the person sitting at the table.

This will not happen with an Indian. Indians tend to speak very loud. When they phone long distance, you wonder whether they really need the telephone at all. When driving, people will use the horn more than they use the accelerator. There is sound or there is noise!

"How are you?" may be a form of polite greeting in the West but it may be taken for a serious inquiry if used in India. You may be in for a long recounting of all the health problems of various members of the family and you will probably regret that you used the greeting in the first place.

The Gap in Nonverbal Communication

In the world of nonverbal communication, cultural differences are sometimes even bigger. Observing and learning is the key. One can never know and understand enough.

Personal space is a misunderstood area because large personal space is the norm in the West while close space is the norm in the East. The latter can cause great discomfort to those from the West, who keep moving away, but sometimes cannot physically get far enough, in spite of their best efforts.

Head nods have so many different meanings in different countries. When an American returned from a meeting with the Japanese and sent a draft agreement for endorsement and signature, the Japanese politely returned it as unacceptable. "But you nodded agreement at the meeting," protested the American on the telephone. "No, I nodded to say, I follow what you are saying, not I agree to what you are saying!" responded the Japanese.

Finalizing Agreements over Drinks and a Meal

Drinking and eating with people across different cultures is also a challenge. In Europe, you are entertained in style in restaurants with a variety of cutlery and glasses laid out. You are expected to know how and when to use them. In India, there will be the Indian *thali*, a large plate with little bowls for different foods, to be eaten with the right hand. In China, one is expected to eat from an individual bowl with chopsticks or from a common bowl with serving chopsticks. In the Middle East, joint eating of the common unleavened bread with various meats and vegetables placed in the center of the flatbread, for sharing, will be common.

It is said that business is discussed during the day and agreements finalized in the evenings during a meal. If this is so, then learning to adopt and adapt to different eating styles becomes a necessity, not a choice.

Manners Maketh the Businessman

Experts in international business admit that success in managing people on different continents and building relationships and trust depends on interpersonal style and etiquette.

In April 2009, the *The Economist* contained an article that made three significant points:

1. Manners make the businessman.
2. Rudeness is out and civility is the new rule in an uncertain world.
3. It is now all about charm and openness and taking time with people.

There is no great magic in behaving appropriately in various situations; all that is necessary is to remember to show consideration at all times and that in the East, you have to be a friend first and then you do business. In the West, you first do business and then, perhaps, you may become a friend.

CONCLUSION

Marketing experience offers a useful lesson when investing in developing economies. The lesson learned over many years of experience is simple. FDE (frontier, developing, and emerging) economies offer exciting investment opportunities, but only if your product can sell. Selling requires a deep understanding of the consumer, tailoring products and services to fit the developing needs, and marketing to underscore those needs and provide solutions.

This is echoed by the experience of the pioneer days of emerging market investing when rules were less clear and influences more prevalent. The moral that remains today is that working in emerging economies requires exceptional personal compromise at lower and at top levels in order to succeed.

In the same vein, the human aspect and cross-cultural behavior teaches us that in the new (or not so new) global village, technical (financial) knowledge and managerial skills are essential but not enough. You need a higher order of human skills.

About the Author and Editor

Dr. Gordian Gaeta is an active private equity investor and advisor specializing in complex and distressed equity and alternative investments and transactions, predominantly in the developing economies of Asia but also in Europe. He participates on boards, investment and finance committees, and in executive functions of fund managers, investment firms, and financial services companies.

Gordian started his career as a banker in several countries before becoming a management consultant. He was a strategic advisor to Standard Chartered Bank and a managing partner for Booz & Company, where he advised most of the largest global banks and multiple governments and agencies on economic and financial services policy.

A former academic, Gordian lectured at several universities, serves as director, professor, or dean of private academies certifying financial services professionals on investment and co-chairs the Asian Banker Summit. He coauthored *Frontiers in Credit Risk* (Wiley Finance), *Hong Kong 21*, and *Vision Korea*, on the economic vision of these economies, and *Servus Hong Kong* on Austria in Hong Kong. He publishes an investment column and contributes to business publications on investment, risk, strategy, and financial services.

A clinical rationalist and contrarian thinker, Gordian studies long-term macroeconomic developments and framework conditions applicable to developing market and alternative investments.

Gordian studied mathematics at the Institute of Technology, Vienna, law in Vienna and Salzburg where he earned a master and doctorate in law, and postgraduate business sciences at the Institute of Technology, Zurich.

Contact: gordian.gaeta@gmail.com

About the Contributors

NOËL AMENC

Noël is professor of finance and director of EDHEC-Risk Institute. He has a master's in economics and a PhD in finance and has conducted active research in the fields of quantitative equity management, portfolio performance analysis, and active asset allocation, resulting in numerous academic and practitioner articles and books.

He is a member of the editorial board of the *Journal of Portfolio Management*, associate editor of the *Journal of Alternative Investments*, and a member of the scientific advisory council of the AMF (French financial regulatory authority).

Contact: noel.amenc@edhec.edu

CHARLES BREWER

Charles Brewer is the CEO of NaMax DI, a UK/Gulf–based organization specializing in the use of software to promote insight and understanding in large sets of data. After university, he worked for Andersen Consulting, Price Waterhouse, Citibank, and Merrill Lynch, specializing in the development of trading systems and related strategic and operational matters.

Charles has an MBA from Liverpool University (2005), an MLitt from the University of Edinburgh (1977), and a BA(Hons) from Newcastle University (1975). He has worked as an advisor to the UK and Swedish governments and the European Commission on matters relating to the IT impact of the euro and has lived and worked in many parts of the world including the UK, USA, Poland, Switzerland, South Korea, and the UAE.

Contact: charles.brewer@namaxdi.co.uk

ANDREAS BUELOW

Andreas has been based in Bahrain since 2008 and has worked in various contexts within the Gulf region, at present as a senior consultant with Roland Berger Strategy Consultants. His professional interests are in the energy sector as well as in financial services.

Andreas holds a diploma in business administration and economics from the University of Hohenheim in Germany (2002) and an MBA from the International University of Monaco (2006).

Contact: andreasbuelow@gmail.com

MARTIN DESAUTELS

Martin has been advising on legal issues in the Mekong Region since 1999 when he worked on major energy projects in Hanoi, including the first BOT power plant project in Vietnam. He has vast experience advising on a variety of energy, infrastructure, project finance, secured lending, and corporate transactions across the region, with a focus on Vietnam, Laos, and Cambodia.

Martin's practice currently focuses on regional energy and infrastructure projects, financing transactions, investment funds, and other corporate work. He has advised on a variety of infrastructure projects throughout the Mekong Region, notably port construction, railway development, toll bridges, water processing facilities, telecommunications networks, and power plants, including renewable and hydropower.

Martin is managing partner and head of the Banking & Finance Practice Group at DFDL.

Contact: Martin.Desautels@dfdl.com

BERNARD FOREY

Bernard is the founder of CFA Investments in Singapore, focused on new businesses in the Asia-Pacific region. Bernard started as geophysicist/prospector in the Sahara and Mauritanian desert and worked for a mine in Iran. He reviewed hydroelectric and timber opportunities in Java and Sumatra.

In the mid-1960s, he moved to Indonesia where he acquired and developed a 360,000-hectare timber concession with logging, a sawmill, and a plywood factory. Since then, he was instrumental in starting and developing a number of successful businesses in a variety of industries: tuna fishing and canning in Indonesia; a leading mineral water brand in Vietnam and Australia; a hygiene product factory in Burma and a mineral water plant in Cambodia.

In 1977, Bernard was made a knight of the French Legion of Honor.

Contact: bforey@cfa.com.sg

FELIX GOLTZ

Felix is head of applied research at EDHEC-Risk Institute. He carries out research in empirical finance and asset allocation, with a focus on alternative investments and indexing strategies. His work has appeared in various international academic and practitioner journals and handbooks.

He obtained a PhD in finance from the University of Nice Sophia-Antipolis after studying economics and business administration at the University of Bayreuth and EDHEC Business School.

Contact: Felix.Goltz@edhec.edu

THOMAS HUGGER

Thomas Hugger is CFO and managing partner at Leopard Capital LP, which is the first private equity fund in Cambodia. He is also the fund manager of Leopard Asia Frontier Fund and invests in Bangladesh, Bhutan, Cambodia, Laos, Maldives, Mongolia, Myanmar, Nepal, Pakistan, Papua New Guinea, Sri Lanka, and Vietnam. Before joining Leopard Capital, Thomas was the head of portfolio management at LGT Bank in Liechtenstein in Zurich and Hong Kong where he invested in all asset classes.

From 1986 to 2000 he worked for Bank Julius Baer in Zurich and Hong Kong where his last position was head of the Asian equity trading desk. In this capacity he gained extensive expertise to emerging and frontier markets in Asia, Middle East, and Africa when managing the bank's proprietary portfolio. Thomas is a CFIA—(Federal) Certified Financial Analyst and Investment Advisor—in Switzerland, and a certified EFFAS (European Federation of Financial Analysts Societies) financial analyst.

Contact: th@leopardcapital.com

SCOTT ALEXANDER LEWIS

Scott is managing partner and chief investment officer of Leopard Capital's Cambodia Fund and is based in Phnom Penh. He joined Leopard Capital in 2008 and has 19 years' experience in investment banking and private equity.

Prior to Leopard Capital he was a director of Merrill Lynch's Global Energy & Power investment banking group in London, Houston, and Calgary. Earlier he was a member of the investment teams of First Reserve Corp., an energy-focused private equity group, and Sterling Group, a private equity firm investing in the US petrochemical, agribusiness, and manufacturing sectors.

Scott received an MPA and a BBA (Accounting) with high honors from the University of Texas at Austin.

Contact: sl@leopardcapital.com

EMANUEL MARAVIC

Emanuel earned a doctorate of law from the University of Vienna. From 1977 to 1996, he worked for Creditanstalt and Deutsche Bank in Brussels, Hamburg, Sydney, Manila, and Hong Kong followed by New York and London. He served as Credianstalt's head of international credit risk control, managing director of the asset-based lending subsidiary, head of the restructuring and distressed corporate asset unit, and assistant general manager and head of corporate and trade finance.

In 1996, Emanuel joined the European Investment Bank (EIB), Luxemburg, as the first director nominated from the three then-new EU member states. As director for lending operations, he covered Germany and Austria from 1996 to 2000, the accession countries of Eastern Europe from 2000 to 2003, and six member states of Central Europe from 2004 to 2005. From 2006 to 2012 he was appointed the first director of the EIB Office in Vienna covering Austria, the Czech Republic, Hungary, Slovakia, and Slovenia.

In April 2012 Dr. Maravic joined KBR Corporate Finance, Frankfurt, which specializes in corporate advice to enterprises and sovereigns, structured export transactions, and the resolution of distressed corporate and sovereign assets.

Contact: emaravic@kbr-finance.com

GUILLAUME MASSIN

Guillaume has been working in Cambodia as a consultant and a legal adviser since 2005. His practice covers property, corporate and commercial, criminal law and procedures, and technical assistance consultancies. Guillaume is currently team leader on a number of recent and ongoing major real estate–related and agriculture projects in Cambodia.

He has notably played an important role on landmark deals advising international investment groups on land use rights and construction permits, assisting banks and private equity funds for the structuring of property projects, supervising the acquisition and structuring of hotel and resort projects, including for the lease of state land to investors and in respect of land development projects for factories in Special Economic Zones.

Guillaume also advises numerous international and local investors in the retail, agriculture, and construction sectors. Guillaume is managing director of DFDL Cambodia and head of the Real Estate Practice Group.

Contact: Guillaume.Massin@dfdl.com

MOHAMMED MOUSSALLATI

Mohammed is a corporate and commercial lawyer with broad experience in a wide range of areas and sectors, including advising on company formations, acquisitions and disposals and general commercial contracts and matters.

Mohammed graduated with First Class Honors from the University of Manchester with a BA Accounting & Law degree and with Distinctive Honors at BPP Law School.

Mohammed qualified as a lawyer in the United Kingdom with a leading national commercial law firm and has since worked in private practice as a corporate and commercial lawyer in the Sultanate of Oman and as in-house counsel for a prominent corporate in Dubai, United Arab Emirates.

Contact: mmoussallati@live.co.uk

MASAYOSHI MUKAI

Masayoshi is an analyst at EDHEC-Risk Indices and Benchmarks. He attended college at the University of California, Berkeley, where he graduated with high honors and was a Regents' and Chancellor's scholar.

He also holds an MPhil in management from the University of Cambridge, Judge Business School, and is a member of Girton College. His research interests are in the area of equity and fixed income indexing innovation.

PADMANABAN NARASIMHAN

Padmanaban contributed to this report during his tenure as a research assistant at EDHEC Risk Institute–Asia in Singapore. He has a master's of financial engineering from the Anderson School of Management at University of California, Los Angeles, and a bachelor's of technology, computer science, and engineering, from the International Institute of Information Technology, Hyderabad.

MICHAEL PREISS

Michael is founder and chief investment officer of Mongolia Asset Management. He has 17 years' experience in global financial markets having worked in New York, London, Paris, Hong Kong, Dubai, and Singapore in various investment and research functions. Michael held senior positions with HSBC Private Bank as well as Standard Chartered Bank.

Michael is a graduate of the European Business School with a major in finance and international economics, having studied at the school's centers in London, Paris, and Bologna, Italy in their respective languages. In addition he undertook studies in Japan, Korea, and China. He has published extensively on investment and securities, appeared as commentator on major networks and teaches securities-related matters at private academies.

Mr. Preiss was born in Germany and raised in Switzerland. He currently resides in Singapore.

Contact: mpreiss@mongoliaassetmanagement.com

JOSUAH RECHTSTEINER

Josuah is currently establishing a financial business in Central Eastern Europe. Until April 2012, he was an associate at Rising STAR AG where he worked within the operations and controlling department in fund and investment controlling. His areas of responsibility comprised cash and cost controlling as well as currency controlling for Rising STAR's private equity funds. He began his career as part of the Investment Management Team in the role of a research analyst overseeing the hedge fund product line. During the last two years, he was also involved at the Thurgauer Wirtschaftsinstitut (TWI) as research assistant heading the implementation of a long-term project for regional economic research.

Josuah Rechtsteiner holds a diploma in economics (master of science in economics) from the University of Konstanz (Germany).

MALCOLM RIDDELL

As investment banker, lawyer, diplomat, and CIA spy, Malcolm Riddell has participated in China's rise to international economic and political power for over 30 years. A Mandarin speaker, who lived and worked for more than 15 years in China and Taiwan, he is president of RiddellTseng, a boutique investment bank he formed in 1988. The firm advises leading international financial services and real estate companies on business, investment, and joint ventures in China, and works with them to source, negotiate, and close deals there.

Malcolm is editor of CHINA Debate, a media and events platform he created in 2011 that currently hosts the CHINA Debate blog (www.china debate.com).

He is a lawyer, licensed to practice in his home state of Florida since 1976, board certified in international law, and vice chair of the International Law Certification Committee. Malcolm's former government service includes United States delegate to the United Nations, Florida Undersecretary of State for International Affairs, and undercover CIA case officer in China operations.

Among his graduate degrees are an MBA from Harvard Business School (1986) and a master of international affairs at Columbia University (1985). Among his academic activities, he is an associate-in-research at the Harvard Fairbank Center for Chinese Studies, senior visiting fellow at Peking University Law School, and a former Asia fellow at the Harvard Kennedy School of Government. For his full academic profile, please go to: http://execed.gsd.harvard.edu/faculty/riddell-malcolm.

Malcolm is a member of the Council on Foreign Relations.

Contact: malcolm.riddell@riddell-tseng.com

ERIC ROSENKRANZ

Eric Rosenkranz is founder and chairman of e.three (Singapore), a strategic advisory helping organizations in Asia determine and execute their long-term plans. He specializes in helping start-ups from initial fundraising to exit.

Eric is currently director of Caelan Wright & Ass. (Singapore) call center, independent non-executive director of Focus Media (HK and

Singapore) Network Limited (Listed on HKSE), and director of Kingdom Breweries, a microbrewery in Cambodia. He is a member of the Expert Advisory Network of Frontier Strategy Group (US), and serves as senior advisor to West Indochina Consulting (Thailand) focusing on Myanmar. He is Chairman of start-ups PeeplePass (social media travel website) and EspressoGrow (bio-friendly fertilizer).

Eric has an MBA from The University of Chicago (1975) and a BA in economics from The George Washington University (1973). He currently guest lectures at the Singapore campus of the University of Chicago Booth School of Business in marketing and venture financing. Previously, Eric worked for 21 years for Grey Global Group; in his last position he was President of Asia-Pacific.

Eric has appeared as a panelist and moderator at the World Economic Forum, and in The Asian *Wall Street Journal*. He is a regular host/commentator on CNBC Asia's *Squawk Box*. Eric writes a monthly column on strategy for *The Nation* in Thailand since 2004.

Contact: er@ethree-asia.com

TORD STALLVIK

Tord has 21 years of experience in asset management and investment banking. He was previously senior managing director and president at Protégé Partners. Prior to Protégé, he was a principal and manager of an Asian joint venture at Pequot Capital and served as director of sales and product development of the firm's global business.

He has been in the alternative asset management industry since 1995 when he joined Merrill Lynch & Co., Inc. as director of investments in the Private Advisory Services Group. He holds a BA with distinction and high honors in economics from the University of Michigan, Ann Arbor. He is fluent in Norwegian.

Contact: ts@evcap.com

KENNETH STEVENS

Ken joined Leopard Capital in 2007 and has over 21 years of operational and investment experience in Southeast Asia. After serving as research head and investment banker at CLSA Securities in Thailand, he spent ten years managing proprietary private equity investments in Thailand and Vietnam.

Ken's specific operational experience includes project design, construction and management, product distribution, aquaculture production, and service businesses.

He holds an MIM from Thunderbird and a BA from Cornell University, and is a CFA charter holder.

Contact: ks@leopardcapital.com

PAUL STEWART

Paul is a Colombian national with working experience in the building materials industry in Colombia, and other industries in the US. He currently works as an analyst for a private equity fund in Colombia.

Paul has a BA from the Universidad de los Andes and a masters in marketing and commercial development from the Universidad de Catalunya (Barcelona). He is fluent in German, English, and Spanish.

Contact: paulstewart673@hotmail.com

LIN TANG

Lin is a senior research engineer at EDHEC Risk Institute–Asia in Singapore. She has contributed to industry surveys on ETFs, green investing, and private wealth management and to a publication on dynamic asset allocation with ETFs.

She has a master's in risk and asset management from EDHEC Business School. Prior to joining EDHEC, Lin worked as a product engineer for one year after receiving her bachelor's in engineering, with first-class honors, from Nanyang Technological University in Singapore.

FUNGAI TARIRAH

Fungai is the Head of Africa ex-SA Investments at Momentum Asset Management a division of MMI Holdings South Africa. MMI Holdings Limited (MMI) is a South Africa–based financial services group listed on the Johannesburg Stock Exchange with a presence in over 14 African countries and involved in insurance, asset management, savings, investment, healthcare administration, and employee benefits.

Fungai runs portfolios that invest in listed equity across Africa as well as balanced portfolios for MMI's life businesses across the continent. He has been investing in African markets for over ten years and has travelled the continent extensively. He graduated from the National University of Science and Technology in Zimbabwe with a bachelor of commerce degree with honors in finance in 2001 and is currently completing a master's in development finance for Africa with the University of Stellenbosch in South Africa.

Contact: fungai.tarirah@momentum.co.za

CHRIS TELL

Chris Tell is a self-made investor who spends his time investing in businesses and markets, to which he devotes an extraordinary amount of time performing due diligence. Raised in Southern Africa, having lived in seven different countries, and now residing in multiple Australasian countries Chris has a background and education in law, investment banking, and financial planning, Chris has been a successful entrepreneur, investor, and speculator for many years.

Chris studied commerce through UNISA, obtained a graduate diploma in financial markets at the Securities Institute of Australia, and a British SFA futures and options representative qualification. He worked for a number of Investment houses including Invesco, Lehman, Robert Fleming and Co., Chase Manhattan, and JP Morgan before becoming an independent investor managing his own capital. Chris is focused on private equity in frontier markets and holds the majority of his net worth in this space.

Chris developed his insights and expertise on developing and emerging markets from entrepreneurial activities on the ground, being an avid student of the world always attempting, but not always succeeding, in understanding how and why it functions the way it does.

Chris is the cofounder of www.capitalistexploits.at, and you can follow Chris's and his friend and business partner Mark Wallace's activities on the site.

Contact: chris@capitalistexploits.at

ROBERT-JAN TEMMINK

Robert read law at Cambridge University and then at the Inns of Court School of Law in London, England. He was called to the bar of England and

Wales in 1996 and to the bars of Northern Ireland, the Dubai International Financial Centre Courts, and the bar of the State of New York as a foreign legal consultant in 2007. He works from Quadrant Chambers in London and frequently appears in courts and tribunals in the United States, UAE, and the Far East.

His particular areas of expertise include contract and partnership law, particularly in financial services, insolvency, insurance, shipping and aviation law, and he is acknowledged as a leading barrister in the global legal directories.

Robert is a fellow of the Chartered Institute of Arbitrators and has sat as sole or joint arbitrator in ICC, LCIA, and other arbitral institutions' references as well as in domestic arbitrations. He has published articles in several international banking journals and has contributed to a number of legal text books and journals. Robert is a trustee and director of three charitable institutions concerned with music and musical education and performance.

Contact: Robert.Temmink@quadrantchambers.com

WALTER VIEIRA

Walter Vieira is president of Marketing Advisory Services, India, which provides consultancy, research, and training services to corporations, governments, and the NGO sector. He founded the company in 1975, after a 14-year stint as a corporate manager in large multinationals. Walter is a fellow of the Institute of Management Consultants, India, and was given the lifetime achievement award for consulting in 2005, and lifetime achievement award for marketing in 2009.

He is the author of 11 books on marketing and management, and over 900 articles in the business and general press. He has lectured at well-known business schools like Kellogg, Cornell, and NYU in the United States and other institutions around the world. He was invited to address three consecutive World Congresses of Management Consultants in Yokohama, Rome, and Berlin.

Walter was the founder chairman of the Asia Pacific Conference of Management Consultants, and the chairman of the 42-nation apex body, the International Council of Management Consulting Institutes. He is now involved in contributing his expertise to worthwhile causes such as the Consumer Union, WWF for Nature, and others.

Contact: www.waltervieira.com

TOBIAS M. WEINERT

Tobias Weinert is an associate in the investment management team of Rising STAR AG, based in Switzerland. He is responsible for the corporate economic research. Besides the research, he monitors the external private equity management partners and is responsible for the investment reporting of Rising STAR's closed-ended private equity and private equity real estate funds.

In June 2011 Tobias took over the public relations work for the company. Before starting at Rising STAR he worked as student trainee in the corporate finance and mergers and acquisitions boutique albatross invest, where he was part of the mergers and acquisitions team.

Tobias Weinert holds a diploma in economics (master's of science in economics) and studied at the University of Konstanz (Germany) and Cardiff University (United Kingdom).

Contact: t.weinert@risingstar.ch

Bibliography

Agtmael, Antoine van. *The Emerging Markets Century*. New York: Free Press, 2007.

Ahn, D. H., Conrad, J., and Dittmar, R. F. "Basis Assets." *The Review of Financial Studies* 22, no. 12 (2009).

Aisen, A., and Veiga, F. J. "How Does Political Instability Affect Economic Growth?" IMF Working Paper 11/12, January 2011.

Akamatsu, K. "A Historical Pattern of Economic Growth in Developing Countries." *Journal of Developing Economies* 1, no. 1 (March–August, 1962): 3–25.

Allen, M., Rosenberg, C., Keller, C., Setser, B., and Roubini, N. "A Balance Sheet Approach to Financial Crisis." IMF Working Paper 02/210, December 2002.

Altman, E. I. "Financial Ratios, Discriminant Analysis, and the Prediction of Corporate Bankruptcy." *Journal of Finance.* 23, no. 4 (1968): 589–609.

Amenc, Noel, Goltz, Felix, et al. EDHEC Risk Indexing Survey. EDHEC Risk Institute, 2012.

Autor, D. H., Dorn, D., and Hanson, G. H. "The China Syndrome: Local Labor Market Effect of Import Competition in the United States. IMF Working Paper 02/210, March 2011.

Bakaert, G., and Harvey, C. "Foreign Speculators and Emerging Equity Markets." *Journal of Finance* 55 (2000): 565–613.

Barro, R. and Redlick, C. J. "Macroeconomic Effects from Government Purchases and Taxes." NBER Working Paper No. 15369, September 2009.

Basu, Moni. "Haiti's New Leader Makes Rounds in Washington, Vows Transparency." CNN World, April 21, 2011.

Batjargal, B. and Liu, M. "Entrepreneur's Access to Private Equity in China: The Role of Social Capital." Organization Science 15, no. 2 (March/April 2004): 159–172.

Benning, J. "Benchmarking Fixed-Income Returns." Chicago Board of Trade, Working paper, 2006.

Bernstein, Ann. *The Case for Business in Developing Economies*. Johannesburg, South Africa: Penguin Books, 2010.

Blitzer, David. "Emerging Liquidity." *Journal of Indexes* (September/October) 2008, www.journalofindexes.com.

Bloomberg Markets. Bloomberg Rankings, network release, February 8, 2012. Bloomberg, March 2012.

Boer, Kito de, and Turner, John M. "Beyond Oil: Reappraising the Gulf States." *McKinsey Quarterly*, January 2007.

Boston Consulting Group, The. "Building on Success. Global Asset Management 2011," The Boston Consulting Group Inc, 2011. www.bcg.com.

Boogle, John C. *The Clash of Cultures: Investment vs. Speculation* (Hoboken, NJ: John Wiley & Sons, 2012).

Bourdet, Yves. *The Economics of Transition in Laos: From Socialism to ASEAN Integration* (Northampton, MA: Edward Elgar Publishing, 2000).

Briand, Remy, and Subramanian, Madhusudan. "Emerging Markets: A 20-Year Perspective." *Journal of Indexes* (September/October 2008), www.journalof indexes.com.

Bruton, G. and Ahlstrom, D. "An Institutional View of China's Venture Capital Industry—Explaining the Differences between China and the West." *Journal of Business Venturing* 18, no. 2 (2003): 233–259.

Bruton, G., Fried, V. H. and Manigard, S. "Institutional Influences on the Worldwide Expansion of Venture Capital." *Entrepreneurship Theory and Practice*, 29, no. 6 (2005).

"Business Principles for Countering Bribery." www.transparency.org.

Cambridge Associates LLC. Highlights from "The Case for Diversified Emerging Markets Exposure." Massachusetts, 2011.

Campani, H. C., and Goltz, F. "A Review of Corporate Bond Indices: Construction Principles, Return Heterogeneity and Fluctuations in Risk Exposures." EDHEC Risk Institute Publication, 2011.

Caribbean Export Development Agency. "Doing Business with Haiti." May 2007.

Chemla, G. "The Determinants of Investment in Private Equity and Venture Capital: Evidence from American and Canadian, Pension Funds." SSRN Working Paper 556421, 2005.

ChiefExecutive.net, "Designing a China Business Framework."

CIA, *The World Factbook, 2010*, various editions. Central Intelligence Agency, https://www.cia.gov/library/publications/the-world-factbook/geos/la.html.

City of London, Global Financial Centers Index (GFCI). The City of London and Z/Yen Group, London, 2012.

CityUK, The, *Fund Management*. TheCityUK Research Centre, October 2011.

Claessens, Stijn, Djankov, Someon, and Klinebiel, Daniela. "Stock Markets in Transition Economies." Financial Sector Discussion Paper 5 (Washington: The World Bank, September 2000).

Clear Path Analysis. "Investing in Frontier Markets." (London: Clear Path Analysis, December 2010).

Cornelius, P., Langelaar, B., andvan Rossum, M. "Big Is Better: Growth and Market Structure in Global Buyouts." *Journal of Applied Corporate Finance* 19, no. 3 (2007).

Cottarelli, C., and Schaechter, A. "Long-Term Trends in Public Finances in the G-7 Economies." IMF Staff Position Note (Washington: International Monetary Fund, September 1, 2010).

Deloitte and US Council on Competitiveness—2010 Global Manufacturing Competitiveness Index. Deloitte Touche Tohmatsu, June 2010.

DFDL. *Legal, Tax & Investment Guide 2011–2012*, (Phnom Penh, Cambodia: DFDL Legal & Tax, March 2011). Edition Cambodia 2011–2012; Edition Laos 2011–2012; Edition Myanmar 2011–2012; Edition Thailand 2011–2012; Edition Vietnam 2011–2012.

DFDL. "Legal & Tax, Mergers & Acquisitions in Laos P.D.R." www.dfdl.com/easyblog/entry/mergers-a-acquisitions-in-lao-pdr.

Dubai, Government of. "Dubai Economic Council, Migration, Labor Markets and Long Term Development Strategy for the UAE." Dubai, 2011.

EIU. "Haiti: Country Report." *Economist* Intelligence Unit (London, February 2011).

EIU. "Myanmar: Country Report." *Economist* Intelligence Unit (London, April 2012).

EIU. "Myanmar: White Elephant or New Tiger Economy?" Special report, *Economist* Intelligence Unit (London, April 2012).

EIU. "The Search for Growth, Looking to Emerging Markets."*Economist* Intelligence Unit (London, December 2011).

Ellatari, L., Sultanate of Oman. "Major Business Sectors." The Embassy of Switzerland, September 2011, www.oesc.ch

Elton, E. J., and Green, T. C. "Tax and Liquidity Effects in Pricing Government Bonds." *Journal of Finance* 53, no. 5 (1998).

EMPEA. *Industry Statistics, 2011* (Washington, DC: Emerging Markets Private Equity Association, March 15, 2012).

EMPEA. *Asian LP Sentiment Towards Private Equity.* Special Report, Emerging Markets Private Equity Association, 2012.

Ernst & Young 2010 Global Private Equity Watch (London: Ernst & Young, 2010).

Errunza, V., Hogan, K., and Hung, M. W. "Can the Gains from International Diversification Be Achieved without Trading Abroad?" *Journal of Finance* 54 (1999).

European Banking Coordination Initiative. Working Group Report on NPLs, March 2012.

Fama, E. F., and French, K. "Common Risk Factors in the Returns on Stocks and Bonds." *Journal of Financial Economics* 33, no. 1 (1993).

Farag, H., Hommel, U., and Wright, M. "Contracting, Monitoring, and Exiting Venture Capital Investments in Transitioning Economies: A Comparative of Eastern European and German Markets." *Venture Capital* 6, no. 4 (2004).

Fernando, Rodriguez, et al. "Assessment of Haitian Coffee Value Chain." Catholic Relief Services.

Ferreira, A. "The Importance of Industry and Country Effects in the EMU Equity Markets." *European Financial Management* 12, no. 3 (2006).

Florén-Romero, Marisol. "Researching Haitian Law." New York University GlobaLex (May/June 2008).

Food and Agriculture Organization of the United Nations. Low-Income Food-Deficit Countries (LIFDC)—List for 2011.

Fox, Tim. Chief Economist Emirates NBD, GCC Economic Overview, private presentation (October 2011).

Gauci, Geoffrey and Fisher, Jessica, "The UK Bribery Act and the US FCPA, Bristows Law Firm." In: QuickCounsel, Association of Corporate Counsel, 2010, www.acc.com.

Goldman Sachs. "Building Better Global Economic BRICs." Global economic Paper (November 2001).

Goldman Sachs. "N-11: More than an Acronym." Global economic paper (March 2007).

Gottschalg, O., and Zipser, D. "The Changing Face of Risk in Emerging Markets." Working paper (2006).

Groh, A. P. "Private Equity in Emerging Markets." IESE Working Paper WP-779 (February 2009).

Haiti, Government of. "Action Plan for the National Recovery and Development of Haiti," March 2010.

Haiti, Government of. "Haiti Earthquake PDNA: Assessment of Damage, Losses, General and Sectoral Needs." (March 2010).

Haiti Libre. "Haiti – Economy: The Budget of Haiti 2010–2011, Passes the 100 Billion Gourdes" (December 14, 2010).

Hamelink, F., Harasty, H., and Hillion, P. "Country, Sector or Style: What Matters Most when Constructing Global Equity Portfolios?" Working paper, FAME (2001).

Harvard Business Review. Thriving in Emerging Markets (Boston: Harvard Business Review Press, 2011).

Heritage Foundation and *Wall Street Journal*. 2012 Index of Economic Freedom (Washington DC, 2012).

Himalayan Times. "Share Market Not Ready for Foreign Investors" (December 21, 2011).

Holdsworth, P. "Foreign Direct Investment in Oman Improved by 128 Percent." Gulf Jobs Market, January 2011, www.gulfjobsmarket.com

Hogan Lovells. "Change and Opportunity in Myanmar." Hogan Lovells International LLP (April 2012).

Hornbeck J. F. "The Haitian Economy and the Hope Act." Congressional Research Service (June 24, 2010).

Hsu, J. "Cap-Weighted Portfolios Are Sub-Optimal Portfolios." *Journal of Investment Management* 4, no. 3 (2006).

IIA, 12th Annual Internal Auditor Software Survey. Internal Auditor, 2006.

Inter-American Development Bank (IDB). "History of the IDB in Haiti." Inter-American Development Bank. www.iadb.org/en/countries/haiti/history-of-the-idb-in-haiti,1009.html.

International Development Bank for Reconstruction and Development. "Doing Business." (Washington, DC: International Bank for Reconstruction and Development/The World Bank, 2012).

International Monetary Fund. "World Economic Outlook Database." International Monetary Fund (April 2011).

International Trade Administration. "Haiti Uses a Bit of MAGIC to Energize their Textile Industry."

Jaeger, M. "Schwellenländer und Finanzmarktliberalisierung, Aktueller Kommentar." *Deutsche Bank Research* 7 (September 2009).

JP Morgan. "EM Moves into the Mainstream as an Asset Class." JPM Emerging Markets Research (October 2010).

JP Morgan. Market Pulse: Alternative Assets Survey Key (2010).

Kang, Xiaowei, Nielsen, Frank, and Fachinotti, Giacomo. "Some Like it Hot." *Research Insights* (MSCI Inc., January 2011).

Kang, Xiaowei, Nielsen, Frank, and Fachinotti, Giacomo. "The 'NewClassic' Equity Allocation." (MSCI Inc., October 2010).

Kaufmann, Daniel, Kray, Aart, and Mastruzzi, Massimo. "The Worldwide Governance Indicators: A Summary of Methodology, Data and Analytical Issues." World Bank Policy Research Report, Working Paper 5430 (Washington, DC, 2011).

Kelley, Martha N. "Assessing the Investment Climate in Haiti: Policy Challenges." OECD, Workshop on Foreign Direct Investment in the Caribbean Basin and Latin America (Curacao, April 5–6, 2001).

Khanna, Tarun, and Palepu, Krishna G. *Winning in Emerging Markets* (Boston: Harvard Business Press, 2010).

Khanna, V., "Law Enforcement & Stock Market Development: Evidence from India." Stanford University Working paper, 2009.

Kruck S. E., S. S. "Spreadsheet Accuracy Theory.", *Journal of Information Systems Education* 93–108.

Kunio, Yoshihara. *The Rise of Ersatz Capitalism in South East Asia* (Singapore: Oxford University Press, 1988).

Laovoices.com, "Lao Indochina Group Prepares for IPO," http://laovoices.com/lao-indochina-group-prepares-for-ipo/.

Leeds, R., and Sunderland, J. "Private Equity Investing in Emerging Markets." *Journal of Applied Corporate Finance* 15, no. 4 (2003): 8–16.

Levine, Ross. "Stock Markets, A Spur to Economic Growth, World Bank Conference, Stock Markets, Corporate Finance and Economic Growth," not dated, www.worldbank.org/fandd.

Lewellen, J., Nagel, S., and Shanken, J. "A Sceptical Appraisal of Asset-Pricing Tests." *Journal of Financial Economics* 96, no. 2 (2010).

Luise, Marc de. "What Are Frontier Markets?" *Journal of Indexes* (September–October 2008).

Magus, George. *Uprising—Will Emerging Markets Shape or Shake the World Economy?* (London: John Wiley & Sons Ltd., 2011).

Makarenko, A. V. Phenomenological Model for Growth of Volumes Digital Data, 2011, http://arxiv.org/ftp/arxiv/papers/1102/1102.5500.pdf.

Malevergne, Y. P., Santa-Clara, and Sornette, D., "Professor ZIPF Goes to Wall Street." Working paper, National Bureau of Economic Research, 2009.

McGregor, Richard. *The Party: The Secret World of China's Communist Rulers.* (HarperCollins e-books, Kindle edition).

McKinsey & Company, "The Value and Challenges of Good Corporate Governance" (Kiev, 2004).

Menchero, Jose, and Morozov, Andrei. "The Relative Strength of Industry and Country Factors in Global Equity Markets." MSCI Research Insight, (April 2011).

Ministry of Information, Sultanate of Oman, "Useful Information," www.omanet.com

Mobius, Mark. *The Little Book on Emerging Markets* (Hoboken, NJ: John Wiley & Sons, 2012).

Myanmar Legal Services, "Doing Business in Myanmar." March 2012, www.myanmarlegalsevices.com.

News 24, "Haiti's Martelly Vows 'Rule of Law,'" April 6, 2011.

Nexant. "Caribbean Regional Electricity Generation, Interconnection, and Fuels Supply Strategy Final Report" (March 2010); submitted to the World Bank.

Nienaber Georgianne. "Haiti's Michel Martelly: The Election, Fraud, and the Future." *La Progressive* (December 8, 2010).

Olsen, K. "Indexed Assets Surge 25%." *Pension and Investments* (September 19, 2011).

Organisation for Economic Co-operation and Development. "Good Practice Guidance on Internal Controls, Ethics, and Compliance," at paragraph 12, February 18, 2010, www.oecd.org.

Organisation for Economic Co-operation and Development. Convention text, www/oecd.org.

Organisation for Economic Co-operation and Development. "Laos Securities Exchange LSX." Organisation for Economic Co-operation and Development, 2001, www.lsx.com.la.

Panko, R. "What We Know about Spreadsheet Errors." *Journal of End User Computing* (1998, revised Spring 2008).

PEI, Asia Pacific Private Equity Review. Private Equity International, PEI Surveys (March 2012).

Phongpaichit, Pasuk, and Baker, Chris. *Thai Capital: After the 1997 Crisis* (Chiang Mai: Silkworm Books, 2008).

Pratt, S. *Guide to Venture Capital Sources*, 5th ed. (Wellesly: Capital Publishing, 1981).

Pula, G. and Santabárbara, D. "Is China Climbing Up the Quality Ladder? Estimating Cross Country Differences in Product Quality Using Eurostat's Comext Trade Database," Working Paper 1310, European Central Bank, Frankfurt, (March 2011).

Ramey, V. A. "Identifying Government Spending Shocks: It's All in the Timing." NBER Working Paper 15464, October 2009.

Rising Star AG, (Switzerland), Rechsteiner, Josuah, and Weinert, Tobias. "Investments in Schwellenländer kurzlebige Gelegenheit oder säkulares Thema?" (Bottighofen, 2011).

Rodrik, Dani. "The Inescapable Trilemma of the World Economy," June 2007, www.rodrik.typepad.com.

Roubini, Nouriel B. S. "Bailouts or Bail-Ins? Responding to Financial Crises in Emerging Economies." Washington, DC: Peterson Institute, 2004.

Rubin, J., and Tal, B. "Will Soaring Transport Costs Reverse Globalization?" *StratEco*, CIBC World Markets Inc. (May 2008).

Ruby, V., de, and Debnam, J. "Does Government Spending Stimulate Economies?" *Mercatus on Policy* 77, George Mason University, July 2011.

Schumpeter, Joseph A., *History of Economic Analysis* (New York: Oxford University Press, 1954).

Sharma, Ruchir. *Breakout Nations: In Pursuit of the Next Economic Miracles*, (New York: Norton, 2012).

Sharpe, William F. "The Arithmetic of Active Management." *The Financial Analysts' Journal* 47, no. 1 (January/February 1991).

Shelby-James, T., A. A. "Handheld Computers for Data Entry: High Tech Has Its Problems Too." BioMed Central, 2007, www.ncbi.nlm.nih.gov/pmc/articles/PMC1804282.

Siegel, L. B. "Benchmarks and Investment Management." The Research Foundation of the Association for Investment Management and Research, Charlottesville, Virginia, 2003.

S&P. Standard and Poor's documentation, www.indices.standardandpoors.com.

S&P. Standard and Poor's Select Frontier index documentation, www.indices.standardandpoors.com.

S&P. "Standard and Poor's Global Equity Indices Methodology."

S&P. "Standard and Poor's Country Rating Framework, Sovereign Government Rating Methodologies and Assumptions." Standard and Poor's literature.

Standard Chartered Bank. "The Super Cycle." Standard Chartered Global Research, London, 2010.

Stiglitz, J. E. *Globalization and Its Discontent* (New York: Norton, 2002).

Tabner, I. "Benchmark Concentration: Capitalization Weights versus Equal Weights in the FTSE 100 Index." Working paper, University of Stirling, 2007.

UBS. "On the Ground in Myanmar." UBS Investment Research, Global Equity Research, March 2012, UBS Securities (Thailand) Ltd.

UNDP, Human Development, "Five Arab Countries among Top Leaders in Long-Term Development Game," November 2010, www.undp.org

United Nations, News & Media: UN/HAITI DONORS 3.

United Nations. Handbook on the Least Developed Country Category: Inclusion, Graduation and Special Support Measures, November 2008.

United Nations Commission on International Trade Law, about UNCITRAL.

UNU-IHDP and UNEP, Inclusive Wealth Report 2012, Measuring Progress toward Sustainability. Cambridge: Cambridge University Press, 2012.

US Department of State, Bureau of East Asian and Pacific Affairs, www.state.gov/r/pa/ei/bgn/2770.htm.

US Department of State. "Background Note: Haiti." Bureau of Western Hemisphere Affairs, August 10, 2011.

US Embassy. Port-au-Prince, Fact Sheet: North Industrial Park, January 11, 2011.

Utkus, Stephen P. "Market Bubbles and Investor Psychology." Vanguard Research, Vanguard, February 2011.

Ward, Karen. "The World in 2050." HSBC Global Research, The Hong Kong and Shanghai Banking Corporation, January 2011.

Weidig, Tom, and Mathonet, Pierre-Yves. The Risk Profile of Private Equity, Luxembourg, 2004.

Wickam, H. *Elegant Graphics for Data Analysis* (London: Springer, 2009).

Wilton, David. "The Case for Emerging Markets Private Equity." IFC, presentation, February 2011, www.ifc.org.

Wilton, David. Emerging Markets Private Equity: The Opportunity, the Risks & Ideas to Manage Them." IFC, presentation, January 2012, www.ifc.org.

Wilton, David. "Perspectives of an LP in Emerging Markets Private Equity." EMPEA, www.ifc.org.

Wilton, David. "IFC's Experience in Emerging Markets Private Equity." EMPEA, *Quarterly Review* VI, issue 1 (Q1 2010), www.ifc.org.

WEF. "The Arab World Competitiveness Report 2011–2012." The World Economic Forum, Geneva, 2012.

WEF. "The Global Competitiveness Report 2011/2012." The World Economic Forum, Geneva, 2011.

WEF. "Private Sector Development in Haiti: Opportunities for Investment, Job Creation and Growth." The World Economic Forum, Geneva, 2011.

World Bank, "Haiti: Recent Progress in Economic Governance Reforms." The World Bank, http://siteresources.worldbank.org/INTHAITI/ . . . /Governance_reforms_Haiti.pdf.

World Bank, The Asian Miracle, World Bank Policy Research Report, The World Bank, Oxford University Press, New York, 1993.

World Bank, The Worldwide Governance Indicators, 2011 update, The World Bank, www.govindicators.org.

World Bank, "One Year Later: World Bank Group Support for Haiti's Recovery." The World Bank, January 2011.

World Bank, Financial Sector Discussion Paper No 5. The World Bank, Washington DC, 2000.

World Bank, Lao PDR Overview, The World Bank, www.worldbank.org/en/country/lao/overview.

World Bank, Chronology, www.worldbank.org.

World Bank, Haiti: Trade Brief, The World Bank, 2008

WTTC. "Haiti: The Economic Impact of Travel and Tourism." World Travel and Tourism Council, 2011.

Zopounidis C.D.M. "Multi-Group Discrimination Using Multi-Criteria Analysis: Illustrations from the Field of Finance." *European Journal of Operational Research* 139, no. 2 (2002): 371–389.

Index